PUBLIC PROTECTION
OR **REPRESSION?**

**Russia's Anti-Extremism
Law Enforcement**

PUBLIC PROTECTION
OR REPRESSION?

Russia's Anti-Extremism
Law Enforcement

MARIA KRAVCHENKO AND **NATALIA YUDINA**

EDITED BY **ALEXANDER VERKHOVSKY**
INFOGRAPHICS BY **TATIANA TSVIROVA**

East View Press
Minneapolis, USA

Public Protection or Repression? Russia's Anti-Extremism Law Enforcement

Published by East View Press, an imprint of East View Information Services, Inc.
10601 Wayzata Blvd, Minneapolis, MN 55305 USA
www.eastviewpress.com

Library of Congress Cataloging-in-Publication Data

Names: Kravchenko, Mariia (Human rights worker), author. | I͡Udina,
   Natalʹia, author. | Verkhovskiĭ, Aleksandr, editor. | Tsvirova,
   Tatiana, illustrator.
Title: Public protection or repression? : Russia's anti-extremism law
   enforcement / authors: Maria Kravchenko, Natalia Yudina; editor:
   Alexander Verkhovsky ; infographics by Tatiana Tsvirova.
Description: First edition. | Minneapolis, MN : East View Press, an imprint
   of East View Information Services, Inc., 2023. | Includes
   bibliographical references.
Identifiers: LCCN 2023031722 (print) | LCCN 2023031723 (ebook) | ISBN
   9781879944381 (paperback) | ISBN 9781879944374
Subjects: LCSH: Terrorism--Prevention--Russia (Federation) | Hate
   crimes--Law and legislation--Russia (Federation) | Radicalism--Russia
   (Federation) | Law enforcement--Russia (Federation)
Classification: LCC HV6433.R9 K743 2023 (print) | LCC HV6433.R9 (ebook) |
   DDC 363.3250947--dc23/eng/20230808
LC record available at https://lccn.loc.gov/2023031722
LC ebook record available at https://lccn.loc.gov/2023031723

Front and back cover photos © Ilya Varlamov, CC-BY-SA 4.0, Wikimedia Commons
Cover design, book design, and composition by Ana K. Niedermaier

Printed in the United States of America
First Edition, 2024
1 3 5 7 9 10 8 6 4 2

Contents

Foreword from the Publisher

When Alexander Verkhovsky, director of the SOVA Center for Information and Analysis, contacted us in late 2019 to propose a book on human rights in Russia, we were quite interested. The studies that SOVA has been producing for over two decades fall squarely within the purview of East View, as they represent research done about Russia, in Russia, by Russian researchers.

Since Verkhovsky's proposal, of course, our world has changed substantially, and it would be no exaggeration to say that Russia's political landscape in particular has changed drastically. In 2020, a package of constitutional amendments, approved by national referendum, gave President Vladimir Putin the option to run for an unprecedented fifth term. Throughout 2021, the Russian military amassed more and more troops near the Ukrainian border. And February 2022 marked the start of what the Kremlin called a "special military operation," which is in fact the bloodiest conflict in Europe since World War II.

Meanwhile, on the domestic front, the Moscow government has been systematically silencing human rights advocates. In 2022, it shut down the Memorial Human Rights Center, and also revoked the registrations of Human Rights Watch and Amnesty International. In January 2023, a court ordered the closure of the Moscow Helsinki Group, the country's oldest human rights organization. And the most recent target has been the SOVA Center itself: On April 27, 2023, the Moscow City Court approved a request filed by the Russian Ministry of Justice to liquidate SOVA, on the grounds that the organization had taken part in events outside its region of registration.

That judicial decision brought added urgency to the publication of this book, which focuses on a marked trend that has emerged in Russia in the "post-Crimea" period (since 2014): Anti-extremism legislation – ostensibly designed to protect ethnic, religious and other minorities from hate crimes and violence – is increasingly being applied to protect the Russian government from individuals and organizations that dare to speak out against its policies.

This publication is based mainly on SOVA's annual reports from 2014 to 2020, supplemented by an epilogue that summarizes further developments that have emerged with the constitutional changes and the ongoing conflict in Ukraine. We publish this book for two main purposes. The first is to highlight the work of one of Russia's most long-standing and courageous nonprofits, which has provided valuable data to authoritative sources abroad such as Human Rights Watch, The Guardian and The New York Times. The second purpose is both more targeted and further-reaching: to contribute to a better understanding of how Russia's judicial and law-enforcement apparatus has come to affect the ways in which ordinary citizens exercise (or refrain from exercising) their basic human rights, particularly freedom of speech, in both public spaces and private social media.

This collection will be of interest to scholars engaged in human rights and legal protections; post-Soviet history, politics and civil society; and the relationship between foreign policy and domestic practices. It is also relevant to anyone interested in the development of governments – the Russian one in particular – and the strategies they deploy to retain their authority.

Laurence H. Bogoslaw
Chief Editor and Publishing Director
East View Press

Introduction

This book focuses on xenophobia-motivated illegal activities in Russia, government policies for counteracting extremism (that is, various direct, ideologically motivated threats to state and public security), and abuses that systematically arise in the implementation of these policies.

The work is based on the annual reports by SOVA Center for Information and Analysis and can be viewed as a guide to events in this sphere from 2014 to 2020. This particular time frame was chosen because it was these dates that marked substantial changes in counter-extremism policy within Russia. Of course, this policy has experienced other substantial shifts, but the year 2014 strikes us as the most appropriate starting point for our analysis: This was the beginning of Russia's intervention in the Ukraine crisis, which in many respects served as a turning point in domestic policy as well.

The year 2020 was when a large package of amendments to the Constitution were approved by nationwide referendum. Technically, none of those amendments had to do with counter-extremism policy, but there is a broad consensus that this year marked a watershed in domestic policy. As for counter-extremism policy per se, it too underwent a profound change – one that was not detected until a year later. The number of new criminal cases for crimes of an extremist nature rose by 70% or more over the previous year, an acceleration that had not been seen since 2012. A roughly proportional rise occurred in prosecutions for extremist public statements – however, for the first time in all of these years, the most common targets of those prosecuted statements were representatives of governmental authority, not "ethnic enemies."[1] Subsequent events showed that these changes were not a fluctuation, but a turning point.

---

1. Natalia Yudina. Protecting Oneself: The State against the Incitement of Hatred and the Political Participation of Nationalists in Russia in 2021 // SOVA Center. 2022. March 18 (https://www.sova-center.ru/en/xenophobia/reports-analyses/2022/03/d45954/).

Of course, the year 2022, when the large-scale armed conflict in Ukraine began, brought changes that were no less noticeable. However, we cannot fully assess them as yet, so we decided to choose the landmark year of 2020 as our stopping point.

The scope of our review requires further clarification.

First, the book does not include any descriptions of the strictly political – that is, legitimate – activities of the ultra-right. We also excluded the topic of ultra-right xenophobic propaganda, since assessments of its legality may vary widely. Thus, the subject matter has been limited to hate crimes – i.e., ordinary crimes committed for ideological motives associated with xenophobic views.

Second, we present our annual reviews of the enforcement of anti-extremist legislation –including prosecutions against hate crimes, incitement to hatred or other public statements deemed extremist by law enforcement agencies, and against organizational activities that law enforcement recognizes as extremist. We start with a general overview of the practice, and then examine in more detail cases of abuse and excessive restriction of civil liberties in the application of anti-extremist legislation.

Third, due to space limitations, we omitted law enforcement problems that are related in one way or another to religion – an extensive subject that includes bans against religious organizations, persecution of minorities, criminalization of "insulting the feelings of believers," and so on. These issues are mentioned only occasionally in connection with other topics. Finally, we skipped some less significant aspects of anti-extremist law enforcement related to administrative measures taken by the authorities.

The book as a whole is composed of five parts. In Part One, Trends and Data, we provide key statistics on hate crimes and anti-extremist law enforcement, based on our own information and Supreme Court data. These charts should give readers an immediate sense of the dynamics of various kinds of crimes and law enforcement during the years of our analysis.

Part Two briefly outlines the legal framework for countering extremism in Russia. This framework differs significantly from its European (not to mention American) counterparts, so it is worth special attention early in the book.

The remainder of the book is divided into three major parts (Three, Four, Five), each of which is subdivided into chapters devoted to a specific year (2014-2020).

Part Three focuses on legislation. The information presented here comprises excerpts from SOVA Center annual reports that cover the changes in the legal framework for combating extremism.

Part Four is devoted to hate crimes – against persons and material objects (property).

Part Five, which is the most voluminous, is devoted to law enforcement. The chapters for each year follow the same structure, giving an overview of bans against organizations, followed by an overview of criminal law enforcement broken down by types of "crimes of an extremist nature," This summary is followed by a subchapter (section) on inappropriate persecution of political and civil activists for extremism. Each year's chapter then concludes with an overview of updates to the Federal List of Extremist Materials, a review of policy for blocking extremist content on the Internet, and examples of abuse in its implementation. In the sections on inappropriate prosecutions, we list only completed cases and those that were in progress by the end of 2020. We omitted some sections if the corresponding information for a specific year was insufficient or insignificant.

We hope that this book will contribute to a better understanding of how political extremism has been interpreted in "post-Crimean" Russia and how anti-extremist policies have been built.

PART ONE

Trends and Data

In the first years after the adoption of the law "On Combating Extremist Activity," law enforcement was focused on two principal issues.

The first one was the fight against neo-Nazi groups, with the main emphasis on suppressing xenophobic violence. These activities of law enforcement agencies were not sufficiently systematic or effective in the early 2000s. However, starting in the middle of the decade, and especially since 2008, when the Russian Ministry of Internal Affairs launched its specialized Centers for Countering Extremism ("E" Centers), the authorities began to focus much more on this issue. According to SOVA Center, the largest number of sentences for violent hate crimes was handed down in 2010; the numbers have been steadily decreasing since then. The number of hate attacks recorded by SOVA over this time period consistently declined as well.[1] Thus, it can be concluded that the introduction and application of anti-extremist legislation successfully suppressed the wave of xenophobic violence in Russia.

The second issue – prosecution of participants in banned organizations, such as the National Bolshevik Party (NBP), neo-Nazi groups or the radical Islamic Hizb ut-Tahrir party (recognized in Russia as terrorist) – was also taking shape.

Cases of unjustified prosecution for public statements were reported as early as the first half of the 2000s.

Countering extremism on the Internet remained a marginal law enforcement area throughout the 2000s. However, in the 2010s, with the widespread penetration of the Internet into the life of Russian citizens and the growing popularity of social media networks, law enforcement agencies began to pay more attention to online content. It soon became clear that identification of online crimes and offenses is an easy process allowing to generate favorable statistics on the fight against extremism. At the same

---

1. In both cases, the results come not from the official statistics, but from the SOVA Center monitoring.

time, security officials widely believed that, since imprisonment was not often imposed under anti-extremist articles, a criminal record could be viewed as a preventive measure. This line of thinking resulted in a rapid increase in the number of people convicted for "extremist" statements on the Internet (mainly under Art. 282 of the Criminal Code); the number of sentences for offline propaganda has not increased. As a result, according to the SOVA Center estimates, the share of "Web propaganda" offenders amounted to more than 80% of those convicted of speech crimes in 2014, and did not fall below this level in the subsequent years.

General trends can be observed in the tables and graphs below. Details are presented in the corresponding chapters of the book.

These tables and graphs represent general trends and should not be assumed as fully accurate. Our data are incomplete, but often becomes fuller over time, which is why the numbers we now know, reflected in the tables below, somewhat differ in almost all categories from those that we knew and analyzed when writing the reports. Due to the reporting specifics, the Supreme Court data also not entirely accurate.

Infographics

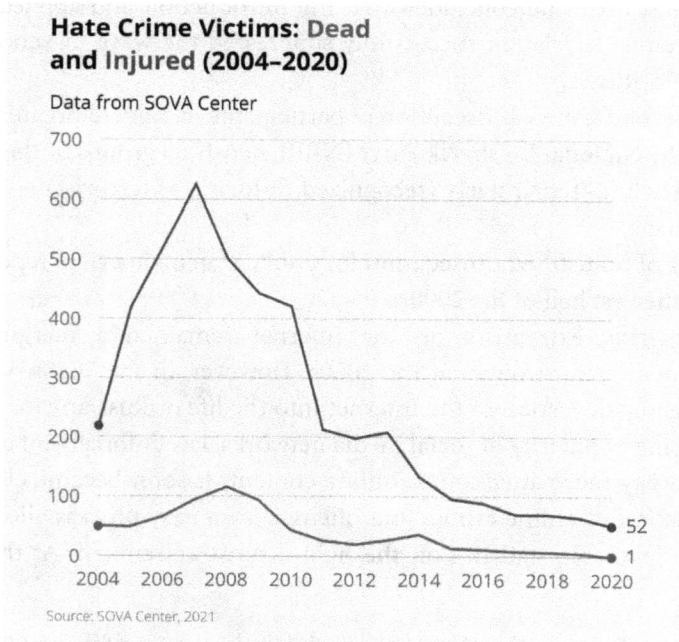

Hate Crime Victims: Dead and Injured (2004–2020)

Data from SOVA Center

Source: SOVA Center, 2021

Hate Crime Victims by Type (2014–2020)

Data from SOVA Center

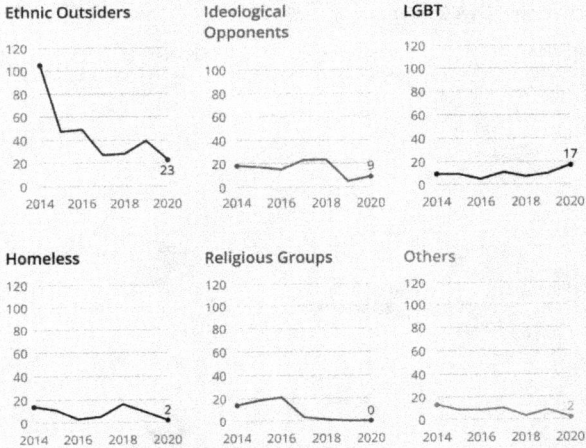

Ethnic Outsiders

Ideological Opponents

LGBT

Homeless

Religious Groups

Others

Source: SOVA Center, 2021

Hate Crimes Against Property: from Explosions and Arsons to Graffiti and Other Damage (2007–2020)

Data from SOVA Center

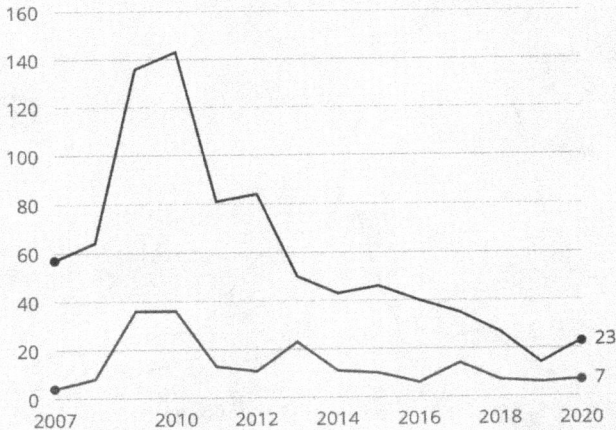

Source: SOVA Center, 2021

Desecrated Religious and Ideological Sites by Type (2014–2020)

Data from SOVA Center

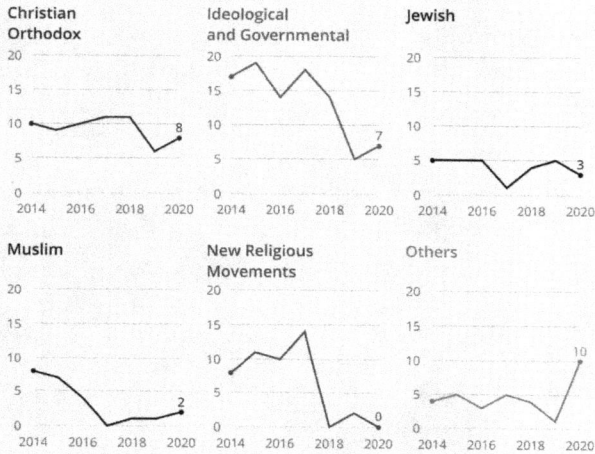

Source: SOVA Center, 2021

Violent Hate Crimes: Victims and Convicts (2004–2020)

Data from SOVA Center

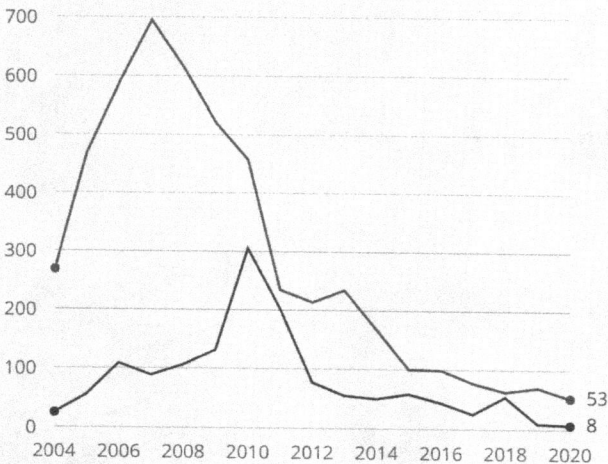

Source: SOVA Center, 2021

Criminal Penalties for Ideologically Motivated Violence (2014-2020)

Data from SOVA Center

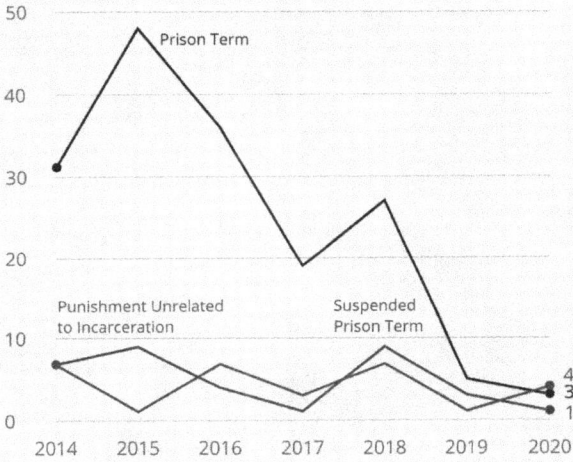

Source: SOVA Center, 2021

Convicted of "Crimes of Extremist Nature"

Data from SOVA Center

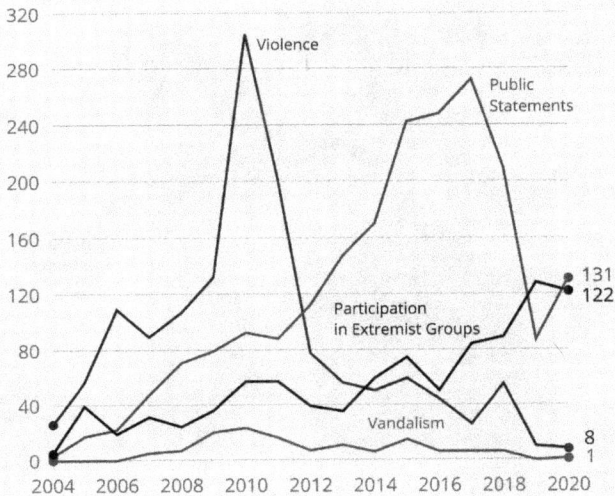

Source: SOVA Center, 2021

Appropriateness of Punishments for Public Statements (2018–2020)

Data from SOVA Center

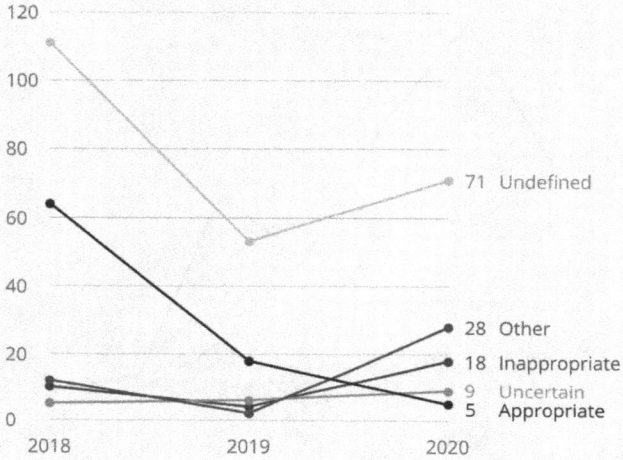

```
120

100

 80
                                        71  Undefined
 60

 40

                                        28  Other
 20                                     18  Inappropriate
                                         9  Uncertain
  0                                      5  Appropriate
    2018          2019          2020
```

Source: SOVA Center, 2021

Sentences for Public Statements (2014–2020)

Data from SOVA Center, in % of the Total Number

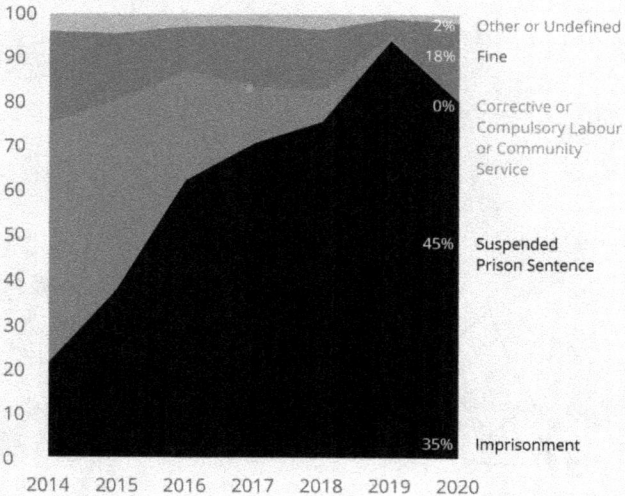

```
100
                                  2%   Other or Undefined
 90                              18%   Fine

 80                               0%   Corrective or
                                       Compulsory Labour
 70                                    or Community
                                       Service
 60

 50                              45%   Suspended
 40                                    Prison Sentence

 30

 20

 10
                                 35%   Imprisonment
  0
   2014  2015  2016  2017  2018  2019  2020
```

Source: SOVA Center, 2021

Federal List of Extremist Materials Dynamics (2014–2020)

Data from the Ministry of Justice, Classification by SOVA Center

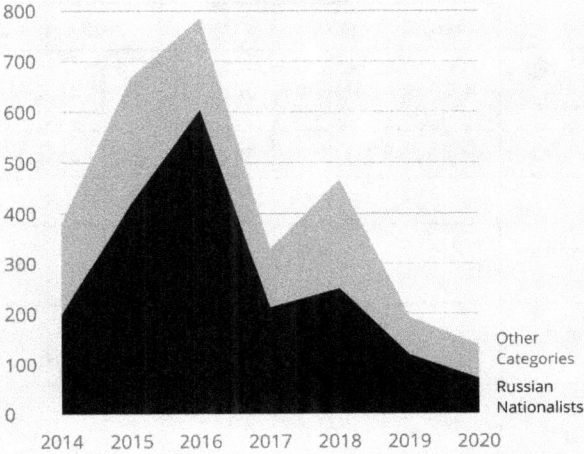

Other Categories

Russian Nationalists

Source: SOVA Center, 2021

Federal List of Extremist Materials Dynamics (2014–2020)

Data from the Ministry of Justice, Classification by SOVA Center

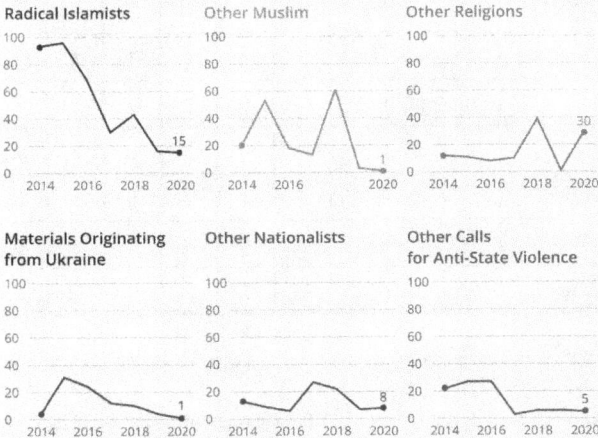

Source: SOVA Center, 2021

Summary Statistics of Crimes and Punishments
Data as of February 26, 2023

Types of Violence and Victims of Violent Hate Crimes

K – killed, B – beaten, wounded	2007		2008		2009		2010		2011		2012	
	K	B	K	B	K	B	K	B	K	B	K	B
Total *	94	625	116	501	94	443	44	421	27	213	20	198
Dark-skinned	0	34	2	26	2	59	1	28	1	19	0	26
People from Central Asia	36	95	57	133	40	92	20	86	10	38	8	38
People from the Caucasus	27	77	22	71	18	78	5	45	8	18	4	15
People from the Middle East and North Africa	1	22	0	15	0	2	0	2	0	5	0	2
From other Asian countries	9	76	9	40	14	37	3	19	0	15	0	5
People of "non-Slav appearance"	9	67	13	57	9	62	7	104	1	26	1	16
Ideological opponents	8	174	3	103	5	77	3	67	1	40	1	57
Homeless	1	3	4	1	4	0	1	3	3	3	6	2
Russians	0	22	3	12	0	7	1	8	1	9	0	5
Jews	0	9	0	6	0	3	0	3	1	2	0	0
Religious groups	0	9	0	6	1	2	0	22	0	24	0	10
LGBT	0	7	1	6	0	0	0	3	0	3	0	12
Others or unknown	3	30	2	25	1	24	3	31	1	11	0	10

* Not including the victims of mass clashes; not including the victims in the North Caucasus republics and in the Crimea prior to 2016.

We have not included serious death threats. In 2010, we have information about 6 persons who received such threats, in 2011 – 10, in 2012 – 2, in 2013 – 10, in 2014 –2, in 2015 – 8, in 2016 – 3, in 2017-18 – 0, in 2019 – 3, in 2020 – 5.

2013		2014		2015		2016		2017		2018		2019		2020	
K	B	K	B	K	B	K	B	K	B	K	B	K	B	K	B
28	**209**	**37**	**134**	**14**	**96**	**12**	**89**	**9**	**70**	**9**	**79**	**9**	**72**	**1**	**54**
0	7	0	15	0	6	1	0	1	0	0	1	0	1	0	2
15	62	14	30	7	7	4	24	0	11	2	3	3	12	0	4
3	28	3	14	0	8	2	1	0	4	0	0	0	1	1	8
0	1	0	6	1	3	0	0	0	0	0	4	0	0	0	0
0	7	1	5	0	2	1	4	0	3	0	3	0	2	0	1
0	34	3	8	0	10	1	8	0	8	4	11	0	19	0	8
0	7	0	18	0	17	0	15	4	19	0	23	0	5	0	9
2	3	13	1	3	8	2	1	4	1	1	15	1	8	0	2
0	4	0	5	0	0	0	4	0	2	0	0	0	1	0	0
0	2	0	1	2	1	0	3	0	0	0	0	0	1	0	1
0	21	2	12	0	18	0	21	0	3	0	1	0	0	0	0
2	25	0	9	0	9	1	4	0	11	2	15	5	14	0	17
6	8	1	12	1	7	0	4	0	8	0	3	0	8	0	2

Ideologically Motivated Attacks Against Property

D – dangerous assaults O – other assaults *	2009		2010		2011		2012		2013	
	D	O	D	O	D	O	D	O	D	O
Total	36	136	36	142	13	81	11	84	23	48
Religious targets	14	45	17	43	12	53	10	61	23	41
Russian Orthodox	5	11	8	8	3	9	5	33	12	19
Muslim	3	5	2	7	1	16	1	5	5	4
Jewish	1	21	1	14	1	13	1	7	3	7
New religious movements	1	3	4	10	5	11	2	11	2	9
Catholic	0	1	0	0	0	0	0	1	0	0
Protestant	2	2	2	1	2	3	1	4	1	0
Armenian	2	2	0	2	0	0	0	0	0	0
Other religious **	0	0	0	1	0	1	0	0	0	2
Other targets	22	91	19	99	1	28	1	23	0	7
State facilities	9	0	12	1	0	0	0	0	0	0
Ideological targets	13	91	5	95	1	27	1	23	0	7
Other ***	0	0	2	3	0	1	0	0	0	0

* The most dangerous assaults are explosions and arson, others – various breakdowns, as well as other damage, including graffiti (but excluding individual graffiti on the walls).

This table does not include data on Crimea prior to 2016 and on the North Caucasus.

** These include Buddhist targets and other religions that were not mentioned and religious objects that could not be attributed.

*** These include objects that do not fall into any of the other categories or those that could not be attributed.

2014		2015		2016		2017		2018		2019		2020	
D	O	D	O	D	O	D	O	D	O	D	O	D	O
11	43	10	46	6	40	14	35	7	27	6	14	7	23
6	26	9	24	6	25	9	21	7	13	6	9	7	11
2	8	4	5	2	8	4	7	4	7	3	3	3	5
4	4	2	5	0	4	0	0	0	1	0	1	0	2
0	5	1	4	1	4	1	0	3	1	1	4	1	2
0	8	2	9	3	7	3	11	0	0	1	1	0	0
0	0	0	0	0	0	0	0	0	0	1	0	0	0
0	1	0	0	0	0	1	1	0	2	0	0	2	0
0	0	0	0	0	0	0	0	0	1	0	0	0	0
0	0	0	1	0	2	0	2	0	1	0	0	1	2
5	17	1	22	0	15	5	14	0	14	0	5	0	12
1	4	0	4	0	1	0	0	0	0	0	0	0	1
4	13	1	18	0	14	4	14	0	14	0	5	0	7
0	0	0	0	0	0	1	0	0	0	0	0	0	4

Guilty Verdicts for "Crimes of an Extremist Nature"

In addition to hate propaganda and crimes that are directly related to the concept of "extremism," this table includes sentences for ordinary hate crimes. We can assess the sentences as fully or largely appropriate, or as fully or largely inappropriate; sometimes, we are unable to determine the extent of appropriateness**. Three numbers in each column refer to sentences that we consider appropriate, inappropriate, and indeterminate.

Year	Number of verdicts (in which at least one defendant was found guilty)				Number of convicts	
Crimes	against persons	against property	Public statements	Membership in a group *	against persons	against property
2004	9/0/0	-***	3/0/0	3/2/0	26/0/0	-
2005	17/0/0	-	12/1/0	2/4/8	56/0/0	-
2006	33/0/0	-	17/2/0	3/1/3	109/0/0	-
2007	38/0/0	4/0/0	30/1/1	2/0/8	89/0/0	5/0/0
2008	33/0/0	8/0/0	49/2/1	3/0/4	107/0/0	7/0/0
2009	52/0/1	10/0/0	56/4/0	5/13/2	130/0/2	20/0/0
2010	91/0/0	13/0/1	69/8/3	9/6/8	305/0/0	22/0/1
2011	62/1/3	9/0/0	72/6/1	12/7/7	195/4/3	16/0/0
2012	32/2/2	5/0/0	87/4/1	6/9/3	70/4/3	7/0/0
2013	32/1/0	8/0/0	130/7/3	7/8/6	55/1/0	11/0/0
2014	22/0/2	4/0/0	153/4/6	7/9/14	47/0/3	6/0/0
2015	24/1/0	8/1/0	211/14/9	11/16/3	58/1/0	14/1/0
2016	17/2/0	5/0/0	207/17/9	8/22/1	39/2/0	6/0/0
2017	10/0/0	4/0/0	216/17/21	4/27/3	24/0/0	6/0/0
2018 **	16/0/2	2/0/0	60/11/140	4/25/3	48/0/7	6/0/0
2019	5/0/0	0/0/0	15/6/92	7/27/6	11/0/0	0/0/0
2020 *	5/0/0	1/0/0	6/11/106	3/41/13	8/0/0	1/0/0

* This includes participation in an "extremist community" or an organization banned for extremism, as well as in Hizb ut-Tahrir under Art. 205.5 of the Criminal Code.

** Since 2018, we have been using the "undeterminate" category in the assessment of the verdicts in a much broader manner (see the report); in the table above, this category includes the verdicts that are not related to countering nationalism and xenophobia.

*** The hyphen means that the data for this period has not yet been collected.

Number of convicts		Suspended sentences or released from punishment				
Public statements	Membership in a group *	against persons	against property	Public statements	Membership in a group *
3/0/0	3/2/0	5/0/0	-	2/0/0	2/0/0
15/2/0	2/18/19	5/0/0	-	6/0/0	0/1/9
20/2/0	15/1/3	24/0/0	-	7/1/0	0/0/0
41/1/5	4/0/27	12/0/0	5/0/0	9/0/0	0/0/6
67/3/0	10/0/14	22/0/0	6/0/0	27/3/0	2/0/7
74/5/0	9/25/2	35/0/1	7/0/0	33/1/0	2/12/1
78/9/5	32/6/19	119/0/0	5/0/1	35/5/4	5/5/8
80/7/1	26/12/19	77/4/1	4/0/0	33/2/1	3/7/4
100/11/1	9/24/13	13/0/2	1/0/0	15/6/0	1/12/4
136/7/4	8/16/11	14/0/0	1/0/0	14/3/3	1/3/3
158/4/8	15/22/26	7/0/1	0/0/0	14/2/0	2/5/4
220/16/9	25/44/6	12/0/0	2/0/0	41/2/3	7/20/0
226/18/9	22/38/2	3/0/0	0/0/0	101/4/3	14/1/0
235/18/22	6/76/11	1/0/0	0/0/0	116/7/9	4/6/0
71/12/140	9/76/6	9/0/0	0/0/0	25/5/82	1/1/0
20/6/93	15/94/18	4/0/0	0/0/0	9/2/41	4/10/1
7/17/117	8/78/31	1/0/0	1/0/0	4/1/102	1/28/6

Anti-Extremist Legislation

Anti-extremist legislation, as a comprehensive legislation in the sphere of state and public security, emerged in Russia in 2002. On the one hand, it includes elements that exist or formerly existed in the legislation of Russia, in one form or another. On the other hand, it represents an ambitious attempt at a comprehensive solution to problems usually linked in the realm of social sciences rather than in the realm of law.

A brief description of this legislation is provided here, given that the transformations that have taken place since 2014 will be discussed below.

The Framework Law

Russian anti-extremist legislation consists of a framework law "On Combating Extremist Activity," related criminal and administrative norms, as well as relevant provisions of several other laws.

A systematic state policy on countering extremism in Russia can be said to have originated on July 25, 2002 with signing of Federal Law No. 114-FZ "On Combating Extremist Activity."[1] It actually defines the concept of "extremism" ("extremist activity"),[2] as well as the related concepts of "extremist organization," "extremist materials" and "symbols of an extremist organization." In addition to the general principles that underlie the anti-extremist policies, the law established particular mechanisms for holding public organizations and the media responsible for their extremist activities.

Extremism is defined in Art. 1 of the law as a set of various actions. This list has been modified several times – in 2006, 2007, 2012 and 2020. As of July 2021, it includes the following:

- forcible change of the foundations of the constitutional order and (or) violation of the territorial integrity of the Russian Federation (including alienation of part of the territory of the Russian Federation) with the exception of delimitation, demarcation or re-demarcation of state borders of the Russian Federation with neighboring states;

- public justification of terrorism and other terrorist activity;

- stirring up of social, racial, national or religious enmity;

- propaganda of the exceptional nature, superiority or deficiency of persons on the basis of their social, racial, national, religious or linguistic affiliation or attitude to religion;

- violation of human and civil rights and freedoms and lawful interests in connection with a person's social, racial, national, religious or linguistic affiliation or attitude to religion;

- obstruction of the exercise by citizens of their electoral rights and rights to participate in a referendum or violation of voting secrecy, combined with violence or threat of the use thereof;

- obstruction of the lawful activities of state authorities, local authorities, electoral commissions, public and religious associations or other organizations, combined with violence or threat of the use thereof;

- committing of crimes with the motives set out in Paragraph "f" ["e" in the Russian original] of Art. 63, Part 1 of the Criminal Code of the Russian Federation;

- propaganda and public show of Nazi emblems or symbols, as well as of emblems or symbols confusingly similar to Nazi emblems or symbols, or public show of the emblems or symbols of extremist organizations;

- public calls inciting the carrying out of the aforementioned actions or mass dissemination of knowingly extremist material, and likewise the production or storage thereof with the aim of mass dissemination;

- public, knowingly false accusation of an individual holding state office of the Russian Federation or state office of a Russian Federation constituent entity of having committed actions mentioned in the present Article and that constitute offenses while discharging their official duties;

- organization and preparation of the aforementioned actions and also incitement of others to commit them;

- funding of the aforementioned actions or any assistance for their organization, preparation and carrying out, including by providing training, printing and material/technical support, telephony or other types of communications links or information services.

The feature of the Russian definition of extremism is that not all of its components are related to violence and the threat of its use.

Legal understanding of extremism in Russia is characterized by the fact that, from the very beginning, this term has encompassed acts against the security of the state and actions threatening vulnerable groups of society (i.e., hate crimes and hate speech). The impetus to combine these phenomena of a different nature into a single notion can, most likely, be found in Art. 13 of the Constitution of the Russian Federation, which prohibits activities instigating social, racial, national and religious strife and anti-state activities of public associations in the same sentence.[3] Presidential decrees of the 1990s, in which the term "extremism" was first mentioned, contain references to this constitutional norm. Vague wording of the definition of extremist activity in the framework law, such as "forcible change of the foundations of the constitutional system and violation of the integrity of the Russian Federation" and "undermining the security of the Russian Federation" came from the same source (the 2007 amendments excluded the latter from the definition).

It should be noted that acts directed against the state and against vulnerable groups of the population were individually recognized as illegal even before they were united under the umbrella of "extremism."

Countering extremist activities, understood in accordance with the definition provided in the law, implies additional restrictions on civil rights and freedoms as compared to the ordinary fight against crime. However, according to the International Covenant on Civil and Political Rights (ICCPR), such restrictions must be established by law, pursue the legitimate aim of respecting the rights and reputations of others, protecting national security, public order, or public health or morals, and be necessary in a democratic society. Both the Russian definition of extremism described above and the legal norms associated with it raise questions regarding their compliance with the international legal standards, since they use vague terminology and can be interpreted broadly. This applies to freedom of expression in particular, but also to freedom of association. Coupled with the law enforcement practice, characterized, among other features, by a formal approach to establishing the illegality of an act in court, application of these standards often leads to state-imposed restrictions on civil liberties that cannot be recognized as necessary in a democratic society.[4]

Until the summer of 2021, the law "On Combating Extremist Activity" defined extremist materials as "documents intended for publication or information on other media calling for extremist activity to be carried out or substantiating or justifying the necessity of carrying out such activity, including works by leaders of the National Socialist Workers' Party of Germany or the Fascist party of Italy, publications substantiating or justifying ethnic and/or racial superiority or justifying the practice of committing war crimes or other crimes aimed at the full or partial destruction of any ethnic, social, racial, national or religious group."

Such materials are prohibited for mass distribution by courts on the basis of prosecutorial claims. Descriptions of materials recognized as extremist are assembled by the Ministry of Justice into the Federal List of Extremist Materials. Next, access to these materials, if they are found on the Internet, as well as to other materials with "signs of extremism," is blocked – giving rise to a large-scale practice of blocking online resources.

The practice of individual blocking orders was gradually supplanted by two mechanisms that were introduced later.

The first operating mechanism of Internet filtering, based on the Uniform Registry of Banned Web Sites, exists since November 2012. Initially, The Federal Service for Supervision of Communications, Information Technology and Mass Communications (Roskomnadzor) simply added to it the online materials, which had been recognized as extremist and included in the Federal List. Since 2014, courts started issuing decisions to enter Web sites into the Registry without recognizing them as extremist, based on the fact that they contained materials similar to the ones already recognized as extremist.

The second blocking mechanism was established by the amendments known as the Lugovoi law, which entered into force in February 2014 and allowed the Prosecutor-General's Office to demand that Roskomnadzor immediately, without a trial, block Web sites containing "incitement to mass riots, extremist activity, incitement of ethnic and (or) sectarian strife, participation in terrorist activities, or participation in public mass events held in violation of the established order."

Certain prosecutor's offices can issue a notification to public or religious associations or other organizations about the inadmissibility of extremist activity, if prosecutors have information about upcoming actions that show signs of extremism. If the fact of such activity has already been established, a prosecutor's office or the Ministry of Justice issues a warning. If violations are recognized as serious, or are not eliminated, or if new ones are discovered within a year, the organization is subject to liquidation by a court decision, which recognizes it as extremist.

Criminal Law

The reference to Art. 63 Part 1 Paragraph "f" ["e" in the Russian original] of the Criminal Code in the definition of extremism means that extremist activity includes carrying out of a crime with such aggravating circumstances as the motive of "political, ideological, racial, national or religious hatred or hostility" or the motive of "hatred or hostility in relation to any social group." Moreover, these same motives are indicated as qualifying features in Arts. 105 (murder), 111, 112, 115 (intentional infliction of grave injury, injury of average gravity, or light injury to health respectively), 116 (battery), 117 (torture), 119 (threat of murder or infliction of grave injury to health), 150 (involvement of a minor in the commission of a crime), 213 (hooliganism), 214 (vandalism), 244 (outrages upon bodies of the deceased and their burial places).

An entire block of existing criminal articles is aimed at countering extremism.

Art. 280 of the Criminal Code provides for liability for public incitement to extremist activity.

According to the decision of the plenary meeting of the Supreme Court of the Russian Federation on judicial practice in cases involving "extremist" crimes,[5] calls for genocide, repression, deportation, for ethnic or religious violence in general are acts aimed at inciting hatred which fall under Art. 282 of the Criminal Code (see below). However, investigators often prefer to qualify calls for xenophobic attacks under Art. 280 of the Criminal Code, rather than Art. 282. Such calls may be more or less clear about the object and the method of an attack.

Art. 282 Part 1 of the Criminal Code, in its current version, stipulates responsibility for public actions aimed at incitement of hatred or hostility, as well as abasement of dignity of a person or a group of persons on the basis of "sex, race, nationality, language, origin, attitude to religion, as well as affiliation to any social group." Penalty for the first such violation takes the form of a fine under an equivalent administrative article (Art. 20.3.1 of the Code of Administrative Offenses), and criminal liability follows for a repeated violation within a year. Until 2019, there was no corresponding administrative article, and citizens faced criminal prosecution for their very first violation of the law. People previously convicted under Art. 282 Part 1 could apply for review of their cases in 2019 and get their sentences annulled; the cases under investigation as of the beginning of 2019 were closed.

Art. 282 Part 2 covers the cases, when hatred is connected to the use of violence or a threat of such use; it does not provide for administrative punishment for the first violation.

Art. 282 has been widely used to counter the spread of xenophobic propaganda.

Art. 280.1, introduced into the Criminal Code in 2013, separately establishes liability for public calls for action aimed at violating the territorial integrity of the Russian Federation (i.e., separatism). The problematic nature of this norm stems from the fact that the definition of extremism and, accordingly, the disposition of Art. 280.1 of the Criminal Code contain no indication that violation of territorial integrity is illegal specifically if and when it includes the use of force.

In late 2020, this article underwent a revision similar to that described above for Art. 282 (see details below).

A whole series of Criminal Code articles is related to organizing. **Art. 282.1** provides punishment for organizing an extremist community, recruiting for it and participation in it. Such a community is understood as an organized group of people gathered to plan "crimes of an extremist nature." The note to this criminal article indicates that this term only refers to hate crimes. In practice, however, "crimes of an extremist nature" – as also reflected in the Supreme Court decision in 2011[6] – include all the crimes qualified under Arts. 280, 280.1, 282, 282.1, 282.2, and 282.3 of the Criminal Code.

Art. 282.2 of the Criminal Code establishes sanctions for organizing an extremist organization, recruiting for it and participating in it. In contrast to the previous legal norm, Art. 282.2 of the Criminal Code refers to organizations already banned by the court as extremist and included on a special list published by the Ministry of Justice. Therefore, this is a formally defined crime – the very fact of participation in a banned organization makes a person liable regardless of whether or what kind of socially dangerous consequences it entailed or did not entail.

Both of these articles also covered terrorist communities and organizations until 2013, when separate articles that provide for much more stringent sanctions for these actions – **205.4** (for communities) and **205.5** (for organizations) – were added to the Criminal Code.

Art. 282.3 of the Criminal Code relates to the financing of extremist activities.

Without going into much detail about the criminal liability for terrorist activities, we would like to bring attention to an anti-terrorism legal norm that restricts freedom of expression – **Art. 205.2** of the Criminal Code (public calls for committing terrorist activities, public justification of terrorism or propaganda of terrorism).

Art. 354.1 Parts 1 and 2 of the Criminal Code (rehabilitation of Nazism) addressed in 2014-2020 punishment for publicly denying the facts established by the International Military Tribunal, approving the crimes mentioned therein and "disseminating knowingly false information about the activities of the USSR during World War II." Part 3 of the same article provided liability for disseminating information about the memorable dates that expresses "obvious disrespect for society" and for desecrating symbols of Russia's military glory.

In Russia, minor offenses are classified not under the Criminal Code, but under the Code of Administrative Offenses (CAO, already mentioned above). In addition to the already mentioned Art. 20.3.1, some other norms of the Code of Administrative Offenses, were also used in 2014-2020 in the course of anti-extremist law enforcement.

Art. 20.3 of the Code of Administrative Offenses (CAO RF) provides penalties for publicly displaying Nazi symbols and paraphernalia, or attributes or symbols confusingly similar to them, symbols of extremist organizations, and other prohibited symbols. In addition, it covers the production and sale of such symbols for propaganda purposes.

Art. 20.29 CAO RF pertains to mass distribution of extremist materials and their storage for the purpose of mass distribution. Responsibility arises only with respect to materials already included in the Federal List of Extremist Materials on the basis of court decisions (see above). The context and purpose of the distribution of prohibited materials are not taken into account when someone is held accountable under Art. 20.29 of the Code of Administrative Offenses, and, in some cases, the intent to distribute materials has been established only nominally.

NOTES

1. Federal Law of July 25, 2002, N 114-FZ "On Combating Extremist Activity" (as amended) // Garant. URL: https://base.garant.ru/12127578/.

2. These terms are equivalent in the law and, therefore, in the Russian legislation overall.

3. The Constitution of the Russian Federation // Site of the President of Russia. URL: http://www.constitution.ru/en/10003000-02.htm.

4. See: Rights in extremis: Russia's anti-extremism practices from an international perspective // ARTICLE 19, SOVA Center. 2019. URL: https://www.sova-center.ru/files/books/a19_sova_eng.pdf.

5. Ruling of the plenary meeting of the Supreme Court of the Russian Federation No. 11 "On Judicial Practice in Criminal Cases Regarding Crimes of Extremism" of June 28, 2011 (as amended by the plenary meeting decisions No. 41 of Nov. 3, 2016 and No. 32 of September 20, 2018) // The Supreme Court of the Russian Federation. Sept. 20, 2018. URL: https://www.vsrf.ru/documents/own/27145/.

6. Ruling of the plenary meeting of the Supreme Court of the Russian Federation No. 11 [see above].

PART THREE

Development of Legal Framework

In February, the bill "On Amendments to the Criminal Code of the Russian Federation (with regard to increasing liability for extremist action)" was signed into law. The law toughens punishments under the Criminal Code Art. 280 (calls for extremist activity), Art. 282 (incitement to hatred and enmity), 282.1 (organizing an extremist community) and Art. 282.2 (organizing the activity of an extremist organization). The fines were increased and the terms of forced labor extended under all articles; the upper limits for prison terms were also raised under three of them (except 282). Prior to the commencement of this law, the crimes covered by the Criminal Code Arts. 280 Part 1, 282.1 Part 2, and 282.2 were considered minor offenses. Now they have been transferred to the category of major and mid-level offenses, with corresponding procedural consequences. The main drawback of the new law is the raising of the upper limit for a prison term – a measure, unwarranted by the practice of anti-extremist law enforcement in Russia. Meanwhile, the increase in fines appeared appropriate.

On May 5, 2014 the President signed an anti-terrorism legislation package, proposed in January 2014 by a group of parliamentarians from all four factions. These laws affected far more than just terrorist activities. Below, we outline the innovations related to the issue of counteracting extremism.

The first out of three laws in the package was the law "On Amendments to Certain Legislative Acts of the Russian Federation (relating to improvements in counteracting terrorism)." Prison terms under the Criminal Code Art. 212 (mass public unrest) were increased from 4-10 years to 8-15 years. The wording of the criminal code article was amended; punishment is now stipulated not only for organizing mass unrest, but also for preparing it, while the list of methods used in mass unrest ("the use of firearms, explosives or explosive devices") was supplemented by "substances and objects that pose a threat to those in the vicinity," thus expanding the notion of "unrest" in principle. The article was supplemented by Part 4 which criminalized "the acquisition of knowledge and practical skills in the course of physical and psychological preparation" for organizing mass unrest.

Additions were also introduced to the Criminal Code Arts. 282.1 and 282.2. Now they include potential liability (from one to six years of imprisonment) for "the inducement, recruitment or other involvement of a person" in the activities of an extremist community or organization. Such broad formulas criminalized activities of people who are not themselves members of extremist organizations or communities and failed to clarify what should be considered "an inducement to participate," if the inducing person does not participate in the entity himself/herself.

The "Law on Bloggers" from the same "anti-terrorist package" amended the laws on information and communication to increase the state control over the Internet in order to counter extremism. Service providers now must notify Roskomnadzor (Federal Service for Supervision in the Sphere of Telecom, Information Technologies and Mass Communications) about the start of their business activity; they must store data about all user activity for six months after the end of providing service and supply this information to law enforcement authorities in cases, specified by law. They must also comply with the requirements relating to certain equipment and software/hardware that facilitates operational and investigative activities. The law also provided a legal definition of the term "blogger" as an owner of an Internet site or page, not registered as mass media, that is accessed by 3,000 or more users on a daily basis. Roskomnadzor has been designated to provide clarifications.[1] These "bloggers" must disclose their own actual names; they shared the obligations of the mass media but not the rights, and must be listed in a special register. As of early 2015, the register included only about 500 bloggers.

On the same day, the bill "On the Rehabilitation of Nazism," proposed by a group of members of parliament headed by Irina Yarovaya (United Russia), was also signed into law. A new Art. 354.1 was added to the criminal code; it sets a hefty fine or up to five years of imprisonment for "denial of facts established by the verdict of the International Military Tribunal for the trial and punishment of the major war criminals of the European Axis countries, approval of the crimes established by this verdict, as well as the dissemination of knowingly false information about the activities of the USSR during the years of World War II combined with accusations of crimes established by the said judgment, committed in public." The penalties vary from a fine (up to 300,000 rubles) to five years in prison. From our perspective, the law could not help to counteract neo-Nazi propaganda, since all the necessary legal tools had already been provided by the Criminal Code Art. 282.

Meanwhile, due to the new law's infelicitous and vague language, it opened possibilities for restricting freedom of expression, especially in historical debates.

A law on combating extremism on the Internet and in finance was signed in June and introduced a new Art. 282.3 (financing of extremist activity) into the Criminal Code. The wording of the article was as follows: "Financing or collection of funds or providing financial services wittingly intended to finance extremist organization, preparation, and commitment of at least one extremist crime or support an extremist community or extremist organization." Penalties for these offenses range from a fine of 300,000 rubles to imprisonment for up to three years under Part 1 and up to six years under Part 2. In our opinion, the introduction of a new article in the Criminal Code was unjustified because providing funds for extremist activities had already been regarded as a form of complicity in extremism.

In its part pertaining to online activities, the law added the words "Information and telecommunications networks, including the Internet" to the text of the Criminal Code Arts. 280 and 282, thus giving the Internet the same status as media outlets.[2] Including this amendment into Art. 282 does not effect any actual changes, in Art. 280, on the other hand, an online publication moved from Part 1 to a more severe Part 2. In our opinion, equating the Internet to mass media in the sense of Arts. 280 and 282 with regard to anti-extremist law enforcement is inappropriate, inasmuch as the information posted online can differ widely in its degree of public exposure and may be intended for a small group of users. We should also note that prosecution for unlawful statements online was practiced quite widely even prior to the adoption of this law.

In the second half of July, the President signed the Law "On Amendments to Art. 280.1 of the Criminal Code of the Russian Federation," which further toughens recently introduced punishment for "public calls for action aimed at violating the territorial integrity of the Russian Federation" and treats any statements posted on the Internet similarly to statements published via mass media. This article now stipulates penalties ranging from a fine of 100,000 rubles to five years of imprisonment. We view the entire Criminal Code Art. 280.1, introduced in 2013, as a negative development, and continue to insist that only violent separatism should entail criminal prosecution. Increasing the severity of the article even further, in our opinion, constituted an attack on the freedom of speech, particularly in view of the inevitable debates regarding the annexation of Crimea.

In November, the President signed the law expanding application of the Code of Administrative Offenses Art. 20.3, pertaining to banned symbols (i.e., Nazi symbols). The law establishes legal responsibility for propaganda and public demonstration of attributes or symbols of "organizations, which cooperated with fascist organizations or movements and cooperate with international or foreign organizations and their representatives who deny the verdict of the International Military Tribunal (Nuremberg Tribunal) as well as national, military or occupation tribunals, based on the judgment of the Nuremberg Tribunal." As clearly stated in the explanatory memorandum to the bill, this formulation refers to the organizations that use "symbols and attributes of the Banderite organization in Ukraine." From our point of view, the law, adopted solely due to foreign policy reasons, was redundant, while its broad interpretation, which seems highly probable, can lead to various legal oddities and inappropriate prosecution. The legislative body de facto delegated the implementation of this law to the government, which has been charged with compiling a list of relevant organizations. Notably, the list still does not exist.

In December, the government introduced to the State Duma a draft bill proposing fines of up to a million rubles for media outlets that propagate extremist materials, incitements to extremist activities, justification of terrorism, and so on. The draft was approved in the first reading in February 2015.

The Constitutional Court made in 2014 a number of important decisions in our area of interest in the course of the year. Unfortunately, all these decisions only strengthen the existing trend toward gradual shrinking of civic freedoms.

In mid-September 2014, it became known that the Constitutional Court of the Russian Federation refused to consider an appeal against the law "On Information, Information Technologies and Protection of Information." The appeal was filed by director of the Association of Internet publishers Vladimir Kharitonov after his Web site digital-books.ru had been blocked due to having the same IP-address as the Web site that promoted illegal drugs. Kharitonov claimed that the practice of blocking IP addresses de facto takes away the right to distribute non-prohibited information and constitutes a punishment for the site owners, who committed no infringements against the law. However, the Constitutional Court has stated in its definition that the rights of owners of the Web sites that happened to be blocked along with the resources that contained banned information, were violated not by including their network address on the register, but by "improper actions (or inaction) of their hosting service provider." Thus, the Constitutional Court refused to recognize an error in the law and shifted responsibility onto hosting providers.

In late October, the Constitutional Court upheld the ban on any display of Nazi symbols and symbols similar to them to the point of confusion. The determination was issued in response to a complaint filed by Vladimir Murashov, sentenced to an administrative fine for such acts. Murashov argued that, in various cultural traditions, symbols and signs in question have meaning not associated with the ideology of Nazism, and, therefore, the ban on their use and dissemination violates his constitutional rights. The Constitutional Court rejected the complaint, not finding any ambiguity in the ban, despite its glaring obviousness. The determination used the following argument: "In itself, the use of Nazi attributes (symbols), as well as attributes (symbols), similar to Nazi attributes (symbols) to the point of confusion – regardless of their genesis – can cause distress to people whose relatives were killed during the Great Patriotic War, which also entails the right of a legislative body to take measures in accordance with Art. 55 (Part 3) of the Constitution of the Russian Federation." Thus, the Constitutional Court refused to bring any clarity to the issue of interpreting the symbols, and inappropriate prosecution under the Code of Administrative Offenses Art. 20.3 for displaying swastikas and other symbols, regardless of context and objectives of these actions, continued (see below).

Similarly, the Constitutional Court refused to see any ambiguities in the language and use of the Criminal Code Art. 213 (hooliganism), when considering a complaint by Nadezhda Tolokonnikova, member of the Pussy Riot punk band. As Nadezhda Tolokonnikova pointed out, the Criminal Code Art. 213 "disproportionately restricts freedom of expression, allows one to declare a public nuisance what, in fact, is a violation of religious norms, and to establish the criminal nature of acts on the basis of them being perceived as unacceptable by the majority of the population." The Constitutional Court disagreed with Tolokonnikova's position, stating that "the challenged provisions of criminal law contain no ambiguity that could cause a person to be deprived of the opportunity to realize the wrongfulness of his/her actions and anticipate eventual responsibility for its commission, and which could prevent uniform understanding and application of the rule by the law enforcement authorities, and can not be viewed as constituting a violation of the applicant's rights." According to the Constitutional Court judges, in cases when the information is propagated in a manner, based on "gross and demonstrative neglect toward accepted societal notions of acceptable behavior in particular locations, including religious Web sites, is devoid of any aesthetic and artistic value and is in and of itself offensive," such activity falls outside the legitimate scope for freedom of expression. As we see it, the history of use of the Criminal Code Art. 213 indicates lack of common understanding of this article (including the interpretation of the hate motive) among various law enforcement agencies. Regretfully, the Constitutional Court failed to notice this problem as it failed to notice defects in the overall wording of Art. 213 in its 2007 edition. The issues pertaining to the extent of exhibited disregard for social norms, or the degree of social danger of particular incidents of hooliganism, not to mention aesthetic and artistic aspects of an event, are all debatable.[3]

NOTES

1. Roskomnadzor has, in fact, developed a definition of "user visit" and a rather complicated method for determining the number of visits (number of users) per day. For details, see: Roskomnadzor has developed methodology to identify a "blogger" // SOVA Center. June 10, 2014 (http://www.sova-center.ru/misuse/news/lawmaking/2014/06/d29705/).

2. Changes were also introduced into the law "On Combating Extremist Activity" to the articles, describing the role of the various authorities, including the text of Art. 13 of the Law, which stipulates procedural deadlines, associated with recognizing materials as extremist.

3. The consistent position of the Constitutional Court in the assessment of anti-extremist norms was, once again confirmed in March 2015; the Constitutional Court confirmed the ban against the swastika and asserting the verity of only one religion // SOVA Center. March 4, 2015 (http://www.sova-center.ru/misuse/news/lawmaking/2015/03/d31422/).

The year of 2015 turned out to be much less productive with regard to updating anti-extremist legislation than the previous few years. Perhaps, at some point, the people in charge of the real legislative process realized that increase in severity of legislation needs to be halted in order to give the enforcement system a chance to master the changes of the preceding three years.

Notably, the most significant changes of this year pertained not to the criminal law, but to softer instruments. In this respect, we need to discuss, first of all, two legislative norms, one of which is only partly related to our area of interest.

The first one is the law on "undesirable foreign organizations," that is, the new amendments to the notorious Dima Yakovlev's Law. On May 23, the president signed the amendment proclaiming that "activities of foreign or international non-governmental organization that represent a threat to the foundations of the constitutional system of the Russian Federation, the country's defense or security of the State may be considered undesirable in the Russian Federation."

The decision that activities of an organization are undesirable on the territory of the Russian Federation is made by the Prosecutor General's Office with input from the Foreign Ministry and the Ministry of Justice, but without any input from the court. Cooperation with "undesirable organizations" is an administrative offense, and repeated cooperation, and, especially, heading their work in Russia is a criminal offense. Observers could have assumed that the new amendment pertained to threats that could be classified as terrorist or extremist. In this case, the amendments could have been regarded as an additional instrument of anti-extremist legislation. However, this conclusion begged a reasonable question – why was an extrajudicial procedure provided in this case, if the only way to recognize organizations, including foreign ones, as extremist is through the courts.

However, the practice of law enforcement has followed another expected scenario – the status of "undesirable" has been applied to Western funds for supporting social activity, which fails to meet the legal definition of extremism even in its broadest interpretation.

Another important innovation of 2015 was administrative responsibility introduced for extremist activities in the mass media – obviously, not instead of criminal responsibility but in addition to it.

On May 2, the following amendments were made to the Code of Administrative Offenses: Art. 13.15 (abuse of freedom of mass media) came to include the new sixth part, which introduces fines for legal entities (publisher, and so on) for the "production and manufacturing of media that contains public incitement to terrorist activity, and (or) materials, publicly justifying terrorism, and (or) other materials calling for extremist activity, or justifying or excusing the need for such an activity." The fines range from 100,000 to 1 million rubles with confiscation of the offending object. The wording is similar to Art. 205.2 (public calls for committing terrorist activities, public justification of terrorism or propaganda of terrorism) and Art. 280 (public calls for extremist activity), so it implies punishment for the same act, but for the publishers rather than the authors. A question arises as to whether this provision of the Code of Administrative Offenses should be used only if a related criminal case has been initiated, or regardless of it.

Exceptions were provided for the offenses covered under the Code of Administrative Offenses Arts. 20.3 (distribution of banned symbols) and 20.29 (distribution of banned materials) since these activities were already covered by previously established penalties. On the other hand, the law increased the amount of a fine under Art. 20.29 of the Administrative Code (mass distribution of extremist materials) for legal entities to 100,000 and up to 1 million rubles (previously, they ranged from 50,000 to 100,000 rubles).

In 2015, we have information about only one case of utilizing the new rules of the Administrative Code (see below). In principle, holding publishers responsible for criminal propaganda offenses published in their media outlets does not constitute a legally inappropriate innovation. However, if a criminal conviction is not required for its use, this new Administrative Code article becomes an independent instrument for punishing the media and, thereby, creates additional opportunities for arbitrary enforcement. It is much easier to bring a person to administrative responsibility than to criminal one – there are fewer instruments of defense, and it becomes possible to ruin a media outlet by fines.

As for penalties for the mass distribution of prohibited materials, it should be taken into account that the length of the Federal List of Extremist

Materials, which provides the basis for these verdicts, has exceeded 3,200 items by the end of 2015, and, for the most part, it is impossible to understand. Thus, punishing citizens on the basis of the cryptic list is becoming increasingly problematic. A radical increase of fines, given such problematic law enforcement, seemed altogether inappropriate.

A series of scandals related to bans against religious materials led to an unexpected result – in 2015, President Putin proposed a bill (which was, of course, adopted immediately), prohibiting to prohibit the fundamental religious texts. Perhaps, the intentions were good, but as a result, the bill, signed on November 23, amended the Law on Combating Extremist Activity to include Art. 3.1 "Specifics of applying legislation of the Russian Federation on combating extremist activity with regard to religious texts" which reads as follows: "The Bible, the Koran, the Tanakh, and the Kangyur, their contents, and quotations from them cannot be recognized as extremist materials."

Although religious leaders had welcomed the amendment, admittedly, it made no practical sense. The amendment failed to clarify the issues regarding translations and various versions of the Bible, the Koran, the Tanakh and the Kangyur, and whether or in what format these can be subject to a ban, in whole or in part.

Thus, the problem of bans against old religious texts, which, far from being subject to prohibition, should not even be subject to interpretations based on the modern day concepts of extremism and tolerance, persisted.

On February 17, the Constitutional Court confirmed the prohibition against using the swastika in a religious context, where it had a clearly Buddhist origin, and motivated its decision by the fact that "the use of Nazi attributes (symbols) in and of itself… – regardless of their genesis – may cause suffering to people, whose relatives were killed during the Great Patriotic war."

Development of Legal Framework

The package of anti-terrorist laws, known as "Yarovaya's Package," submitted to the Duma in early April 2016, became the most significant legislative innovation of 2016. The initiative introduced by Deputy Irina Yarovaya and Senator Viktor Ozerov caused a heated discussion, which resulted in removal of several proposals from the legislative package under public pressure. The Deputies decided against dropping all forms of punishment other than imprisonment from the Criminal Code articles related to extremist crimes. They also rejected the proposed introduction of a new Criminal Code article on providing support to an extremist activity, the restrictions on leaving the country for those previously convicted under terrorist and extremist articles. Another rejected proposal suggested loss of citizenship for dual citizens convicted for crimes of terrorist or extremist nature, or serving in the army or law enforcement agencies of another state without prior authorization, or working in international structures that do not include Russia.

Nevertheless, the package as a whole was adopted and signed by the president on July 7, 2016. It launched the mechanisms that directly invaded the areas of freedom of speech and of protection of privacy and other rights and freedoms of citizens. The part of the package, related to control over the Internet caused a particularly strong resonance. The amendments require all communication providers to store information on the fact of communication between people for one year, and the actual content of calls and correspondence for up to six months (this part will only enter into force in the summer of 2018). The amendments further demand that "the organizers of information dissemination on the Internet" provide the FSB with keys to decrypt their users' correspondence or be subject to a fine, and that providers terminate contracts with subscribers upon request of law enforcement agencies, unless the user's identity is confirmed within 15 days (in case of anonymous SIM-cards).

Another important part of the package substantially restricts missionary work and has been applied most actively, starting in 2016; dozens of people faced administrative responsibility (SOVA Center covers this subject in greater detail in its 2016 report on the problems of exercising freedom of conscience in Russia). The amendments, essentially, make it possible to issue a fine for any religious statement not authorized in writing by an officially registered religious association. This section of the package was supposedly intended against the Salafi preaching, but the wording has been taken from the old "anti-cult movement," so that the Protestants, the Hare Krishnas, etc. became its first victims.

Yarovaya's Package significantly increased penalties for crimes of terrorist or extremist nature, as well as for organizing illegal migration. The age of criminal responsibility for a number of crimes (mainly of terrorist nature) was lowered. The Criminal Code came to include such questionable offenses as failing to report a terrorism-related crime or encouraging organization of mass disorders. From our point of view, prior law enforcement practice indicated no need for all these innovations, so there is little reason to think that they would be useful in fighting real threats; on the other hand, new abuses under the aegis of combating radicalism are already evident, and we can expect more of them.[1]

The bill "On the Basics of the Prevention of Offenses in the Russian Federation" was signed into law on June 23, 2016. The authorities of different levels and law enforcement agencies have been entrusted with such prevention; however, according to the law, citizens, public associations and other organizations legally possessing such rights, can participate in it. Prevention should be conducted in a number of areas, including fight against terrorism and extremist activities. In essence, the law merely sums up the established practices, but it has aroused certain suspicions by introducing (or reintroducing) vague expressions such as "antisocial behavior," "educational influence," and "a person intending to commit a crime" into the legal terminology. Preventive monitoring or participation of various kinds of social groups in crime prevention are not objectionable in and of themselves, but there is reason to fear that law enforcement agencies could interpret this law as a signal to an "excessively intensive" prevention campaign that would violate the rights of citizens (privacy, freedom of speech, religion, movement, etc.), as it happens, for example, in Dagestan. In addition, all kinds of citizens' registries, aimed at prevention, have a tendency to transform in our system from preventive to repressive tools, as happened in the 2000s with the Watchdog (*Storozhevoy control*) system, and later with the Rosfinmonitoring Registry.

On June 24, 2016, the president signed the law regulating the activity of online news aggregators in Russia. News aggregators with an audience of more than a million people a day now can only be owned by Russian nationals or legal entities and are somehow obligated to prevent "dissemination of materials containing public calls for terrorist activities or publicly justifying terrorism, or other extremist materials," as well as materials "of defamatory intent against a citizen or certain categories of citizens on the basis of sex, age, race or ethnicity, language, attitude toward religion, occupation, place of residence or work, or in connection with their political beliefs." This means that aggregators must delete news on a substantiated request from Roskomnadzor, and the refusal to comply entails responsibility under new Art. 19.7.10-1 of the Code of Administrative Offenses. A fine of up to 1 million rubles has been suggested for legal entities, increasing up to 3 million for a repeated violation. At the same time, aggregators are exempt from sanctions for the word-for-word distribution of materials, if these materials come from the sources registered as mass media – obviously, this clarification was made in order to encourage aggregators not to accumulate any other news sources. This law resulted in one tangible development in 2016 – news.yandex.ru has stopped publishing stories from unregistered media Web sites on its front page.

In March 2016, the Prosecutor General's Office issued an order providing a new procedure of banning materials for extremism. In accordance with it, the city and district-level prosecutor's offices and the military and specialized prosecutor's offices of equal status lost their right to file such lawsuits in courts. This right has been transferred to the prosecutor's offices of the Russian Federation constituents and to the military and specialized prosecutor's offices of equal status, albeit with the use of information coming from the lower-level prosecutors. Moreover, under the order, prior to court filing, the prosecutor's offices of the Federation's constituents are required to coordinate their prepared cases with the Department of the Prosecutor General's Office for supervision of enforcement of the laws on federal security, interethnic relations, countering extremism and terrorism (military prosecutors must coordinate their lawsuits with the Chief Military Prosecutor's Office). The order also contained a call to refrain from actions that could provoke adverse social consequences, and, in particular, take into account the law prohibiting recognition of the scriptures of the world religions and quotations from them as extremist.

On November 3, 2016, the plenary meeting of the Supreme Court of the Russian Federation adopted a new ruling on the use of anti-terrorist and anti-extremist articles of the Criminal Code ("On Amending the decisions of Ruling No. 1 of the plenary meeting of the Supreme Court of the Russian Federation 'On Certain Issues of Judicial Practice in Criminal Cases Regarding Crimes of Terror' " of February 9, 2012 and Ruling No. 11 of the plenary meeting of the Supreme Court of the Russian Federation "On Judicial Practice in Criminal Cases Regarding Crimes of Extremism," of June 28, 2011).[2] The ruling contained clarifications on a number of issues faced by Russian courts in their application of legislative norms aimed at combating extremism and terrorism.[3] The courts now have to base their decisions under the relevant Criminal Code articles on these clarifications.

Among other issues, the Supreme Court drew attention to the fact that, when applying Art. 280.1 of the Criminal Code (public calls for actions aimed at violating the territorial integrity of the Russian Federation), one should distinguish such calls from incitement to crimes aimed at violating the territorial integrity of the Russian Federation, since "calls should not be aimed at inducing specific individuals to commit particular criminal acts." Thus, from the point of view of the Supreme Court, a rather severe "anti-separatist" article of the Criminal Code should be applied precisely in the cases when an offender made no calls for illegal actions in order to achieve the goal.

An important clarification pertained to evaluating online publications: "When deciding on the nature of actions of an individual, who posted any information or expressed their attitude toward it on the Internet or other information and telecommunications networks, as aimed at incitement of hatred or enmity, as well as violation of the dignity of a person or group of persons, the decision should be based on the totality of all the circumstances of the deed and, in particular, take into account the context, form and content of the posted information, the existence and content of comments or other expressions of their attitude toward it." The Supreme Court's comment is more than relevant, but there is a clear need for more detailed explanations, as to what kind of context should be taken into account (it should be both the historical context and the circumstances, in which the utterance was made), how exactly comments of the information-sharer and other users (the latter can't be imputed to the original poster per se, but demonstrate the understanding of his/her statement by the audience), what is meant by "form" of a statement (for example, the court must learn to recognize the cases when the statement was ironic). In addition, it is necessary to take into account the quantitative and qualitative composition of the real target group of a given statement and the authority of its author within this group. This clarification about re-posting has had little practical impact until now, but it was unexpectedly used in March 2017 as an argument in the retrial of the notorious Yevgeniya Chudnovets case, unrelated to extremism.

The following thesis of the Supreme Court regarding extremist propaganda and calls for terrorism also merits attention – in case of public calls via mass message campaigns via mobile communication networks or the Internet, the crime should be considered completed "from the moment when calls are placed on these public networks (for example, on Web sites, forums or blogs), or sending messages to other persons." Until now, law enforcement agencies based their decisions on an assumption that a crime was still in progress for as long as the material in question remained online, even if this publication had been there for several years, and both the publisher and his readers have long forgotten about its existence.

NOTES

1. Additional details on the content and history of the adoption of the law can be found on our Web site: Putin signed the "Ozerov-Yarovaya package" // SOVA Center. July 7, 2016 (http://www.sova-center.ru/misuse/news/lawmaking/2016/07/d34993/).

2. Ruling of the Plenary Meeting of the Supreme Court of the Russian Federation No. 41 on issues of judicial practice in criminal cases of terrorist and extremist nature // SOVA Center. November 28, 2016 (http://www.sova-center.ru/racism-xenophobia/docs/2016/11/d35905/).

3. SOVA Center Comments on the Ruling of the Plenary Meeting of the Supreme Court on extremist and terrorist crimes // SOVA Center. November 3, 2016 (http://www.sova-center.ru/misuse/publications/2016/11/d35761/).

In 2017, the government continued its prior course on tightening its control over the Internet.

In February 2017, the president approved changes to the Code of Administrative Offenses (CAO) that increased the liability of Internet providers for failure to fulfill their obligations to block pages based on information received from Roskomnadzor. A new Art. 13.34 was introduced in the Code, establishing their liability in the form of a fine in the amount of 3,000 to 5,000 rubles for government officials, 10,000 to 30,000 rubles for individual entrepreneurs, and 50,000 to 100,0000 rubles for legal entities.[1]

The law banning the use of anonymizers and VPN-services for access to blocked Web sites in Russia was signed in July and entered into force in November. The Federal Law on Information added a new Art. 15.8, which requires such services to implement restrictions against banned materials under threat of sanctions, starting with blocking access to their own Web sites. At the same time, the regulations regarding the bloggers' registry and their duties[2] were removed from the Law on Information and the Code of Administrative Offenses due to their lack of effectiveness. The Art. 15.8 has not been used yet, as of late February 2018.

The draft legislation that seeks to fine search engines operators for failure to stop providing the links to prohibited Web sites (5,000 rubles for citizens, 50,000 rubles for officials, and 500,000 to 700,000 rubles for legal entities), introduced in the State Duma simultaneously with the above-described bill, passed the first reading in October; the second reading has not yet taken place.

In November, amendments were made (and immediately came into force) to the laws "On Information" and "On Mass Media" with regard to "foreign agents" media; among their other effects, the amendments created the widest opportunities for blocking Internet resources. They make extrajudicial blocking possible not only with respect to Web sites that contain calls for extremist activity, riots, or participation in actions without permits, as previously stipulated by the Lugovoi law, but also of Web sites that contain materials from "undesirable organizations" as well as "information, allowing to access" to any of the above. The meaning of the phrase "information allowing to access" is not entirely clear. At the very least, it implies hyperlinks to the Web sites or any publications of "undesirable organizations" or to calls (even extremely dated ones) to participate in non-permitted actions – and such links can be found on numerous Web sites of all kinds. Probably, a Web site can also be blocked for posting instructions on obtaining anonymous access to problematic resources via VPN or anonymizers.[3]

New restrictions for media outlets, primarily the foreign ones or the ones using foreign funds, fit the same trend of strengthening control over the flow of information.

The amendments to the Law on Mass Media, signed in July, imposed a ban on establishing media outlets for persons who are deprived of their liberty, or have a criminal record for committing crimes using the media or the Internet, or a criminal record "for committing crimes related to carrying out extremist activities." The amendments also allow Roskomnadzor to refuse permission to distribute a foreign periodical or to revoke such a permission, if the publication fails to comply with the article of the law on misuse of the media or with anti-extremism legislation in general.

A number of measures were taken in 2017 to increase the severity of the anti-terrorist and anti-extremist legislation.

In May, amendments were made to the Law on Administrative Supervision of persons released from correctional institutions. The amendments introduced changes to the provisions on administrative post-prison supervision, which affect, in particular, the fate of those convicted under anti-extremist and anti-terrorist articles. Now, offenders, convicted of serious and most serious crimes under a number of the Criminal Code articles – including Arts. 205.2 Part 2, 205.5, 278, 282 Part 2, 282.1, and 282.2, which, in our opinion, are often used in inappropriate verdicts – could remain under administrative supervision until their conviction is expunged.[4]

In July, a law was signed allowing to revoke an earlier act on acquiring Russian citizenship for some of those convicted of extremist and terrorist crimes. Supposedly, the court verdict regarding such crimes proves that, at the time of obtaining citizenship, an applicant falsely claimed that s/he was committed to respect the Constitution and legislation. Meanwhile, it is quite obvious that criminal intent could have been formed at a later point. There is a reason to fear that the law will be used to revoke the citizenship of (and subsequently deport) some immigrants or residents of Crimea.[5]

In November, a plenary meeting of the Supreme Court of the Russian Federation adopted a ruling that clarified certain aspects of the legislation on protecting the interests of children when resolving related disputes. In particular, the Supreme Court expanded the list of acts seen as falling within the definition of "abuse of parental rights," which can be used as the grounds for termination of parental rights under the Family Code. The Supreme Court recommends adding to the list such acts as involving children "in activities of a public or religious association or other organization, with respect to which an enforceable court decision on its liquidation or prohibition of activities has been issued (Art. 9 of Federal Law No. 114- FZ 'On Combating Extremist Activity' of July 25, 2002; Art. 24 of the Federal Law No. 35-FZ of March 6, 2006 'On Counteraction to Terrorism')." We would like to point out that the concept of "involving children in activities of the organization" has not been defined in the legislation, providing opportunities for its expansive interpretation by law enforcement agencies and courts. Moreover, the Supreme Court failed even to indicate that termination of parental rights should be preceded by a court verdict for involving a child in the activities of a banned organization. Thus, believers and political activists find themselves in a situation, in which they are facing not only potential inappropriate criminal charges for being involved in banned organizations, but also the threat of their children being removed from the family for no valid reason. We would like to remind readers that, in our opinion, a number of religious associations and organizations of a political nature are prohibited in Russia inappropriately. Even if the courts refrain from wide application of this Supreme Court ruling in their practice, the very existence of such recommendations creates an additional "preventive" instrument for exerting pressure on citizens and pushing them to abandon the beliefs, which the authorities find objectionable, or to give up their protest activity.

NOTES

1. For additional information on this law see: "Putin Approved Fines for Internet Providers for Evasion of Blocking Web Sites" // SOVA Center. February 22, 2017 (http://www.sova-center.ru/misuse/news/lawmaking/2017/02/d36452/).

2. For additional information on this law see: "The Bill to Ban the Means of Circumventing the Internet Blocking Was Adopted in the Second Reading" // SOVA Center. July 19, 2017 (http://www.sova-center.ru/misuse/news/lawmaking/2017/07/d37523/).

3. For additional information on this law see: "The Law on Access to Materials of "Undesirable Organizations" and on "Foreign Agents" Media Has Entered into Force" // SOVA

Center. November 27, 2017 (http://www.sova-center.ru/misuse/news/lawmaking/2017/11/d38355/).

4. For additional information on this law see: "The President Signed the Law on Administrative Supervision of Persons Guilty of Extremist and Terrorist Crimes after Their Release from Correctional Institutions" // SOVA Center. May 29, 2017 (http://www.sova-center.ru/misuse/news/lawmaking/2017/05/d37181/).

5. For additional information on this law see: "Putin Signed the Law on Revoking Citizenship for Those Convicted of Extremist and Terrorist Crimes" // SOVA Center. July 31, 2017 (http://www.sova-center.ru/misuse/news/lawmaking/2017/07/d37585/).

The year 2018 was marked by important initiatives, some of which were aimed at liberalizing the legislation, while the other provided for new and very significant restrictions.

The President's amendments to Art. 282 of the Criminal Code became the most notable event of the year. The problem with using Art. 282 of the Criminal Code – increasingly visible in recent years as its application has expanded – remained in the center of public attention throughout 2018. During the "Direct Line with the President" in June, Deputy Sergei Shargunov (the author of yet another initiative to change the article) spoke on the need to reform the anti-extremist legislation and law enforcement practice. Following Putin's instructions, *Obshcherossiysky narodny front* (All-Russia People's Front, ONF) took up the task of drafting possible changes, and the Supreme Court of the Russian Federation issued new clarifications on the use of anti-extremist legal norms.

The Supreme Court ruling, published in September, indicated that, when anti-extremist articles are applied, the fundamental freedoms could be restricted only in extreme cases, in accordance with the Constitution and international law. The court recommendations mostly pertained to the cases under Art. 282 of the Criminal Code for online publications. The Supreme Court clarified the process of evaluating the context of a public statement when deciding on the motive of a defendant, charged with incitement to hatred. In particular, the Court recommended taking into account the form, content and extent of the statement, presence of any commentary describing the publisher's attitude toward the material, the overall content of the defendant's account and information about their personality and activities.

When analyzing a statement to decide whether it represents a danger to society or whether it is an insignificant act that does not merit prosecution, the Supreme Court suggested taking into account the size and makeup of the post's audience and its reaction to the published statement. The Court also indicated the possibility of appeals, citing the above circumstances, against the decisions to initiate court proceedings. All these explanations were made only with respect to Art. 282 of the Criminal Code, although the same should obviously apply to other articles that deal with public statements.

The Supreme Court also commented on the issue of using expert opinions in cases involving Art. 280 (public calls for extremist activity), Art. 280.1 (public calls for undermining the territorial integrity of the Russian Federation) and Art. 282 of the Criminal Code. The Supreme Court indicated, once again, that an expert opinion in these cases had no predetermined validity and no advantage over other evidence, whereas the task of evaluating public statements for possible liability under the provisions of the anti-extremist Criminal Code articles falls within the exclusive competence of a court.

The Prosecutor General's Office followed the Supreme Court's example. An order to strengthen prosecutorial oversight over the investigations related to extremist crimes was signed by the Prosecutor General in late September. Following the lead of the Supreme Court, the Prosecutor General's Office stressed the need to examine the motive of the supposed perpetrators and establish the intent of inciting hatred; it further required that not only distributors, but also creators of such content be held accountable. The document specifically emphasizes that prosecutors need to put an end to the cases of unreasonable prosecution; but, at the same time, they should examine the legal validity of criminal case terminations and report back to the Prosecutor General's Office. Prosecutors should also maintain detailed regional-level registries of extremist crimes and of reports on such crimes. Finally, the prosecutor-general's order paid particular attention to the need to investigate violent hate crimes and cases related to extremist communities and organizations.

The Prosecutor General's Office, once again, emphasized the need to involve academic experts in investigating extremist cases (although the Supreme Court has stated that requests for such an expert opinion are not always appropriate). The document also discussed the quality of expert opinions in such cases. The agency recommended that, when assessing the legality of procedural decisions, *the opinions of specialists and experts be examined carefully, paying particular attention to the following: correspondence of their conclusions to the content of their analytical part and to questions reflected in the request for an expert opinion (examination); completeness and comprehensiveness of their conclusions; qualifications of experts (specialists) and the extent of their authority to evaluate the stated facts.* Hence, the Prosecutor General's Office recommended avoiding the currently widespread practice of automatically copying the experts' conclusions with "no reason to doubt" their competency.

Ambiguously worded project to reform Art. 282 of the Criminal Code, submitted to the State Duma by deputies Shargunov and Zhuravlyov, received negative reviews and was not considered. However, it served as the basis for a package of bills developed by the ONF on behalf of the President and submitted to the parliament by Vladimir Putin in October. It was adopted in record time, signed on December 27, 2018 and entered into force on January 7, 2019. The reform introduced partial decriminalization of Art. 282 Part 1 of the Criminal Code – the first violation is now punished administratively under the new Art. 20.3.1 of the Code of Administrative Offenses, which corresponds exactly to the wording of Art. 282 Part 1. Administrative responsibility has been extended to legal entities. Criminal liability is incurred only if the law is violated for a second time within a year following the administrative prosecution. The only amendment made in the second reading on December 19 was related to establishing a one-year limitation period for administrative liability under Art. 20.3.1 (as opposed to the three months period after the offense, currently established for administrative offenses that require court proceedings). The proposals of the Ombudsman and the President's Human Rights Council – to exclude the clause on belonging to a social group from Arts. 282 and 20.3.1, to exclude criminal prosecution for violation of dignity and to introduce criminal liability only for the third, rather than the second, violation within one year – were not taken into account.

Partial decriminalization of Art. 282 allowed many citizens accused of inciting hatred to avoid overly harsh punishment and a criminal record. The Supreme Court ruling and the expected amendments to the article already led to revision and closing of a number of cases in late 2018. However, a number of emerging concerns has to be noted as well.

First, the procedures for initiating an administrative offense cases are much simpler than in criminal proceedings, and the burden of proof is much lighter; therefore, we can expect a significant increase in the number of prosecutions for inciting hatred, most of which will take place within the framework of the Code of Administrative Offenses. The provision, stipulating that only prosecutors and not the police have the right to open administrative proceedings under Art. 20.3.1 could, to some extent, serve as a sole possible deterrent to the rapid proliferation of prosecutions under the new article.

Next, one should not forget that the Criminal Code still contains the unmodified Art. 280, which covers calls for extremist activities. Since the definition of extremist activities includes incitement of hatred, law enforcement agencies can bring charges under this article, if they so desire. The established practice is to file charges under two articles at once in the cases where the incitement of hatred is accompanied by calls for violence. However, belligerent xenophobes are not the only ones who should keep their vigilance – let's not forget that the elastic formulation of Art. 280 creates ample opportunities for criminal prosecution of activists.

Many abuses of anti-extremist norms are caused by flaws in their wording and the corresponding wording in the Law on Combating Extremist Activity. The reform addressed only Art. 282; it failed to include the clarifications and corrections proposed for the problematic provisions of the anti-extremist legislation. The Supreme Court ruling may have a positive impact on enforcement, but only if law enforcement agencies and courts actually follow it. Experience shows that the prior Supreme Court recommendations on the extremism-related cases have often been ignored even by the Supreme Court itself. Obviously, future development of law enforcement in this area depends on the political will of the authorities.

A certain positive effect can be expected from a change in the procedure for banning materials as a result of the new amendments to the procedural legislation that were approved by the President in November, but entered into force in the fall of 2019. Among other norms, the innovations will also affect the court procedures with regard to claims on deeming materials as extremist or on recognizing information as prohibited. According to the new law, the cases pertaining to recognition of materials as extremist are transferred from the civil proceedings to the administrative sphere. When considering a prosecutorial claim to recognize certain materials as extremist, the court is obligated to involve persons, whose rights and legal interests may be affected by the judicial decision. In addition, "if a person, whose actions have led to filing of an administrative claim, has been identified" the court shall involve them in the case as a defendant and impose legal costs on them. If such a person has not been identified, the Ombudsman of the Russian Federation (or of a respective unit of the Federation) will be involved in the consideration of the case "for providing an opinion." In addition, the court will be able to take "preliminary protective measures in the form of restricting access to extremist materials" while the case is under consideration, and, if the claim is satisfied, the decision regarding the ban will take effect immediately. The cases on recognizing certain information as prohibited will proceed in a similar fashion. The key procedural difference for these cases is mandatory participation of Roskomnadzor in the proceedings. Thus, the favorable conditions have been created to terminate the practice of banning materials without adversarial proceedings – the change that can reduce the number of inappropriately banned materials. However, this reform will not make the Federal List of materials, whose length approaches 5,000 entries, into an acceptable and effective mechanism for countering the spread of radical ideology.

All the remaining legislative innovations and initiatives of 2018 related to regulation were proscriptive.

In late June, the president signed a law establishing the responsibility of Web search engines for showing links to banned Web sites and for failure to connect to the information system containing data on blocked Web sites. The law introduced Art. 13.40 (failure to perform duties by a search engine operator) into the Code of Administrative Offenses; citizens operating the offending search engines may be fined 5,000 rubles, officials – 50,000 rubles, and legal entities – from 500,000 to 700,000 rubles. At the time of writing the report, Yandex was already connected to the Roskomnadzor system, while Google refused to do so and continued to review the agency's blocking decisions on the case by case basis.

In addition, the Administrative Code article on failure to submit information to Roskomnadzor was augmented with a new part, which punishes hosting providers for failing to submit to Roskomnadzor, in a timely manner, the information identifying their clients who own anonymizing Web sites or VPN-services. A fine of 30,000 to 50,000 rubles has been established for individuals, and of 50,000 to 300,000 rubles for legal entities.

In December, Deputy Dmitry Vyatkin (*Yedinaya Rossiia* [United Russia]) and Senators Aleksandr Klishas and Lyudmila Bokova (the heads of the Federation Council Committee on Constitutional Law) submitted to the State Duma two draft legislative packages seeking to punish citizens for dissemination of objectionable information on the Internet. This was the first time, when the sanctions specifically punishing online behavior were introduced in the Duma.

The first of the proposed projects was intended to prevent the dissemination of online information targeting an unlimited number of people and "expressing obvious disrespect in indecent form" toward society, the state, the official state symbols, the Constitution and the agencies exercising state power in the Russian Federation, "if these actions do not constitute a criminal offense." The authors suggested adding Part 3 to Art. 20.1 (petty hooliganism) of the Code of Administrative Offenses. The new provision would punish for the offense described above by imposing an administrative fine ranging from 1,000 to 5,000 rubles or an administrative detention for up to fifteen days. Introduction of a procedure for extrajudicial blocking of such information is expected as well. The draft contains vague formulas ("expressing disrespect in indecent form" has not been clearly defined) and suggests excessive legislative norms duplicating the existing articles of the Criminal Code on socially dangerous statements. Furthermore, it creates the risk of excessive interference of the authorities in the Russian citizens' right to freedom of opinion and expression on the Internet, where communication has its own stylistic peculiarities and is governed by the rules established by the social media networks administration.

The second package of bills suggests imposing sanctions for distribution of deliberately inaccurate socially significant information, disseminated under the guise of reliable messages, that creates a threat to the life and (or) health of citizens, threat of mass violation of public order and (or) public safety, of breakdown in the functioning of the essential services, transport or social infrastructure, or other grave consequences via mass media or the Internet. The authors propose adding Part 9 to Art. 13.15 of the Code of Administrative Offenses (abuse of freedom of the media), which would stipulate a punishment for such violation – an administrative fine ranging from 3,000 to 5,000 rubles for individuals, from 30,000 to 50,000 rubles for officials, and from 400,000 to 1 million rubles with confiscation of means of committing the offense for legal entities. We regard the use of the term "deliberately inaccurate" in the legal sphere in relation to socially significant information as problematic. It will be almost impossible to establish the presence of intent in the relevant cases, that is, to prove the fact that a violator knew for a fact that the incriminating information was unreliable and that its dissemination would lead to the named or even to certain unnamed "grave" consequences. On the other hand, the courts' failure to pay due attention to determining such an intent would inevitably lead to violations of the citizens' rights to freedom of receiving and disseminating information, freedom of expression and freedom of assembly. In addition, according to the existing legislation, if a person publicly urged citizens to engage in illegal activity or shared prohibited information, such publications fall under the relevant articles – criminal

Art. 280 (incitement to extremism), 205.2 (incitement to terrorism), 212 (mass riots), or administrative Art. 20.29 (dissemination of extremist materials) and others – regardless of whether the disseminated information was false or truthful. Thus, the proposed law is redundant.

Despite criticism from the Prosecutor General's Office, the Ministry of Communications and Mass Media, the Ministry of Justice and Roskomnadzor, the bills eventually received the necessary positive feedback from both the government and parliamentary committees. In January 2019, both packages were approved by the lower house in first reading. We can possibly expect substantial amendments to the text of the draft laws in the second reading, but improvements to individual formulas in the Klishas bills will not make the proposed norms expedient.[1]

Yet another round of tougher measures, introduced in 2018 for different categories of individuals accused and convicted under anti-terrorist or anti-extremist articles, is also worth noting.

Thus, in June, a plenary meeting of the Supreme Court of the Russian Federation adopted a ruling "On Certain Issues Related to Using Confiscation of Property in Criminal Proceedings." In the draft ruling, the Supreme Court inter alia indicated that "any property belonging to the defendant that is an instrument, equipment or other means of committing a crime" (including cell phones, computers, etc.) is subject to confiscation in the criminal cases on extremist or terrorist activity. At the same time, as the Supreme Court noted, if money, valuables or other property were intended for "financing terrorism, extremist activity, an organized group, illegal armed formation or a criminal association (criminal organization)," then in accordance with Art. 104.1 Part 1 Paragraph "c" of the Criminal Code, such items are subject to confiscation "regardless of their ownership." Accordingly, seizure of property for the purpose of securing possible confiscation can be applied not only to the suspects, defendants or individuals materially responsible for their actions, but to any persons, if "there are sufficient grounds to believe" that it was used as an instrument of crime. In its reasoning for the relevant ruling, a court has to justify its choice of property rights restrictions as "necessary and sufficient" for ensuring the preservation of the property in question.

In October, Putin signed a law allowing to ban foreigners, who are on the Rosfinmonitoring list of extremists and terrorists (as well as those whose bank accounts were frozen by a court or by the Interdepartmental Commission on Counteracting the Financing of Terrorism) from entering

Russia. It should be noted that, in practice, foreigners included on the extremists' list were regularly barred from entering the country even prior to these amendments "in order to ensure the defense capability or security of the state."

A package of bills, signed in December, stipulated harsher conditions of serving the sentences for offenders convicted under a number of the Criminal Code articles (primarily pertaining to terrorism) or offenders, who have a "destructive impact" on their cellmates. The package expands the list of conditions that allow courts to decide on imprisonment for at least part of the term, to specify initial mandatory prison term under a number of Criminal Code articles and to prohibit the early transfer of inmates with positive characteristics to penal colonies. In addition, the new legislation gives the Federal Penitentiary Service of Russia discretion to determine the location for offenders to serve their sentences (regardless of their crime), if they are noticed to have a "negative impact" on their cellmates or engage in propaganda of terrorist ideologies. These provisions do not pertain to ordinary members of extremist groups or organizations convicted under Art. 282.1 Part 2 and Art. 282.2 Part 2.

NOTE

1. In March 2019, i.e., beyond the reporting period, both of Klishas bills were approved by the Duma in the second reading with certain amendments, then upheld by the Federation Council and signed by the President.

Development of Legal Framework 2019

In July, Russia ratified the Shanghai Cooperation Organization (SCO) Convention on Countering Extremism, signed in 2017; the convention entered into force for Russia in October 2019. Among other provisions, it expands the definition of extremism previously adopted at the SCO level. While the definition of extremism in the Shanghai Convention of 2001 was tied to violence, the new definition also came to include "other unconstitutional actions." It also introduces a list of "extremist acts," largely corresponding to the definition of extremism used in the Russian law "On Combating Extremist Activity." This list includes, inter alia, incitement to political enmity, which is absent in the Russian definition; in principle, this opens the way to increasing the severity of the current Russian legislation. The Convention imposes on SCO members obligations to establish penalties for extremist acts and for a number of related actions. The document provides for close cooperation between law enforcement agencies in their investigation of extremist cases, including travel to the territory of other participating states to attend operational search activities. In addition, the Convention imposes on participating countries an obligation to deny refugee status to all those involved in extremist crimes. We view strengthened cooperation of the kind as alarming since it may lead to further deterioration of the already problematic situation of dissidents in the SCO countries.

The number of legal norms restricting the rights of people viewed by the Russian authorities as involved in terrorism and extremism kept growing in 2019. These include the laws signed in March, one of which requires lawyers and accountants to freeze the funds of their clients if the latter were placed on the so-called Rosfinmonitoring (Federal Financial Monitoring Service) list of extremists and terrorists. Another law prohibits persons included on this list from working at nuclear facilities. Since July, they are also not allowed to operate railroad trains, and, since August, they are banned from owning crowdinvesting platforms or using them to solicit funds under the law on crowdinvesting. We would like to remind readers that the Rosfinmonitoring list includes not only convicted offenders but also individuals charged with or suspected of involvement in extremist and terrorist activities.

In addition, the government submitted a draft bill to the State Duma extending the ban on creating non-profit organizations and on membership in such organizations to include individuals whose funds were frozen by the Interdepartmental Commission on Countering the Financing of Terrorism.

In 2019, the authorities finally addressed the need to limit the total ban on displaying prohibited symbols. In December, the president signed the law "On Amending Art. 6 of the Federal Law 'On Immortalization of the Victory of the Soviet people in the Great Patriotic War of 1941-1945,' and Art. 1 of the Federal Law 'On Combating Extremist Activity,' " developed by a group of deputies led by Elena Yampolskaya of the United Russia party at the initiative of the All-Russia People's Front. The newly adopted law replaces the legislative ban on "propaganda and public display" of Nazi symbols (as well as attributes and symbols of extremist organizations) with a ban on its "use," except for the use that "forms a negative attitude toward the ideology of Nazism and extremism and contains no signs of propaganda or justification of Nazi or extremist ideology." A similar note will be added to Art. 20.3 of the Code of Administrative Offenses (public display of Nazi symbols) in accordance with the corresponding bill approved by the State Duma in February 2020.

We welcome the abolition of the blanket prohibition against demonstrating banned symbols, but it is not clear how the fact of forming a "negative attitude" toward Nazi or extremist ideology is to be established. In addition, this clause will not cover all the cases, in which banned symbols can be displayed without the purpose of advocating the corresponding ideology. In order to prevent inappropriate prosecutions, we proposed that federal laws and Art. 20.3 of the Code of Administrative Offenses explicitly state that display of forbidden symbols is punishable only if it is aimed at such propaganda. This suggestion was included in a legislative proposal submitted by Senator Anton Belyakov, which contained an alternative plan for reforming Art. 20.3, but was rejected by the State Duma in December 2019.

A number of laws pertaining to the sphere of information and aimed at further restricting the right to freedom of expression in Russia were signed in 2019. We also saw some new legislative initiatives of the same kind.

In March, the president signed a package of laws targeting indecent behavior on the Internet and dissemination of inaccurate socially significant information. This legislation was introduced by Dmitry Vyatkin, a deputy of the United Russia party, and by senators Aleksandr Klishas and Lyudmila Bokova. Roskomnadzor (the Federal Service for Supervision of Communications, Information Technology, and Mass Media) received the right to block "unreliable socially significant information disseminated under the guise of reliable messages," upon request of the Prosecutor General's Office, if the information poses a threat to citizens, public order, etc. At the same time, registered online media outlets were given the opportunity to quickly remove such information in order to avoid blocking. The laws introduced administrative responsibility under Art. 13.15 of the Code of Administrative Offenses (abuse of freedom of mass information) in the form of large fines for disseminating "knowingly inaccurate" information. The fines are differentiated depending on the degree of the alleged or actual harm and reach 1.5 million rubles for legal entities.

Information that expresses clear disrespect for society, the state, state symbols and authorities "in the indecent form, which insults human dignity and public morality," is to be blocked as well. Web site owners are given 24 hours to remove such information. Citizens may face administrative punishment for its distribution in the form of fines of up to 300,000 rubles and/or arrests of up to 15 days under the new parts of Art. 20.1 of the Code of Administrative Offenses (disorderly conduct).

In our opinion, these laws operate with ambiguous concepts, introduce redundant norms and imply unreasonable interference with the right of Russian citizens to freedom of expression in order to suppress criticism of the authorities.

A law that increases liability for violations of the information-related legislation, proposed by deputies from United Russia, was signed in December. Under this law, Art. 13.11 of the Code of Administrative Offenses (violation of the legislation of the Russian Federation on personal data) was supplemented by a norm establishing liability for refusal to store personal data of Russian citizens in Russia and imposing large fines for citizens and multi-million dollar fines for legal entities. In addition, large fines were established for repeated violations of the Law on Information that fall under Arts. 13.31, 13.35, 13.36, 13.37, 13.39 and 13.40 of the Code of Administrative Offenses, which include anti-extremist restrictions, among others. According to the law, cases of repeated violations under these articles should be tried in courts, rather than reviewed by Roskomnadzor inspectors.

Also in December, the president approved the law "On Amending the Law of the Russian Federation 'On Mass Media' and the Federal Law 'On

Information, Informational Technologies and the Protection of Information.' " This new legislation provides for the possibility of recognizing individuals as "foreign agent" mass media and establishes the procedure for disseminating information by the media recognized as "foreign agents." Individuals can be branded a "foreign agent mass media" resource, if they distribute any messages or materials to an unlimited number of people, and, at the same time, but not necessarily in connection with this activity, receive money from any foreign sources. In addition, this status can be imposed for participating in the creation of materials by "foreign agent mass media," if a participant also receives money from abroad or from a "foreign agent mass media" outlet. Russian physical and legal entities engaged in such activities will be included on the Foreign Agent Mass Media Register and might fall under the provisions of the law "On Non-Profit Organizations" that apply to "foreign agent" non-profits. The Ministry of Justice has been entrusted with keeping the new register, but the decision to add a particular individual is supposed to be made in consultation with the Ministry of Foreign Affairs. Imprints, messages and materials of both "foreign agent mass media" resources and their corresponding Russian "foreign agent" legal entities will have to indicate this status. A similar indication should be included in the output of a registered mass media outlet established by such a legal entity. If a decision in an administrative case on violation of the procedure committed by a "foreign agent" mass media outlet or by its Russian legal entity enters into force, Roskomnadzor is to block the offender's resource in the manner determined by the government. Another law, signed in the same month, introduced new Art. 19.34.1 in the Code of Administrative Offenses, which stipulates the fines for violating the law on foreign agent mass media that range from 10,000 to 100,000 rubles for citizens, from 50,000 to 200,000 rubles for officials and from 500,000 to 5 million rubles for legal entities. Both legal norms entered into force in February 2020; at the time of releasing this report, we have no information on their application.

2020 turned out to be so rich in legislative innovations in the sphere covered by this report that we divided them into several blocks. The first one includes changes directly related to anti-extremist legislation as a whole, the second covers norms that are presented as instruments for countering Nazism, the third deals with blocking online information, and the fourth one is the legislation on "foreign agents." In general, we can conclude that only a small minority of these new norms can be interpreted as attempts to correct the shortcomings of the existing legislation, while the bulk of them are clearly repressive.

Countering Extremism

In May, Putin signed a law that bans people convicted under certain anti-extremist and related articles of the Criminal Code (Art. 205.2 Part 1, Art. 207.2 Parts 1 and 2, Art. 212.1, Art. 239 Part 1, Art. 243.4 Part 2, Art. 244 Part 1, Art. 280 Part 2, Art. 280.1 Part 2, Art. 282 Part 1, and Art. 354.1 Part 2) from running for elected office for five years after expunction or clearing of their criminal record. Previously, offenders convicted for "crimes of extremism" could not run until their criminal record has been cleared (with the exception of those convicted for grave and especially grave crimes, who, after clearing of their criminal record, continue to be restricted from running for 10 and 15 years respectively). We see no valid reasons for additional restrictions on the right to stand for election, including for those convicted of any of the Criminal Code articles listed above. In addition, we believe that prosecutions under many of these articles are frequently inappropriate.

Also in May, the President approved a new version of the Strategy for Countering Extremism until 2025. Among other considerations, the Strategy clarified certain concepts (including "radicalism") and defined the concept of "ideology of violence." The document, on the one hand classifies "destructive activities" of NGOs (including "the use of techniques and scenarios of the so-called 'color revolutions' ") as extremism, and calls for paying attention to the "informational-psychological influence" of foreign intelligence services aimed at destroying the traditional values. On the other hand, when discussing the migration policy priorities related to countering extremism, the Strategy proposes to focus not on combating "illegal migration," but on adaptation programs, on counteracting social exclusion, formation of ethnic enclaves, and spatial segregation, and on involving civil society institutions. Finally, for the first time, the Strategy defines quantitative indicators that include the percentage of violent crimes among "the crimes of extremist nature."

In July, a law was signed on amendments to Art. 1 of the Law "On Combating Extremist Activity." The law replaced the wording *forcible change of the foundations of the constitutional order and violation of the integrity of the Russian Federation* in the definition of extremism with the following: *forcible change of the foundations of the constitutional order and (or) violation of the territorial integrity of the Russian Federation (including alienation of part of the territory of the Russian Federation) with the exception of delimitation, demarcation or re-demarcation of state borders of the Russian Federation with neighboring states.* Thus, the law "On Combating Extremist Activity" was brought in line with the new edition of the Russian Constitution.

The law amending the Code of Administrative Offenses and the Criminal Code of the Russian Federation as they relate to separatism was approved by the President in December. Criminal liability was established for the separatist actions per se; for this, a new Art. 280.2 of the Criminal Code (actions aimed at violating the territorial integrity of the Russian Federation) was introduced with the maximum incarceration sentence of 10 years. Publishing calls for separatism for the first time now entail administrative liability under the new Art. 20.3.2 of the Code of Administrative Offenses, which can also apply to legal entities; liability under already existing Art. 280.1 of the Criminal Code is only triggered by a repeated offense committed within a year. We believe that calls for changing country borders should only be considered illegal if combined with calls for violent action, but the Supreme Court is of the opposite opinion.[1] Taking into account the fact that the litigation in administrative cases is much more superficial than in criminal proceedings, we cannot presume that the number of inappropriate sanctions will decrease with the introduction of Art. 20.3.2; it may even increase instead. So far, Art. 280.1 was invoked in no more than ten sentences a year. As for Art. 280.2, it uses the wording "other actions aimed at violating the territorial integrity," which is quite vague and may turn into an expansive interpretation and lead to prosecution, in particular, for expressing an opinion on the status of certain territories.

In October, Vladimir Putin signed a government-developed law amending Arts. 9 and 10 of the Federal Law "On Combating Extremist Activity"; the courts that make decisions to ban or suspend an organization's activities as extremist now must send their decision to the Ministry of Justice within three days for it to be included on the relevant list. Previously, this period was not defined, so, in practice, it took up to five years for a banned organization to appear on the list.

In December, the government bill on amendments to the federal law "On Freedom of Conscience and on Religious Associations" was adopted in the first reading. Among other legislative innovations, the amendments stipulate that the following types of persons are not allowed to be leaders or members of religious groups: a foreign citizen or a stateless person, whose continued stay in the Russian Federation has been deemed undesirable; a person included on the Rosfinmonitoring List of Extremists and Terrorists; a person in respect of whom a court decision established that their actions amounted to extremist activity; an individual whose accounts are frozen by the Interdepartmental Commission on Countering the Financing of Terrorism. Thus, the requirements already present in the legislation on non-profit organizations, including religious ones, are being extended to include the leaders and members of religious groups. In our opinion, these new restrictions represent yet another unjustified intrusion into the exercise of the right to freedom of religion. The law was adopted in 2021.

"Fight Against Nazism"

In March 2020, Vladimir Putin signed a law amending Art. 20.3 of the Code of Administrative Offenses (public display of Nazi symbols). Disposition and sanctions of Art. 20.3 of the Code of Administrative Offenses have remained unchanged – only a note was added to clarify that the provisions of the article *do not apply to cases in which Nazi attributes or symbols, or attributes or symbols similar to Nazi attributes or symbols to the point of confusion, or attributes or symbols of extremist organizations are used to form a negative attitude toward the ideology of Nazism and extremism, and there are no signs of propaganda or justification of Nazi or extremist ideology.* Similar amendments to the laws "On Immortalization of the Victory of the Soviet people in the Great Patriotic War of 1941–1945," and "On Combating Extremist Activity" were adopted in late 2019. As expected, this clause did not cover all the cases, in which banned symbols could possibly be displayed without the purpose of advocating the relevant ideology; the courts invoked it only in some of the applicable cases. In our opinion, explicitly stating in federal laws and Art. 20.3 of the Code of Administrative Offenses that the display of forbidden symbols is punishable only if intended as propaganda of the corresponding banned organizations ideology would have been more effective in decreasing the number of inappropriate enforcement cases.

In April, a law was signed to prevent demolition of Soviet monuments abroad. A new Art. 243.4 of the Criminal Code (destruction or damage to military graves, as well as monuments, stelae, obelisks, other memorial structures or objects, which immortalize the memory of those who died defending their Fatherland or its interests, or are dedicated to the days of Russia's military glory) with punishments that include multimillion ruble fines and imprisonment, among others. It should be noted that, although the introduction of this article is motivated primarily by foreign policy considerations, it can be applied to Russian citizens as well. At the same time, the actions described in the text of this norm were already punishable under the existing articles of the Criminal Code; therefore, there were no need to create it; meanwhile, the stipulated sanctions, especially large fines, are, in our opinion, disproportionately severe.

In November, Deputy Irina Yarovaya introduced two draft bills in the State Duma to amend Art. 354.1 of the Criminal Code (rehabilitation of Nazism) and the Code of Administrative Offenses of the Russian Federation. One of them proposes to make responsibility for online dissemination of information aimed at rehabilitation of Nazism equal to responsibility for dissemination of such information via mass media – that is, to qualify such activities under the more severe Part 2 of Art. 354.1. The second bill seeks to introduce administrative punishment for the rehabilitation of Nazism in mass media; for this purpose, a related part, which stipulates a fine for legal entities of up to 3 million rubles with or without confiscation of the offending item, should be added to Art. 13.15 of the Code of Administrative Offenses. We would like to remind readers that we view Art. 354.1 of the

Criminal Code as excessive and imprecisely formulated legal norm, some provisions of which excessively limit the historical discussion; we oppose increasing in severity and expanding the sanctions for the rehabilitation of Nazism. The bill was adopted in the first reading in February 2021, and, by the second reading, it will be expanded to add the new vaguely formulated restrictions prohibiting dissemination of knowingly false information about veterans, abasement of their honor and dignity and insult against the memory of defenders of the Fatherland. The law was signed in 2021.

Regulating the Internet

In April, the president signed amendments, which included expanded and more severe punishments for distributing fake news in mass media and over the Internet. Art. 13.15 of the Code of Administrative Offenses has been supplemented by a new Part 10.1 that punishes dissemination of "deliberately unreliable information under the guise of reliable messages" with regard to emergency situations and measures to counter them. Such actions will incur heavy fines, but only for legal entities. Legal entities are also liable under the new Part 10.2 for distribution of false information resulting in death, damage to health, violation of public order or security, and so on. Part 11 of the new version covers repeated offenses under Parts 10, 10.1 and 10.2, also increasing the severity of sanctions for legal entities. The same amendments also indicate that individuals can be criminally liable under new Art. 207.1 (public dissemination of knowingly false information about circumstances posing a threat to the life and safety of citizens), which provides for punishment of up to three years behind bars, and Art. 207.2 of the Criminal Code (public dissemination of knowingly false socially significant information that entailed grave consequences), with the maximum imprisonment term of five years. We believe that there is no need for criminal prosecution for disseminating false information about emergencies, and the proposed sanctions appear disproportionately harsh.

Throughout the year, new norms were adopted to expand the grounds for extrajudicial blocking of information and increase the severity of sanctions for evading it. We believe that this area of legislation has systemic shortcomings, and the use of extrajudicial blocking procedures in practice often unreasonably and disproportionately restricts freedom of speech.

However, the Russian authorities are not inclined to listen to the European Court of Human Rights, which in its decisions, including the ones made in 2020, drew attention to the fact that this legislation did not comply with the requirements of the European Convention (see below).

In early June, Vladimir Putin signed a law that obligates hosting providers to carry out extrajudicial blocking of Web sites. The amendments, which entered into force on October 1, introduce changes in the extrajudicial blocking mechanism described in Art. 15.3 of the Federal Law "On Information." Previously, upon receiving a request from the Prosecutor General's Office, Roskomnadzor ordered telecom operators to block the indicated Web site; then a hosting provider received a notification that the Web site has been blocked, and had to notify the site owner of the need to delete the problematic information within 24 hours. Now, a hosting provider has to notify the owner immediately after receiving the notification from Roskomnadzor. If the site owner fails to delete the information within 24 hours, the provider will have to block the information resource indicated in the notification (the blocking obligations of telecom operators remain unchanged). Previously, a site owner could delete the information indicated in the notification and inform Roskomnadzor, and then telecom operators had to unlock his resource. The amendments, despite imposing on hosting providers the obligation to block Web sites, fail to provide for any obligations to remove such restrictions.

In December, a law was signed on sanctions for hosting providers and Web site owners for failure to remove or block content. According to Art. 13.41, newly added to the Code of Administrative Offenses, large fines are to be imposed for failure to take measures on restricting access to Web sites, access to which has to be limited in accordance with the requirements of the law (except in cases of copyright infringement): up to 100,000 rubles for individuals, up to 400,000 for officials, up to 4 million for legal entities; fines for repeated offenses are doubled for individuals and officials, and for legal entities they range from 1/20 to 1/10 of revenue, but no less than 4 million rubles. Fines for failure to block exceptionally dangerous content, including extremist content (along with child pornography and information about drugs) range from 100,000 to 200,000 rubles for individuals, from 400,000 to 800,000 for officials, and from 3 to 8 million for legal entities. In case of repeated offense fines range from 200,000 to 500,000 rubles for individuals, from 800,000 to 1 million rubles for officials, and from 1/10 to 1/5 of the proceeds, but no less than 8 million rubles for legal entities.

Also in December, the president approved a law on mandatory filtering of inappropriate content on social media networks. For the purposes of this law, the authorities will grant the status of a social media network to services with a monthly audience of more than 500,000 Russian users. Social media networks are obligated to independently monitor information, the dissemination of which is prohibited in Russia and which is subject to extrajudicial blocking (including information that contains calls for mass riots, carrying out extremist activities or participation in unpermitted rallies, as well as alleged fakes, materials of "undesirable organizations" and links to them and statements "offensive for the authorities and society"), accept complaints about such content and block it. In disputable cases, the content will be temporarily blocked and submitted through Roskomnadzor to the competent authorities, so that the latter could make a decision on whether it should be restricted permanently. In case of non-compliance social media networks are to be punished in accordance with Art. 13.41 described above.

However, in addition to the above-listed requirements for content removal or blocking, social media networks are required to make sure that their resources are not used to violate the electoral legislation restrictions (which have not yet been added to the list of information subject to extrajudicial blocking, see the corresponding bill below) or "to defame a citizen or certain categories of citizens" based on their belonging to a certain group, including their place of work and political convictions. In addition, obscene language and attacks against honor, dignity, or business reputation of citizens or organizations are unacceptable (the latter case also mentions the possibility of filing civil claims, but it is not clear whether the claims should be filed against offenders or against a social media network). Consistent compliance with all these requirements will obviously end not just political discussions, but any kind of polemics on social media network pages.

Simultaneously with the legislative proposal described above, aimed at forcing foreign social media networks to comply with Russian law, a law was signed to prevent social media networks from censoring information that comes from pro-government Russian media. The explanatory note to the relevant bill explicitly stated that the need for such a measure was made obvious by the fact that, since April 2020, about 20 instances of "discrimination" have been recorded for such media as RT, RIA Novosti, and Crimea 24 by foreign Internet sites such as Twitter, Facebook, and YouTube. The law "On Measures of Influence on Persons Involved in Violations of Fundamental Human Rights and Freedoms, Rights and Freedoms of Citizens of the Russian Federation" was supplemented by an article, according to which the owner of an information resource used by Russian citizens and legal entities is recognized as involved in human rights violations if the resource restricts dissemination of socially significant information in Russia *on the basis of nationality, language, origin, property ownership or job title, profession, place of residence or work, attitude toward religion and (or) in connection with the introduction by foreign states of political or economic sanctions against the Russian Federation, citizens of the Russian Federation or Russian legal entities,* or restricts the right of Russian citizens to freely seek, receive, transmit, produce and distribute information by any legal means. The decision to recognize a resource owner as implicated in human rights violations is made by the Prosecutor General of Russia or his deputies in consultation with the Ministry of Foreign Affairs. The decision is then forwarded to Roskomnadzor, which must, within 24 hours, add the owner of the resource to the appropriate list, and then issue a warning. Upon eliminating the violations, the owner must notify Roskomnadzor, and the latter sends a notification to the Prosecutor General's Office, which, together with the Ministry of Foreign Affairs, decides whether or not to cancel the imposed "sanctions." If the owner of the resource fails to comply with the requirements of the Russian authorities within the time frame specified in the warning, Roskomnadzor restricts access to this resource completely or partially. Partial restriction in this context can mean slowing down the Internet traffic. A law introducing sanctions for non-compliance with the requirements described above was proposed in November 2020 and signed in February 2021. The fine under the new article of the Code of Administrative Offenses, which punishes for its violation, ranges from 50,000 to 100,000 rubles for individuals, 200,000 to 400,000 rubles for officials, and 600,000 to 1 million rubles for legal entities. The fine for repeated failure to comply with the requirements of the law is set for 200,000 to 300,000 rubles for individuals, 500,000 to 700,000 for officials, and from 1.5 to 3 million rubles for legal entities.

The State Duma commission to investigate the facts of interference by foreign states in Russia's internal affairs submitted to the parliament a bill on amendments to the Federal Law "On information, information technology and the protection of information." In July. The amendments pertain to Art. 15.3 Part 1 of the law – now not only information containing "calls for mass riots and carrying out extremist activities" (current version), but also the one "containing justification for and (or) excuse of extremist activities, including terrorist activities" will be subject to extrajudicial blocking. We believe that the proposed amendments with their vague wording will only aggravate the situation, making both academic research and public discussion a possible target under the law. The government fully supported the bill and proposed, for good measure, that the extrajudicial blocking mechanism be extended to "Internet resources spreading false messages about acts of terrorism." The legislation was adopted in 2021.

In November, another bill was introduced to the State Duma, expanding the list of online information subject to extrajudicial blocking; it proposes that election commissions be instructed to make decisions on temporary blocking of illegal campaign propaganda. Following a report by election commissions about the presence of such information on the Internet, Roskomnadzor would be expected to immediately send to a provider a request to temporarily block the offending site (subject to immediate compliance). According to the bill, blocking can start no earlier than the day of the announcement of the elections, and ends five days after the date their results are determined. The bill passed in 2021. Given that illegal campaign propaganda is most likely to appear on social media networks, and selective blocking of social media messages by the authorities is technically impossible, the existence of such a law increases the risk of complete blocking of certain social media networks during the electoral campaign.

"Foreign Agents" Legislation

During 2020, several laws were developed and adopted to provide for more stringent regulation of the activities of so-called "foreign agents" in Russia. Although this area of legislation is not directly related to the fight against extremism, it fits the general trend of imposing, under the pretext of protecting national or public security, unreasonable and excessive restrictions on freedom of speech, which are in fact aimed at suppressing criticism of government's policy. In addition, since SOVA Center, along with other Russian NGOs that focus on legislation and law enforcement issues in Russia and receive foreign funding, has been recognized as a "foreign agent," we must point out that the increased severity of this legislation directly affects our ability to continue our work.

In December, the president signed the Law "On Amendments to Certain Legislative Acts of the Russian Federation regarding the Establishment of

Additional Measures to Counteract Threats to National Security," which was submitted to the State Duma in November and rapidly passed all stages of approval. This law added to the "Foreign Agent" status, already existing for an NGO, similar status designations for public associations with no corresponding legal entity and for individuals. The "foreign agent" status is still assigned based on a combination of two criteria. The first one is foreign support from governments, international organizations or individuals, even if received through a Russian "intermediary." For individuals designated as "foreign agents" not only financial, but also methodological assistance counts as foreign support. The second criterion is "political activity" in its current definition, which covers any notable public activity. Moreover, an individual can become a "foreign agent" even without "politics" if engaged in "purposeful collection of information in the field of military or military technology activities" (the law does not specify the kind of information; the FSB will do it later) without the purpose of espionage.

Similarly to NGOs, unregistered public associations and individuals who meet these criteria will be obligated to register as "foreign agents" with the Ministry of Justice, but the Ministry of Justice can also assign this status to people or associations directly. All types of "foreign agents" must submit regular reports on their "political activity," receipt and expenditure of money, as well as disclose their "foreign agent" status in any situation that can be interpreted as political activity, when making any statements or appeals to government agencies and organizations. Mass media also need to cite their status every time they mention "foreign agents."

It should be noted that the adopted law directly limits the rights of individuals recognized as "foreign agents" – they cannot be admitted to state and municipal public service and to state secrets.

In December, a law was signed to amend Art. 330.1 of the Criminal Code now renamed "Malicious Evasion from the Fulfillment of Duties Imposed by the Legislation of the Russian Federation, in Connection with Being Recognized as a Person Performing the Functions of a Foreign Agent." The sanctions for such evasion are:

- for leaders of NGOs and unregistered public associations – up to two years of imprisonment;

- for leaders of foreign media "foreign agents,"[2] their subsidiary Russian "foreign agents" legal entities, as well as for individuals already listed in the register of "foreign agents" and facing administrative responsibility for repeated violation of the operating procedures for "foreign agents" media, – also up to two years' imprisonment;

- for individuals recognized as "foreign agents" who carry out political activities and have already been brought to administrative responsibility for it, or who collect the aforementioned military-technical information – up to five years in prison.

In addition, by the end of the year, the State Duma passed on first reading a bill introducing or increasing administrative liability for all categories of "foreign agents" for violation of operating procedure – absent labeling on their materials or failure to provide information about themselves and their status. The bill was passed by parliament and signed by the president in early 2021. The changes also affected Art. 13.15 of the Code of Administrative Offenses on abusing freedom of mass information, which now includes the fines for disseminating information by or about "foreign agents" in the mass media without the appropriate labeling.

In December, a draft law under which candidates in elections would have to self-report as a "foreign agent," or "a candidate affiliated with a person acting as a foreign agent," if the candidate received money from any "foreign agent" within the preceding two years, passed on first reading. According to the bill, these labels should accompany all signature lists and all types of electoral information, including debates. The bill extends the ban on participation in election campaigns, already in force for "foreign agent" NGOs, to unregistered "foreign agent" public associations and "foreign agent" media. The law was signed in 2021.

NOTES

1. See: The SOVA Center commentary on the Ruling of the Plenary Session of the Supreme Court on Extremist and Terrorist Crimes // SOVA Center. November 3, 2016 (https://www.sova-center.ru/misuse/publications/2016/11/d35761/).

2. This status was introduced in the preceding year. See: Inappropriate Enforcement of Anti-Extremist Legislation in Russia in 2019 // SOVA Center. April 21, 2020 (https://www.sova-center.ru/en/misuse/reports-analyses/2020/04/d42333/).

PART FOUR

Hate Crimes

This section is focused on the phenomenon known as hate crimes – that is, on ordinary criminal offenses committed on the grounds of ethnic, religious or other similar enmity or prejudice.[1]

Of course, our data is quite incomplete, especially for the year preceding each annual report, as we often do not find out about crimes until much later. Unfortunately, we cannot compare our numbers with official or any other data because no statistics on hate crimes exist in Russia. We can only rely on the stability of our methodology – which, we believe, allows us to adequately assess the trends.

Information about such crimes is becoming more fragmented with every passing year. For a while now, the way the media has been describing crimes has made it impossible to determine whether they were motivated by hatred. More often than not, the media simply does not report such incidents. The victims rarely, if ever, turn to social organizations, let alone the police, since they are rightly apprehensive about getting in trouble with law enforcement agencies. The attackers, who merely a few years ago used to brazenly publish videos of their deeds," have become more cautious.

The data below do not include victims of mass clashes, victims in republics of the North Caucasus or victims in the Crimea prior to 2016.

1. Hate Crime Law: A Practical Guide. Warsaw: OSCE/ODIHR, 2009 (available on the OSCE Web site in several languages, including Russian: http://www.osce.org/odihr/36426).

Alexander Verkhovsky. Criminal Law on Hate Crime, Incitement of Hatred and Hate Speech in OSCE Participating States. The Hague: 2016 (available on the SOVA Center Web site: http://www.sova-center. ru/files/books/osce-laws-eng-16.pdf).

Systematic Racist and Neo-Nazi Violence

In 2014, at least 27 people were killed and about 123 people were injured as a result of racist and neo-Nazi violence; two people received serious death threats. These data show that the number of racist and neo-Nazi attacks dropped in 2014, while the number of murders rose. In 2013, 23 people were killed, 203 were wounded or beaten, and 10 received death threats.[1] It is possible that, against the background of official rhetoric about "Ukrainian fascists," the activities of domestic ultra-rightists were being covered up to a greater extent than usual. Mass media paid less attention to them as well. It is also possible that, due to the events in Ukraine, there actually was a drop in racist violence; many nationalists switched their attention to events in the neighboring country, and quite a few representatives of the militant ultra-right travelled there in order to participate in the hostilities.

In the past year, attacks occurred in 26 regions of the country (compared to 35 regions in 2013). Moscow (13 killed, 42 injured), St. Petersburg (three killed, 10 injured) and Krasnodar Territory (one killed, 10 injured)[2] still topped the list. In addition, a significant number of victims were reported in Novosibirsk Province (nine injured), Moscow Province (one killed, eight injured), Sakhalin Province (eight injured), Voronezh Province (six injured)[3] and Perm Territory (one killed, six injured). Voronezh Province and Sverdlovsk Province also appeared in our 2013 statistics. In comparison to the year 2013, the situation has improved in Chelyabinsk Province, Omsk Province and Samara Province. The data for the other regions mentioned above have not changed significantly.

Compared to 2013, our statistics came to include new regions (Arkhangelsk, Irkutsk, Kostroma, Leningrad, Nizhny Novgorod, Ryazan, Sakhalin, Tomsk and Tula Provinces, as well as the republics of Karelia and Tatarstan and the Jewish Autonomous Region,). At the same time, a number of regions left our charts (Volgograd, Ivanovo, Kaliningrad, Kirov, Lipetsk, Omsk, Samara, Smolensk, Tambov, Tver and Chelyabinsk Provinces, Transbaikal and Kamchatka Territories, as well as the republics of Buryatia, Mari El, and Mordovia and the Khanty-Mansi Autonomous Region). Unfortunately, we cannot confidently declare an improvement of the situation in the regions since information about such attacks is probably just not reported.

Attacks Against Ethnic "Outsiders"

The largest group of victims was, as usual, those perceived by the attackers as "ethnic outsiders." Our records showed a total of 102 victims of ethnically motivated attacks (compared to 163 in 2013). Information on this particular group is the most difficult to obtain, because the victims of such attacks usually shy away from publicity and rarely contact the police, community organizations or the media. In the overwhelming number of cases, even the names of the victims remain unknown.

Migrants from Central Asia, as usual, constituted the largest group of victims with 12 killed and 23 injured (compared to 14 killed and 61 injured in 2013). In addition, 10 victims (two killed, eight injured) were of unspecified "non-Slavic" appearance, usually described as "Asian," so most likely, migrants from Central Asia constituted the vast majority of this group as well (this group numbered 31 injured victims in 2013). Many victims – three killed and 14 injured – came from the Caucasus region (compared to three killed and 27 injured in 2013).

The number of attacks against dark-skinned people has doubled to 13 injured victims (compared to seven in 2013). For the most part, this information was gathered thanks to the Moscow Protestant Chaplaincy, which has been systematically tracking these kinds of attacks, and to the Civic Assistance Committee, which has started a special hotline for victims or witnesses of hate crimes.[4]

The cases of openly antisemitic attacks are quite rare in our statistics, simply because Jews are not that easy to spot in the crowd. However, the antisemitic rhetoric within the right-wing radical segment of the Internet shows no signs of decreasing; the Jews have been a principal target of hate speech for many years, and this fact indicates a potential threat of violence. In the past year, a violent incident of this kind took place on the night of Dec. 1-2 in the Ramensky District of Moscow Province – Shlomo (Fyodor) Romanovsky, a student of Yeshivat Torat Chaim, was severely beaten while returning to his religious seminary from Moscow.

There were also some known cases of attacks against other "ethnic aliens" under xenophobic slogans – against Palestinians in Voronezh (six injured), Gypsies in Ryazan Province (four injured), a native of Bangladesh and a citizen of China in Moscow, two Japanese nationals in Moscow Province, and citizens of Kyrgyzstan in Moscow and Irkutsk. Ethnic Russians were also victims of attacks motivated by ethnic hatred – we know about five injured people in Moscow and Rostov-on-Don.

In the year under review, attacks against lone passers-by as well as cases of gang attacks against members of Caucasus ethnic groups were reported. The most notorious example was an attack against "non-Slavic" visitors of "Master Pizza" pizzeria in Krasnodar on the night of May 10-11. At least eight people suffered injuries in the aggressive attack by the gang of masked young men; one person – 25-year-old Adyghe Timur Ashinov – died in the hospital. Possible criminal underpinnings of the incident do not cancel out its racist nature. Far-right raids on commuter trains and subway cars (so-called "white cars") also continued throughout the year. We know of at least five such actions by right-wing radicals in 2014.

When speaking of cases of ethnic attack, we usually discuss organized violence, but casual xenophobic violence also never disappears. However, the trends in this violence cannot be evaluated even approximately due to its remarkable latency. Our records showed about ten such attacks each year.

Attacks Against Political Adversaries

The number of attacks by the right wing against their political, ideological or "aesthetic" adversaries almost doubled in 2014 (15 injured compared to seven in 2013).[5] The victims included hardcore and rock music fans in Novosibirsk, members of informal youth movements in Yekaterinburg, punks in St. Petersburg, and participants of antifascist activities and rallies in Moscow.

Despite the almost complete cessation of street warfare between neo-Nazi and militant antifascists, such attacks do occur.

Here we also need to point out people battered "by association" – those who tried to stand up for the "non-Slavs." For example, a female passenger on a Moscow suburban train in Khimki tried to stand up for a man who was being beaten up in the car and suffered injuries as a result. People on the streets who dared to show their disapproval of the ultra-right's behavior could also be victims of attacks. Thus, eight young men on Prospekt Mira in Moscow attacked a passerby who reprimanded them for using the Nazi salute.

In 2014, we were faced with a new kind of political violence by right-wing radicals – attacks against those whom they considered "national traitors" or the "fifth column."

Most prominent in this category were the actions of activists of the National Liberation Movement (*Natsionalno-Osvoboditelnoye Dvizhenie*, NLM), led by Duma Deputy from United Russia Yevgeny Fyodorov. In June, NLM activists tried to disrupt the Congress of the Intelligentsia, which was being held in the House of Journalists in Moscow. Not only did they picket the House of Journalists holding signs, but they also sprayed gas inside the building. Maria Katasonova – a participant in the provocation – later posted about it on the social media network VKontakte. In August 2014, NLM activist Sergei Smirnov beat up Arseny Vesnin, a journalist from Echo of Moscow, in St. Petersburg, when the latter was covering a rally in support of Ukraine.[6] Finally, in December, NLM members attacked a picket by the Solidarity (*Solidarnost*) movement in Sokolniki Park in Moscow. Police detained an activist known as Gosha Tarasevich (Igor Beketov) at the scene.

The Other Russia (*Drugaya Rossiya*) also became active in its fight against the "fifth column"; they disrupted a concert by famous rock musician Andrei Makarevich in Moscow's House of Music on Rosh Hashanah in September. A group of young men sprayed pepper gas while shouting "Makarevich is a traitor, he sold out his Motherland!"[7] In October 2014, police arrested Oleg Mironov (born in 1987, a native of the Komi Republic) on suspicion of disrupting the concert.

A group of about 10 people carrying the flags of the Donetsk people's republic (DPR), "Novorossiya," the National-Bolshevik Party (a "limonka" grenade in a circle), and the SERB (South East Radical Block)[8] group attacked participants of the opposition Peace March on Sept. 22 in Moscow. Russian Orthodox activists, in particular Kirill Frolov, head of the Corporation for Orthodox Action (*Korporatsiya pravoslavnogo deistviya*) also participated in the attack.

Attacks Against LGBT or Homeless People

The number of attacks against members of the LGBT community (eight injured) decreased significantly in comparison with 2013 (two killed and 25 injured).

This decline in homophobic violence is partly explained by the fact that 2013 was a year of an active homophobic campaign, and LGBT activists had made themselves noticeable as well. Throughout almost the entire year, the latter group engaged in protests against the bill to ban "homosexual propaganda;" right-wing radicals of all stripes went to them to beat up the protesters, and their actions were de facto condoned by the police.

The LGBT movement organized fewer demonstrations in 2014. However, these events were hardly safer for the participants. Over the past year, our records showed attacks on participants of the LGBT events as well as on participants in other demonstrations who were carrying LGBT symbols.

LGBT non-protest events also faced challenges. For example, a group of "Orthodox activists" led by Dmitry "Enteo" Tsorionov and chanting "Moscow is not Sodom!" pelted with eggs a security guard and the Sakharov Center building in Moscow, where a LGBT community event was taking place in October. In September, supporters of the Duma Deputy Vitaly Milonov twice tried to disrupt the opening of the annual LGBT Queerfest in St. Petersburg.

Statistics for this group also include the victims of "pedophile hunters" from the neo-Nazi project Occupy Pedophilyai.[9]

Victims of attacks included not only members of the LGBT community, but also those perceived as such: two girls in the St. Petersburg metro whom an attacker took for lesbians, and teachers and students of an English school in Irkutsk who were celebrating St. Patrick's Day and were dressed "in historical costumes, particularly in kilts," so they were taken for gays.

Unfortunately, we have received no information or have been unable to establish any details about the majority of such attacks. For example, a video of two young people being beaten up as their attackers shouted homophobic slurs surfaced online in early 2015. It was clear from the context that the incident took place on May 1, but even establishing the location proved impossible.

The number of attacks against homeless people was higher in 2014 than in the preceding year with six killed and one wounded (compared to three killed and two injured in 2013). The brutality of these attacks is simply appalling. For example, an attacker in Birobidzhan ("motivated by hatred against people leading a vagabond lifestyle") doused a victim's clothes with gasoline and set them on fire, then kicked the homeless man down the stairs.

Unfortunately, such attacks take place much more often than we know, since we only keep records of cases in which the hate motive has already been recognized by the prosecution. Alas, this seldom happens.

Violence Motivated by Religion

The number of religion-based xenophobia victims was lower than in 2013, but the attacks were more violent, with two killed and 12 injured (compared to 21 injured in the year before).

Jehovah's Witnesses, who constituted the largest group among the victims, have been subjected to a government-organized repression campaign for the past six years. In 2014, at least 11 followers of the Jehovah's Witnesses denomination were injured; at least 12 were injured in 2013.

Islam as a religion and Muslims as a religious group are constant targets of xenophobic attacks on social media. However, Muslims per se (that is, as members of a religious group, not as "ethnic outsiders") are rarely targets of xenophobic violence. There was a record of this kind of violence in 2014, when a woman passerby, dressed in traditional Muslim clothes (a long dress and a headscarf) was beaten up in Moscow.

Other victims include parishioners and a nun of a Russian Orthodox church in Yuzhno-Sakhalinsk, who were shot by a "pagan" motivated by his "hostile feeling against Abrahamic religions, particularly Christianity."

Other Kinds of Right Radical Violence

The police stepped up their efforts to protect popular public spaces during the holidays. Perhaps that was why the Airborne Forces Day on Aug. 2 – accompanied for many years by mass attacks by drunken paratroopers, including openly racist ones – was more subdued than in the preceding year. However, Aug. 2, 2014, did not pass completely incident-free: Two former paratroopers beat a citizen of Côte d'Ivoire in Tomsk, and paratroopers in St. Petersburg tried to take away a flag from an LGBT activist who was coming out to Palace Square. However, after only a few seconds, the gay activist was taken into police custody and put into a squad car that had quickly pulled up. Two paratroopers were detained, and the crowd prevented the OMON riot police from arresting the others involved in the incident. At least 10 people were injured on that day in 2013.

Raids by the ultra-right in search of "illegal migrants" continued throughout the year 2014, although, compared to the preceding year, the number of them was much more modest. These raids did not always proceed peacefully, despite the fact that the police were often present and occasionally even acted as partners. On July 20, activists of the National Socialist Initiative (*Natsional-sotsialisticheskaya initsiativa*, NSI) destroyed one of the shops in the area of the Primorskaya and Pionerskaya metro stations in St. Petersburg; on Sept. 21 nationalists seized fruit from fruit sellers of "non-Slavic appearance" in Primorsky shopping center and threw it into the trash. In Syktyvkar, members of the organizations Frontier of the North (*Rubezh Severa*) and Guestbusters-Komi (Guestbusters is a project of the "Russians" (*russkiye*) movement) found out the addresses of 13 apartments in which migrant workers were registered, affixed Guestbusters stickers on the apartment doors, photographed the doors with stickers on them, and published the images and the addresses on the Frontier of the North Web site.

Explosions and arson that targeted government buildings continued in 2014. On the night of April 20 (Hitler's birthday),[10] nationalists threw two "Molotov cocktails" at the police station in Cheboksary; a prosecutor's office in Chelyabinsk was set on fire on April 21. In early April, unknown people tried to set fire to the building of the Maritime Territory Court in Vladivostok. However, this last case of arson was probably associated not with Hitler's birthday, but with the fact that the court at that time was considering the case of the notorious Maritime Territory Guerillas (*Primorskie partizany*) – a group popular among the ultra-right.

Crimes Against Property

Crimes against property include damage to cemeteries, monuments, various cultural sites and property in general. They are categorized under several different articles of the Criminal Code, but the enforcement is not always consistent. Such acts are usually referred to as vandalism.

Our statistics do not include isolated cases of neo-Nazi graffiti and drawings on buildings and fences, but it does include serial graffiti (law enforcement considers graffiti to be either a form of vandalism or a means of public expression).

In 2014 vandals motivated by religious, ethnic or ideological hatred were less active than the previous year: In 2014, there were at least 53 such acts of vandalism in 35 regions of the country, compared to at least 71 in 35 regions in 2013.

Most acts of vandalism in 2014 had a pronounced ideological character: the desecration of memorials to soldiers killed in the Great Patriotic War, monuments to the fighters of the Revolution, Lenin's monuments, etc. – 17 incidents in total, including four cases of arson. In 2013, there were seven such incidents.

[Attacks on] Orthodox sites take second place, with 10 of them attacked by vandals in 2014, including two cases of arson. A year earlier, Orthodox facilities suffered the largest number of attacks (32 cases).

Sites of new religious movements were third on this list, with eight cases, all of them buildings owned by Jehovah's Witnesses (compared to 12 in the preceding year). They were followed by Muslim sites (seven incidents, including three cases of arson, compared to nine in the preceding year) and Jewish sites with five incidents (compared to nine in the preceding year). In addition, five government buildings and the Protestant church Word of Life (*Slovo zhizni*) came under attack. Thus, the number of attacks on all religious sites decreased in comparison with 2013.

The number of the most dangerous acts (arson) was rather small and amounted to 19% [of attacks on property] (10 of 53) compared to 19 of 72 in 2013.

The situation in the regions showed some changes. In 2014, acts of vandalism were reported in new regions (Transbaikal and Khabarovsk Territories, Ivanovo, Kaliningrad, Kemerovo, Orenburg, Rostov, Saratov, Tambov, Tver and Tyumen Provinces and the republics of Kalmykia and Udmurtia). On the other hand, a number of regions (Altai and Stavropol Territories, the Jewish Autonomous Region, Novgorod, Ryazan, Sakhalin, Sverdlovsk, Smolensk, Tomsk, Tula and Ulyanovsk Provinces and the republics of Kabardino-Balkaria, Adygea, Karelia, and Komi) appeared in our statistics for 2013, but not for this year.

The geography of vandalism largely coincides with the geography of racist violence (in 17 regions), but xenophobic vandalism was more widespread (35 regions) than violence (25 regions).

NOTES

1. Data as of March 7, 2015.
2. Krasnodar Territory has been a hotbed of ethnic tension for many years.
3. Voronezh Province showed up in our statistics in 2013, 2008, 2007 and 2005.
4. Maria Rozalskaya, You Will No Longer Be the Silent Majority // Mediazona. Jan. 9, 2015 (http://www.zona.media/agenda/molchalivym-bolshinstvom/).
5. These attacks peaked in 2007 (seven killed, 118 injured) and have been declining slowly ever since; they dropped abruptly in 2013 (seven injured) after a number of leaders of the

antifascist movements gave up their political activity or left the country fearing government persecution for participation in the protests of 2011–2012.

6. After A. Vesnin filed a complaint, the police found the actions of the attackers fall under Art. 144 of the Criminal Code (impeding the legitimate activities of journalists with violence), but the Investigative Committee, to which the journalist's case was referred, found no crime in this case. S. Smirnov was brought to administrative justice under the Art. 20.1 of the Code of Administrative Offenses (petty hooliganism).

7. On Aug. 12, 2014, Andrei Makarevich went on a humanitarian mission to the Donetsk Basin at the invitation of President of the Ukrainian Volunteers Fund. The musician gave a concert in the town of Svyatogorsk for refugees from Donetsk and Lugansk. This caused a negative reaction in the Russian media. Makarevich's concerts were canceled in several Russian cities, including St. Petersburg, Novosibirsk and twice in Samara.

8. The SERB group is led by abovementioned Gosha Tarasevich.

9. "Occupy Pedophilyai" was a project of the "Restruct!" neo-Nazi movement created in 2011 by Maksim "Tesak" Martsinkevich. Activists lured suspected pedophiles with live bait, beat and humiliated them, then published video reports of the attacks. Such groups existed in many Russian cities. In 2014, after Martsinkevich's arrest and the opening of numerous criminal cases against members of "Restruct!," the movement announced it was dissolving.

10. We know at least two racist attacks that happened around April 20. Makhmadkarim Dzhalilov, a citizen of Tajikistan, was stabbed on April 18 in Moscow, and a crowd of young men attacked two representatives of a youth subculture on April 23 in Yekaterinburg.

Systematic Racist and Neo-Nazi Violence

According to our preliminary estimates, at least 11 people were killed and approximately 82 people were injured in 2015 as a result of racist and neo-Nazi violence; six people received credible death threats. As you can see, the number of racist and neo-Nazi attacks dropped dramatically. In 2014, 36 people died and 133 were injured; two received death threats.[1] We can say with a high degree of probability that the number of racially motivated attacks dropped – an undeniably positive result.

In the past year, attacks occurred in 23 regions of the country (compared to 29 regions in 2014). As before, the highest levels of violence were observed in Moscow (three killed, 31 injured), St. Petersburg (three and 14) and Moscow Province (none and five). In addition, a significant number of victims were reported in Khabarovsk Territory (four injured), Volgograd Province, Kursk Province and Samara Province (three victims in each). Compared to the preceding year, the situation in Krasnodar Territory improved.

A number of regions included in our 2014 statistics have disappeared this year. However, in comparison to 2014, crimes were reported in a number of new regions: Volgograd Province, Kaliningrad Province, Kirov Province, Kursk Province, Murmansk Province and Samara Province.

Attacks Against Ethnic "Outsiders"

The largest group of victims was, as usual, those who were perceived by the attackers as "ethnic outsiders." Our records showed a total of 38 victims of ethnically motivated attacks. This number constitutes only 1/3 of the corresponding data point from the previous year (101 persons). This drop could be partially explained by the active practice of migrant deportations and bans against re-entry[2] by the FMS (Federal Migration Service). However, this factor is unlikely to have played a significant role. It may have affected the number of random attacks on the streets. However, migrants were still present on the streets in sufficient numbers to be involved in targeted attacks on ethnic grounds. More likely, [the decline occurred because] the state further intensified its efforts to prosecute right-wing radicals, and this movement was going through a serious crisis, which also undoubtedly affected its militant wing.

Migrants from Central Asia, as usual, constituted the largest group of victims with four people killed and six injured (14 and 29 in 2014). In addition, 11 victims (one killed, 10 injured) were of unspecified "non-Slavic" appearance, usually described as "Asian," so migrants from Central Asia most likely constitute the vast majority of this group as well (this group numbered one killed and 17 injured victims in 2014). There were five victims among migrants from the Caucasus region (compared to three killed and 13 injured in 2014).

The number of attacks against dark-skinned people also decreased significantly – six victims were injured in 2015 (compared to 15 in 2014). In the year 2015, we saw an example of antisemitic violence in the Voronezh Province. The data for 2014 were identical to 2015 (two wounded). Attacks under xenophobic slogans against other "ethnic others" – a native of Sudan in Moscow, a visitor from Kalmykia in St. Petersburg, a native of Kazakhstan in Volgograd Province – were reported as well.

In the year under review, our records showed both attacks against lone passers-by and cases of gang attacks. For example, a mass brawl "accompanied by nationalist slogans" took place on the night of Oct. 14-15, 2015, in St. Petersburg, near the Metro Club.[3]

We know of at least one far right raid on a commuter train (a so-called "white car") in 2015. In January 2015, a group of 15-20 masked young men entered the car on Kratovo Station of the Moscow regional commuter train Kazan line and started beating up people of "non-Slavic appearance." Right-wing radicals also continued their raids at markets and other places.

Attacks Against Political Adversaries

In 2015, the number of right-wing attacks against political, ideological or "aesthetic" opponents decreased slightly to 13 injured (compared to 15 in 2014).[4] The victims include participants of the Franz Kafka and George Orwell forum in Kaliningrad Province, attendees of a punk metal concert in St. Petersburg and a punk concert in Moscow, and antifascists in Cherepovets.

The number of the victims of attacks by pro-Kremlin nationalist movements against people they regarded as a "fifth column" and "traitors" increased.

In October, members of the SERB group attacked elderly activist Vladimir Ionov, who was holding a one-person picket near the Historical Museum in Moscow.[5] Gosha Tarasevich unsuccessfully tried to organize an attack against the Sakharov Center, which was hosting a charity evening on June 27 in support of prisoners of conscience.

In January, NLM activists attacked participants of the Jan. 19 marches in memory of slain lawyer Stanislav Markelov and journalist Anastasia Baburova in Moscow and Irkutsk, and, in June 2015, they also attacked the participants of the opposition picket who were holding a banner "Freedom for the prisoners of May 6."[6]

Anti-Maidan Supporters, after their march in the capital, which was held on the anniversary of the February [2014] events on the Maidan, attacked a young man on Petrovka Street in Moscow who had shouted "Glory to Ukraine!" They also attacked participants of the Spring March in memory of Boris Nemtsov in Voronezh.

This category also includes people who were beaten up "by association." Passerby Roman Muzichenko reprimanded a group of young people who were throwing up their arms in a Nazi salute on the Silikatnaya Station platform (the Moscow regional commuter trains Kursk line). In response, he was beaten to death. Soccer fans stabbed a young man who tried to defend a girl in a hijab in Moscow. In the Volgograd Province, a woman was punched in the face for stopping a group of young men from beating up a native of Kazakhstan.

Attacks Against LGBT or Homeless People

The number of attacks against LGBT people remains the same as a year earlier[7] – nine people injured. Over the past year, our records showed cases of attacks against participants of LGBT events, as well as attacks against participants of any other demonstrations in which symbols of the LGBT community were displayed. Members of the God's Will (*Bozhya Volya*) movement, headed by Dmitry "Enteo" Tsorionov, were especially zealous in this regard. For example, they attacked participants of the unauthorized LGBT rally in central Moscow on May 30.

LGBT meeting places were also under threat – on April 13, unknown perpetrators sprayed suffocating gas with a pungent odor in the office of the Murmansk regional civic organization Maximum: The Center for Social and Psychological Assistance and Legal Support to Victims of Discrimination and Homophobia. Two people were injured. Notably, "The police officers' attitude toward the victims was dismissive."

Attacks took place against people "taken for" LGBT, as well. A young man wearing a multi-colored scarf with no symbols or LGBT colors was beaten in a subway car in St. Petersburg in October 2015.

The number of attacks against homeless people was lower in 2015 than the year before – three killed and seven injured (compared to 13 and one in 2014). All of them were victims of the Moscow "Cleaners Gang," which has a mission of killing the homeless and people sleeping on park benches.

Violence Motivated by Religion

The number of victims of religious xenophobia was greater than in the preceding year, but the attacks were less brutal: 18 injured (compared to two killed and 12 injured in 2014). Four people received credible murder threats.

As usual, [many victims were] Jehovah's Witnesses. At least 14 of them were injured in 2015.

Muslims per se (that is, as members of a religious group rather than as "ethnic outsiders") are rarely targets of xenophobic violence. However, such incidents did take place in 2015: A group of soccer fans tried to attack a young woman in a hijab in Moscow on Nov. 21.

The group of victims also includes an Orthodox priest from Volgograd.

Crimes Against Property

In 2015, the activity level of vandals motivated by religious, ethnic or ideological hatred remained almost the same as in the preceding year. In 2015 there were at least 52 such acts of vandalism in 32 regions of the country compared to at least 53 in 35 regions in 2014.

Similarly to the preceding year, most acts of vandalism in 2015 had a pronounced ideological character: the desecration of monuments to heroes of the Great Patriotic War, to Lenin, to People's Will revolutionaries etc. – 19 incidents, including one arson (compared to 17 incidents in 2014).

Sites of new religious movements (all of them belonging to Jehovah's Witnesses) took second place with 11 cases (compared to 12 in 2014),

Orthodox and Muslim sites shared third place for the number of attacks by vandals. In each case, six religious sites were attacked (10 Orthodox sites and seven Muslim sites were affected in 2014) with two cases of arson in each group.

Jewish sites took fourth place (four sites, one of which was attacked twice), including one bombing (compared to nine in the preceding year) followed by the Korean wooden totem poles (a year earlier, there were no attacks against pagan sites).

In addition, four government institutions were attacked (compared to five in the preceding year).

As can be seen from the above data, the number of attacks on religious sites decreased slightly to 29 in 2015 (down from 32 in 2014).

The number of the most dangerous attacks (arson or bombing) decreased slightly in both absolute and relative terms; it was down 15%, that is, eight out of 44, compared to 10 out of 53 in 2014.

The geographic spread of xenophobic vandalism was wider (32 regions) than that of violence (23 regions). The geographic distribution of vandalism overlaps with that of racist violence only in 10 regions – Moscow, St. Petersburg, Volgograd Province, Vologda Province, Kirov Province, Murmansk Province, Nizhny Novgorod Province, Samara Province, Sverdlovsk Province and Tula Province.

NOTES

1. Data as of Jan. 29, 2016.

2. Deportation of Migrants: Figures and Facts // Web site of the Civic Assistance Committee. Sept. 29, 2015. (http://refugee.ru/news/vydvorenie-migrantov-tsifry-i-fakty/).

3. Mass brawl near Metro Club in St. Petersburg // SOVA Center. Oct. 16, 2015 (http://www.sova-center.ru/racism-xenophobia/news/racism-nationalism/2015/10/d33050/).

4. These attacks peaked in 2007 (seven killed, 118 injured), and were gradually decreasing in quantity before they fell sharply in 2013 (seven injured). See: V. Alperovich, N. Yudina. Ibid.

5. SERB activists attacked a man in a one-person picket // SOVA Center. Oct. 24, 2015 (http://www.sova-center.ru/racism-xenophobia/news/racism-nationalism/2015/10/d33105/).

6. Pro-government movement activists beat up participants of an opposition picket // SOVA Center. June 25, 2015 (http://www.sova-center.ru/racism-xenophobia/news/racism-nationalism/2015/06/d32282/).

7. Our records showed a sharp rise in homophobic violence in 2013 (2/25) during an active homophobic campaign and at a time when LGBT activists were very noticeable. See: Vera Alperovich, Natalia Yudina, The Ultra-Right Shrugged: Xenophobia and Radical Nationalism in Russia, and Efforts to Counteract Them in 2013 // SOVA Center. Feb. 17, 2014 (http://www.sova-center.ru/racism-xenophobia/publications/2014/02/d29004/).

Systematic Racist and Neo-Nazi Violence

In 2016, at least nine people were killed by racist and neo-Nazi violence, 72 were injured, and three people received credible death threats. Our data does not include victims of incidents in the North Caucasus and the Crimea or victims of mass brawls. Compared to 2015, the number of racist and neo-Nazi attacks dropped, although not as dramatically as it did the year before. (In 2015, 12 people were killed, 96 were injured, and eight received credible death threats;[1] in 2014, 36 people were killed, 134 were injured, and two received credible death threats.)

We often do not find out about what happened until much later. For example, in 2017 a native of the Republic of Chad was killed in Kazan. Those suspected of his murder were quickly arrested, and an investigation is under way. The police have been checking whether the suspects had participated in other attacks carried out in 2013-2014. However, the details of these other attacks were only being reported in the media in 2016.

In the past year, attacks occurred in 18 regions (compared to 26 regions in 2015). As before, the highest levels of violence were recorded in the cities of Moscow (three killed, 26 injured) and St. Petersburg (three killed, 16 injured), and in Moscow and Vladimir Provinces (none killed, six injured in each). In addition, a significant number of victims were reported in Omsk Province (one killed, two injured) and in the Republic of Tatarstan (one killed, two injured).

In comparison to the previous year, the situation in Khabarovsk Territory slightly improved (none killed, two injured).

A number of regions that figured in our 2015 data set no longer do so this year (Volgograd, Voronezh, Kaliningrad, Kaluga, Kirov, Kurgan, Kursk, Murmansk, Nizhny Novgorod, Samara and Tver Provinces, Perm Territory, and the Republic of Karelia). However, crimes were reported in a number of new regions (the Vladimir, Omsk and Chelyabinsk Provinces and Transbaikal, Krasnodar and Stavropol Territories).

Attacks Against Ethnic "Outsiders"

As before, those perceived by the attackers to be "ethnic outsiders" made up the largest group of victims, and the proportion of attacks on this group rose significantly: in 2016, our records showed 44 victims of ethnically motivated attacks (seven of whom died), compared to the 38 recorded in 2015. Migrants from Central Asia, as usual, constitute the largest group of victims, with two killed and 22 injured (compared to four killed and six injured in 2015). In addition, there were victims of unspecified "non-Slavic appearance" (one killed and seven injured; in 2015, this group numbered one killed and 10 injured). Victims from the Caucasus region include two killed and one injured (compared to none killed and five injured in 2015).

Additionally, an Indian citizen was killed in Kazan, a Bangladeshi citizen suffered battery in Moscow, and Korean citizens suffered battery in St. Petersburg and Tula.

Last year, our records showed three victims of antisemitic attacks in Moscow and St. Petersburg (compared to two Jewish victims in 2014 and two in 2015).

Some attacks (especially those against adolescents and women) were marked by their extreme cruelty. For example, a 20-year-old African woman was raped and brutally murdered in December 2016 in Moscow. One of the suspects arrested, nicknamed "Kolyuchka" (Spike) stated that what had motivated him were "his radical views."[2] The young men claimed that they considered the victim to be "dirty." In August 2016, a 17-year-old boy from Tajikistan was found near a 24-hour shop on Lensky Street, St. Petersburg, with multiple knife wounds to the back and two severed fingers. Three young suspects, armed with bats, knives and machetes, were detained.

This year our records have shown multiple incidents of group attacks on people from Central Asia and the Caucasus in subway and commuter train cars (the so-called "white cars"). We know of at least five such incidents. However, attacks in subway cars were also carried out by lone individuals. An incident that took place on April 8, 2016, caught media attention: A subway passenger in Moscow attacked two immigrants from Tajikistan, Mukhammadzhon Khakimov and Sulaimon Saidov, inside a train car at Kaluzhskaya Station.

Ultra-right raids on markets and other public spaces continued. Thus, in St. Petersburg, Dmitry Bobrov carried out a so-called Russian Purge (*Russkaya zachistka*) – a number of raids in search of places of illegal trade. The ultra-right group North-Slavic Village (*Stanitsa Severo-Slavianskaya*) organized raids in areas where migrant workers live. Approximately 10 people, together with the police, broke into flats in derelict apartment buildings and forced Central Asian migrants out onto the street. In Moscow, activists from the National Conservative Movement (*Natsionalno-Konservativnoye Dvizhenie*, NCM) checked the registration and sanitation paperwork of kebab vendors. In Podolsk, they also raided the places where melons and watermelons were sold. In Moscow, the Citadel project led by Vladimir Ratnikov carried out raids in search of illegal melon and watermelon sellers.

Attacks Against Ideological Opponents

In 2016, the number of ultra-right attacks against political, ideological or "aesthetic" opponents decreased slightly to eight injured (compared to 13 in 2015).[3] Those targeted included a Greenpeace volunteer in Krasnodar Territory and an "emo" teenager in Vladimir. A number of "inappropriately dressed" schoolchildren[4] were beaten up by neo-Nazis in Vladivostok.

This category also includes those seen as "fifth column" or "traitors." On July 11, an employer of the Russian social media Web site VKontakte, Denis Samsonov, was attacked in St. Petersburg. The attackers shouted, "National traitor, Jew, fifth column."[5]

In Moscow, on April 28, 2016, activists from the NLM attacked the attendees at a ceremony for the winners of Russia's annual research project competition for senior high school students: "Man in History: Russia – 20th Century."[6]

Some victims were "victims by association." For example, this was the case when a native of Kyrgyzstan, Nurik (Atabek) Munduzov was killed near Ryazansky Prospekt Metro Station in Moscow in August 2016. A 29-year-old man, a passerby, was riding his motorcycle when he heard shouting. He pulled over and ran after the attackers but was struck with a knife in the shoulder.

Attacks Against LGBT and Homeless People

Attacks on members of the LGBT community decreased slightly (one killed and five injured in 2016 compared to nine injured in 2015).

However, the attacks became more serious. On March 31, 2016, the journalist Dmitry Tsilikin was brutally murdered. A suspect, Sergei Kosirev, was detained. Kosirev referred to himself as a "cleanser," his life's purpose being to "crusade against a certain social group." What drove him to kill Tsilikin was "not dislike – as your report states – but hatred."[7]

Attacks were not limited to people participating specifically in LGBT demonstrations and events; participants in any demonstration where LGBT symbols were displayed could find themselves targeted. On Jan. 19, for example, 10-15 members of God's Will, headed by Dmitry "Enteo" Tsorionov, turned up at a rally in memory of the murdered human rights lawyer Stanislav Markelov and reporter Anastasia Baburova.[8] They intended to "beat up gays," but were stopped by the police.

Aggressive soccer fans, aside from jeering and displaying racist symbols during games[9] (including European Championship matches[10]), also attacked members of the LGBT community. In the early hours of June 15, 2016, a group of soccer fans attacked customers at the "Mono" gay bar in Yekaterinburg.

The infamous "Khabarovsk flesher-girls" (*khabarovskie zhivoderki*) also bullied and attacked LGBT people. Investigations confirmed that the two teenage girls and their male accomplice, who were accused of torturing and killing animals, were involved in the incitement of hatred and insulting the feelings of religious people. According to investigators, one of the girls and an 18-year-old man recorded and edited a video of a man. This video was judged to be "aimed at the violation of the dignity of a person or a group of persons on the basis of affiliation to a social group." (The investigative committee's report left it unclear which social group was being referred to; however, the girl's social media page contains posts about violent attacks on homeless and LGBT people in 2016.)[11]

Fewer attacks on homeless people came to our attention in 2016 than in 2015 (one killed and one injured, compared to three killed and seven injured in 2015). Intoxication and unkempt appearance were cited as the reasons for the murder of Aleksandr Chizhikov, the leader of the Bryansk rock band Otvet Chemberlenu (Response to Chamberlain), on July 28, 2016. The suspects, aged 19 and 21 years old, were "supporters of an informal movement aggressively advocating intolerance toward people outside of society." They stabbed the musician, who had been sleeping near a heating system pipe.[12]

Violence Motivated by Religion

The number of victims of religious xenophobia was greater than in the preceding year (20 injured, compared to 18 in 2015). One other person received a credible death threat.

Most of the victims were Jehovah's Witnesses. In 2016, at least 18 Jehovah's Witnesses were targeted. Other victims include Pentecostals in Aleksandrov, Vladimir Province.

Crimes Against Property

In 2016, there was a lower rate of vandalism motivated by religious, ethnic and ideological hatred than in the previous year. There were at least 44 cases of such vandalism in 26 regions in 2016, compared to at least 56 cases in 32 regions in 2015.

As in 2015, most cases of vandalism in 2016 were distinctly ideological in nature: the defilement of monuments to Marx, Lenin, and the Revolution, as well as graves of local World War II heroes, the Federal Security Service (FSB) Museum, etc. (14 incidents in total compared to 19 in 2015).

Russian Orthodox religious sites were the second most commonly vandalized with 10 incidents, two of which involved arson (compared to nine incidents in 2015 and 10 in 2014). Sites of new religious movements (all of them belonging to Jehovah's Witnesses) were third with nine incidents, including one bombing and two arson attacks (compared to 11 incidents in 2015). Jewish sites were fourth with five incidents, the same as the previous year, including one arson attack. Muslim sites were fifth with four incidents of vandalism (compared to seven in 2015). Two Buddhist sites were vandalized: a temple in St. Petersburg and a statue of Buddha in Elista, Kalmykia. No Buddhist sites were targeted in 2015.

The data show that the number of attacks on religious sites did not change significantly between 2015 and 2016 (30 incidents in 2016 compared to 29 in 2015).

However, the proportion of more dangerous incidents – fires and explosions – fell slightly to 13% [of all incidents]: six out of the total of 44, compared to 10 out of the 56 in the previous year.

The geographic distribution changed somewhat. A number of new regions reported acts of vandalism in 2016: Amur, Arkhangelsk, Ivanovo, Kaliningrad, Kursk, and Rostov Provinces, the republics of Karelia, Kalmykia, Crimea, Tatarstan, and Chuvashia, and Stavropol, Altai, Transbaikal and Khabarovsk Territories). Meanwhile, some previously featured regions disappeared from our 2016 statistics: Moscow, Bryansk, Volgograd, Vologda, Kostroma, Lipetsk, Murmansk, Novosibirsk, Samara, Sverdlovsk,

Tver, Tomsk, Tula, Ulyanovsk and Chelyabinsk provinces, Krasnodar and Krasnoyarsk Territories, the republics of Bashkortostan and Khakassia and the Komi Republic.

The geographic distribution of xenophobic vandalism was broader (26 regions) than that of violence (18 regions). The geographic distribution of vandalism overlaps with that of racist violence in only six regions (compared to 10 in 2015): St. Petersburg, Rostov Province, the Republic of Tatarstan and Stavropol, Transbaikal and Khabarovsk Territories.

NOTES

1. Our data for 2015 and 2016 are as recorded on March 11, 2017.

2. Girl's body with multiple knife wounds found in south-east Moscow // life. Dec. 23, 2016 (https://life.ru/t/новости/951185/tielo_zhiestoko_ubitoi_dievushki_naidieno_v_moskvie).

3. These attacks had peaked in 2007 (seven killed, 118 injured) and were consistently decreasing in number. The lowest point was in 2013 (seven injured).

4. Group of young men in Snegovaya Pad beats up schoolchildren, extorts money, attempts to establish white supremacy // Novosti Vladivostoka. May 11, 2016 (http://www.newsvl.ru/vlad/2016/05/11/147231/#ixzz48KF7rjjV).

5. VKontakte employee battered and robbed in St. Petersburg; attackers shouted "national traitor, Jew, fifth column" // Mediazona. June 13, 2016 (https://zona.media/news/2016/12/06/s-krikami).

6. For more information see: Feel the epoch for yourself: "patriotic" activists throw eggs at children taking part in competition // Meduza. April 28, 2016 (https://meduza.io/feature/2016/04/28/pochuvstvovat-epohu-na-sebe).

7. Man from ultra-right suspected of killing journalist Tsilikin // SOVA Center. April 28, 2016 (http://www.sova-center.ru/racism-xenophobia/news/racism-nationalism/2016/04/d34258/).

8. See SOVA report for more information on the story: Hundreds March in Memory of Markelov and Baburova in Moscow Jan. 24, 2016 // SOVA Center. Jan. 24, 2013 (http://www.sova-center.ru/en/xenophobia/news-releases/2013/01/d26273/).

9. Right-football // SOVA Center. May 20, 2016 (http://www.sova-center.ru/racism-xenophobia/publications/2016/05/d34534/).

10. Marseille Fans: racism on top of all // SOVA Center. June 16, 2016 (http://www.sova-center.ru/racism-xenophobia/publications/2016/06/d34799/).

11. For more information see: Khabarovsk flesher-girls accused of inciting hate and insulting religious sentiment // SOVA Center. Nov. 11, 2016 (http://www.sova-center.ru/racism-xenophobia/news/counteraction/2016/11/d35813/).

12. New accusation for the defendants in criminal case about murder of Bryansk Musician // Office of Investigations, Russian Federation Investigative Committee, Bryansk Region. Dec. 21, 2016 (http://www.sova-center.ru/racism-xenophobia/news/counteraction/2016/12/d36056/).

Systematic Racist and Neo-Nazi Violence

In 2017, at least 71 people were victims of violence motivated by racist or neo-Nazi-ideology. Fewer than six people died; the others were injured. We saw a drop in numbers compared to 2016, when 10 people were killed, 82 injured and three more threatened with murder.[1]

The attacks of 2017 occurred in 19 regions of the country (compared to 18 regions in 2016). Unexpectedly, St. Petersburg had the highest level of violence (one killed, 24 injured), while victims in Moscow were uncharacteristically few (nine injured). A significant number of people were attacked in Novosibirsk Province (five injured), the Republic of Tatarstan (one killed, four injured), Rostov Province (two killed, two injured), Oryol Province (three injured), and Khabarovsk Territory (two killed, one injured). When compared to 2016, the situation improved in Moscow Province (two people injured in 2017 compared to six in 2016) but deteriorated in Tatarstan (one killed, two injured in 2016).

According to our data, in addition to Moscow, St. Petersburg and Moscow Province, the centers of ethnic tension in the past seven years (2011-2017) can be identified as Novosibirsk Province, Orenburg Province, Rostov Province, Sverdlovsk Province, Tula Province and the Republic of Tatarstan. However, it is possible that these regions simply do a better job of informing the public about such crimes.

Attacks Against Ethnic "Outsiders"

People perceived by their attackers to be "ethnic outsiders" constituted the largest group of victims. In 2017, our records showed 28 attacks motivated by ethnic considerations. In comparison with the preceding year, the percentage of such attacks decreased: We reported 44 such victims (seven of them dead) in 2016.

Migrants from Central Asia were the most numerous group in this category of victims with 11 injured (compared to three killed and 25 injured in 2016), followed by individuals of unidentified "non-Slavic appearance" (five injured); most likely, the overwhelming majority of these people were also from Central Asia, since their appearance was described as "Asian" (compared to two killed and eight injured in 2016). Migrants from the Caucasus take the next place with three injured (compared to three killed and one injured in 2016).

Additionally, in August 2017, three students from Iraq were beaten up in Oryol. Mahjub Tijani Hassan, a 24-year-old student of Kazan Federal University from the Republic of Chad, was brutally murdered in early February 2017 in Kazan.[2] This murder was the focus of significant media attention in early 2017. Two Russian victims of violence motivated by ethnic hatred were reported in Novosibirsk.

In addition to attacks on the streets, we know of at least two cases of group attacks in subway and commuter train cars against migrants from Central Asia or the Caucasus (the so-called "white cars"). For example, in December 2017, a group of young people armed with nunchucks and a knife entered the train at Technological Institute Station in St. Petersburg and proceeded to beat up two passengers of "non-Slavic appearance," pushing one of them out onto the platform with the shout, "This car is for Russians!"[3]

Despite all the anti-Ukrainian rhetoric of the recent years, attacks against Ukrainians are quite rare, apparently because ethnic Ukrainians are hard to identify in a crowd. However, we encountered one attack against a Ukrainian citizen in the period under review. Five young skinheads beat up an 18-year-old Ukrainian citizen – a trainee at Dynamo Football Club (Kyiv) – while yelling xenophobic anti-Ukrainian slogans; the incident took place outside the Garage Underground nightclub in Chelyabinsk in July 2017.[4]

The Neo-Nazi group Citadel conducted a number of raids in Moscow early in the year. However, in contrast to the previous years, anti-migrant raids had almost disappeared by the end of 2017, especially after most of their perpetrators faced criminal prosecution.

Videos of attacks also appeared on the Internet, but it was impossible to establish where and when they occurred. The neo-Nazi videos with scenes of racist violence by the infamous Sparrows' Crew gang, as well as the new Vigilance Committee (*Komitet Bditelnosti*), were shared online in early 2017. Unfortunately, recognizing the circumstances of the incidents from these videos was impossible.

Moreover, while law enforcers managed to bring down the level of systematic racist violence by organized Nazi groups, ordinary xenophobic violence seemed to have remained at the same level. Our records show three to five such incidents each year.

Attacks Against Ideological Opponents

The number of attacks by ultra-right against their political, ideological or "aesthetic" opponents increased noticeably in 2017 bringing the count of victims up to 21, including three deaths (compared to nine injured in 2016).

The victims of the attacks included representatives of youth subcultures, both politicized (antifascists, anarchists) and apolitical (attacks against anime fans, or shaving the head of a teenager as an objection against his dreadlocks).

The number of people beaten up because they were perceived as the "fifth column" and "traitors to the homeland" increased; the victims included independent journalists,[5] volunteer guards at the Boris Nemtsov memorial and participants in opposition pickets or rallies against corruption (primarily supporters of Aleksei Navalny). There were six such attacks in 2017 compared to three in 2016.

Attacks of this nature were carried out by representatives of nationalist pro-Kremlin groups, of which the SERB group was the most prominent. The most well-known incident took place in Moscow in April, when Aleksei Navalny had antiseptic green dye (supposedly mixed with another substance) thrown into his face. As a result, he suffered a chemical burn to his eye and had to receive medical treatment in Spain. Internet users identified the person who committed the attack as Aleksandr Petrunko, a SERB group activist.[6]

The same category also includes the attacks by the ultra-right against state employees. An armed attack on the FSB reception room, which occurred in Khabarovsk on April 21, 2017, was one of the resonant events of the year. The attack ended with the death of two people and of the perpetrator, 17-year-old Anton Konev; one man was wounded.[7] It soon became clear that Konev was a member of Schtolz Khabarovsk, a small neo-Nazi group (which collaborated with the local cell of the Occupy Pedophilyai project led by Maksim "Tesak" Martsinkevich). His social media network page was found to contain the posts regarding his intention to go to Valhalla (German and Scandinavian mythology is traditionally very popular among neo-Nazis). Later, FSB officers detained Konev's alleged accomplice, an "experienced neo-Nazi."[8]

Journalists and academic experts who worked on cases related to incitement to hatred also faced threats from the ultra-right. In early 2017, Dmitry "Schulz" Bobrov published the name, the photo and the place of employment of a staff member of St. Petersburg State University; in another case, a statement containing threats against a female journalist from Novaya Gazeta was posted online.

Other Attacks

The number of attacks against LGBT [people and activists] exceeded the corresponding indicator for the preceding year; our records showed 11 injured in 2017 compared to one killed, four injured in 2016. Most of the victims were attending LGBT demonstrations, such as the Yaroslavl commemoration of the victims of hate-motivated murders of transgender individuals[9] or the LGBT Pride event in St. Petersburg.[10] Fortunately, the participants in the demonstrations and the journalists covering these demonstrations only received minor injuries.

Attacks against the homeless increased slightly in 2017 in comparison to the preceding year – two killed, one injured (compared to one killed and one injured in 2016). We count only the cases in which the hate motive was officially recognized by the investigators, as happened, for example, in the case of the murder of two homeless people (a man and a woman) at the Bratskoye Cemetery of Rostov-on-Don. A resident of Tyumen Province, detained on suspicion of the murder, confessed to the act and declared himself a "cleaner" of the city from "worthless people."[11]

The number of victims of religious xenophobia was almost impossible to estimate. As usual, the majority of the known victims were Jehovah's Witnesses. In 2017, the data on cases related to the attacked Jehovah's Witnesses were closed, probably due to shutting down of the Jehovah's Witnesses' organizations as extremist on April 20, 2017.[12] Nevertheless, we have information about two attacks against representatives of this group (compared to about 18 in 2016).

In 2017, we also have information about an attack on Muslims. For example, in February 2017, four young people verbally attacked a Tatar woman in a head scarf on a minibus in Saransk, uttering insults and threats.[13]

Some individuals who tried to intervene and defend others from being beaten up, also ended up among the victims – seven such people were reported in 2017. Examples include a minibus passenger in Saransk who stood up for the abovementioned Tatar woman in a Muslim headdress, and two subway passengers in St. Petersburg who tried to stop the violence against the non-Slavs in the subway car.[14]

Racism Among Soccer Fans

In connection with the upcoming FIFA World Cup in the summer of 2018, the Russian soccer leadership paid greater attention to the racist antics of soccer fans. The post of Inspector for Fighting Racism was restored in February 2017 and filled by well-known former soccer player Aleksei Smertin. In July, the Russian Football Union (RFU) presented a monitoring system for matches, and this system genuinely identifies incidents of racism at stadiums.

However, despite all the measures taken by the authorities, racist prejudices, expressed as insults and incitement to ethnic hatred, were still evident in Russian soccer and its affiliated groups. Booing, as well as racist, aggressively nationalistic (including antisemitic) and homophobic chants were heard from the fan sections of various teams throughout the year.[15] The characteristic insulting gestures addressed to dark-skinned players of opposing teams were also observed on several occasions.

In addition, we encountered openly discriminatory statements coming not only from individual fans, but from entire fan groups. Thus, in Krasnoyarsk, the requirements for entering the fan stands at the Yenisey-Arsenal soccer match were posted in the "Fan-Sector – Krasnoyarsk" VKontakte group in May 2017. The message stated that "only fans dressed in red" and people "only of Slavic appearance" could gain entrance into the sector. A representative of the movement told journalists that this unspoken rule "has been working for a long time" in Krasnoyarsk; he added that he would not want "non-Slavs to be seen" among the Yenisei fans in photos from the match.[16]

In 2017, we know of at least two attacks involving soccer fans that seemed ideologically motivated. These were the cases of attacks against students from Iraq in Oryol and against the Ukrainian trainee of FC Dynamo Football Club in Chelyabinsk.

Unfortunately, we can't overlook the possibility that the true number of such violent actions involving soccer fans was much higher, given the presence of neo-Nazis directly or indirectly influencing the fan environment. For example, the suspects in the murder of the student from the Republic of

Chad met each other at the stadium, and their group included "those who come from the environment of soccer hooligans, fan sections; that's where they picked [people]."[17]

Crimes Against Property

In 2017, the number of crimes against property motivated by religious, ethnic or ideological hatred was slightly higher than a year earlier; there were at least 48 incidents in 25 regions of the country compared to at least 46 in 26 regions, recorded in 2016.

As in the preceding years, the majority of the 2017 attacks were directed against ideological targets rather than religious or any other sites – our records showed 18 instances (compared to 14 in 2016) of graffiti and damage affecting the Lenin and Yeltsin monuments, the monument to TU-214 aircraft, the war monuments, and so on.

Sites, associated with other ideological enemies of the far right (specifically, with the liberal opposition) – the Sakharov Center, the editorial office of the online newspaper Lenta.ru and the director's office of the movie *Matilda* – should also be viewed as part of this group.

Second place went to Jehovah's Witnesses buildings with 14 incidents, of which three were arson (compared to nine incidents in 2016). Orthodox sites were in third place with 11 incidents, two of them arson (compared to 10 in the preceding year). Protestants took fourth place with two incidents, including one explosion (compared to none in the preceding year). Jewish, neo-Pagan and Buddhist sites split fifth place with one incident for each group (in 2016, there were five incidents related to Jewish sites, two related to Buddhist sites and no incidents related to neo-pagans). Notably, we have no information on any Muslim sites targeted in 2017 (there were four of those in 2016).

Overall, the number of attacks against religious sites remained stable at 30 per year in 2017 and 2016 (and 29 in 2015). But the percentage of the most dangerous acts – arson and explosions – exceeded those in the preceding year and comprised 29% (that is, 14 out of 48), compared to 13% (six of 44) a year earlier.

The regional breakdown for the attacks changed significantly. In 2017, such crimes were reported in 18 new regions (in Moscow, Volgograd, Vologda, Voronezh, Leningrad, Lipetsk, Moscow, Murmansk, Penza, Rostov, Sverdlovsk, Smolensk, Tula and Chelyabinsk Provinces, in Krasnoyarsk Territory, in the Jewish Autonomous Region, in the Komi Republic and in Tatarstan), but, on the other hand, 16 previously cited regions did not make our statistics in 2017 (Ivanovo, Kirov, Kursk, Nizhny Novgorod, Pskov, Saratov and Chelyabinsk Provinces, the republics of Kalmykia, Karelia and Chuvashia, Altai, Stavropol, Transbaikal, Perm and Maritime Territories and the Khanty-Mansi Autonomous Region (Yugra)).

The geographic spread was wider for xenophobic vandalism (25 regions) than that for acts of violence (18 regions). Seven regions reported both violence and vandalism – Moscow, St. Petersburg, Moscow Province, Rostov Province, Sverdlovsk Province, the Chelyabinsk Province, and the Republic of Tatarstan – compared to six regions in the preceding year.

NOTES

1. Data for 2016 and 2017 cited as of Jan. 18, 2018.

2. Kazan: the student from Chad murdered // SOVA Center. March 7, 2017 (http://www.sova-center.ru/racism-xenophobia/news/racism-nationalism/2017/03/d36533/).

3. Neo-Nazi with nunchucks beat up several people in the St. Petersburg subway shouting "Russia for Russians" // Mediazona. Dec. 11, 2017 (https://zona.media/news/2017/12/11/white).

4. For more details see: "A Ukrainian soccer player from Dynamo Kyiv brutally beaten in Chelyabinsk" // Chel.pro. July 15, 2017 (http://chel.pro/2978/).

5. For example, on Jan 10, 2017, in downtown Rostov-on-Don, neo-Nazis beat up Vladislav Ryazantsev, a journalist affiliated with the independent regional news Web site *Caucasian Knot*. See: National socialists of Rostov Province took responsibility for the attack against the journalist with *Caucasian Knot*. Jan. 16, 2017 (http://www.sova-center.ru/racism- xenophobia/news/racism-nationalism/2017/01/d36191/).
Several attacks against Galina Sidorova, a lecturer with the School of Journalistic Investigations, took place in Yoshkar-Ola on April 26 and 27, 2017. See: A journalist from School of Journalistic Investigations attacked in Yoshkar-Ola // SOVA Center. April 27, 2017 (http://www.sova-center.ru/racism-xenophobia/news/racism-nationalism/2017/04/d37096/).

6. SERB Activists attacked Aleksei Navalny // SOVA Center. May 2, 2017 (http://www.sova-center.ru/racism-xenophobia/news/racism-nationalism/2017/05/d36957/).

7. Khabarovsk: Neo-Nazi attacked a shooting club and the FSB reception room? // SOVA Center. April 24, 2017 (http://www.sova-center.ru/racism-xenophobia/news/counteraction/2017/04/d36889/).

8. The alleged accomplice of the attack against the FSB in Khabarovsk detained // SOVA Center. April 26, 2017 (http://www.sova-center.ru/racism-xenophobia/news/counteraction/2017/04/d36912/).

9. Attack against LGBT demonstration in Yaroslavl // SOVA Center. Nov. 21, 2017 (http://www.sova-center.ru/racism-xenophobia/news/racism-nationalism/2017/11/d38324/).

10. Attack against journalists and participants of the LGBT Pride event // SOVA Center. Aug. 23, 2017 (http://www.sova-center.ru/racism-xenophobia/news/racism-nationalism/2017/08/d37713/).

11. The killer of the homeless at the Bratskoye Cemetery in Rostov declares himself a "cleaner" // Svobodnaya Pressa. Jan. 13, 2017 (http://yug.svpressa.ru/accidents/news/143597/?rss=1).

12. The Supreme Court decides to shut down the Administrative Center of Jehovah's Witnesses in Russia // SOVA Center. April 20, 2017 (http://www.sova-center.ru/misuse/news/persecution/2017/04/d36871/).

13. Saransk: A young Tatar woman attacked on a minibus // SOVA Center. Feb. 5, 2017 (http://www.sova-center.ru/racism-xenophobia/news/racism-nationalism/2017/02/d36322/).

14. St. Petersburg: The "White Car" action in the subway // SOVA Center. Dec. 11, 2017 (http://www.sova-center.ru/racism-xenophobia/news/racism-nationalism/2017/12/d38456/).

15. Fare and SOVA publish a monitoring report on the issues of racism and xenophobia in Russian soccer for the seasons of 2015/16 and 2016/17 // SOVA Center. June 20, 2017 (http://www.sova-center.ru/en/xenophobia/reports-analyses/2017/06/d37316/).

16. The Yenisei fans only admitted "people of Slavic appearance" to their sector for the match against Arsenal // Prospekt Mira. May 26, 2017 (https://prmira.ru/news/fanaty-eniseya-na-match-s-arsenalom-puskali-v-svoj-sektor-tolko-lic-slavyanskoj-vneshnosti/).

17. The Kazan "avenger" looked up to the St. Petersburg nationalist: "Any white man must act" // Realnoye Vremya. March 8, 2017 (https://realnoevremya.ru/articles/58596-kazanec-ravnyalsya-na-nacistov-v-borbe-za-beluyu-rasu).

Systematic Racist and Neo-Nazi Violence

At least 57 people suffered from racist and other ideologically motivated violence in 2018: at least four of them died; the rest were injured. Our statistics continued to indicate a decrease in the number of serious ideologically motivated attacks: Nine people died and 69 were injured in 2017.[1] Of course, our 2018 data were far from final, so evidently, it would be more accurate to say that the number of victims remained fairly stable over the past four years. This number was, of course, an order of magnitude lower than it was a decade ago, but still, the current level of ideological violence cannot be deemed insignificant.

The attacks of 2018 occurred in 10 regions of the country (compared to 20 regions in 2017. The levels of violence in Moscow (two killed, 28 injured) and St. Petersburg (one killed,[2] 10 injured) top the list as usual.

In 2018, a number of regions disappeared from our statistics (Belgorod, Kirov, Orenburg, Oryol, Rostov, Tula, Chelyabinsk and Yaroslavl Provinces, Transbaikal, Krasnodar, Perm and Khabarovsk Territories and the republics of Mari El, Mordovia and Tatarstan), but on the other hand, crimes were reported in several new places, which were not on our radar in 2017 (Kaluga Province, Kursk Province, Tyumen Province and Samara Province).

Attacks Against Ethnic "Outsiders"

People perceived by their attackers to be "ethnic outsiders" still constituted the largest group of victims. Our records showed 20 ethnic attacks motivated by ethnic considerations in 2018. In 2017, we reported 28 such victims.

Victims in this category include migrants from Central Asia (two killed, three injured compared to 11 injured in 2017), dark-skinned people (one person injured, same as in 2017),[3] and individuals of unidentified "non-Slavic appearance" (12 injured compared to seven injured in 2017) who most likely were also from Central Asia, since their appearance was described as "Asian" by eyewitnesses. Attacks against other "ethnic outsiders" accompanied by xenophobic slogans were reported as well. For example, a beating of a person accompanied by anti-Chinese slurs took place in Moscow.

In addition to the street attacks, we encountered several cases of group attacks in the subway and commuter train cars. For example, in June 2018, three videos from the so-called "white car" campaign appeared on the Internet; they show groups of aggressive young people beating up commuter train passengers of "non-Slavic appearance."[4]

Cases of ordinary xenophobic violence are usually qualified by the media and law enforcement agencies as incidents of ordinary hooliganism. Nevertheless, three to five such incidents are reported per year. Incidents such as a swastika and offensive statements being found on the car of a migrant from Tajikistan, or xenophobic graffiti on a pavilion owned by a migrant from Uzbekistan, profoundly testified to the presence of xenophobic attitudes in Russian society.

The events that took place in August 2018 in the village of Urazovo in Belgorod Province illustrated such prejudices even more vividly. About 150-200 Roma residents left the village in fear of pogroms. Their concerns proved to be justified. On the following day, several houses in the village where Roma families used to live were set on fire. The flight and the arson were triggered by detention of a Roma man on suspicion of the rape and murder of a local nine-year-old girl.[5]

Attacks Against Ideological Opponents

The number of attacks by the ultra-right against their political, ideological or "aesthetic" opponents increased slightly in 2018, bringing the number of injured victims to 14 (compared to three dead and nine injured in 2017).[6]

The victims of beatings in this group also included individuals perceived by their attackers to be "fifth column" and "traitors to the Motherland," such as protest participants and people standing guard at the Boris Nemtsov memorial. There were four such attacks in 2018, compared to six attacks in 2017. In addition to assaults and provocations against the picketers, the attackers also targeted the offices of alleged "traitors." Thus, in the month of October alone, SERB activists attacked the office of Lev Ponomarev's "For Human Rights" movement twice.

Nationalist pro-Kremlin groups, the SERB and the NLM, were known to have used violence against the opposition. However, they were not the only ones to have done so. A particular incident, which took place on May 5, received significant media attention. During Aleksei Navalny's "He is Not Our Tsar" protest, people in Cossack uniforms showed up and started beating up event participants, including with the use of their nagaika whips. The Cossacks of the Central Cossack Host (*Tsentralnoye Kazache Voisko*) later confirmed that they had been present on Tverskaya Street during the demonstration. However, the attackers also included NLM activists dressed in camouflage uniforms and carrying a flag; they snatched protesters from the crowd and dragged down opposition activists who were trying to climb onto the pedestal of a monument.[7]

The anti-Ukrainian rhetoric of recent years also bore fruit. Attacks against Ukrainians are quite rare, apparently due to the fact that ethnic Ukrainians are hard to identify in a crowd. However, politicized anti-Ukrainian incidents do occur. Last year, our records showed two attacks related to the display of the Ukrainian flag. Both incidents took place in St. Petersburg. In one case, a passer-by attacked activists of the St. Petersburg Solidarity and Democratic Petersburg movements who were returning from a rally carrying posters and Ukrainian flags.[8] The other incident was an attack against an activist of the Solidarity movement who was standing in a solitary picket on the Anichkov Bridge with a Ukrainian flag and the poster "Freedom to the Political Prisoner."[9]

The Internet page of the Russian Imperial Movement (*Russkoye Imper-skoye Dvizhenie*, RID) and the online group "Veterans of Novorossiya" published threats against artist Sergei Zakharov, "a Kiev character distinguished by his anti-Russian and anti-DPR position." The nationalists called on their audience to come to the Sakharov Center (which was hosting the festival "Muse of the Recalcitrant" and was presenting Zakharov's works)[10] on May 1 for a "preventive conversation." As a result, on May 1, several dozen people – including some men in Cossack uniform, some activists from the Lugansk people's republic, several members of the Donetsk Basin Volunteers Union and SERB activists – tried to break into the Sakharov Center and started a fight.[11]

The issue of threats by the far right was present throughout the year. In addition to the episodes mentioned above, ultra-right Web sites published photographs, personal data and threats targeting independent journalists, law enforcement officers, prosecutors, and judges presiding over the nationalists' trials. In some cases (the Dina Garina case),[12] the emphasis was placed on the "non-Russian names and surnames" of their relatives.

Threats against the "traitors" – defendants in group trials related to racist attacks who testified against their "comrades-in-arms" – took place as well. Their personal information was published on the Internet. The actions were not limited to threats. The far-right Internet sites also posted video clips with scenes of brutal beatings. The Firstline Nevograd movement (a St. Petersburg neo-Nazi movement, allegedly under the leadership of Andrei Link) published a video of a young man lying on the ground bleeding, being kicked by his attackers. The video included an explanation that the movement had "found a rat" – the victim "leaked information using his position in the group***and committed impermissible acts."

Other Attacks

The number of attacks against the LGBT was lower than in the preceding year – one killed,[13] five injured (compared to 11 injured in 2017). The victims in 2018 included LGBT conference volunteers in Moscow, a young woman beaten up near a gay club in Yekaterinburg, and participants of the LGBT pickets in Volgograd who were beaten up by Cossacks who were also yelling "There should be no gays in Volgograd."

Fourteen attacks against the homeless were recorded in 2018 (one killed, 13 injured compared to four killed and one injured in 2017). We learned about these victims on October 30, 2018, when the links to two videos appeared online. The videos were made by neo-Nazis[14] and contained the scenes of murders and attacks against at least 15 people; the victims were mostly drunk or drug impaired. The publishers of the videos called themselves "the orderlies" (*sanitary*) and mentioned a certain "Project Sanitäter-88." The videos showed the attackers beating the victims, cutting them with knives, and spraying them in the face. The time and place of filming were impossible to determine for most of the episodes, but we assume that these attacks took place in 2018.

Official media outlets pointed out that teenage attacks on the homeless had become widespread,[15] but no statistics are publicly available on this topic. Moreover, when deceased homeless people are discovered, the causes of their deaths and the motives for the attacks are hard to determine. For example, a homeless person died from multiple stab wounds in Chelyabinsk in August 2016, and, only in September 2018 was it reported that the investigators had qualified this attack as a hate murder, and that two right-wing activists, Maksim Sirotkin and Nikita Yermakov from the ultra-right movement Misanthropic Division (recognized as extremist back in 2015), were the defendants in this case.[16]

In 2018, there was almost no mention of any attacks motivated by religious hatred. This state of affairs could possibly be explained by the fact that the leadership of the Jehovah's Witnesses, preoccupied by the flood of criminal cases, no longer published information about attacks against their co-religionists – these attacks previously constituted the overwhelming majority of cases in this category. In any case, the number of such attacks dropped – the Witnesses had no buildings left, and they cannot engage in open missionary work, so the typical situations in which violent attacks used to occur no longer happen. We know of only one incident in which a dispute about the proper way of wearing a cross took place in the subway and ended with serious stab wounds.[17]

Individuals who tried to intervene and defend others from being beaten up, or who expressed their disapproval of the aggressive young people's behavior, were also part of our unfortunate statistics. For example, on the night of Aug. 31-Sept. 1, 2018, at the Mendeleyevskaya Metro Station in Moscow, a young woman rebuked a group of young men who were loudly singing "Moscow Skinheads," a song by the ultra-right band Kolovrat. One of the "soloists" started hitting her in the head and yelling neo-Nazi slogans. When another passenger stood up for her, the attacker began to threaten him with a knife. After sharing her experience on Facebook, the victim started receiving threatening personal messages "You didn't get enough; we'll add some more!"[18]

Racism Among Soccer Fans

In connection with the FIFA World Cup in the summer of 2018, law enforcement agencies paid special attention to the racist antics of soccer fans. In July 2017, the Russian Football Union (RFU) presented a monitoring system for matches, and this system genuinely accurately identified the incidents of racism at stadiums. According to the data of SOVA Center and the Fare network, the total number of discriminatory incidents dropped during the 2017-2018 season. The number of recorded cases of displaying ultra-right banners at stadiums showed a particularly dramatic fall. However, after a period of relative quiet, the frequency of discriminatory chants increased. The chants in question include racist "booing," neo-Nazi slogans, and outbursts against natives of the Caucasus region.[19]

A racist shouting incident also occurred during the World Cup. On June 16, 2018, in Moscow, a soccer fan yelled "Denmark, White Power!" at Danish fans who at that time were giving interviews to Eurosport journalists.[20] Xenophobic statements from the fan stands were also heard once the World Cup was over. For example, Spartak fans started chanting racist slogans directed at the Brazilian-born Lokomotiv goalkeeper Marinato Guilherme during a match at the Otkritie Arena stadium in Moscow on Dec. 2, 2018.[21]

The problem of hate-motivated attacks committed by Russian ultra-right soccer fans also persisted. We know of three attacks involving soccer fans in 2018 that appear to be ideologically motivated.

Crimes Against Property

In 2018, the number of crimes against property motivated by religious, ethnic or ideological hatred was significantly lower than a year earlier: there were at least 34 incidents in 23 regions of the country in 2018 compared to at least 49 in 26 regions in 2017. The majority of these actions continue to be directed against religious sites.

Fewer ideological sites suffered in 2018 – the number was 14 compared to 18 episodes in 2017. Unknown perpetrators defaced with graffiti a World War II Victory monument, an obelisk in memory of the young victims of the concentration camps, a monument to the Cheka officer Ksenia Ge, Immanuel Kant's grave and monument, and so on. Another set of broken and destroyed sites was associated with ideological opponents of the ultra-right and included Ksenia Sobchak's office in St. Petersburg, and memorials to deceased American rapper XXXTentacion.

The number of affected Orthodox Christian churches and crosses turned out to be almost on par with ideological sites: 11 incidents, four of which were arson (in 2017, there were 11 incidents as well). Jewish sites took third place with four incidents, two of them arson (compared to one incident a year earlier). Two incidents were related to Protestant sites (there were two in 2017, as well). Muslim, Armenian and pagan sites suffered one incident each (in 2017, there were two episodes related to pagan sites, and no information about any damage to Muslim or Armenian sites).

However, sometimes the perpetrators' ignorance takes comic forms and creates problems with classifying the damaged site for our purposes. Thus, in February 2018, unknown persons painted a swastika on a monument to Russian-Armenian friendship in Novokuznetsk (Kemerovo Province); the swastika was accompanied by an explanation – "To the Jews." Apparently, the attackers mistook the Armenian alphabet for Hebrew.[22]

Overall, the number of attacks against religious sites decreased. There were 20 such incidents in 2018 (we reported 30 both in 2016 and in 2017). Apparently, this was due largely to the disappearance of an entire class of sites – Jehovah's Witnesses buildings. The percentage of the most dangerous acts – arson and explosions – also decreased in comparison to the preceding year. In 2018, they comprised 20%, that is, seven out of 35 (a year earlier, the most dangerous acts comprised 29% or 14 out of 49), possibly for the same reason.

The geographic distribution changed as well. In 2018, such crimes were reported in 10 new regions (Novosibirsk, Ryazan, Samara, Ulyanovsk and Yaroslavl Provinces, Stavropol Territory, Khanty-Mansi Autonomous Region and the republics of Karelia and Khakassia and Crimea). On the other hand, 13 regions previously on this list, disappeared from our statistics (Arkhangelsk, Volgograd, Vologda, Irkutsk, Lipetsk, Moscow, Penza, Rostov and Ulyanovsk Provinces, Transbaikal and Krasnoyarsk Territories, the Jewish Autonomous Region and the Komi Republic).

In Moscow and St. Petersburg, as well as in Arkhangelsk, Voronezh, Kemerovo, Leningrad, Murmansk, Sverdlovsk, Tula and Chelyabinsk Provinces and in the Republic of Tatarstan (that is, in 11 regions total) such crimes were reported in both 2017 and 2018.

The geographic spread of xenophobic vandalism turned out to be wider (23 regions) than that for acts of violence (10 regions). Five regions reported both problems (compared to seven regions a year earlier): Moscow, St. Petersburg, Novosibirsk Province, Samara Province and Sverdlovsk Province.

NOTES

1. Data for 2017 and 2018 are cited as of Jan. 8, 2019.

2. One person was killed in the preceding year as well.

3. See: Kursk: A student from Nigeria was attacked // SOVA Center. March 1, 2018 (https://www.sova-center.ru/racism-xenophobia/news/racism-nationalism/2018/03/d38937/).

4. New videos of the neo-Nazi "White Car" action appeared on the Internet // SOVA Center. July 4, 2018 (https://www.sova-center.ru/racism-xenophobia/news/racism-nationalism/2018/07/d39661/).

5. Murder of a 9-year-old girl nearly triggered anti-Roma pogroms // SOVA Center. Aug. 7, 2018 (https://www.sova-center.ru/racism-xenophobia/news/racism-nationalism/2018/08/d39822/).

6. These attacks peaked in 2007 (seven killed, 118 wounded), and were in a constant decline since then, reaching a minimum in 2013 (seven wounded); the trends have been unstable since then.

7. Nationalists at the Protest of May 5 // SOVA Center. May 8, 2018 (https://www.sova-center.ru/racism-xenophobia/news/racism-nationalism/2018/05/d39325/).

8. St. Petersburg: Passer-by attacked activists because of the Ukrainian flag // SOVA Center. Aug. 21, 2018 (https://www.sova-center.ru/racism-xenophobia/news/racism-nationalism/2018/08/d39869/0.

9. In St. Petersburg, a passer-by attacked a solitary picketer // SOVA Center. March 12, 2018 (https://www.sova-center.ru/racism-xenophobia/news/racism-nationalism/2018/03/d38982/).

10. Racism and xenophobia. Findings. April 2018 // SOVA Center. April 29, 2018 (https://www.sova-center.ru/racism-xenophobia/publications/2018/04/d39295/).

11. Attack on the Sakharov Center in Moscow // SOVA Center. May 1, 2018 (https://www.sova-center.ru/racism-xenophobia/news/racism-nationalism/2018/05/d39299/).

12. St. Petersburg: Verdict handed down in Dina Garina's case // SOVA Center. December 19, 2018 (https://www.sova-center.ru/racism-xenophobia/news/counteraction/2018/12/d40438/).

13. Actor Yevgeny Sapayev, who had undergone sex reassignment surgery. See: Murder in Moscow // SOVA Center. April 2, 2018 (https://www.sova-center.ru/racism-xenophobia/news/racism-nationalism/2018/04/d39123/).

14. Two videos with scenes of neo-Nazi murders and beatings were found on the Internet // SOVA Center. Oct. 30, 2018 (https://www.sova-center.ru/racism-xenophobia/news/racism-nationalism/2018/10/d40212/).

15. Naive cruelty: why teenagers attack the homeless // Moskva 24. Jan. 24, 2016 (https://www.m24.ru/articles/podrostki/14012016/94481).

16. Chelyabinsk: Verdict handed down in the case of the local Misanthropic Division cell // SOVA Center. Sept. 14, 2018 (https://www.sova-center.ru/racism-xenophobia/news/counteraction/2018/09/d40015/).

17. Subway dispute about faith ended with a knife wound // SOVA Center. Sept. 17, 2018 (https://www.sova-center.ru/religion/news/extremism/murders-violence/2018/09/d40024/).

18. A young man beat up a young woman while yelling neo-Nazi slogans // SOVA Center. Sept. 1, 2018 (https://www.sova-center.ru/racism-xenophobia/news/racism-nationalism/2018/09/d39945/).

19. Discriminatory incidents in Russian soccer, 2017 – 2018 // FARE. May 2018 (http://farenet.org/wp-content/uploads/2018/05/FINAL-SOVA-monitoring-report_2018-6.pdf).

20. Russian skinheads: A wild incident occurred at the 2018 World Cup // Obozrevatel. June 16, 2018 (https://www.obozrevatel.com/sport/football/russkie-skinhedyi-na-chm-2018-proizoshel-dikij-intsident.htm).

21. The racist chants of Spartak fans directed at the Lokomotiv goalkeeper // SOVA Center. Dec. 2, 2018 (https://www.sova-center.ru/racism-xenophobia/news/racism-nationalism/2018/12/d40364/).

22. Vandals in Novokuznetsk take the Armenian alphabet for the Jewish one // SOVA Center. Feb. 26, 2018 (https://www.sova-center.ru/racism-xenophobia/news/racism-nationalism/2018/02/d38916/).

Systematic Racist and Neo-Nazi Violence

In 2019, at least 45 people were victims of racist and other ideologically motivated violence; at least five of them were killed and the others were injured or beaten; two people received death threats. The number of people killed increased in 2019 compared to the previous year, although the total number of hate-motivated attacks decreased: in 2018, four people died and 55 were injured or beaten.[1]

On Dec. 31, 2019, an ultra-right Telegram channel wished everyone a Happy New Year by publishing a video showing a series of arson attacks and beatings of people in the streets and in train cars, two of the attacks involving use of knives. The video ended with a young man wearing a mask writing "Happy New Year NS/WP" on the wall and raising his hand in a Nazi salute. From this video, it was absolutely impossible to establish where and when these acts were being committed. Therefore, such videos, unfortunately, cannot be included in our statistics.

In the past year, our records showed attacks in 18 regions of the country (in 2018, [they took place] in 12 regions). Moscow (two killed,[2] 11 injured and beaten) and St. Petersburg (nine injured and beaten) led in terms of the level of violence, as usual. A significant number of victims (three) were reported in Sverdlovsk Province.

In the past year, our records did not show any hate crimes in Kaluga, Kirovsk, Novosibirsk, Samara, and Tyumen Provinces. At the same time, assaults were reported in regions where they were not reported for the previous year, namely, Vologda, Voronezh, Leningrad, Nizhny Novgorod, Rostov, and Tula Provinces, Altai Territory, Maritime Territory, Khabarovsk Territory, Sakha Republic (Yakutia), and the Khanty-Mansi Autonomous Region (Yugra).

Attacks Against Ethnic "Outsiders"

Those whom attackers perceived as "ethnic outsiders" remained the largest group of victims, and their numbers increased compared to the previous year. In 2019, our records showed 21 ethnically motivated attacks. In 2018, we reported 20 victims.

Victims in this category include natives of Central Asia (three killed, 11 beaten compared to two killed, three beaten in 2018) and the Caucasus (one beaten, none reported in 2018) and individuals of unidentified "non-Slavic appearance" (three beaten compared to 12 in 2018).

Unfortunately, threats and violence by the police, including those made under xenophobic pretext, are not uncommon. Law enforcement officers harbor the same prejudices and biases as common citizens and often abuse their positions. But information about the details is almost always classified, making analysis of the trends in motivated violence by the police force impossible. Only the most egregious cases become public knowledge, such as the December 2019 police raid in Khabarovsk, when more than a hundred migrants were beaten by cops who were shouting xenophobic slurs such as "Narrow-eyed people, we are sick of you! Get out of here and don't let us see you here again!"[3]

We are aware of only one attack on a black man[4] that occurred in the course of the past year (one person was killed in each of the years 2017 and 2018). However, it is likely that many more such attacks were happening, since the level of intolerance toward black people in Russia is quite high. This was clearly demonstrated by what happened in Stavropol, where some of the local [business-]owners simply refused to allow black patrons in their establishments. Egidio Nanga, a student from Angola, reported such a situation and said that he and his friends had been repeatedly turned away from several restaurants and clubs, such as the Goldy club, the Forbs restaurant, and the Yes café.[5]

One case of an antisemitic attack was reported in St. Petersburg.[6]

A 2019 poll by the Levada Center[7] showed that the Roma were the most unpopular ethnic group in Russia: the number of individuals wishing to expel them from the country was 50% higher than the number of those supporting the expulsion of Africans and natives of Central Asia.

The largest ethnically charged mass riots of 2019 were directed against the Roma. One person was killed in a mass brawl that erupted on June 13 in the village of Chemodanovka in Penza Province. The reasons for the fight are still unknown. According to some Penza media, it all started after Roma had harassed a daughter or daughters of local residents; after that, several [local residents] came to a Roma house to "set up a protest." Nadezhda Demeter, the head of the Federal National and Cultural Autonomy of Russian Roma, claimed that the incident had occurred because of a children's quarrel, after which the villagers came to the Roma house. In a mass brawl that occurred the next day at a pond, five people were injured. One of them, Vladimir Grushin, born in 1985, later died. There were no police in the village, and the clash was only stopped by riot police called in from the provincial capital. Internal affairs agencies took in 174 people for questioning, and three Roma who had participated in the conflict were arrested. The following day, the local residents held a "people's rally" and blocked a federal road, demanding the eviction of the Roma. On June 15, a Roma house in the neighboring village of Lopatki went up in flames. After that, a message spread, citing the head of the village council, that the authorities had forcibly removed all the local Roma; this was promptly refuted by a spokesperson for the Penza Province governor, but the Roma really virtually disappeared from both villages.[8]

The events in Penza Province elicited a massive response on social media: There was talk of the start of "war" against the Roma and fake news reports alleging that the Roma had set July 1 as the day of revenge and were marching toward Chemodanovka with gasoline. Roskomnadzor even demanded that social media networks delete information about the conflict in the village that the Prosecutor General's Office had deemed false. For instance, VKontakte blocked the "Chemodanovka on Fire" community "due to calls for violence."

It was not only in connection with what had happened in Chemodanovka that threats against the Roma were spread on social media. A Cossack community page and far-right pages in the VKontakte social media network posted a photo of a Roma man with a link to his VKontakte page and a call to all Cossacks "to give him the full treatment."

Another major example of mass riots against migrants resulting from local violence was the protests in Yakutsk in March 2019, where the rape of an ethnic Yakut woman by migrants from Kyrgyzstan provoked a series of threats to migrants and the destruction of their vegetable stands.[9]

Very little is known about organized racist groups among ethnic minorities (like the Kyrgyz "Patriot" gang that would beat up Kyrgyz girls for allegedly going out with non-Kyrgyz young men).

One such group surfaced in connection with the Yakutsk riots. "Us Tumsuu," a local vigilante nationalist movement[10] that cooperates with the local authorities and advocates for conservative values, was suspected of being involved. For instance, in the first days of 2019, the members of the movement joined police in raiding Yakutsk nightclubs with the aim of intimidating the migrants and admonishing Yakut girls, who, according to the activists, should "return to their own kind – the Yakut."[11]

In 2019, yet another ethno-nationalist organization For the Good of the Common Nation (*Vo Blago Obschego Naroda*, FGCN), came to light. This Azerbaijani movement, which promotes traditional values and a healthy lifestyle, became infamous after videos of beatings and screenshots bearing threats against "those who insult the Azerbaijani people," signed with the acronym FGCN, spread via social media and a Telegram channel. The assaults and threats committed in Russia[12] were motivated by hatred toward both the Armenians and "the insulters" of the Azerbaijanis.[13]

In addition to the abovementioned, 2019 witnessed assaults on other "ethnic outsiders" accompanied by xenophobic slogans. For example, a student from India was beaten in Barnaul and a resident of Kalmykia [was beaten] in Volgograd.

Attacks Against LGBT People

The number of attacks against the LGBT community was higher than in the preceding year: one killed,[14] seven injured and beaten (compared to one killed and five injured and beaten in 2018). In 2019, the victims were comprised primarily of picketers or participants of other events associated with LGBT people; but there were also street attacks on individuals who were mistaken for LGBT people due to their appearance, as happened in Yekaterinburg when a group of aggressive young men attacked a man they suspected of being gay[15] and in St. Petersburg when girls mistaken for lesbians were beaten.[16]

The murder of activist Elena Grigorieva in St. Petersburg on the night of July 19 was widely reported in the media. Grigorieva, who was openly bisexual, was an LGBT rights activist prominent in the St. Petersburg LGBT movement. Her name was on the hit list published on the Web site of the homophobic group *Pila* (Saw).[17] Grigorieva was also receiving threats from the well-known St. Petersburg homophobic activist Timur Bulatov and some nationalists. She had contacted the police more than once because of the threats but "there was no reaction whatsoever [by the law enforcement agencies]." Yet the final working theory of the murder was drunken homicide.

Police detained a suspect with whom the activist had had a personal conflict that led to her death, according to investigators.[18]

In addition to physical assault, LGBT activists regularly face threats from anti-gay individuals and right-wing radicals of all sorts. For example, threats from Bulatov continued even after Grigorieva's murder, with Karolina Kana- yeva, an activist from Saransk, being one of the recipients.[19] On July 1, the abovementioned *Pila* group published a hit list of the activists that it was threatening. On July 17, the LGBT Resource Center in Yekaterinburg received a letter signed by *Pila* demanding that the Center shut down by the end of July and the transfer of its funds to the charity Gift of Life (*Podari Zhizn*).[20]

The NCM, led by Valentina Bobrova and Mikhail Ochkin, was very actively engaged in anti-gay acts throughout the past year. Together with Archpriest Vsevolod Chaplin, the NCM opposed "the LGBT lobby and anti-Christian trends offensive against Russia" by holding various anti-gay demonstrations and pickets. And on Aug. 28 in Moscow, a play at Teatr.doc about the situation of homosexuals in Russia was disrupted by the NCM, the pro-Kremlin SERB group, and NLM activists.[21]

Attacks Against Ideological Opponents

In 2019, the number of attacks by the ultra-right against their political, ideological, or "aesthetic" opponents – four beaten – decreased significantly compared to the 19 beaten in the previous year of 2018.[22]

Acts by the pro-Kremlin SERB group were very visible in the past year. Fortunately, there were virtually no serious assaults; the activists limited them- selves to provocations, verbal insults and shouting at protesters. In particular, in February, they disrupted the screening of the film *Prazdnik* (Holiday), at the Memorial Society; in April, they interfered with members of the protest group "Against Torture and Discrimination," led by Lev Ponomarev, which was holding a series of solitary pickets in front of the FSB building and in Manezh Square in support of those detained in the Network (*Set*) case; finally, in December, they tried to prevent an opposition rally in Pushkin Square.

Other Attacks

In 2019, our records showed seven attacks on the homeless (one killed, six injured), which was half as many as in the previous year (one killed, 13 injured in 2018).

We are not aware of any religious hate attacks committed in 2019.

Jehovah's Witnesses, who previously made up the vast majority of the victims of these attacks, do not report attacks anymore. It is possible that, since their properties were seized and their missionary activities were banned, they became less visible and the frequency of attacks on them genuinely decreased. However, there were some signs of the repressive campaign against this religious group: For instance, at the end of December 2019, a car belonging to a resident of the Sukhobuzimskoye village of Krasnoyarsk Territory, Kirill Mikhailin, had its windshield smashed, and a handwritten note with profanities against Jehovah's Witnesses was thrown inside the car. Mikhailin states that his family received threats because of their religion throughout the whole past year.[23]

Our statistics customarily include those who tried to intervene and protect the victims. For example, during the abovementioned homophobic attack in Yekaterinburg, two passersby were injured when they went to the aid of the man who was being attacked.

Crimes Against Property

Compared to 2018, 2019 witnessed a significant decrease in the number of religious, ethnic and ideological hate crimes against property: at least 20 in 17 regions in 2019 compared to at least 34 in 23 regions in 2018.

The number of ideological sites and facilities damaged in 2019 was also lower – five compared to 14 in 2018. In the past year, monuments to victims of World War II, a Sino-Soviet Friendship Monument, and a memorial to the Rapper XXXTentacion were damaged.

As before, most of these acts targeted religious sites and facilities. Russian Orthodox churches and crosses were the most frequent target of desecration (six incidents in 2019 compared to 11 in 2018). Jewish sites come in second with five instances (four in 2018). New religious movements experienced two incidents of building damage (none were reported in 2018). Muslim and Catholic sites and facilities had one incident each; in 2018, one act of desecration against a Muslim site was reported, and none [were reported] against Catholic sites.

Overall, the rates of attacks against religious sites went down from 30 in 2017 and 20 in 2018 to 15 in 2019. On the other hand, the share of the most dangerous acts – arson and bombings – increased to 30%, or six out of 20 (in 2018, it was seven out of 35). The highest-profile attack came on May 16 when the People's Resistance Association (PRA) assaulted the patriarchal residence on Chisty Pereulok in Moscow. PRA members placed a banner that said "Apologize for EKB" (EKB stands for "Yekaterinburg") on the gates and threw smoke bombs onto the grounds, which also house the office of the Moscow Patriarchate. The attack was in support of protests against the construction of a new church on the site of a park in Yekaterinburg.[24]

The regional distribution changed noticeably over the course of the year. In 2019, this type of crime was reported in the following 11 regions where it had not occurred before: Astrakhan, Vladimir, Volgograd, Irkutsk, Moscow, and Tver Provinces, Altai Territory, Krasnoyarsk Territory, Maritime Territory, the Kabardino-Balkaria Republic, and Sevastopol; on the other hand, the following 17 regions where such crimes had previously been reported went off the list in 2019: Arkhangelsk, Voronezh, Kemerovo, Leningrad, Murmansk, Ryazan, Samara, Sverdlovsk, Smolensk, Tula, Ulya-novsk, Chelyabinsk, and Yaroslavl Provinces, the Republic of Karelia, the Republic of Khakassia, Khanty-Mansi Autonomous Region and Crimea.

For the first time in our experience, the geographical spread of acts of violence (18 regions) turned out to be wider than that of xenophobic vandalism (17 regions). Both types of crimes were reported in five regions (same as in 2018): in Moscow, St. Petersburg, Altai Territory and Vologda and Moscow Provinces.

NOTES

1. Data for 2018 and 2019 are provided as of Jan. 22, 2020.

2. A year earlier, two people were killed.

3. In Khabarovsk, police beat migrants while shouting xenophobic insults // SOVA Center. Dec. 23, 2019 (https://www.sova-center.ru/racism-xenophobia/news/racism-nationalism/2019/12/d41885/).

4. An African man beaten in Kudrov // SOVA Center. Jan. 16, 2019 (https://www.sova-center.ru/racism-xenophobia/news/racism-nationalism/2019/01/d40524/).

5. Stavropol Obscshepit [public catering] against African students // Kavkaz.Realii. Dec. 11, 2019 (https://www.kavkazr.com/a/30319758.html).

6. St. Petersburg: musician beaten and insulted by taxi driver // SOVA Center. May 20, 2019 (https://www.sova-center.ru/racism-xenophobia/news/racism-nationalism/2019/05/d41032/).

7. Monitoring of xenophobic sentiments // Levada-Center. Sept. 18, 2019 (https://www.levada.ru/2019/09/18/monitoring-ksenofobskih-nastroenij-2/).

8. Anti-Roma riots in Chemodanovka // SOVA Center. June 17, 2019 (https://www.sova-center.ru/racism-xenophobia/news/racism-nationalism/2019/06/d41149/).

9. Anti-migrant protests in Yakutsk. Restrictions introduced on the employment of foreigners // SOVA Center. March 19, 2019 (https://www.sova-center.ru/racism-xenophobia/news/racism-nationalism/2019/03/d40783/).

10. Officially registered as the Center for Civic-Patriotic Education of Youth in Sakha Republic "Tri."

11. Taisiya Bekbulatova. The People Are Sleeping Like a Bear – Do Not Wake Them // Takie Dela. April 5, 2019 (https://takiedela.ru/2019/04/narod-spit-kak-medved/).

12. At least one attack by the members of FGCN on four gay men in Baku on Aug. 6 was also reported.

13. Attacks and threats by the FGCN movement // SOVA Center. Oct. 25, 2019 (https://www.sova-center.ru/racism-xenophobia/news/racism-nationalism/2019/10/d41622/).

14. The brutal murder of transgender woman Nika Surgutskaya. For additional information see: Kursk: brutal murder of transgender woman // SOVA Center. April 24, 2019 (https://www.sova-center.ru/racism-xenophobia/news/racism-nationalism/2019/04/d40936/).

15. A homophobic attack in Yekaterinburg // SOVA Center. Sept. 16, 2019 (https://www.sova-center.ru/racism-xenophobia/news/racism-nationalism/2019/09/d41469/).

16. Several young men attack a group of girls, mistaking them for lesbians // SOVA Center. Dec. 10, 2019 (https://www.sova-center.ru/racism-xenophobia/news/racism-nationalism/2019/12/d41822/).

17. Ksenia Morozova. *Pila* Against LGBT: What Is Known About the Homophobic Movement That Is Believed to Have Been Involved in the Death of Elena Grigorieva // Sobaka. July 24, 2019 (http://www.sobaka.ru/city/society/94002/).

18. Activist Elena Grigorieva is murdered. Suspect arrested // SOVA Center. July 23, 2019 (https://www.sova-center.ru/racism-xenophobia/news/racism-nationalism/2019/07/d41276/).

19. After the murder of Elena Grigorieva, her friend receives threats // OVD-info. July 27, 2019 (https://ovdinfo.org/express-news/2019/07/25/posle-ubiystva-eleny-grigorevoy-ee-znakomoy-postupayut-ugrozy).

20. Yekaterinburg LGBT Resource Center About Threats of Violence by *Pila* // The Village. July 17, 2019 (https://www.the-village.ru/village/city/news-city/356591-lgbt-ugroza).

21. NCM (National-Conservative Movement), SERB, and NLM (National Liberation Movement) disrupt Teatr.doc play // SOVA Center. Aug. 29, 2019 (https://www.sova-center.ru/racism-xenophobia/news/racism-nationalism/2019/08/d41410/).

22. Attacks of this type peaked in 2007 (seven killed, 118 injured); the numbers then steadily declined. After 2013, trends have been unstable.

23. In Krasnoyarsk Territory, vandals smashed the windshield of the car belonging to a Jehovah's Witness and threw in a note with profanities // SOVA Center. Jan. 9, 2020 (https://www.sova-center.ru/racism-xenophobia/news/racism-nationalism/2020/01/d41917/).

24. PRA activists hang banner and throw smoke bombs onto the ground of the patriarchal residence // SOVA Center. May 17, 2019 (https://www.sova-center.ru/religion/news/community-media/communities-conflicts/2019/05/d41022/).

Systematic Racist and Neo-Nazi Violence

In 2020, at least 43 people were victims of ideologically motivated violence: One of them died, and the others were injured or beaten; five people received serious death threats. The total number of hate-motivated attacks decreased: In 2019, seven people died, and 64 were injured or beaten.[1]

In the past year, our records showed attacks in 11 regions of the country (in 2019, [they took place] in 20 regions). Moscow (12 injured and beaten) and St. Petersburg (20 injured and beaten) led in terms of the level of violence, as usual. And this was a rare occasion in our history of data collection when our records showed more victims in St. Petersburg than in Moscow. Just like the year before, a significant number of victims (three) were reported in Sverdlovsk Province.

In the past year, assaults were reported in the regions where they were not reported before, namely, in Arkhangelsk, Kaluga, Novosibirsk, and Saratov Provinces.

According to our data, in the past ten years, in addition to Moscow, St. Petersburg, and Moscow and Leningrad Provinces, crimes were recorded practically every year in Volgograd, Vologda, Voronezh, Kaluga, Kirov, Nizhny Novgorod, Novosibirsk, Omsk, Rostov, Samara, Sverdlovsk, Rostov, and Tula Provinces, Maritime Territory, Krasnodar Territory and Khabarovsk Territory. However, it is also possible that incident reporting was simply better organized in these regions.

Attacks Against Ethnic "Outsiders"

Those perceived to be "ethnic outsiders" by attackers remained the largest group of victims, though their numbers were slightly lower compared to the previous year. In 2020, our records showed 19 ethnically motivated attacks, a bit lower than the 21 victims reported in 2019.

Victims in this category include natives of Central Asia (four beaten, compared to three killed, 11 beaten in 2019) and the Caucasus (one killed, eight beaten, compared to one beaten in 2019);[2] and individuals of unidentified "non-Slavic appearance" (two beaten, compared to three beaten in 2019). A brutal murder in Volgograd stands out from the rest: On June 13, 2020, Timur Gavrilov, a 17-year-old medical student from Azerbaijan, died of 20 stab wounds. The murder suspect was a member of a far-right organization and attacked the student as he set out to "kill a non-Russian" that day.

In addition to these, a native of Buryatia was beaten at a train station in Yekaterinburg. The attacker did not like his "narrow eyes."

The echo of the events related to the US Black Lives Matter movement reached Russia. Fortunately, there were few direct attacks on black people, but there were still a few more than a year earlier. We have information about at least two attacks in 2020 (between 2017 and 2019, there was one attack per year, with one person beaten in each). For example, in a subway car in St. Petersburg, a group of aggressive young men sprayed aerosol from an UDAR gas pistol in the direction of Africans and began to beat them. The level of intolerance toward black people in Russia is quite high, as was clearly demonstrated by routine and rather large-scale online racist campaigns. For example, on June 8 in Bryansk, a Yandex Taxi driver refused to take black student Roy Ibonga and responded affirmatively when asked whether he was a racist. The video of the conversation was published in the VKontakte group Overheard in Bryansk and widely distributed on social media. After the scandal broke, Yandex Taxi removed the driver and publicly condemned his behavior. However, the story did not end there: Kirill Kaminets, a blogger living in Germany, the author of Sputnik and Pogrom and the founder of the Vendee project, launched the hashtag #YandexCuckold on Twitter, asserting that Yandex Taxi had "infringed on the rights of Russian drivers and denied them the right to choose customers." The hashtag was posted by many other users.

Mixed-race St. Petersburg resident and blogger Maria Magdalena Tunkara routinely received racist threats in her blog; as proof, she shared screenshots of some of the threats she was receiving, including references to "monkeys" and comments like "Negroes do not belong in Russia." The blogger was insulted not only in far-right social media network groups and the Telegram channel of Vladislav Pozdnyakov, the founder of the group Men's State, but also, for example, in the popular apolitical imageboard 2ch, also known as *Dvach*. On the eve of the Without Borders Fest, the NCM reported that Maria Tunkara had "insulted nationalists" and was planning to speak at the festival organized by "leftists and feminists" On June 20. As a result, Tunkara was forced to cancel her participation in the event.

It's not just black people who face hate campaigns. In February 2020, the media reported that Elena Melnik, a resident of Kogalym in Tyumen Province who tried to publicly stick up for her Chechen husband, who had been abducted in Grozny, received more than 100 xenophobic messages with threats and insults on the social media network VKontakte over the course of just one night. She "was accused of causing the degeneration of the 'Russian nation,' of betraying 'the blue-eyed Slavic blood' and 'the Russian traditions for which our Orthodox grandfathers have been giving their lives for many centuries.' " They called her a "stinking degenerate" and "a whore" and wrote that they would gladly cut her throat, etc.[3]

According to the results of a 2020 poll by the Levada Center,[4] 44% of Russian respondents supported the idea of not allowing the Roma into the country. And in the past year, we saw anti-Roma riots. After a 16-year-old Roma driver hit a 15-year-old girl in one of the villages of Stavropol Territory on Aug. 13, local residents came together for a town meeting and demanded that the Roma community be evicted from the village. The ultra-right immediately took advantage of the situation and attempted to stoke the local conflict into an ethnic one; on right-wing Internet resources, this news was published under the headline "I Hate Gypsies."

In December, some excitement was caused by the 10th anniversary of the events on Manezh Square in Moscow.[5] All the ceremonies were held online: Memorial speeches were streamed online, and the memorial evening for the killed Spartak fan Yegor Sviridov[6] was held on the VKontakte social media network. However, on the eve of the anniversary, that is, on Dec. 6, a video of an attack on Dagestan natives by a "group of Russian nationalists" spread on the far-right Internet. According to the comments to the video, it was "in Yegor's memory."

Fear of the coronavirus provoked an increase in xenophobic anti-migrant sentiment in society. Numerous offensive and racist comments were posted on social media about Chinese people and nationals of other Asian countries. Fortunately, direct attacks did not materialize, probably due to the increased mobilization of the police, who were strictly monitoring quarantine compliance. However, the far-right was very active on the Internet. Since the end of winter, anti-migrant materials were distributed on nationalist Web sites talking about robberies and murders, "Guest worker gangs" operating in various areas of Moscow, and "pregnant Tajik women" with infections in maternity hospitals. Petitions appeared in far-right online resources demanding a tougher immigration regime. The National Democratic Party (NDP) published a petition titled "Let Us Protect the Labor Market and the Security of Russian Citizens!" proposing to deport migrants who had lost their jobs and introduce a visa regime for the Central Asian countries. Konstantin Malofeyev, a well-known Orthodox nationalist, also spoke out in support of the immediate deportation of all migrants left without work. And the Volgograd "Russian Corps" organization promised to "put our vigilantes on the streets of our glorious city."

Such vigilantes patrolling markets appeared in Yekaterinburg. Patrols arrived in the largest market known as Tagansky Row, located in the Seven Keys residential district, home to many Chinese, to "check for coronavirus" only among nationals of Asian countries. According to Ataman Gennady Kovalev of the Ural Cossacks non-profit partnership, similar groups were patrolling the streets of Ryazan and Tula.[7]

The armed conflict in Nagorno-Karabakh caused ethnic clashes between Armenians and Azerbaijanis on Russian soil. On July 27, 2020, in St. Petersburg, several Azerbaijani citizens attacked two Armenian citizens while shouting anti-Armenian slogans and recording it on video.[8] On July 24, Moscow also saw clashes between natives of Armenia and Azerbaijan.[9]

Attacks Against LGBT People

The number of attacks against the LGBT community was, once again, higher than in the previous year. SOVA Center records showed 16 beaten (in 2019, there were one killed, seven injured and beaten). It seems to us that the increase in the attacks on LGBT people was not accidental. On the one hand, it was connected with a high level of domestic homophobia in Russian society, which has been recorded in annual surveys. According to the results of a 2019 poll by the Levada Center,[10] 56% of the respondents perceive LGBT people "mostly negatively." In part, negative attitudes toward LGBT people have been fueled by the authorities, since a law passed in 2013 prohibited "propaganda of non-traditional sexual relationships" among minors. At the same time, homophobic context has always been inherent in neo-Nazi movements (both during the Third Reich and among Russian neo-Nazis since the early 2000s), whose ideology is based on biological postulates and arguments about blood and soil.

In 2020, homophobic attacks were provoked by the death of a well-known neo-Nazi, the former leader of the far-right "Restruct!" movement and the founder of the Occupy Pedophilyai movement Maksim "Tesak" (Hatchet) Martsinkevich.[11] In October 2020, in Arkhangelsk, a group of young men held a "pedophile hunt" in his memory: posing as a minor, they met a man online and set up a sex date. The group showed up on the date with a video camera and recorded their interrogation of the man, whom they afterwards forced to drink urine.[12] According to Vladislav Pozdnyakov of Men's State," the attack on Theater Institute student Ilya Bondarenko near the Uzbechka restaurant in Saratov in December 2020 was also organized by the local far-right from Occupy Pedophilyai, who "caught a pedophile."[13]

Included among the number of attacks targeting LGBT people were attacks against those who were mistaken for LGBT people. This happened, for example, in January 2020 in St. Petersburg, when attackers did not like a man's appearance; or in Moscow, when a teenagers' dyed hair aroused suspicion about their "non-traditional" sexual orientation.

Attacks Against Ideological Opponents

In 2020, the number of attacks by the ultra-right against their political, ideological, or "aesthetic" opponents – five beaten – increased significantly compared to the four beaten in 2019.[14] One antifascist and participants of the protest organized by the SocFem Alternative activist group were among the victims.

The topic of threats by the ultra-right remained relevant throughout the year. The personal data of an expert witness who testified in court at extremism trials, and the names of the judges and witnesses, were published on Telegram channels.

Other Attacks

We are aware of one attack on a homeless person in 2020 (in 2019, we reported one murder and six beatings). However, the statistics for this group are particularly unreliable. The media reports beatings and deaths of the homeless, but it was impossible to extract any details from these reports.

The topic of hazing in the military with a xenophobic element is off-limits, and we do not have any detailed information about any such incidents. The military itself actively denies such incidents. A video message about ethnic discrimination in the army, posted on Instagram by a Tuvan conscript on Jan. 10 2021, may be considered indirect evidence. Private Shoigu Kuular claimed that he and other conscripts from Tuva were humiliated by unit commanders in Rostov Veliky.[15] Characteristically, many readers complained about xenophobic threats and attacks in comments on the post.

Crimes Against Property

In 2020, the numbers of religious, ethnic, or ideological hate crimes against property were higher than in 2019: 29 incidents in 21 regions in 2020 compared to at least 20 in 17 regions in 2019.

The number of ideological sites and facilities damaged in 2020 – six ideological sites and one national – was slightly higher than a year earlier (five ideological sites in 2019). The sites that sustained damage included monuments to military glory, monuments to Lenin, and a monument to Gulag victims.

The desecration of images of and monuments to "ethnic enemies" deserve a separate mention: In Chelyabinsk, "Not our hero" was written in black paint on an image of the Dagestani athlete Khabib Nurmagomedov, in Astrakhan, paint was poured and a swastika was drawn on a bust of the ethnographer and Nogai educator Abdul-Hamid Dzhanibekov, and a monument to the Tatar poet Gabdulla Tukai was smeared with blue paint and a white swastika was drawn over it.

As usual, most of these acts targeted religious sites and facilities. As in 2019, Russian Orthodox churches and crosses were the most frequent target of desecration (eight incidents in 2020 compared to 16 in 2019). Jewish sites come in second with three instances (five in 2019). Pagan sites take third place with three attacks (none in 2019). Muslim and Protestant sites and facilities had two incidents each (in 2019, one attack against a Muslim site, and none against Protestant ones), and a Buddhist site had one incident (none in 2019).

Overall, the number of attacks against religious sites increased slightly: 19 in 2020 (in 2019, we reported 15 incidents, down from 20 in 2018). The share of the most dangerous acts – arson and explosions – somewhat decreased compared to the previous year and represents 24%, or seven out of 29 (in 2019, it was six out of 20).

The regional distribution changed noticeably over the course of the year. In 2020, this type of crime was reported in 13 new regions: Arkhangelsk,

Vologda, Voronezh, Kaluga, Murmansk, Nizhny Novgorod, Ryazan, and Chelyabinsk Provinces, the Altai Republic, Bashkortostan, Komi, Khakassia and the Khanty-Mansi Autonomous Region (Yugra).

For the second year in a row, the geographical spread of the xenophobic vandalism (21 regions) turned out to be wider than that of the acts of violence (11 regions). Both types of crimes were recorded in five regions (the same number as in 2019 and 2018): in Moscow, St. Petersburg, and Arkhangelsk, Voronezh and Kaluga Provinces (these last three regions were different in 2020 from those in 2019 and 2018).

NOTES

1. Data for 2020 and 2019 are provided as of Jan. 20, 2021.

2. Remarkably, this year the number of Caucasus natives was higher than that of the natives of Central Asia, whereas typically, it is the opposite.

3. A resident of Kogalym is threatened by social media users because she is married to a Chechen // SOVA Center. Feb. 7, 2020 (https://www.sova-center.ru/racism-xenophobia/news/racism-nationalism/2020/02/d42056/).

4. Xenophobia and Nationalism // Levada-Center. Sept. 23, 2020 (https://www.levada.ru/2020/09/23/ksenofobiya-i-natsionalizm-2/).

5. Riots on Manezh Square in Moscow // SOVA Center. Dec. 12, 2010 (https://www.sova-center.ru/racism-xenophobia/news/racism-nationalism/2010/12/d20481/).

6. Galina Kozhevnikova. Iz ze unique moment // SOVA Center. Dec. 8, 2010 (https://www.sova-center.ru/racism-xenophobia/publications/2010/12/d20452/).

7. In Yekaterinburg, the Cossacks conduct raids to find people of Asian appearance with cold symptoms // SOVA Center. Feb. 21, 2020 (https://www.sova-center.ru/racism-xenophobia/news/racism-nationalism/2020/02/d42118/).

8. Azerbaijani national detained in St. Petersburg in extremism criminal case for attack on Armenians // Mediazona. Aug. 6, 2020 (https://zona.media/news/2020/08/06/spb).

9. Human rights activists warn about the risk of the Azerbaijani-Armenian conflict escalation in Moscow // Kavkazsky Uzel. July 30, 2020 (https://www.kavkaz-uzel.eu/articles/352464).

10. Attitudes toward LGBT People // Levada-Center. May 23, 2019 (https://www.levada.ru/2019/05/23/otnoshenie-k-lgbt-lyudyam/).

11. Maksim "Tesak" Martsinkevich in brief // SOVA Center. Oct. 1, 2020 (https://www.sova-center.ru/en/xenophobia/news-releases/2020/10/d42991/).

12. Arkhangelsk: Martsinkevich's fans hold a raid in his memory // SOVA Center. Oct. 5, 2020 (https://www.sova-center.ru/racism-xenophobia/news/racism-nationalism/2020/10/d43004/).

13. The attack in Saratov // SOVA Center. Jan. 11, 2021 (https://www.sova-center.ru/racism-xenophobia/news/racism-nationalism/2021/01/d43477/).

14. Attacks of this type peaked in 2007 (seven killed, 118 injured); the numbers then steadily declined. After 2013, trends have been unstable.

15. "His last name is not Shoigu": Details of the scandal with a conscript who revealed discrimination in the army // 76.ru. Jan. 13, 2021 (https://76.ru/text/incidents/2021/01/13/69694056/).

PART FIVE

Law Enforcement

Banning Organizations as Extremist

The Federal List of Extremist Organizations, published on the Ministry of Justice Web site,[1] added three entries in 2014.

The first two were inappropriately banned religious organizations: the "Faizrakhmanist" group in Kazan, recognized as extremist by the Sovetsky District Court of Kazan in Tatarstan in February 2013, and "The Muslim religious organization of the Borovsky village in the Tyumen District of Tyumen Province" recognized as extremist by the Tyumen Province Court in May 2014.

The third case was a far-right organization – "The Community of Indigenous Russian People of Shchyolkovsky District in Moscow Province" – recognized as extremist by the Shchyolkovo City Court in February 2014. The organization was known as the organizer of Shchyolkovo Russian Runs (*Russkie Probezhki*); it was also collecting humanitarian aid "for the residents of the Luhansk and Donetsk republics." The prosecutors based their claims on the statement in the Charter of the Community that reads "the organization is part of the territory of the Rus state formation within Russia."

Criminal Prosecution

For Violence

The number of convictions for violent racist crimes in 2014 was over 30% smaller than in the preceding year. In 2014, there were at least 21 convictions, in which courts recognized the hate motive in 19 regions of Russia (compared to 32 convictions in 24 regions in 2013), according to which 45 people were found guilty (compared to 59 in 2013).

When prosecuting racist violence, the judiciary used the Criminal Code articles that contained a hate motive as an aggravating circumstance:

Art. 105 Part 2 Paragraph "l" (murder motivated by hatred), Art. 116 Part 2 Paragraph "b" (battery), Art. 115 Part 2 Paragraph "b" (infliction of a light injury), Art. 111 Part 4 (infliction of a grave injury), Art. 213 Part 2 (hooliganism), Art. 119 Part 2 (threat of murder), etc.

Art. 282 of the Criminal Code (incitement to hatred) was utilized in four convictions in 2014. In accordance with Ruling No. 11 of the plenary meeting of the Supreme Court of the Russian Federation "On Judicial Practice in Criminal Cases Regarding Crimes of Extremism," adopted on June 28, 2011, the application of Art. 282 to violent crimes is considered appropriate if the crimes were aimed at inciting hate in third parties, for example, through a public and provocative ideologically motivated attack. The ruling implies that Art. 282 should be used in conjunction with another appropriate Criminal Code article (such as murder, bodily harm, etc.). In such cases, we consider the use of this article in convictions for violent crime to be justified. In three of the convictions, including the verdict against skinheads from the neo-Nazi group NS/WP, which received the most media attention, it was used for isolated episodes of ultra-right propaganda. The fourth verdict, handed down in the Stavropol Territory, utilized Art. 282 Part 2 Paragraph "a" (incitement to hatred with the use of violence or the threat of violence) for attacking a passer-by while shouting xenophobic slogans and insults. The attack happened in a public place, and the victim didn't suffer significant harm.

Penalties in violent crime cases were distributed as follows:

- Seven people received suspended sentences;
- Two people were sentenced to mandatory labor;
- Four people were sentenced to corrective labor;
- One person received a suspended corrective labor sentence;
- Four people received a prison sentence of up to one year;
- Eight people – up to three years;
- Eleven people – up to 10 years;
- Five people – up to 15 years;
- Two people – up to 20 years;
- One person received a prison sentence of 24 years.

We only know of two verdicts in which the offenders were ordered to pay financial compensation to their victims for moral harm and medical expenses. Regretfully, we rarely see any reports about such measures. Meanwhile, victims frequently need expensive medical help and have no financial means to cover the expenses; their offenders should face material liability for the incident.

As you can see from the above data, 16% of convicted offenders (seven out of 45) only received suspended sentences. In some cases, such decisions could be justified. For example, in 2014, Roman Veits of NS/WP accepted a deal with the investigation and is unlikely to attempt a racist crime in the future. We have doubts about the second verdict handed down against a resident of Samara, who threatened his victim with a stationery knife while uttering anti-Semitic slurs. Perhaps the fact that the attacker had inflicted no actual injuries accounts for this lenient sentence. However, some suspended sentences for openly racist violence seem inappropriately lenient. For example, two neo-Nazis in Novosibirsk, who beat up a native of Armenia and threw him down on the railroad tracks, or three young men in the town of Kasimov in the Ryazan Region, who committed a racist attack against an apartment with Roma residents.

We believe that suspended sentences for violent racist attacks tend to engender the sense of impunity and do not stop offenders from committing such acts in the future.

Nevertheless, the majority of the offenders (31 people) were sentenced to actual prison terms of varying length. Among others, the members of abovementioned neo-Nazi group NS/WP Nevograd received long sentences behind bars. Nikita Tikhonov was sentenced to 18 years in prison for plotting, as a member of the Military Organization of Russian Nationalists (*Boyevaya organizatsiia russkikh natsionalistov*, BORN), the assassination of Moscow City Court judge Edward Chuvashov and several other murders. Nikita Tikhonov already received a life sentence in May 2011 for the murder of Stanislav Markelov and Anastasia Baburova.

In two more cases, members of the ultra-right organizations were convicted, but the verdict did not cite the hate motive. A St. Petersburg court sentenced nationalist Aleksei Voyevodin, who had previously received a life sentence,[2] to six years in a maximum-security penal colony for beating a young man to death; the hate motive was not part of the charge.

Members of ultra-right association Perun's Warriors – SS (*Voiny Peruna – SS*) were convicted in Yekaterinburg; they were sentenced to long prison terms for their murder of a homeless person. Earlier, the investigation believed that the murder had been motivated by ideological hatred, but the case was reclassified during the trial, and the ideological motive was ruled out.

Prosecution of Members and Leaders of Ultra-Right Organizations

In the year under review, law enforcement authorities actively prosecuted activists of the most notorious nationalist organizations. The leaders and members of organizations affiliated with "Restruct!" and the "Russians" (*russkiye*) movements were most severely affected.

In August 2014, the Kuntsevsky District Court of Moscow found leader of the neo-Nazi "Restruct!" movement Maksim "Tesak" Martsinkevich guilty of inciting ethnic hatred with the threat of violence and sentenced him to five years' imprisonment in a maximum-security penal colony. The charges were based on the fact of Martsinkevich's publication of three videos "Throw the churki out! The Election Campaign!" "Tesak on the movie *Stalingrad* and the situation in Biryulyovo," and "Tesak on the movie *Okolofutbola.*" Such a harsh sentence (five years for three videos) produced a mixed public reaction. The verdict was probably handed down to reflect "the accumulation of effort" and "taking into account the identity of the defendant,"[3] – perhaps the most notorious neo-Nazi. On Nov. 11, 2014, having considered the cassation appeal, the Moscow City Court reclassified the charges from Part 2 of Art. 282 to Part 1 of Art. 282 and reduced Martsinkevich's sentence from 5 years of imprisonment to two years and 10 months. Martsinkevich is currently a defendant in at least two more criminal cases.[4]

In addition to their leader, law enforcement also expressed interest in other activists of "Restruct!" In June 2014, a criminal case was opened in Moscow under Art. 111 Part 4 (causing serious bodily injury resulting in the death of the victim), after activists had beaten to death 37-year-old citizen of Azerbaijan Zaur Alyshev, whom they took for a drug dealer.[5] The court ordered detained three "Restruct!" members suspected in the attack, including 17-year-old Kirill Filatov. After that, the authorities began a large-scale investigation into the activities of "Restruct!" activists. On July 13, 2014, the quarters of activists Yevdokim Knyazev (leader of Occupy Drug Addiction (*Occupy-narkofilyay*) movement) and Yelizaveta (Lyutaya) Simonova were searched in Moscow. On June 28, 2014, the riot police dispersed a "Restruct!" conference in Izmailovo concert hall.

Later, all the cases initiated in relation to different incidents were combined into a single court case. The case against members of the "Restruct!" movement pressed charges against about 20 people, who are accused of attacking vendors of prohibited smoking substances, hooliganism and robbery. About 10 people were arrested.

Another movement which attracted law enforcement's attention is the Russian National Union "Attack" (*Russkoye Natsionalnoye Obiedinenie "Ataka"*), founded in the summer of 2013 by several activists who had left "Restruct!"[6] The Presnensky District Court in Moscow ordered detained leaders of the Attack movement Stanislav Mityaev and Vladimir Tkach on Oct. 29. In November, three more new suspects appeared in the Attack case – Roman Chernikov, Tomas Paipalas and Sergei Sukhanov. One of them was detained, another one is under house arrest, and the third one is under travel restrictions. The young people, depending on their respective roles, were facing charges under Art. 282 Part 1 and Art. 282.1 Parts 1 and 2 of the Criminal Code (organization of an extremist community and participation in it, respectively), and Art. 214 Part 2 (vandalism motivated by ethnic hatred). According to the investigators, the suspects participated in organizing the ultra-right Attack movement "whose main task was the forcible overthrow of the present government in Russia." The defendants promoted their ideas via social media, by disseminating leaflets and by posting stickers.

Ultra-right activists close to the "Russians" Ethnic-Political Association were actively persecuted as well.

On Oct. 15, 2014, a leader of the "Russians" Association and one of the most famous Russian nationalists Aleksandr Belov (Potkin) was detained in Moscow on suspicion of laundering money stolen from the Russian and Ukrainian depositors of BTA Bank of Kazakhstan. Actually, former head of the bank Mukhtar Ablyazov (then in detention in France) had been accused of embezzling funds, while A. Belov, according to the investigation, was engaged in laundering some of the money moved out of the bank.[7] Belov was taken into custody. His associates claimed that his detention was politically motivated, and the charges had been fabricated.[8]

Interestingly enough, Aleksandr Belov was also a defendant in a criminal case, opened in Kazakhstan under Art. 164 (inciting ethnic hatred) of the Kazakh Criminal Code. According to the investigators, Belov met with representatives of Slavic and Cossack organizations in Kazakhstan in February 2012 and suggested organizing a military training base for young Cossacks in Kyrgyzstan. A month later, according to the investigators, Belov conducted closed training events in Kyrgyzstan, this time for activists of the Kazakh national-patriotic youth organization Ult Azattığı. The group of Kazakhs, sent to Kyrgyzstan, was allegedly put together by member of the Kazakh Popular Front Zhanbolat Mamai, while Stan-TV Internet portal, owned by Mukhtar Ablyazov, sponsored the trainings. Allegedly, Belov tried to "destabilize the situation in the country and create political chaos utilizing the 'Angry Kazakh' political technology project, launched upon Ablyazov's initiative, the essence of which is to discredit the current Kazakh government and oligarchic groups in front of representatives of the titular nation."[9]

The St. Petersburg group Russian Sweep also didn't escape the attention of law enforcement. On Sept. 26, 2014, the Petrogradsky District Court of St. Petersburg sentenced ultra-right activist Dmitry "Besheny" Yevtushenko (Slavic Force (*Slavyanskaya sila*), the Russian Sweep) to 160 hours of mandatory labor under Art. 282 Part 1. According to the investigation, in 2010-2013, Yevtushenko "repeatedly posted materials aimed at inciting hatred and enmity on the basis of nationality and religion."[10] In October 2014, a new criminal case against Yevtushenko was opened under Arts. 282 and 212 of the Criminal Code (incitement to mass riots) for posts on his VKontakte page, which contained "incitement to riots and incitement to hatred against persons of non-Slavic ethnicity or natives of the Caucasus, and against government representatives."

Another ongoing court case in St. Petersburg targeted another famous St. Petersburg nationalist Nikolai Bondarik, charged under Art. 282 Part 1 for planning provocations on the Kurban Bayram (Eid al-Adha) in October 2013.

Already in 2015, well-known St. Petersburg right-wing activist and one of the principal organizers of the Russian Runs Maksim Kalinichenko and leader of the Rights for European Development Vitaly Shishkin were detained. Nationalist activist Oksana (Voyelva) Borisova was subjected to administrative detention.

All these people and organizations have been widely known and active for a long time. Their actions have also deserved attention for a long time. However, on prior occasions, their actions were almost fully condoned by the authorities. Why did the authorities choose this particular moment to actively prosecute them? The theory that the persecution has to do with the difference from the official position in their views on Ukraine does not quite explain the dynamics. After all, members of these organizations differ in their opinions on the Ukrainian question. The "Russians" and their allies clearly oppose the "Russian Spring" movement, while "Restruct!" prefers to avoid this subject.

While these nationalists have no common position regarding the government in Ukraine, they all are in clear opposition to the current Russian authorities. So, unfortunately, the political character of the persecution is obvious. For the most part, all these nationalists demonstrated very high levels of engagement in 2012-2013 related to nationalist raids in search of "illegal migrants" and the "hunt for pedophiles." The "Russians" movement was playing a leading role among radical nationalist organizations until recently and still remains quite active – it is possible that the authorities simply decided to neutralize such a dangerous and hard-to-predict force.

Most of these nationalists have been charged under "propaganda" articles of the Criminal Code. On prior occasions, we repeatedly spoke out against prosecuting harmless Internet users who have no influence among the far right, for propaganda and called for paying attention to the well-known agitators. In this case, we are talking about popular right-wing media figures. However, we suspect that the incriminating episodes and articles for the criminal charges were selected at random; no one seriously analyzed the actions of these people (the verdict for Martsinkevich was very revealing – he was convicted for statements that were definitely not the most incendiary by his standards) and the prosecution was triggered not by their propaganda but by political causes. The authorities, while solving their possibly quite legitimate political problems, would do well not to forget that legal tools should be used appropriately and not superficially.

For Crimes Against Property

In 2014, the prosecution of ethno-religious and neo-Nazi vandalism was less active than in the preceding year – we know of four sentences handed down to six people in four regions (compared to eight convictions of 11 people in eight regions in 2013).

In all of these cases, the charges were brought under Art. 214 of the Criminal Code (vandalism motivated by ethnic or religious hatred). A verdict for swastikas in an elevator in Surgut used only this article; a sentence for the desecration of a mosque in the Ivanovo aggregated Art. 214 with Art. 282 Part 1; in a sentence for arson against a prosecutor's office in Chelyabinsk, Art. 214 was aggregated with Arts. 280, 213 and 167 (intentional damage to property); in a sentence for a series of bombings and arson in Novomoskovsk (Tula Province), it was aggregated with Paragraphs "a" and "b" of Art. 244 Part 2 (desecration of burial places motivated by ethnic hatred), Art. 213 Part 2, Art. 30 Part 3 and Art. 167 Part 2 (organization of attempted premeditated destruction of property by arson).

Uncharacteristically, all of the convicted offenders received prison sentences ranging from two months to three years. Four people in the Tula and Chelyabinsk Provinces received sentences for arson and bombings, that is, for truly dangerous acts. The Ivanovo vandal received three years for making insulting inscriptions on the Grand Mosque and placing a pig's head on the mosque fence – perhaps with some previous acts committed by this person taken into consideration. The real prison term for the Surgut vandal for xenophobic inscriptions in the elevator seems debatable, but we may not be aware of all the circumstances of the case.

By the way, the majority of such crimes (desecration of buildings, houses or fences) in the past year, were customarily qualified not as vandalism but as propaganda under Art. 282 (see the next section). Apparently, the difference is due to the fact that, in the above cases, the xenophobic graffiti appeared on objects that, unlike religious buildings or monuments, could not be vandalized. However, even indisputable acts of vandalism were frequently qualified as propaganda, as happened in the conviction for "extremist inscriptions" made on a mosque in Udmurtia. Due to the dual nature of such offenses, the decision on which specific article to be used is left to the discretion of law enforcement agents, and Art. 282 is better known to law enforcement and more advantageous in terms of media coverage.

For Public Statements

The number of sentences for statements has increased. In 2014, it far exceeded the number of all other extremism-related convictions combined. At least 153 guilty verdicts for xenophobic statements were handed down in 2014 to 158 people (and one more individual released from punishment due to active remorse) in 54 regions of the country. In 2013, 133 verdicts were handed down against 136 people in 59 regions.[11]

Art. 282 of the Criminal Code was utilized in 136 convictions against 141 people. An overwhelming majority of them (114 people) were convicted under this article only; 13 people were convicted under Art. 280 only; and 12 more cases involved the aggregation of Arts. 282 and 280. One person – the vandal who damaged the mosque in Ivanovo – was convicted under Arts. 214 and 280 (see also the section on penalties for vandalism). Two more – guilty of arson targeting a prosecutor's office in Chelyabinsk – were convicted under the aggregation of Art. 167 Part 2 (intentional damage to property), Art. 213 Part 2 (hooliganism), Art. 214 Part 2 (vandalism), Art. 280 Part 1 and Art. 282 Part 1.

Five sentences for nine people involved the Criminal Code articles pertaining to violence in aggregation with the articles for statements. Such are the cases of the members of the far-right NS/WP group in St. Petersburg (Vladimir Mumzhiev, Roman Veits, and Kirill Prisyazhnyuk) or of neo-Nazi Gleb Tsyba, who had attacked an anti-fascist in Moscow.

In some verdicts, Art. 282 was utilized in combination with general nonviolent Criminal Code articles, such as Art. 228 (illegal possession of drugs) or Art. 161 (robbery).

Two people were convicted under Arts. 280 and 205.2 (public calls for terrorist activity or public justification of terrorism): Roman Solovyov in Lipetsk for the publication of recorded performances by Said Buryatsky, and Michael Ture in Moscow for acting as administrator for a Web site that published news and articles about the activities of the Caucasus Emirate (*Imarat Kavkaz*). Earlier, sentences under Art. 205.2 were imposed exclusively for radical Islamist propaganda. The verdict, in which Art. 205.2 Part 2 of the Criminal Code (preparation for the public justification of terrorism through the media) was aggregated with Art. 280 Part 1, Art. 282 Part 1, Art. 205.2 Part 1 (justification of terrorism) and Art. 30 was no exception to this rule; neither was the Moscow case of Boris Stomakhin, the editor-in-chief of the *Radical Politics* newsletter – despite the fact that Stomakhin is not an Islamist, he specifically praised Islamist violence.

At least five verdicts utilized Art. 282 for sharing and linking to materials from the Federal List of Extremist Materials.[12] We wrote earlier about the lack of standards that allows prosecutors to press either criminal or administrative charges for the same offenses.[13] We do not see these sentences as fully legitimate, because they represent a clear case of an administrative issue that should be resolved by applying the corresponding Administrative Code article. However, among the huge number of people convicted for public statements, many were only guilty of posting a single item; moreover, these items were not very dangerous and not (yet!) included on the Federal List. In any case, we view such acts as presenting so little danger that they are altogether not worthy of law enforcement attention.

The court sentences for the propaganda cases were distributed as follows:
- One person was released from punishment due to remorse;
- Two people were released from punishment because the statute of limitations had expired;

- Three people were referred for compulsory medical treatment;
- Twenty-one people received prison sentences;
- Thirteen people received suspended sentences without additional punishment;
- Thirty-two people were sentenced to various fines;
- Forty-eight people were sentenced to mandatory labor;
- Thirty-six people were sentenced to corrective labor;
- Three people received suspended corrective labor sentences.

In 2014, convictions that involved real prison terms were handed down in conjunction with Criminal Code articles other than propaganda. As already mentioned, these were for racist violence, arson, etc.

We have strong doubts about the validity of several prison sentences handed down in Vladimir, Saratov, Sverdlovsk and Rostov Provinces for xenophobic videos and anti-Caucasian statements on social media, as well as racist songs and shouts. However, we do not know all the circumstances in these cases – it is possible that the offenders had prior suspended sentences, or that their indictments included other charges as well.

A prison sentence that we view as exceedingly harsh is the decision of the Butyrsky District Court in Moscow in the case of Boris Stomakhin, who was sentenced to six and a half years in prison for publishing several articles on the Internet and in his newsletter. Even considering the fact that his writings indeed contain statements that might qualify under the cited Criminal Code articles, and that this was not the first time Stomakhin broke the law (he was sentenced to five years of imprisonment under Art. 282 Part 1 and Art. 280 Part 2 of the Criminal Code in 2006),[14] the punishment is excessive, in our opinion, not only because it was imposed for "words only," but also because the audience for the outlets that published the incriminating articles was obviously small, so the articles presented no significant public danger.

The trend of a diminishing share of suspended sentences for propaganda has persisted since 2012. Such sentences represented only 8% in 2014 (13 of 158 convicted offenders). We see this trend as unambiguously positive, since, in our experience of many years, the majority of convicted propagandists do not view a suspended sentence as a serious punishment and are not being deterred from similar illegal activities in the future.

For example, Viktor Korchagin – a famous preacher of anti-Semitism and anti-Christianity and former director of the Vityaz publishing house – received a suspended sentence of two years in Moscow for publishing and distributing of the book *Generals on the Jewish Mafia* by General Grigory Dubrov. We believe that a sentence restricting his professional activities[15] and barring him, at least for a period of time, from acting as a publisher would have been wiser, particularly since this was far from the first time Viktor Korchagin had appeared as a defendant in court.[16] However, the defendant claimed that he no longer served as director of the publishing house and was not engaged in book distribution.

The majority of convicted offenders (119 people) received penalties that did not involve the loss of freedom, which we believe to be more effective, such as fines, mandatory labor or corrective labor.

Following the trend of the three preceding years, propaganda convictions overwhelmingly pertained to online publications (135). As expected, their proportion only keeps increasing. The number of convictions for online propaganda in 2014 was over six times greater than the number of convictions for offline propaganda (22). Four cases included both online and offline offenses; these cases are included in both totals and in both breakdowns below.

The materials were posted on the following Internet resources:

- Social media – 120 (VKontakte – 86, unidentified social media networks – 28; Odnoklassniki – six);
- Articles on Web sites – three;
- Maintaining Web site of an organization – one;
- Forums, comments to articles – four;
- Blog post – one;
- Email messages – one;
- Unspecified Internet resources – five.

As you can see from these data, law enforcement officers continue to search for extremism primarily on the VKontakte social media network, which is popular among Russian youth (including its ultra-right segment). The enforcement mechanism is routine, since page owners have to provide their personal data and phone number during registration, and it is easy for network administrators to provide this information upon request from law enforcement. Thus, the number of convictions related to VKontakte keeps growing.

All the shortcomings of Internet-related law enforcement remain un-changed. The key issue for the Criminal Code "propaganda" articles, namely the lack of clarity on quantitative assessments of public exposure, still has not been addressed. It is characteristic that when reporting about all these convictions, nothing is said about the audience of the defendant's alleged statements. Meanwhile, the audience size obviously has varied widely from one case to another. The number of "visitors" and "friends" of the accused has been mentioned extremely rarely. Of course, VKontakte or Odnoklassniki are very popular in Russia, and theoretically anyone can see what is published there. And this is the main argument of law enforcement when making this type of decision. In the news from prosecutor's offices about convictions for statements on social media or blogs, they almost invariably add that the incriminating materials were freely or openly available. However, in practice, law enforcement agencies are most often the first to visit the "seditious" pages, save for a few friends.

However, it is worth noting that in 2014 law enforcement paid attention not only to ordinary and rarely visited social media network users, as had been the case earlier, but also to individuals who are well-known among the ultra-right. In addition to Dmitry (Besheny) Yevtushenko and Maksim "Tesak" (Hatchet) Martsinkevich, propaganda-related convictions were handed down to Oleg Gonchar, the head of the South Siberian Cossack District press service from Khakassia, to Nikolai Babushkin, the coordinator of the Russian National Union (*Natsionalny soyuz Rossii*) and administrator of the VKontakte group "The Russian March 2013" from Norilsk, and to the administrator of the Slavic North (*Slavyansky Sever*) VKontakte group in Murmansk. Unfortunately, sentences against such prominent actors are still lost in the rising tide of convicted small-scale social media users.[17]

Genre distribution of the criminal online materials also remained largely unchanged from the year before (one verdict can pertain to several genres):

- Videos and films (including the notorious "The Execution of a Tajik and a Dagestani" [*Kazn Tadzhika i Daga*]) – 48;
- Audio (including songs by Kolovrat [an old Russian name of a solar symbol similar to a swastika]) – 11;
- Images (photo or drawings) – 33;
- Articles or other complete texts (including re-publications of *Mein Kampf*) – 29;
- Statements, comments, forum posts – 26;
- Creating or administering online groups and communities – two;
- Unspecified – 11.

Similarly to the preceding year, sentences for audiovisual materials predominate (members of the music bands Trupny yad (Ptomaine), Yarovit, and O.T. were convicted, among others). This can be easily explained by the fact that audiovisual materials are far more effective propaganda tools than texts. The law enforcement agents could also locate them faster. In addition, linking to videos is technically simple, and the verdicts have mostly been handed down for links to materials posted elsewhere (e.g., on YouTube). Unfortunately, the numerous reposters of these videos are the only ones facing responsibility (Martsinkevich's verdict is something of an exception). Meanwhile, it would have been much more appropriate, albeit more difficult, to focus on identifying those who created and uploaded these videos, or, better yet, on those who committed the crimes displayed in the videos – especially when it comes to violence, since such recordings are not always staged.

As for the texts, they are almost never available for our review, and the reports by the prosecutors or the Investigative Committee rarely provide sufficient information. It is also notable that individual comments on social media, or comments on articles/videos yield almost the same number of convicted offenders as publications of original texts.

We view the verdicts related to administering and creating ultra-right groups on social media as appropriate; these groups are often created specifically in order to coordinate violent activities. Organizing Internet communities that systematically incite to hatred, is, in our view, a much more serious offense than individual posts or reposts on users' personal pages.

There were far fewer (22) convictions for offline propaganda. They were distributed as follows:

- Graffiti – 11;
- Songs during concert – one;
- Leaflets – one;
- Text publications – one (B. Stomakhin, who was charged for both online and offline publications);
- Publisher, for distribution of books – one (V. Korchagin);
- Public shouts and insults – three;
- Members and leaders of ultra-right and other groups as well as individual activists for specific (but sometimes unspecified) incidents of propaganda – four.

We have no reason to view these verdicts as inappropriate (although we definitely have doubts about some of them), but we believe that criminal prosecution for the nationalist or racist street graffiti is an excessive reaction on behalf of society and the state. Such verdicts constituted 50% of those handed down for "offline" propaganda (11 out of 22). In other cases, we can agree that specifically criminal prosecution was warranted for xenophobic propaganda in the form of newspaper articles (depending on the circulation), distribution of books, posting leaflets, singing songs or other incendiary public statements (obviously, depending on their content), especially if they occur in the course of an attack.

For Participation in Extremist and Banned Groups and Organizations

Prosecution under Art. 282.1 of the Criminal Code (organizing an extremist community) and Art. 282.2 (organizing the activity of an extremist organization) was slightly less intensive in 2014 than in the preceding year. We know of six such verdicts against 14 people in four regions of the country (compared to seven verdicts against eight people in seven regions in 2013). We are not including obviously inappropriate verdicts or the verdicts against Hizb ut-Tahrir.

Art. 282.1 appeared in two cases and was appropriately applied to the founders of ultra-right groups. One of the ideologists and founders of the Northern Brotherhood (*Severnoye bratstvo*)[18] Valery Vdovenko, a former KGB officer, who had previously played an ambiguous role in the history of the Motherland party, was convicted in Moscow. In aggregation with other articles, he was sentenced to two and a half years in prison. Other members of the Northern Brotherhood – Anton "Fly" Mukhachyov, Oleg Troshkin and Pyotr Khomyakov – were already convicted in 2012 and 2013. In Murmansk, member of White Cross (*Belyi krest*) right-wing military-patriotic club Yevgeny Filimonov was sentenced to two years and one month in a penal colony in aggregation with charges under other articles (including violence).[19]

In other cases, the courts utilized Art. 282.2. The best-known verdict was handed down in March 2014, when Dmitry Dyomushkin, the leader of Slavic Force,[20] was sentenced to a fine of 200,000 rubles for continuing the activity of the banned Slavic Union but was released from payment due to the statute of limitations. It is unclear why the case was under investigation for such a long period of time and why other charges were dropped.

The article was once again applied to the neo-pagan right-wing radical organization the Spiritual and Tribal Rus Sovereignty (*Dukhovno-rodovaya derzhava Rus*); members of this organization mail their propaganda to various government offices, including prosecutor's offices, on regular basis. In December 2014, Spiritual and Tribal Rus Sovereignty activist Aleksandr Shiroky was found guilty of racist propaganda, continuing the work of an extremist organization and the storage and distribution of drugs and was sentenced in Arkhangelsk to five years and two months in prison.

Other cases pertain to Islamist associations that were directly involved in violence. Five people were sentenced to lengthy prison terms in a case for collaboration with the banned organization Al-Takfir wa al-Hijra in Tatarstan in aggregation with other charges. Five people were sentenced to lengthy prison terms in Bashkiria for creating a cell of the banned organization Caucasus Emirate, robbery, theft and illegal purchase of weapons.

Another noteworthy verdict was handed down by the Sverdlovsk Province Court against Aleksandr Yermakov – yet another participant in a cell of the Yekaterinburg Minin and Pozharsky People's Militia (*Narodnoye opolcheniie imeni Minina i Pozharskogo*, MPPM). He was sentenced under the Criminal Code Art. 30 Part 1 in aggregation with Art. 279 (preparation for an armed rebellion), Art. 205.1 (involving people in terrorist activity) and Art. 222 (illegal acquisition and storage of explosives) to 12 years of imprisonment in a maximum security penal colony followed by two years of restrictions on freedom.[21]

Inappropriate Prosecution of Political and Civic Activists

The fight against actions in support of Ukraine and against pro-Ukrainian statements online was the top law enforcement priority in the area of combating extremism in 2014. The fact that the FSB has played a significant role in this process suggests that the authorities were afraid of a potential network of agents of radical Ukrainian groups. Right Sector (*Pravy sector*) is the group most frequently mentioned in this context), or even guerilla groups. But, in practice, we saw that the counteraction primarily targeted citizens whose radicalism, at its worst, was limited to irresponsible chatter on the Internet. A number of criminal cases were opened, which will be discussed below, since the sentences on them were handed down not in 2014, but later.

With regard to unbalanced rhetoric about the events in Ukraine, our position is as follows: We believe that the extreme severity of the crisis inevitably provokes many people into making extreme statements that would not be typical for them in a different context. In this situation, it is more expedient not to resort to criminal prosecution, even for the most abrasive texts, unless the constituent elements of the offense are presented in extremely clear and unequivocal manner. This consideration should be taken into account primarily with regard to appeals addressed to citizens or the authorities of another country – in this case, usually, Ukraine. Otherwise, actions of the law enforcement agencies only increase the tensions that are already running high in society.

The movement of Russian troops into the Crimea has drawn sharp criticism from activists of the Tatar nationalist movement in Tatarstan, who are concerned about the fate of the Crimean Tatars. Fauziya Bayramova, a Tatar writer, activist, and the leader of the Milli Mejlis (the alternative "national parliament") published the Statement of the Milli Mejlis on the Events in the Crimea and Ukraine on her Facebook page. It expressed the Tatar nationalists' solidarity with the Crimean Tatars' yearning for independence and disagreement with the policy of the Russian authorities. The statement contained no appeals that could pose any danger in relation to an ethnic group. However, the text, in conjunction with her other text on persecution against peaceful Muslims in Tatarstan, which also contained no signs of extremism, constituted grounds for charges against Bayramova for inciting ethnic hatred. She received a suspended one-year prison sentence under Art. 282; the text was banned.

The fight against pro-Ukrainian rhetoric still has not completely distracted the police from their usual targets of prosecution on charges of inciting hatred or calls for extremist activities.

Eduard Mochalov, the editor-in-chief of the newspaper *Vzyatka* (Bribe) in the Chuvash Republic, was found guilty under Art. 282 Part 1 of the Criminal Code (incitement of hatred or hostility, and violation of human dignity on the basis of nationality) and Art. 315 Part 1 (failure to comply with a verdict, judgment or other judicial act) and sentenced to 400 hours of mandatory labor. Besides failure to obey the court (consisting of failing to publish in his newspaper the refutations of information "discrediting the honor and dignity of individual officials"), Mochalov was also charged under Art. 282 for reprinting Fauziya Bayramova's article "We are Tatars, not Russians."[22] Bayramova was charged under the same Art. 282 Part 1 for distributing via a social media network the Milli Mejlis statement of her own authorship, which called for boycotting the Universiade and for actions against the persecution of Muslims in Tatarstan (Bayramova had already been sentenced in 2014 under the same Art. 282 for her other texts – see above.) We found no inflammatory slogans against members of another ethnicity or religion in this text. The statement contained sharp criticism of the authorities and the high clergy of Tatarstan, as well as of the Russian security services, whom Bayramova accused of an assassination attempt against Mufti Ildus Faizov and murder of his deputy Waliullah Yakupov as a pretext for a new persecution of Muslims. None of this qualifies to be considered under Art. 282.

Vasily Purdenko, the editor of the blog *Svobodnoye Slovo Adygei* (Free Speech of Adygea) was sentenced to a fine of 100,000 rubles under Art. 282 Part 1. In our opinion, the article "Being a Russian in Adygea is Possible, but Hopeless" for which Purdenko has been convicted and which has been banned for extremism, was clearly written from the nationalist perspective and criticized local authorities for their "anti-Russian" policies, but the material contained no signs of incitement to hatred or enmity toward the Adyghe people and no dangerous incitement deserving of criminal prosecution.

The Federal List of Extremist Materials

In 2014, the Federal List of Extremist Materials was updated 47 times, adding 382 items; two items[23] were excluded from the list without changes in numbering. The list grew from 2,179 to 2,561 positions. However, it must be pointed out that the list was updated less frequently (during the comparable period in 2013, 590 items were added to it, compared to 523 items in 2012 and 318 items in 2011). The additions are thematically distributed as follows (some items included a variety of materials):

- Xenophobic materials by modern Russian nationalists – 198;
- Materials by other nationalists – 13;
- Materials by ideologues and classic authors of fascism and neo-fascism – eight;
- Materials of Islamist militants and other calls for violence issued by political Islamists – 93;

- Other Muslim materials (Said Nursi's books, materials of the banned organizations, including Hizb ut-Tahrir, many others) – 20;
- Other religious materials (from Jehovah's Witnesses, evangelicals, etc.) – nine;
- Various anti-state materials that incite riots and violence (including anarchist materials) – 22;
- Extremely radical anti-Russian statements from Ukraine – one;
- Other materials from Ukrainian media outlets and the Internet – three;
- Historical books – one;
- Orthodox fundamentalist materials – three;
- Partial copies of the Federal List itself – one;
- Materials, obviously banned by mistake – one;[24]
- Materials that could not be categorized – six.

At least 284 out of 379 positions (with two deleted ones taken into account) were items found on the Internet (compared to 333 out of 590 the year before).

Unfortunately, working with the list has long been impossible.[25]

New items were added haphazardly with numerous bibliographic, grammatical and spelling errors. Occasionally, items were described in a way that makes them impossible to identify. For example, it is unclear what material was added to the list as No. 2518 – it is described as "object number three (from file MgISO-Re9hs.jpg) posted by the username 'Igor Vladislavovich' on the Vkontakte social media network on the Web site www.vk.com at the URL http://vkontakte.ru/id8925421." Many items consist of huge lists that include different types of materials and are impossible to navigate. Occasionally, materials were obviously added to the list simply by mistake. For instance, only an error or court oversight could explain adding the de-motivator "Russia for Cats" (clearly a parody) as No. 2234. Meanwhile, the fact that the list also includes scholarly articles by Sebastian Shtopper on the history of World War II guerillas in Bryansk Province once again suggests that courts do not pay attention to the content of items they ban; most likely, neither do prosecutors.

Courts keep adding the same books in different editions to the list, or the same online materials published on different Web sites – their content is identical, but formally they are different and have to be considered separately. At least eight duplicate items[26] were entered in 2014, bringing the total number of duplicates to 88.

Some items, such as materials of Jehovah's Witnesses or books by Said Nursi, have been recognized as extremist inappropriately.

The electronic address (URL) of a resource is intentionally distorted prior to being added to the list. Thus, the list essentially represents a collection of dead hyperlinks. Obviously, the Ministry of Justice does not want to advertise extremist materials, but in this case the agency's actions end up being simply meaningless.

Blocking of Online Resources and Internet Censorship

In the course of the year, prosecutors gained strength in their fight against extremist content on the Internet, utilizing both new and old mechanisms.

Prosecutors continued to issue warnings to school administrators about the inadmissibility of extremist activity due to the lack of content filtering software on school computers. However, this activity decreased in scope compared to the preceding year. We know of at least 24 such representations (35 during the similar period of 2013). We believe such methods of combating extremism are counterproductive, since the content filtering software distributed by Rosobrazovanie in March 2008 cannot cope with the task, and, in any case, ideal content filters do not exist even theoretically.

However, the principal area of activity has long shifted to blocking access to restricted (or supposedly otherwise dangerous) materials.

Throughout the year, prosecutors continued to send requests to local Internet providers demanding restrictions on access to "extremist Web sites." Unfortunately, prosecutors and service providers rarely report on the actions taken, so our data are known to be fragmentary. However, we know of at least 48 such cases in 2014 (compared to 77 in the preceding year), not counting obviously inappropriate ones.

While old blocking methods gradually recede into the background, the system of Internet filtering based on the Unified Register of Banned Web Sites, which has been in operation since Nov. 1, 2012, is gaining momentum with a vengeance. According to preliminary estimates made by the Internet resource Roskomsvoboda,[27] there were at least 128 such resources[28] (out of 1,557 entries total) as of Jan. 1, 2015. According to available data (only

Roskomnadzor has the full information), courts added the following materials to the Register for "extremism" in 2014:

- Xenophobic materials by modern Russian nationalists – 61;
- Materials by the authors of classic fascism and neo-fascism – six;
- Xenophobic materials by other nationalists – one;
- Materials of Islamist militants and other calls for violence issued by political Islamists – 20;
- Other Muslim materials (Said Nursi's books, materials of banned organizations, including Hizb ut-Tahrir, etc.) – 17;
- Peaceful opposition Web sites – one;
- Ukrainian media Web sites – one;
- Conspiracy film about Sept. 11, ideology unclear – one;
- Various anti-state materials that incite riots and violence (including anarchist materials – 11;
- Copies of the Federal List of Extremist Materials Web site with working hyperlinks – seven;
- Online library Web site blocked because of one item – one;
- Unidentified material – one.

Thus, starting in mid-2014, a new (in the legal sense) practice emerged in an attempt to circumvent one of the absurdities of the Federal List. The problem is that prohibition of a book, for example, does not automatically mean a ban on its text online – it should be banned and entered in the list separately; moreover, it has to be done separately for each Web site, as well as for each edition of the same book. In order to avoid endless additions to the list, prosecutors find an online copy or a version of the banned material, petition the court to not ban another item, but to recognize that a particular Web site (or a page or a group of pages) "provides information forbidden for dissemination in the Russian Federation," which corresponds to the wording of the law on the Register of Banned Web Sites. These cases are handled using the expedited procedure, in which the Court merely establishes (or pretends to establish) the equivalence of the materials. Next, the decision is sent to Roskomnadzor for implementation.

This practice was soon expanded. Similar decisions were being made about Web sites that contained materials not previously banned as extremist, although the reasons provided by prosecutors referred specifically to the area of anti-extremist legislation. While the procedure described in the preceding paragraph merely constitutes a "legal trick," these bans are simply not based on law.

It seems that restrictions on materials based on the Register are currently just as meaningless and haphazard as new additions to the Federal List. Some obvious instances of misuse were observed as well. For example, we cannot agree with blocking the *Gramotey* online library due to the presence of one or more extremist materials in it. Restrictions on well-known hate Web sites, such as *Shturm-novosti* (Storm-news) occur along with restrictions on materials inappropriately recognized as extremist, such as Said Nursi's books.

The Law on the Register is supplemented by the "Lugovoi law,"[29] which provides for extrajudicial blocking of Web sites that contain incitement to extremist actions or riots at the request of the Prosecutor General but without trial. The Roskomnadzor Web site added a separate registry to work with this mechanism.

By decisions of the Prosecutor General's Office, 156 resources were blocked under this law in 2014.[30] They include:

- Xenophobic materials by modern Russian nationalists – 19;
- Materials of Islamist militants and other calls for violence issued by political Islamists (videos and statements by Islamist militants, Umma-news, Chechen-news, Vdagestan.com, *Kavkaz-Jihad* and others and their mirrors) – 66;
- Other Muslim materials (Said Nursi's books, materials of banned organizations including Hizb ut-Tahrir, etc.) – nine;
- Peaceful opposition Web sites (*Grani, Yezhednevny zhurnal,* and Kasparov.ru, and their mirrors; Aleksei Navalny's blog, Appeal to the Ukrainian people by Borovoy and Novodvorskaya); however, the Prosecutor General's office emphasized that in this case it did not use the term "extremism" – 46;
- Extremely radical anti-Russian statements from Ukraine addressed to the Russian audience – 13;
- Other materials by Ukrainian media – 11;
- Collection of prohibited materials – one;
- Unidentified material – one.

As you can see from the above list, there are quite a few cases of misuse in this registry. At least one-third of the registry listed blocked opposition Web sites, clearly demonstrating that extrajudicial blocking, based only on suspicion of "sedition," inevitably leads to arbitrariness, abuse of power, and an attack on freedom of speech.

Meanwhile, it is impossible to suppress mobilization for riots by blocking Web sites, even though this was the principal motive for the adoption of the Lugovoi law. This point is illustrated by the incidents when the authorities blocked the videos that called for gathering on Manezh Square in Moscow on May 18 to organize the "new Manezhka," or the Internet resources that contained information about the meeting places for the Russian March on Nov. 4. In these and other similar cases, multiple online distribution channels were involved simultaneously, so that all this information quickly reached its intended audience. A huge number of such materials still remain completely accessible.

Abuse of Blocking

In 2014, the blocking of online content, along with preventing meetings and gatherings, became one of the principal forms of government pressure on Russian society. Not surprisingly, these two forms of pressure were closely linked. Actually, the government has provided a direct link between them in the form of the so-called Lugovoi law, signed by the President in late 2013. The law allows the Prosecutor General to request extrajudicial blocking of Web sites that contain "incitement to mass unrest, extremist activities, incitement of ethnic and (or) interconfessional strife, participation in terrorist activity and participation in mass public events conducted in violation of the established procedure." From our point of view, the provision of the Lugovoi law that calls for blocking information on activities that have no permits is inappropriate due to the fact that the event itself has not been permitted gives no grounds to restrict messages about it. A requirement to block information about events still awaiting a decision on their permit application, is even more inappropriate.

In our opinion, if a nationalist event does not involve obviously forbidden slogans, then preventing it or blocking information about it is inappropriate and violates the rights to freedom of assembly and freedom of speech. In cases where the authorities have reasons to expect violations of the law in the course of an event, they should ensure the presence of law enforcement personnel capable of preventing illegal actions rather than prevent dissemination of information about the event itself.

However, the authorities were uneasy about any kind of opposition demonstration, and the registry has been actively replenished with Web pages – including blog posts and media announcements – that contain information on such events.

Implementation of the Lugovoi law began in late February. In March, on the eve of an unpermitted rally near the Zamoskvoretsky District Court in Moscow focused on the expected verdict on the Bolotnaya Square case, Roskomnadzor, at the request of the Prosecutor General, added the following popular opposition resources to the Register of Banned Materials: Grani.ru, Kasparov.ru, *Yezhednevny zhurnal* (Daily Journal, ej.ru) and the blog of Aleksei Navalny (navalny.livejournal.com). According to the prosecutors, these Web sites contained calls for illegal activities and for participation in public events conducted in violation of the established order. The agency did not inform the owners of Web sites what specific materials they found problematic, so the owners had to go to court in order to clarify the circumstances of the blocking. In three cases out of four, the courts helped to clarify the grounds for the restrictions; the restrictions were upheld in all four cases.

Thus, in the course of the proceedings in the Moscow City Court, it became known that Navalny's blog had been blocked because of two entries. The first one was focused on the events in Ukraine, and, in the end, urged the readers to come out in support of the defendants in the Bolotnaya Square riot case. The second entry also contained a call for the readers to gather near the court where the verdict in the Bolotnaya Square case was to be announced.

In the case of Kasparov.ru, it was discovered that the Prosecutor General and Roskomnadzor had issues with an illustration for the article "Ukrainian State Property to Be Nationalized in Crimea," published prior to the Crimean referendum. It depicted an armed man and the text "Crimea, wake up, invaders and their henchmen are brazenly stealing your money and spoiling your cities. Don't be silent, don't give up."

When the court was considering restrictions against ej.ru, the attorney for the Prosecutor General's Office clarified that illegal information, and, specifically, calls for mass actions without permits, were found in a number of materials related to the Bolotnaya Square case. In addition, the Prosecutor General's Office declared that it viewed many articles published by this outlet as biased. A quote from an article by Yulia Latynina on clashes with riot police at Bolotnaya Square was provided as an example of illegal information.

The agencies were unable to agree on a common version regarding access restrictions on Grani.ru: the Prosecutor General's Office mentioned calls to participate in unsanctioned actions, while Roskomnadzor invoked calls for extremist activity. As a result, Grani.ru filed an appeal with the European Court of Human Rights.

The next wave of restrictions at the request of the Prosecutor General took place in early August, when access was blocked to several dozen pages, including pages from Russian and Ukrainian media Web sites, as well as blogs and social media network pages of a number of users. The authorities used this method to prevent sharing of messages on the planned "March for Federalization of Siberia" in Novosibirsk. The editorial boards of a number of major media outlets received Roskomnadzor warnings or notifications demanding that the corresponding material be removed from their pages. The first item to be blocked was the article "No More Feeding Moscow" by National Bolshevik Platform activist Mikhail Pulin published on the *Novy Smysl* (New Meaning) Web resource; the article contained a theoretical substantiation of the need for such a demonstration. Access to the Vkontakte event page for the march was restricted as well. Large-scale blocking of all messages relating to the upcoming march followed next.

Roskomnadzor representative Vadim Ampelonsky explained the decision by the fact that the materials on this demonstration contained "information about preparations for an unpermitted mass event under slogans that encroach on the territorial integrity of the country." We view the actions of the Prosecutor General and Roskomnadzor as inappropriate. First, at the time of publication, the permit request had been filed with the Novosibirsk authorities, but no decision was issued. Second, the media did not encourage participation in the demonstration, let alone participation in riots; many materials did not even mention the date of the event. Third, the organizers did not come forward with any separatist appeals, but only called for autonomous rights for Siberia within the Russian Federation. However, we do not view attempts to criminalize public discussion on the rights of certain territories, the right to self-determination and even separatist appeals as legitimate. Prohibitive measures can be justified only when applied to calls for violence in support of separatist goals. Note that only one publication was able to challenge the warning – in early 2015, the Central District Court of Novosibirsk acknowledged that the note on federalization published on the portal Sibkray.ru contained no signs of extremism. Most Web sites removed their materials related to the march.

The pages, which kept such materials intact, still remain on the Lugovoi Register.

The situation repeated itself in the second half of December, when, upon request from the Prosecutor General's Office, Roskomnadzor blocked dozens of Web sites and individual pages that contained information about a planned rally in support of Aleksei and Oleg Navalny in connection with their sentences in the Yves Rocher case. Some of these resources still remain in the registry.

In early March, several providers in various regions of Russia blocked access to YouTube.com for a period of time. Their actions were based on the order to restrict access to the video of an appeal to the Ukrainian people by Valeria Novodvorskaya and Konstantin Borovoy, issued by the Prosecutor General's Office in accordance with the Lugovoi law. Novodvorskaya and Borovoy called on Ukraine not to surrender the Crimea without armed resistance; such resistance, in their view, could make the West actively intervene in the conflict, prevent further expansion, and hasten regime change in Russia. As is usually the case, when restrictions affect a major Internet resource, Roskomnadzor and representatives of the Internet service providers later claimed that that access to the entire portal had been blocked by mistake or due to technical reasons. YouTube gradually became accessible to its users once again, along with the video in question.

The most famous and notorious court-imposed bans of 2014 were the bans against jw.org (the Jehovah's Witnesses' Web site) and nurru.com, the site of Said Nursi followers. Many Web sites were only blocked temporarily. For example, in the fall of 2014, Roskomnadzor blocked the Wayback Machine (archive.org) – an automatic aggregator of content all over the Internet since 1996 – and entered it onto the Unified Registry of Banned Web Sites. The resource was blocked because it provided access to the video "The Clash of Swords," which was produced by the Islamic State and recognized as extremist. Obviously, restrictions against this extremely useful resource of over 435 billion pages could only be temporary – otherwise, Russian users would have been the ones punished.

The ban against the Jehovah's Witnesses' Web site revealed a cynical attitude of the authorities toward their own blocking mechanism. Initially, the Web site was blocked because of the fact that it published texts of the pamphlets recognized as extremist. In response, the Web site installed a server-side filter that does not allow users with Russian IP-addresses to see these materials – i.e., they blocked these materials voluntarily. This gave grounds for annulment of the previous court decisions. However, the Supreme Court was then presented with a note from the FSB that the banned texts could still be found by using an anonymizer program, which allows its user to bypass any blocks. The Supreme Court found this to be a sufficient reason for banning the entire site.

In the course of 2014, we counted about 22 cases of inappropriate punishment against Internet providers, who were forced to block inappropriately prohibited resources. This number is about four times smaller than in the preceding year. This drop in prosecutorial activity is apparently related to the introduction of a centralized registry. We are aware of six cases of inappropriately imposed fines under the administrative Art. 6.17 (violation of the laws of the Russian Federation on the protection of children from information harmful to their health and (or) development). The defendants are usually the owners of cafes and Internet clubs held responsible for the absence or imperfection of their content filtering systems.

Schools and libraries still face the brunt of these prosecutorial claims more frequently than other institutions. We would like to remind everyone that all their computers must be equipped with content filtering software that blocks access to prohibited information, including extremist materials. If the system of shielding the user from banned information fails to work properly (and perfect filters simply don't exist), The prosecutor's office issues injunctions to eliminate violations to directors of educational institutions and libraries rather than to software developers and distributors, and then the "guilty" parties face disciplinary measures.

However, the number of inspections in schools and libraries, and prosecutors' various responses based on their results in 2014, comes to only a half of the corresponding number from the preceding year; according to our very conservative estimates, there were 349 cases of punishment in 2013, compared to 178 cases in 2014.[31]

NOTES

1. The official name is: A List of Community and Religious Associations and Other Non-profit Organizations, with Respect to Which a Court Decision Was Made and Entered into Force on Liquidation or Ban on Activities on the Grounds Stipulated by the Federal Law "On Combating Extremist Activity."

2. The verdict in the case of the Borovikov-Voyevodin gang was handed down on June 14, 2011, by the St. Petersburg City Court. Aleksei Voyevodin and Artyom Prokhorenko were sentenced to life in prison. For details, see: The Verdict in the Borovikov-Voyevodin Gang Case handed down in St. Petersburg // SOVA Center. June 14, 2011 (http://www.sova-center.ru/racism-xenophobia/news/counteraction/2011/06/d21872/).

3. Martsinkevich had been an activist of the NSO (National Socialist Society), headed the association "Format 18," recognized as extremist by the decision of Moscow City Court of Dec. 20, 2010. "Format 18" specialized in manufacturing and selling videos that depicted Nazi skinheads torturing homeless persons and Asian migrants. Tesak was convicted in 2008 for nationalistic provocation in the Bilingva club in February 2007, but not for his more serious acts. In 2009, he was convicted again for posting on the Internet a video with the staged hanging of a "Tajik drug dealer." Martsinkevich's prison term ended on Dec. 31, 2010; he was released, and took up some new "projects," including the "Restruct!" movement, which quickly started to gain popularity among neo-Nazi youth, and the "Occupy Pedophilyai" project.

4. A criminal case against Maksim "Tesak" Martsinkevich under Art. 213 (hooliganism) was opened in Moscow in October 2014. The case was based on a video where M. Martsinkevich shaves a young man's head. In November 2014, another criminal case against Martsinkevich was opened in Moscow under Art. 282 Part 1 for writing and publishing the book *Restruct!*

5. According to the information from Occupy Drug Addiction (one of Restruct!'s sister-movements), on the day of the attack young people were conducting an "anti-drug raid." Having decided that Z. Alyshev was selling drugs, they handed him over to the police, but he was soon released from the precinct. After that, he was attacked.

6. In July 2013 the statement of ex-members of "Restruct!" appeared in the ultra-right portion of the Russian Internet, in which they reported their departure from the organization, which had become a vehicle for Martsinkevich's self-promotion. In addition, the statement asserted that its authors were planning to engage in propaganda of National Socialism and also more actively engage in "social" projects, similar to the "Occupy Pedophilyai," Occupy Drug Addiction, etc. The authorship of this statement is now difficult to ascertain, but Vladimir Tkach (as a former political council member of "Restruct!") and Stanislav Mityaev (as the former deputy head for human resources) were among its signatories. According to our data, the members of the Attack movement took part in raids against illegal migrants, at least one of which was held in collaboration with the police.

7. For more on this case, see: Moscow: Aleksandr Belov Detained and Arrested on Suspicion of Money Laundering: // SOVA Center. Oct. 16, 2015 (http://www.sova-center.ru/racism-xenophobia/news/counteraction/2014/10/d30455/).

8. This is not the first criminal case against Belov. In 2006, a criminal case against him was opened under Art. 282 after the events in Kondopoga. Later, the case was closed for lack of evidence. In May 2009, a Moscow court sentenced him under the same article to one and a half years' imprisonment for speaking at a rally during the Russian March of 2007.

9. Victoria Kuzmenko. Do Not Make Kazakhs Angry // Russkaya Planeta. May 21, 2014 (http://rusplt.ru/world/ne-zlite-kazahov-9976.html).

10. Yevtushenko was earlier under house arrest on charges of hooliganism for participating in the Russian Sweep.

11. We cannot claim to know all such verdicts. Sentences handed down in the republics of the North Caucasus and in the Crimea are not included in this report. The report data on prosecutions of members of extremist communities and banned organizations here and in the next section (Participation in Extremist and Banned Groups and Organizations) do not include legitimate sentences handed down under the same articles but not for xenophobic actions or to nationalist defendants (there are very few of these). Nor do they include sentences that we consider inappropriate; the latter are cited explicitly in other sections of this collection, particularly those titled "Inappropriate Prosecution of Political and Civic Activists."

Aside from these qualifications, let's compare our data to the official statistics. Such statistics have not been published for 2014 (only for its first six months). If we compare the 2013 data according to the Supreme Court and according to SOVA Center (summed across all types of convicted people and regardless of the conviction's appropriateness), then the Supreme Court reported 60 convicted offenders under Art. 280 (hereinafter – under both parts of the article, both principal and additional charges), and SOVA reports 28; under Art. 282 the Supreme Court and SOVA report 218 and 145 respectively, under Art. 282.1 – 18 and 12, under Art. 282.2 – 30 and 28. See: Summary Statistics on the Status of Criminal Record in Russia in 2013: Report on number of convictions for all crimes of the Criminal Code of the Russian Federation // Web site of the Supreme Court of the Russian Federation (http://www.cdep.ru/userimages/sudebnaya_statistika/2013/f_10-a-osugd_po_vsem_sostavam_prestupleniy_UK_RF_za_2013.xls); SOVA Center Database (http://www.sova-center.ru/database).

12. The lead singer of the band Yarovit from Tyumen, for sharing songs by Kolovrat; a resident of Abakan for the video "Walks near the Gukovo Dorm 2" (*Progulki vozle gukovskoi Obshchagi-2*); a Kurgan resident for "Catechism of the Jew in the USSR" (*Katekhizis yevreya v SSSR*); a Yekaterinburg resident for a link to *Mein Kampf*; and a Tyumen resident for undisclosed videos from the Federal List.

13. N. Yudina. Combating Extremism in the Virtual World in 2012-2013 // Russia Is Not Ukraine: Contemporary Accents of Nationalism. Moscow, SOVA Center, 2014. pp. 178–206.

14. See: Natalia Yudina, Using a Sledgehammer to Crack a Nut: Review of Law Enforcement Practice under the Criminal Code Art. 280 in 2005–2010 // SOVA Center. Oct. 25, 2010 (http://www.sova-center.ru/racism-xenophobia/publications/2010/10/d20081/).

15. Unfortunately, we only know of one such sentence handed down in 2014. A court in Kurgan deprived a local resident of a right to engage in mass media-related activities for one and a half years as a penalty for xenophobic statements on the walls of buildings. Meanwhile, this is the most effective punishment for people involved in nationalist propaganda professionally in the media, in publishing industry or in the field of education.

16. V. Korchagin was convicted in 2004, after many years of litigation. He received a one-year suspended sentence and was released from punishment due to the statute of limitations without any restriction against engaging in publishing. In April 1995, for similar crimes, he was sentenced to a fine of 16 minimum wages and barred from publishing, editorial and journalistic activities for three years, but at that time Korchagin was eligible for an amnesty. See G. Kozhevnikova, Radical Nationalism in Russia: Manifestations and Responses. Overview of Developments in 2004. // SOVA Center. Jan. 24, 2005 (http://www.sova-center.ru/racism-xenophobia/publications/2005/01/d3386/).

17. The convicted offenders of 2014 include three minors.

18. More on Northern Brotherhood see: Galina Kozhevnikova, Anton Shekhovtsov et al. *Radikalny russky natsionalizm: struktury, idei, litsa.* Moscow, SOVA Center, pp. 231-240 (Radical Russian Nationalism: Structure, Ideas, People).

19. The second defendant in the case for creating an extremist community, organizer of the Russian March in Murmansk Aleksandr Valov fled to Ukraine escaping law enforcement agencies in the region. Valov claims that he does not participate in ATO.

20. The renamed Slavic Union (*Slavyansky soyuz*), banned in 2010.

21. The other "Khabarov group" participants had been convicted earlier. Leonid Khabarov himself was released on parole in July 2014.

22. Earlier, *Vzyatka's* author Ille Ivanov was also prosecuted; his article was banned as extremist, and the newspaper received the Roskomnadzor warning.

23. No. 2342 and 2343.

24. For example, No. 2498 (Information materials contained in the article "Muslim Brotherhood" on the Web site http://ilgid/ru/politics/brothers.html, which represent an information resource of the Muslim Brotherhood (Al-Ikhwan al-Muslimun)) (decision of the Tazovsky District Court of the Yamal-Nenets Autonomous District on July 28, 2014) contains a critical and rather formal description of the Muslim Brotherhood.

25. Galina Kozhevnikova. Radical Nationalism in Russia in 2008, and Efforts to Counteract It // SOVA Center. April 15, 2009 (https://www.sova-center.ru/en/xenophobia/reports-analyses/2009/04/d15763/).

26. Videos "Angry Russia" (*Zlaya Rossiya*), "Cyborg – Glory of Russia" (*Kiborg – slava Rossii*), "Kolovrat – Our Country" (*Kolovrat – nasha strana*), "Instructions from Our Sisters" (*Nastavlenie sester*), the film *Russia with a Knife in Its Back 2* (*Rossiya s nozhom v spine – 2*), the Kavkaz-Jihad Web site, the book *History of the Prophets* (*Istoriya prorokov*) by Osman Nuri Topbaş, the book *The Red Kabbalah* (*Krasnaya Kabbala*) by Georgy Klimov.

27. See: Register of Banned Web Sites // Roskomsvoboda (http://reestr.rublacklist.net/).

28. See the updated list: "Extremist Resources" in the Unified Register of Banned Web Sites // SOVA Center (http://www.sova-center.ru/racism-xenophobia/docs/2014/08/d30056/).

29. Full name: "On Amending the Federal Law 'On Information, Information Technologies and Protection of Information.'"

30. See the updated list: Resources in the Registry of Web Sites Blocked in Accordance with the Lugovoi law. // SOVA Center (http://www.sova-center.ru/racism-xenophobia/docs/2014/10/d30228/).

31. We are sure that we never find out about the majority of such inspections. Often, we know about the series of inspections being conducted, but the number of warnings and other acts of prosecutorial response is not always reported. In such cases, we counted the entire series as a single instance.

Banning Organizations as Extremist

The Federal List of Extremist Organizations published on the Ministry of Justice Web site[1] added 11 entries in 2015, almost twice as many as in the preceding year (six organizations).

In January 2015, five Ukrainian right-wing organizations were added to the list:[2] Right Sector, Ukrainian National Assembly – Ukrainian People's Self-Defense (*Ukrainskaya natsionalnaya asambleia – Ukryinskaya narodnaya samooborona*, UNA-UNSO), the Ukrainian Insurgent Army (*Ukrainskaya povstancheskaya armiya*, UPA), the Brotherhood (*Bratstvo*) and the All-Ukrainian Organization Stepan Bandera's Trident (*Tryzub*) (all were recognized as extremist by the Supreme Court of the Russian Federation in November 2014). The activities of these Ukrainian organizations undoubtedly include elements that meet the definition of extremist activity, so the ban is justified. However, the presence of members of these organizations in Russia in significant numbers is unlikely. It is obvious that they were banned for the sake of making a political statement.

Another new organization on the list, the Misanthropic Division association, was recognized as extremist by the Krasnoyarsk Territory Court on July 17, also in connection with the events in Ukraine.[3]

Other right-wing organizations added to the list include People's Social Initiative (*Narodnaya sotsialnaia initsiativa*, formerly commonly referred to as the National Socialist Initiative, *Natsionalnaya sotsialisticheskaya initsiativa*), recognized as extremist by the St. Petersburg City Court on Sept. 16,[4] and the White Cross Military-Patriotic club, recognized as extremist by the Murmansk Province Court on June 29.[5]

In the course of the year, the list also added three religious organizations, including two Jehovah's Witnesses organizations – one in Samara, the other one in Abinsk (Krasnodar Territory). We view these decisions, as well as the use of anti-extremist legislation against Jehovah's Witnesses overall, as inappropriate.

The final addition to the list was the association of followers of "Yngliism" in Stavropol Province, recognized as extremist by the Stavropol Province Court on Aug. 21.[6]

In October 2015, the Moscow City Court granted the prosecutorial claim and recognized the "Russians" Ethno-Political Association as extremist. The ban against the movement was based on law enforcement's problems with the movement's Manifesto, which the court considered extremist, and the fact that supporters and leaders of the "Russians" had repeatedly faced criminal and administrative responsibility under the articles related to nationalist propaganda. During the trial, the prosecutor stated that the Manifesto, which had been submitted for an expert examination, contained calls for "the creation of a national state and the struggle for national liberation by any means," which, according to experts, can be interpreted as incitement to ethnic hatred. In our opinion, this conclusion relies on arbitrary interpretation, because the founding documents of the "Russians" contain no direct incitements.

As to the second basis for their ban – the criminal and administrative cases against members of the organization – in our opinion, not all of them were justified. Moreover, some of the cases, such as the case against leader of the movement Aleksandr Belov, were still under consideration and, in the absence of a verdict, they could not serve as an argument in the court proceedings. However, the "Russians" Association explicitly carried out xenophobic propaganda, so, in effect, the decision to ban the organization can hardly be considered completely inappropriate, despite these obvious violations.[7]

The list of organizations recognized as terrorist, which is published on the FSB Web site,[8] was also updated during the year. Five organizations were added; some of them were banned as far back as 2013:

- The Autonomous Militant Terrorist Organization (*Avtonomnaya boyevaya terroristicheskaya organizatsiia*) (the first right-wing group that was banned as a terrorist organization, and not just as extremist);[9]
- A branch of Right Sector in the Republic of Crimea;[10]
- The Islamic State (the Islamic State of Iraq and Syria, the Islamic State of Iraq and the Levant, the Islamic State of Iraq and Sham);[11]
- Jabhat al-Nusra (the Victory Front) (a.k.a Jabha al-Nusra li-Ahl ash-Sham (Front in Support of Greater Syria);[12]
- The Minin and Pozharsky People's Militia (MPPM).[13]

The ban against MPPM deserves a separate discussion. The MPPM was founded by Vladimir Kvachkov in 2009. A number of materials by this organization were recognized as extremist. The leader of the organization and members of the Yekaterinburg MPPM cell, the so-called Khabarov group, were sentenced to imprisonment de facto for preparing a revolt. Unfortunately, the evidence base for the decision to recognize the MPPM as a terrorist organization is not known to us. MPPM members were known to possess weapons; they conducted combat training. However, many activists were not involved in these activities. So we can say that certain grounds for the decision to recognize it as a terrorist organization could conceivably exist, but we are not aware of them. However, we also have no reason to regard the court's decision as inappropriate.[14]

Criminal Prosecution

For Violence

In 2015, for the first time since 2011, the number of convictions for violent hate crimes was slightly higher than in the preceding year. In 2015, there were at least 24 convictions in which the courts had recognized the hate motive in 19 regions of Russia (compared to 22 convictions in 20 regions in 2014). As a result of these court cases, 61 people were found guilty (compared to 47 people in 2014).

Art. 282 (inciting ethnic hatred) appeared in seven sentences in relation to violent crimes. According to the Ruling No. 11 of the plenary meeting of the Supreme Court of the Russian Federation "On Judicial Practice in Criminal Cases Regarding Crimes of Extremism" of June 28, 2011, it is appropriate to apply Art. 282 to violent crimes if they are aimed at inciting hatred in third parties, for example, through a public and demonstrative ideologically motivated attack, and in such cases Art. 282 should be used in combination with another appropriate article of the Criminal Code (murder, battery, etc.). We completely agree with the position of the Supreme Court. Indeed, in all such verdicts of 2015 – the most resonant ones were the verdicts against a member of the Yekaterinburg Folksshturm group and against the Yuzhno-Sakhalinsk shooter – Art. 282 was utilized for specific cases of ultra-right propaganda combined with violence.

Penalties in violent crime cases were distributed as follows:

- Three people were sentenced to life in prison;
- Two people received a prison sentence of 24 years;
- Three people – up to 20 years;
- Two people – up to 15 years;
- Fourteen people – up to 10 years;
- Twelve people – up to five years;
- Seven people – up to three years;
- Five people – up to one year;
- Nine people received suspended sentences;
- One person was sentenced to a fine;
- Three people were released from punishment due to reconciliation of the parties;
- One person was acquitted.

As you can see from the above data, 14% of convicted offenders (nine out of 61) received suspended sentences. All these people (some of them minors) were convicted in large group trials, and, probably, their direct involvement in the attacks could not be proved or they accepted a deal with the investigators.

Offenders sent to prison in 2015 included members of well-known nationalist groups such as the Kazan Nazi Crew from Kazan, Folksshturm from Yekaterinburg, Piranha 74 from Magnitogorsk, the Northern Frontier from Syktyvkar (with their leader Aleksei Kolegov), and the Kamensk-Uralsky branch of Occupy Pedophilyai in the Sverdlovsk Province.

Three people were sentenced to life in prison. All of them came from the infamous Military Organization of Russian Nationalists (BORN). Vyacheslav Isaev and Maksim Baklagin were sentenced by the Moscow Province Court on April 21,[15] and the ex-leader of the Russian Image (*Russky obraz*) organization Ilya Goryachev, accused of founding the BORN and planning the murders committed by the group, was convicted by the Moscow City Court on July 24.[16]

For Crimes Against Property

Twice as many sentences were handed down for ethno-religious and neo-Nazi vandalism in 2015 than in the preceding year; we know of eight verdicts against 14 people in seven regions (compared to four verdicts against six people in eight regions in 2014).

Four cases involved charges under Art. 214 of the Criminal Code (vandalism motivated by ethnic or religious hatred). It was the only article utilized in the prosecution only in one case. In the other three verdicts (against Nazi skinheads from Kazan Nazi Crew and Occupy Pedophilyai and against the Yuzhno-Sakhalinsk shooter), it was used in combination with charges under other articles (concerning violence).

Three cases utilized Art. 244 of the Criminal Code (desecration of gravestones). In all cases, it was used in combination with other criminal charges. In one instance, it was combined with Art. 158 (theft), in another one – with Arts. 222 (illegal possession of ammunition) and 222.1 (illegal possession of explosives) and in the third case – with Art. 282.

In 2015, we encountered the first sentence for vandalism handed down under Criminal Code Art. 354.1 (the part on "public desecration of symbols of Russia's military glory"). The Krasnoyarsk Territory Court convicted three local residents for desecrating monuments to military glory in Gvardeisky Park on Jan. 9.

As in the preceding year, the majority of convicted offenders (eight out of 14) were sentenced to imprisonment. Vandalism was not the sole or primary charge against any of these people – they included members of the right-wing groups mentioned above, and their sentences included grave charges, such as violence. The previously mentioned individuals, whose verdicts included Arts. 158 and 222, were sentenced to prison terms as well. The only questionable prison sentence was the court decision in Krymsk in Krasnodar Territory. A 19-year-old young man was sentenced to one and a half years in prison under the combination of Arts. 282 and 244 for desecrating a memorial in honor of heroes of the Great Patriotic War together with his "colleague," filming the act of vandalism with his mobile phone camera and uploading the recording to the Internet; in addition, he wrote an "extremist statement" on a tank with a marker.

As for the other sentences, two individuals (from the Kazan Nazi Crew) received suspended prison sentences. However, we do not know the specific episodes they were charged for.

Three people were sentenced to mandatory labor for a period of 60 to 110 hours (all under Art. 354.1 of the Criminal Code), and one – to restrictions of freedom. We view this level of punishment for graffiti on monuments to military glory or Lenin's statues as adequate.

For Public Statements

The number of convictions for public statements continued to grow. In 2015, they once again significantly exceeded the number of sentences for all the other kinds of extremist crime combined. There were at least 202 verdicts for xenophobic statements in 2015, and 211 people were found guilty (one person has been released due to active repentance) in 60 regions of the country. In 2014, 154 sentences were handed down against 159 people in 54 regions.

Propaganda could be qualified under Arts. 282, 280, 212 (incitement to mass riots) and 205.2 of the Criminal Code.

Art. 282 was utilized in 148 sentences against 156 people. The verdicts exclusively used Art. 282 in the overwhelming majority of cases (127 people, 124 verdicts).

- Seven people were convicted exclusively under Art. 280 (public calls for extremist activity).
- Three people were convicted exclusively under Art. 205.2 (public incitement to terrorist activities or public justification of terrorism);
- Eleven people – under a combination of Arts. 282 and 280;
- Three people – under a combination of Arts. 205.2 and 282;
- One person – under a combination of Arts. 282, 280 and 205.2;
- One person – under a combination of Arts. 282 and 212 (in part relating to incitement to riots);
- One person – under a combination of Arts. 280 and 212.

In nine sentences against 16 people, violence charges were aggregated with propaganda charges (including the sentences we mentioned in the Criminal Prosecution: For Violence section).[17] In addition to these, two more verdicts are worth our attention.

The first was handed down under a combination of Arts. 282 and 359 of the Criminal Code (mercenary activity). The Moscow City Court sentenced member of the Ukrainian Right Sector Aleksandr Razumov to seven years in a minimum-security penal colony for publishing Russophobic material on his VKontakte page. In addition, Razumov belonged to the People's Watch of Zelenograd and used to accompany the police in their arrests of lawbreakers. During one of these missions, he offered cops money to go and fight in the South-East of Ukraine on the side of the government forces. The police reported this recruitment attempt to their superiors. This is the first known conviction of an ultra-right activist for mercenary activities.

The second sentence was handed down in Astrakhan under Art. 280 Part 1 and Art. 318 Part 1 of the Criminal Code (violence against an official representative) for publishing multiple photos and comments on them on VKontakte that called for racist violence against "non-Russians." In addition, as the police were carrying out investigative activity on the case, the suspect entered in a scuffle with one of the police officers. The court fined him 140,000 rubles.

In three verdicts against five people the criminal charges for propaganda were aggregated with those for vandalism.[18]

Some verdicts combined Arts. 282 or 280 with other articles of the Criminal Code.[19]

The share of convictions under Arts. 282 and 280 in relation to the total number of offenders convicted for their statements remained about the same as a year earlier. However, the share of offenders convicted under Art. 205.2 increased significantly. As the data show, 11 people were convicted under these charges. Traditionally, this article was utilized for radical Islamist propaganda. However, last year the practice of using this article has broadened – it was utilized for anti-Russian propaganda in the context of the events in Ukraine.[20]

People convicted under this article include editor of the *Radikalnaya politika* (Radical Politics) newsletter Boris Stomakhin,[21] and activist Robert Zagreyev from Ufa. It should be noted that the penalties in such cases were generally harsher than under other propaganda-related articles.

The court verdicts for propaganda cases in the period under review were distributed as follows:

- Forty-one people received prison sentences;
- Thirty people received suspended sentences without additional punishment;
- Thirty-one people were sentenced to pay various fines;
- Sixty-three people were sentenced to mandatory labor;
- Twenty-six people were sentenced to corrective labor;
- Four people received suspended corrective labor sentences;
- Two people were sentenced to educational intervention;
- One person was sentenced to restriction of freedom;
- Three people were sent for compulsory treatment;
- Two people were released due to statute of limitations;
- One person was acquitted.

As you can see, not only the number of such cases, but the percentage of people who have received sentences of real imprisonment significantly increased in 2015 (19 out of 158 in 2014 compared to 14 out of 133 in 2013). Some 2015 sentences involving imprisonment were handed down in conjunction with charges under other Criminal Code articles. As we already mentioned, it could be racist violence, vandalism, possession of weapons, theft, etc. Other offenders went to prison due to unexpired probationary periods for their prior suspended sentences. Two people were convicted of "propaganda" activities for the second time.

However, a number of sentences seem unduly harsh. At least 14 people (including repeatedly convicted Boris Stomakhin and ex-leader of the Russian Runs Maksim Kalinichenko) faced real prison terms for "words only." Such an increase in this type of punishment has no precedent throughout all the years of our monitoring. For example, our records showed two such "questionable judgments" in 2014, and one in 2013. Of course, most of the statements in question, made by the majority of these offenders, indeed included incitement to violence. As far as we could see, the charges stemmed from their statements against the government, against the President of the Russian Federation personally, or against the Russian armed intervention in the affairs of Ukraine; there were also charges for incitement to violent jihad. Offenders sentenced to prison for their speech included representatives of well-known right-wing organizations such as Vitaly Shishkin (the head of the Kaluga Branch of the "Russians" Association and an ex-leader of the Russian Fascist Order "Memory") or Maksim Kalinichenko, the ex-leader of the Russian Runs. We don't view the fact of these people having been convicted for their statements as inappropriate per se, but punishment in the form of imprisonment seems excessive. The tendency to resort to real prison terms is disturbing – even for legitimate convictions, it violates the principle of proportionality of punishment in such a sensitive area for our society as restrictions against freedom of speech.

On the other hand, the share of suspended sentences also increased in 2015 in comparison to the preceding year and amounted to 18% (38 out of the 2,011 convicted offenders). We have strong doubts about the effectiveness of such sentences, despite the fact that a suspended sentence is a real punishment, as it can cause substantial damage to one's reputation and career opportunities, and most importantly, in cases of repeated offenses, a pending suspended sentence leads to heavier punishment.

In the cases of well-known ultra-right figures, a suspended sentence can have an effect of slowing down their activity. However, some of them perceive this punishment only as an additional advertisement for their actions. For example, well-known St. Petersburg nationalist Nikolai Bondarik received a suspended sentence of one and a half years for his complicity in preparing serious provocations on Kurban Bairam (Eid al-Adha). The Court also gave him three years of probation, which included bans against using the Internet, making statements in the media, and participating even in permitted events and marches. Bondarik violated the ban so quickly that a new criminal case against him – for reposting his own interview, given to one of the Internet portals – was already initiated by the end of December 2015.[22]

We know of at least six verdicts that used the bans against mass media, publications, public speaking and participation in the rallies as additional penalties. Regretfully, this practice has been slow to develop; meanwhile, these punishments are the most effective ones for people engaged in nationalist propaganda, including professionally via the mass media or among their students. In this respect, we would like to point out the case of a fine imposed in March on director of the Algoritm publishing house Sergei Nikolaev and editor-in-chief of the same publishing house Aleksandr Kolpakidi for the publication of books authored by Benito Mussolini and Joseph Goebbels. We believe that, in their case, an additional penalty in the form of a ban against practicing their profession would have been appropriate.

Still, most of the offenders (125 people) were sentenced to real punishments that did not involve deprivation of freedom, such as corrective or mandatory labor, or fines. These penalties seem quite appropriate to us for the offenses.

Following the trend of the three preceding years, the propaganda convictions overwhelmingly pertained to online publications (182 verdicts for 184 people). The number of convictions for online propaganda in 2015 was over nine times greater than the number of convictions for offline statements (20 verdicts for 27 people).

The materials were posted on the following Internet resources:

- Social media – 166 (VKontakte – 113, unspecified social media networks – 51, Odnoklassniki – two);
- Blogs – two;
- YouTube – two;
- Internet publications – two;
- Unspecified Internet resources – 10.

Genre distribution of the criminal online materials also remained largely unchanged from the year before (one verdict could pertain to several genres):

- Videos and films (including the notorious "The Execution of a Tajik and a Dagestani" – 79;
- Audio (including songs by Kolovrat, Bandy Moskvy, Korroziya Metalla and Timur Mutsurayev) – 26;
- Images (photo or drawings) – 55;
- Articles or other complete texts (original or re-published) – 32;
- Statements, comments, forum posts – 12;
- Creating or administering online groups and communities – eight;
- Unspecified – 18.

There were far fewer (20) convictions for offline propaganda. They were distributed as follows:

- Public shouts and insults – one;
- Songs during concert – one (Sergei "Pauk" (Spider) Troitsky for performing his own song "Beat up the Devils");[23]
- Speech at a rally – one (A. Amelin);
- Provocations – one (N. Bondarik);
- Leaflets – one (an activist from the Attack group);
- Posting stickers – one;
- Sermons – one;
- Publishing articles – one;
- Verdicts against book publishers for publishing books – one (editor-in-chief and director of Algoritm publishing house);
- Graffiti – four;
- Verdicts against members and leaders of ultra-right groups and individual activists for particular (but unspecified) incidents of propaganda – seven.

For Participation in Extremist and Banned Groups and Organizations

Prosecutions under Art. 282.1 (organizing an extremist community) and Art. 282.2 (organizing the activity of an extremist organization) of the Criminal Code were more widespread than in 2014. We know of ten such sentences against 24 people in eight regions of the country[24] (compared to four sentences against 12 people in five regions in 2014).

Art. 282.1 was used in six cases and quite appropriately applied to creators and participants of far-right groups. The combination of this and other (violent) articles led to a life sentence for ex-leader of Russian Image (*Russky obraz*) Ilya Goryachev. Four Nazi skinheads from Kazan Nazi Crew group received lengthy prison terms in Tatarstan; so did nine members of the Occupy Pedophilyai movement in Kamensk-Uralskysky of the Sverdlovsk Province.[25]

Member of the Attack movement Vladimir Kudryashov, 28, was convicted in Moscow for creating and leading an extremist community. The court sentenced him to one year of imprisonment in a minimum-security penal colony and loss of the right to engage in activities related to the creation, leadership or operation of non-profit organizations for three years. The Attack movement was founded in the summer of 2014 by several activists who had left "Restruct!" The founders of the group issued a statement regarding their intentions to advocate National Socialism and more actively engage in "social" projects similar to Occupy Pedophilyai and Occupy Drug Addiction. According to our information, Attack members took part in raids against illegal immigrants, of which at least one was conducted jointly with the police. Members of the movement and their associates carried out their propaganda through social media, and also posted leaflets and stickers that fairly explicitly incited violence and hatred. A case against Attack activists was launched in the fall of 2014;[26] it involved a total of 10 people.[27]

In Vladimir, leader of a nationalist group Aleksandr Ptitsyn (known in social media as "Burivoy Liuty") was sentenced to two years and ten months' imprisonment followed by restriction of freedom for one year. In addition, he was deprived of the right to hold administrative positions in state and municipal institutions for five years.

In Nizhny Novgorod, a local resident (born in 1995) attempted to create an ultra-right group and received a suspended sentence of two and a half years.

The remaining cases were qualified under Art. 282.2 (organizing the activity of an extremist organization).

A Kirov court sentenced 29-year-old Aleksandr Zamyatin to two years in a minimum-security penal colony for trying to continue the work of an FC Dynamo fan club[28] that had been banned for extremism.[29]

Art. 282.2 was, as usual, applied to the neo-pagan right-wing radical organization the Spiritual and Tribal Rus Sovereignty. Four such activists were fined in the amounts of 50,000 to 100,000 rubles in Krasnodar Territory.

Another member of the same organization, already serving a sentence in Murmansk Province,[30] received an additional year in prison for trying to recruit his fellow inmates to join the organization; he even managed to convince one person.

Another verdict worth mentioning is the suspended five-year sentence handed down in Vladimir Province against a 34-year-old resident of the city of Kolchugino under Art. 150 Part 4 of the Criminal Code (involvement of a minor in the commission of an offense motivated by ethnic and religious hatred). The perpetrator was de facto acting as a leader of a group of teenagers he created. According to the Investigative Committee of Vladimir Province, the man, "being a supporter of the nationalist ideology, started to impose his views on his 13-year-old son and his peers, calling for violence against people of non-Slavic origin or followers of other religions." He brought the teens to a dormitory residence of Tajik nationals, beat up two of the foreigners with a metal bat, and damaged the car of another citizen of Tajikistan.

Inappropriate Prosecution of Political and Civic Activists

The "Ukrainian Question"

The law enforcement trend that started in the preceding year continued in 2015. The vast majority of inappropriate verdicts and newly initiated prosecutions under anti-extremist Arts. 280 (public calls for extremist activity) and 282 (incitement to hatred), as well as under the new Art. 280.1 (public calls for undermining the territorial integrity of the Russian Federation) were associated with various pro-Ukrainian statements on the Internet.

The most severe sentence, handed down against chairman of the Naberezhnye Chelny branch of the All-Tatar Social Center (*Naberezhnochelninskoye otdelenie Vsetatarskogo Obshchestvennogo Tsentra*, ATSC) Rafis Kashapov under Art. 280.1 Part 2 and Art. 282 Part 1 of the Criminal Code, was imposed in September by the Naberezhnye Chelny City Court. Kashapov received three years' imprisonment in a minimum-security penal colony. The Supreme Court of Tatarstan, having considered his appeal, limited its response to canceling an additional penalty – a two-year ban on the use of social media. The crime attributed to Kashapov consisted of posting four materials on VKontakte in public access. Three texts (the fourth material is a poster with photographs of victims of the Russian military operations) shared the same ideas of solidarity with Ukraine and the Crimean Tatars, the illegality of the annexation of the Crimea and rejection of actions of the Russian authorities. We found no signs of inciting ethnic hatred or calls for violence in these materials. As for the criticism of the Russian authorities, it should be remembered that, according to the clarification provided by the Supreme Court with respect to the enforcement practice of anti-extremist legislation,[31] such criticism should not be construed as incitement to hatred and prosecuted under Art. 282. Kashapov appealed the decision of the Russian courts to the European Court of Human Rights.

In December, the Oktyabrsky District Court of Krasnodar sentenced Kuban activist Darya Polyudova to two years of imprisonment in a penal colony (the decision has not yet entered into force, Polyudova currently remains under house arrest). The criminal case against Polyudova was opened in August 2014, after an attempt by Krasnodar activists to organize the March for Federalization of Kuban. Polyudova was arrested in September of the same year, held in custody for six months, and released on condition of remaining at her approved address in February 2015. She was charged under Art. 280.1 Part 2 of the Criminal Code for sharing a post on the VKontakte social media network that stated that ethnic Ukrainians of Kuban demanded incorporation into Ukraine; under Art. 280.1 Part 1 for a photograph of herself during a one-person protest holding a poster "Not War with Ukraine, but Revolution in Russia"; and under Art. 280 Part 2 for publishing a call to come out on the streets and overthrow the regime. We believe that the criminal case against Polyudova was partly inappropriate and partly disproportionate or debatable (similar to the majority of convictions for abstract calls for revolution and "overthrow") and, subsequently, her verdict was inappropriate.

Aleksandr Byvshev, a teacher from Kromy in Oryol Province, was sentenced in July under Art. 282 Part 1 to 300 hours of mandatory labor with a ban on practicing his profession for two years and confiscation of his laptop for publishing his poem "To Ukrainian Patriots," which encouraged the Ukrainians to meet the "Moskal gang" that invaded their land with armed resistance. From our point of view, the author's hostility, expressed in the poem, was caused not by the ethnicity of the "gang" but by its activities, so Byvshev's incriminating actions cannot be qualified under Art. 282. The fact that Byvshev was found guilty of incitement to violence is also spurious, to say the least; he only encouraged the citizens of Ukraine to defend the territory of Ukraine. The ECHR accepted Byvshev's complaint for consideration.

In July, the Leninsky District Court of Barnaul found Republican Party of Russia – People's Freedom Party (RPR-Parnas) activist Anton Podchasov guilty under Art. 280 Part 1 and Art. 282 Part 1 of the Criminal Code. Podchasov received a suspended sentence of fifteen months imprisonment with a probation period of one and a half years, during which time he will lose the right to engage in activities related to telecommunication networks, including using the Internet. Later, the Altai Territory Court reviewed the verdict and increased its severity, banning Podchasov, a member of the precinct electoral commission, from working in electoral commissions for three years. Podchasov was sentenced for sharing a "Russophobic post" – a text previously published by Andrei Teslenko, an opposition member from Altai, against whom a criminal case had also been opened, precipitating his move from Russia to Ukraine, where he was granted political asylum. The incriminating text is extremely abrasive; it contains a lot of abuse aimed at ethnic Russians and an appeal to the Ukrainian authorities not to grant them citizenship. A fragment of it, disseminated online, has been recognized as extremist in Stavropol Province. Nevertheless, we believe that the prosecution for sharing this text is spurious; in particular, it is doubtful that Russia should prosecute incitement to discrimination if it is uttered in Russia, but this was addressed to the authorities of another country and the proposed discrimination does not pertain to Russian citizens.

In October, the Industrialny District Court of Khabarovsk sentenced LGBT activist Andrei Marchenko under Part 1 Art. 280 of the Criminal Code to a fine of 100,000 rubles and then granted him amnesty. Marchenko was found guilty of having published some statements on his Facebook page that "contain calls for violence, including physical destruction, against a social group, defined by the author as residents of Russia, who, in his opinion, support fascism and terror and have committed a violent takeover of Ukrainian territories." In our opinion, the verdict against Marchenko under Art. 280 is at least partially inappropriate. Calls for the use of violence against groups that have "committed a violent takeover of territories" (of another state) is legitimate per se and stipulated by legislation of all countries as protection of territorial integrity.

Konstantin Zharinov, an activist of the South Ural Civic Movement (*Grazhdanskoye dvizhenie yuzhnogo Urala*), was found guilty under Art. 280 by the Tsentralny District Court of Chelyabinsk in September. He got a suspended sentence of two years' imprisonment with a probation period of two years; he also received an amnesty (later, his sentence was upheld by the province court). Zharinov shared on his VKontakte page an appeal by Right Sector to "Russians and Other Enslaved Peoples," which called for actions of disobedience, organizing guerrilla groups, and other forms of resistance against the regime. According to Zharinov, he quickly removed the entry, but it had been online for a sufficient period of time to attract the attention of the FSB, which opened a criminal case. The intelligence services' interest in Zharinov could possibly be explained by the fact that he was a political scientist specializing in terrorism. In our view, the sentence against Zharinov was inappropriate. He didn't express any solidarity with Right Sector's appeal, and his other activity on social media and blogs has not been characterized by aggressive rhetoric. Taking this into account, the law enforcement authorities could have limited their involvement to a simple request to remove the material (if still on the page); the criminal proceedings were a disproportionate measure.

Opposition activist Sergei Titarenko was sentenced to a fine of 100,000 rubles under Part 1 Art. 280 of the Criminal Code (public calls for extremist activity) in September in Krasnodar. The court found that Titarenko, motivated by hatred of the current political regime and President Vladimir Putin, deliberately shared a message by the Kolomoysky Broadcasting group on his VKontakte page that contained the text under the caption "No Dictator – No Problem," with information about a reward allegedly offered for the elimination of Russian president Vladimir Putin. Titarenko shared this text without any comments indicating his own position, so, in this case, the re-post should not have been interpreted as a call to action. In our view, the police could justifiably demand the removal of this incendiary falsehood, but the original author of the post should be the one to merit criminal prosecution. Titarenko refused amnesty.

In July, the Bakhchysarai District Court of the Republic of Crimea found local resident Mustafa Yagyaev guilty under Art. 282 Part 2 Paragraph "a" of the Criminal Code (incitement to hatred with the use of violence or the threat of violence). Yagyaev was sentenced to two years' imprisonment with "loss of the right to engage in activities related to sharing and dissemination of any information." The prosecution against Yagyaev was based on an essentially interpersonal conflict. Yagyaev, a mechanic, while at work, found himself disagreeing with the views of the female employees of the Housing Maintenance and Utilities Board accounting department regarding the consequences of the Crimea joining the Russian Federation. Yagyaev began to scream at his colleagues and use derogatory epithets against them; according to the investigation, he also said: "we will return the Crimea to Ukraine; there will be a war; we will have to cut and burn, and the Russians will drown in blood in this war, but it is a pity that my Muslim brothers will perish." (The defendant categorically denied ever making such a statement.) Information about the conflict quickly reached the local Center for Combating Extremism, which opened a criminal case. The real reason for the prosecution against Yagyaev was probably his activities as an imam, a civic activist and a member of the Crimean Tatar Mejlis during the 1990s. In our opinion, the verdict under Art. 282 against Yagyaev was inappropriate. He was addressing three women who were in the same room. Therefore, even assuming that he actually made a number of radical statements, this incident can't be qualified under Art. 282, which implies statements made in public.

In August, nationalist Andrei Bubeyev of Tver was sentenced under Art. 282 to 10 months of imprisonment in a penal colony. The prosecution was based on a variety of pro-Ukrainian texts and images he shared via VKontakte social media network. As is the case of Byvshev's poem, we believe that the charge under Art. 282 is inappropriate, since the hostility expressed in Bubeyev's posts was motivated not by the ethnic prejudices of the publisher – obviously a Russian nationalist by ideology – but by the activities of his opponents from among Russian citizens. As for the Russian military and law enforcement officials (one of the charges against Bubeyev was inciting hatred toward these groups), from our point of view, they do not belong to the set of vulnerable social groups and are not subject to protection under Art. 282.

In June, the Tsentralny District Court of Kaliningrad found three Kaliningrad activists, Mikhail Feldman, Oleg Savvin and Dmitry Fonaryov, who put a German flag on a garage of the Kaliningrad Regional FSB Office in March 2014 to express their support for Ukraine, guilty under Art. 213 Part 2 of the Criminal Code (hooliganism committed by a group of people by prior agreement, motivated by political hatred and enmity as well as by hatred against the social group "veterans of the Great Patriotic War") and sentenced to a real loss of freedom; however, taking into account the time spent in a pre-trial facility, the three activists were released in the courtroom. An attempt to challenge the verdict in the second instance was not successful, and Mikhail Feldman subsequently filed a lawsuit with the ECHR.

In September, the Tagansky District Court of Moscow sentenced roofer Vladimir Podrezov under Art. 213 Part 2 and Art. 214 Part 2 of the Criminal Code (hooliganism and vandalism motivated by hatred) in the case of the painted star and the Ukrainian flag raised on the steeple of a high-rise building on Kotelnicheskaya Embankment in Moscow on Aug. 20, 2014. Four base-jumpers, also charged in the case, were acquitted. We would like to remind readers that Ukrainian roofer Pavel Ushivets has taken responsibility for this action. We disagree with the qualification of this case – regardless of the perpetrator's identity, it is unclear who could have been a target of hatred as expressed by painting an object the colors of the Ukrainian flag; furthermore, the action should have been classified as a minor (rather than gross) violation of public order and tried as an administrative offense under Art. 20.1 of the Code of Administrative Offenses (petty hooliganism). In mid-December, the Moscow City Court commuted Podrezov's sentence from imprisonment to restraint of freedom.

Other Cases of "Separatism"

In addition to the issues related to Ukraine, law enforcement agencies continue to react strongly to statements involving "territorial integrity."

We view as definitely inappropriate the verdict handed down in December in the case of Vladimir Zavarkin, a deputy of the Suojärvi Urban Settlement Council who was accused of public incitement to separatism. The Petrozavodsk City Court found the deputy guilty under Art. 280.1 Part 1 of the Criminal Code and sentenced him to a fine of 30,000 rubles. The criminal case was initiated after the deputy addressed an assembly in Petrozavodsk in May 2015 that called for resignation of head of the Republic of Karelia Aleksandr Khudilainen. In his emotional speech, Zavarkin proposed holding a referendum on the secession of Karelia from Russia in response to the inaction of the authorities. The video of Zavarkin's speech was recognized in court as extremist in early November. These statements hardly qualify as separatist propaganda; moreover, we also generally believe that only calls for violent separatism merit prosecution.

Another noteworthy separatism-related case was initiated in Chelyabinsk in the summer of 2015 against Aleksei Moroshkin (online nickname Andrei Breiva) – the founder of the Church of the Chelyabinsk Meteorite and the administrator of the VKontakte group "For Struggling Ukraine! For free Urals! Together Against the Evil!" Moroshkin was charged with 12 instances of posting texts on the group's page that called for secession of the Ural region from Russia and for creation of the Siberian Federative Union. We were not able to review all of Moroshkin's texts, but the ones we have seen did not contain any calls for actual, deliberate activities that could lead to implementation of such plans. Moroshkin was held in custody for two months and then was released by the court from criminal responsibility and sent to a psychiatric hospital for compulsory treatment as a person who does not realize the significance of his actions and presents a danger to society. Given that Moroshkin did not previously suffer from mental disorders and was never under observation by a psychiatrist, we doubt both his diagnosis of "paranoid schizophrenia," delivered by a forensic psychiatric commission, and the need to isolate him from society.

Abuse of Criminalization of Incitement to Hatred

Several sentences for inciting hatred of various kind handed down by the Russian courts in 2015 seem questionable.

The Leninsky District Court of Cheboksary sentenced RPR-Parnas activist Dmitry Semyonov to a fine of 150,000 rubles in September, and then pardoned him, canceling the fine and removing the criminal record. Semyonov was accused of disseminating via his VKontakte page a caricature of Dmitry Medvedev in a Caucasian papakha fur hat, accompanied by the words "Death to Russian Vermin." We view Semyonov's sentence as inappropriate. The de-motivator he had shared was fairly widespread on the Internet; apparently, the creator of the image intended to indicate the fact that the Prime Minister's policies were "anti-Russian." Apparently, Semyonov interpreted the image in precisely the same way, claiming that the Russian government does not support ethnic Russians in the national republics of the Federation or in the former Soviet republics. In this case, it is unreasonable to believe that the image was inflammatory and actually called for the murder of Russians. Semyonov tried to appeal the decision, but the Chuvashia Supreme Court upheld his sentence.

In April, we found out about the sentence handed down by the Moscow District Military Court against resident of Staraya Russa Anton Izokaitis. He was sentenced to two and a half years in a penal colony under Art. 205.2 Part 1 of the Criminal Code (public calls for terrorist activity or public justification of terrorism), Art. 280 Part 1 (public calls for extremist activities), and Art. 282 Part 1 (humiliation on the grounds of nationality). Izokaitis was penalized for a squabble at a police station where he was taken for disorderly conduct during the New Year's celebration (Jan. 1, 2015). When brought to the police station, the detainee began to curse Russians and ended up justifying the terrorist actions of December 2013 in Volgograd. Nevertheless, we view the verdict against Izokaitis as inappropriate. He made these statements inside the police station and was addressing a small group, i.e., his actions can't be considered public. In addition, the date and circumstances of arrest raise suspicions that all these statements should not be qualified as intentional acts described in the corresponding Criminal Code articles. In June, when considering his appeal, the Military Collegium of the Supreme Court merely reduced Izokaitis's prison term to two years.

The Federal List of Extremist Materials

The Federal List of Extremist Materials was updated 79 times in 2015 and added 668 entries (compared to 382 in 2014), five entries were removed from the list without changing the numbering, and it grew from 2,561 to 3,229 positions.[32] Many entries represent lists of diverse materials. The additions are distributed by subject as follows:

- Xenophobic materials produced by modern Russian nationalists – 419;
- Materials of other nationalists – nine;
- Materials by the classic authors of racism – one;
- Materials of Islamist militants and other calls for violence issued by political Islamists – 96;
- Other Muslim materials (Said Nursi's books, materials of banned organizations including Hizb ut-Tahrir, etc.) – 53;
- Other religious materials (materials of Jehovah's Witnesses, evangelicals, Russian Orthodox groups that are not part of the ROC, etc.) – 11;

- Various anti-government materials that incite violence and riots (including Anarchist materials) – 27;
- Very radical anti-Russian statements from Ukraine – 12 (we have been counting them separately from "other nationalists" since 2014);
- Other materials from Ukrainian media and the Internet – 19;
- Non-violent opposition materials – eight;
- History books and other texts by historians – one;
- A large body of various texts, blocked in its entirety – one;
- Parodies banned as serious statements – three;
- Materials obviously banned by mistake – four;
- Unidentified materials – three.

As expected, the share of online materials on the list keeps increasing: At least 594 entries out of 668 refer to materials found on the Internet (compared to 284 entries out of 380 in the preceding year).

All the deficiencies of the list described in each of our reports still persist; its size continues to grow, and working with it has long been impossible. It is worth noting that, in the period under review, about 70 titles of Muslim literature, mainly from the notorious "Orenburg list"[33] were removed from the Federal List, but the overall picture didn't show much improvement.

Sometimes materials are described only by their electronic address (URL), which is also intentionally modified upon addition; thus, the list reflects a non-existent Internet resource. The need to modify the URL can be explained by the reluctance of the Ministry of Justice staff to inadvertently promote extremist materials, but then the actions of the Ministry are simply meaningless.

Certain items, such as Jehovah's Witnesses' materials or books by Said Nursi, have been recognized as extremist inappropriately. Some other materials obviously ended up on the list by mistake, for example a number of informational and clearly critical articles on terrorists.

Courts and prosecutors obviously don't monitor the list – the same materials are recognized as extremist in parallel court decisions (for example, http://kobakbogoder.blogspot.ru was listed under No. 2990 and No. 2926, and *The Path of the Truth* (*Stesya Pravdy*) book by I. Sinyavin – under No. 2061 and No. 3028. At least 13 duplicate items were entered in 2015.[34]

172 | RUSSIA'S ANTI-EXTREMISM LAW ENFORCEMENT

Blocking of Online Resources and Internet Censorship

Prosecutorial injunctions on the impermissibility of extremist activity in connection to lack of content filtering on school computers addressed to school administrations have been gradually tapering off. We are not completely sure about the reasons for this change – either school administrators finally installed the required filtering software in order to avoid further trouble, or law enforcement agents were otherwise occupied. In any case, we only know of 13 such injunctions (compared to 24 a year earlier).

However, this change did not mean that prosecutors' offices scaled down their fight against extremist content on the Internet in 2015. Prosecutorial activity for the past three years has been focused primarily on blocking access to restricted (or otherwise allegedly "dangerous") materials.

The number of injunctions against local Internet service providers with requests to restrict "extremist Web sites" has been decreasing as well. Unfortunately, prosecutors and service providers rarely report on the measures taken; therefore, our data are necessarily fragmentary. Nevertheless, we know of 13 such cases in 2015 (compared to about 48 in the preceding year), not including the obviously inappropriate ones. Local actions are being replaced by additions to centralized blocking registries.

A new system of Internet filtering based on the Unified Register of Banned Web Sites (in operation since Nov. 1, 2012) functions very actively. According to the data on the Roskomsvoboda Web site,[35] preliminary estimates put the number of such resources at no less than 431 as of Jan. 1, 2016.[36] Based on the data available to us (only Roskomnadzor has complete information), 283 resources were added there by court decisions for "extremism" in the year under review (compared to 129 in 2014).

- Xenophobic material of modern Russian nationalists – 125;
- Materials by the classic fascist and neo-fascist authors – 21;
- Xenophobic materials by other nationalists – three;
- Materials of Muslim militants and other calls for violence by political Islamists – 18;
- Other Muslim materials (books of Said Nursi, materials of banned organizations including Hizb ut-Tahrir and others) – 65;
- Materials of the Jehovah's Witnesses, L. Ron Hubbard and other religious materials – six;
- Peaceful opposition Web sites – 10;

- Very radical anti-Russian statements from Ukraine – five;
- Other materials from Ukrainian media and the Internet – 14;
- Orthodox fundamentalist Web sites – two;
- Various materials that incite violence and riots (including Anarchist materials) – seven;
- Peaceful materials critical of the Russian Orthodox Church – one;
- Parodies banned as serious statements – one;
- Materials obviously banned by mistake – four;
- Unidentified materials – one.

The know-how of this year is blocking search engine results for certain keywords, primarily on music Web sites rather than restricting specific Web sites or pages ("page containing download links for various audio files found by searching for keywords 'kill a cop,' 'Dobermann,' 'David Lane,' 'Kolovrat' etc."). This is manifestly inappropriate, because the pages found by a keyword search might contain any kind of resource, not necessarily problematic ones.

The Law on the Register is supplemented by the Lugovoi law.[37] By decision of the Prosecutor General's Office, 133 resources were blocked under this law in 2015.[38] They include:

- Xenophobic material of modern Russian nationalists – 19;
- Various inciting anti-government materials (including Anarchist materials) – four;
- Non-violent opposition Web sites – 18;
- Materials of Muslim militants and other calls for violence by political Islamists – 22;
- Other Muslim materials –17;
- Non-violent Ukrainian Web sites – 32;
- Web sites of banned Ukrainian organizations – 18;
- Parodies banned as serious statements – two;
- A large body of various texts, blocked in its entirety – one.

As far as we know, the two registers partially overlap (judging by the links), which seems to us complete nonsense; it means that they are both blocking the same page. The register already includes many cases of inappropriately banned materials (such as Said Nursi books), and there are more such cases in this register than in the other one. Almost half of it is taken up by nonviolent Web sites from Ukraine and blocked opposition Web sites.

In most cases, there was no evident need specifically for extrajudicial (urgent) restrictions of materials that had been available online for many years (for example, various Islamic literature).

The registry contains references to Web pages created for mobilizing people to participate in mass actions (resources with the assembly points for the Russian March on Nov. 4, Russian May Day, etc.). The need to block such pages had been the primary argument for adopting the Lugovoi law – this mechanism was ostensibly necessary for suppressing mobilization to participate in possible riots. In practice, as we could see, a situational mass mobilization is impossible to suppress by blocking.

Abuse of Blocking

We view about a quarter of cases (specifically, 72) as added to the Unified Register of Banned Web Sites inappropriately. Most of them – 47 Web pages – contain a variety of Muslim materials; politically oppositional pages account for another 15 instances; seven cases pertain to nationalist materials and three – to religious (not Islamic) pages. In addition, we doubt the appropriateness of the ban against eight Web pages with the materials of the Hizb ut-Tahrir religious and political party.

Considering the Web sites and Web pages blocked under the Lugovoi law, in our opinion, about 25 Web pages were blocked inappropriately. These problematic cases included pages with announcements of demonstrations in support of Aleksei Navalny and Darya Polyudova, the spring Anti-Crisis March, and the truckers' strike,[39] an instruction from the Consumer Rights Protection Society (*Obshchestvo zashchity prav potrebitelya*, CRPS), songs by the Ensemble of Christ the Savior and Crude Mother Earth, the Ukrainian band Duet Named After Putin and others. In addition, we doubt the appropriateness of blocking eight pages with Hizb ut-Tahrir materials. Some of these pages were only blocked temporarily, and users' access to them has since been restored.

The following aspect is also worth noting. Throughout the year, Russian law enforcement agencies consistently banned via courts and blocked under the Lugovoi law Ukrainian resources as well as Web sites that relocated to Ukraine after the takeover of the Crimea and the beginning of the armed conflict. The resources in question include big news portals as well as individual Web sites and pages. The reasons for restricting access to these resources are often clear – in the course of an armed conflict, the rhetoric quite naturally tends to escalate all the way up to calls for destruction of the enemy. However, such calls are far from the only thing to attract attention of the Russian authorities on Ukrainian Web sites. Disseminating information about unpermitted demonstrations, publishing interviews with leaders of Ukrainian organizations that are banned in Russia, and other violations of Russian anti-extremism legislation – regulations that in our view unduly restrict freedom of speech – can trigger the restrictions. Theoretically, it would be possible to divide the actions of Russian law enforcement agencies in relation to Ukrainian resources into appropriate and inappropriate according to criteria developed by SOVA Center. However, we believe that the anti-extremist legislation is designed for peacetime use only. It is impossible to apply it in a situation of information warfare that involves both Russia and Ukraine, represented by their leaders, the media and ordinary citizens, and which occasionally resorts to absolutely unacceptable rhetoric. The attempts of the Russian authorities to restrict access to Ukrainian resources are, in fact, part of the information war. Evaluating them in terms of adherence to the peacetime rules makes no sense, in our opinion. However, we are ready to address the issue of bans against Ukrainian Web sites in the event of a substantive change in the situation.

Selected Examples of Access Restrictions

As an illustration, we would like to discuss a few resonant cases of bans and access restrictions on Internet pages in more detail.

In September, the Petropavlovsk-Kamchatsky City Court ruled to recognize the local opposition news site *Express-Kamchatka Online* as extremist; it was included on the Federal List of Extremist Materials and the Unified Register of Banned Web Sites. The decision was based on the fact of publication of three prohibited articles by journalist Igor Kravchuk (deceased in 2014) accompanied by a suggestion to copy them, because they could be blocked. These texts were recognized as extremist in May 2014; the court found them to incite social discord and have a potential to encourage readers to violence. Indeed, Kravchuk's materials were written in an abrasive style more typically used on social media than in the media (including the use of profanity), and expressed negativity toward the current government, including President Putin, but we found no calls for violence or incitement to social hatred in their content, and thus no grounds for the ban. It was even more inappropriate to ban a large Web site (which ended up having to change its URL) for publishing three texts.

CRPS spent several months trying to challenge restrictions against its Web site imposed under the Lugovoi law. The decision to block the site was based on "incitement to extremist activities" found by the Prosecutor General's Office in the document titled "An Instruction for Russian Tourists Going to the Crimea for Vacation." The Prosecutor General's Office was referring to the recommendation, found in the document, to comply with the Ukrainian legislation and obtain permission to visit the Crimea from the Border Guard Service of Ukraine, since the Crimea remained an occupied territory under international law. According to the authorities, this advice called into question the sovereignty and territorial integrity of Russia. From our point of view, the actions of the Prosecutor General and Roskomnadzor related to blocking the Web site were inappropriate. The Instruction was not calling for extremist activity, and prosecuting an entity for providing information on international law is a clear encroachment on freedom of speech. In August the Zamoskvoretsky District Court dismissed the CRPS's appeal, and then, in September, the organization appealed to the Moscow City Court. We do not know whether the claim has ever been considered, but Roskomnadzor unblocked the site in the same month, stating that nothing illegal was found on its pages. Notably, the "Instruction" is no longer posted on the site, and at least six additional Web pages with this text were blocked as well.

In the second half of November, at the request of the Prosecutor General, Roskomnadzor blocked work-way.com, the Web site of the Communist working class movement *Rabochy Put* (The Worker's Path) under the Lugovoi law for posting information about truckers' protests along with their location, schedule of the events and names of the organizers; the site also posted calls for participation in the strike. Access to the site was restored after removal of this information from its pages.

In November, the Watchtower Bible and Tract Society of New York (the US-registered parent structure of the Jehovah's Witnesses) submitted a complaint to the Russian Constitutional Court against the provisions of the federal laws on extremism and on information that formed the basis for the prohibition of the official Jehovah's Witnesses' Web site by the Tsentralny District Court of Tver in September 2013, confirmed by the Supreme court of the Russian Federation. Among other considerations, the Jehovah's Witnesses drew attention to the fact that Russian law allows for recognizing the entire site as extremist even if it features only a few materials deemed extremist. In a case involving Jehovah's Witnesses' Web site, the Supreme Court indicated that "partially" recognizing the site as extremist "leads to a threat of further dissemination" of extremist information through this site, despite the fact that the prohibited materials had already been removed by that time. In addition, the legislation does not specify cases in which entire Web sites should be prohibited by a court, cases in which a court ban should only affect individual pages, and cases which merit pre-trial restrictions. The Jehovah's Witnesses indicated that this legal uncertainty leads to discriminatory treatment, which violates constitutionally guaranteed rights and freedoms. The complaint also stated that Russian law does not provide a procedure for taking a Web site off the Uniform Register of Banned Web Sites and the Federal List of Extremist Materials, thus leading to violations of freedom of speech. The Constitutional Court rejected the complaint in December.[40] Important law enforcement questions raised in the complaint were not considered on the merits and have remained unanswered.

NOTES

1. The official name is "A list of community and religious associations and other non-profit organizations, with respect to which a court decision was made and entered into force on liquidation or ban on activities on the grounds stipulated by the Federal Law 'On Combating Extremist Activity.' "

2. For more details see: Viacheslav Likhachev, Right Sector and Others: Radical Nationalists and Ukrainian Political Crisis of Late 2013-Early 2014 // Russia Is Not Ukraine: Contemporary Accents of Nationalism (*Rossiya – Ne Ukraina: Sovremennye aktsenty natsionalisma*): Moscow: SOVA Center, 2014. pp. 230–275.

3. The Misanthropic Division association has existed since 2013 and supports Right Sector.

4. The organization is headed by Dmitry "Schultz" Bobrov. An inspection has shown that its representatives were "spreading the ideas of National Socialism, similar to the ideology of Nazi Germany, based on the exclusive status and superiority of a person on the grounds of their nationality or origin." Autonomous cells under the leadership of Dmitry Bobrov exist in the Kurgan Province and the Khanty-Mansiysk Autonomous Region-Yugra. In 2011, a court in Cherepovets already recognized a branch of the NSI as extremist.

5. Aleksandr Valov, who also headed the ultra-right association Pan-Slavic National Volunteer Association and organized the Russian Marches in Murmansk, is regarded as the club's founder.

6. Old Believers-Yngliings profess the idea of racial superiority, and the movement uses the swastika as its symbol. According to law enforcement data, the church supporters split into several separate groups with identical ideologies and organized branches in Mineralnye Vody, Yessentuki, Pyatigorsk, Georgievsk and Nevinnomyssk.
Previously, several Yngliing organizations were already eliminated as extremist.

7. Unfortunately, we do not have complete data in this case and are relying only on the facts presented in the media; our position could be updated.

8. The official name is "Unified federal list of organizations, including foreign and international organizations recognized as terrorist in accordance with the legislation of the Russian Federation."

9. Recognized as terrorist by the decision of the Moscow City Court of June 28, 2013; the decision entered into force on Nov. 27, 2013. For more details see: Vera Alperovich, Natalia Yudina. The State Duma Directed Right Radicals Toward New Goals: Xenophobia, Radical Nationalism and Efforts to Counteract It in Russia during the First Half of 2013 // SOVA Center. July 12, 2013 (http://www.sova-center.ru/racism-xenophobia/publications/2013/07/d27507/).

10. Recognized as terrorist by the decision of the Moscow City Court of Dec. 17, 2014; the decision entered into force on Dec. 30, 2014.

11. Recognized as terrorist by the decision of the Supreme Court of Russia of Dec. 29, 2014; the decision entered into force on Feb. 13, 2015.

12. Recognized as terrorist by the same decision as above.

13. Recognized as a terrorist organization by the decision of the Moscow City Court of Feb. 18, 2015; the decision went into force on Aug. 12, 2015.

14. For more details see: Court declared NOMP a terrorist organization. // SOVA Center. Feb. 18, 2015 (http://www.sova-center.ru/racism-xenophobia/news/counteraction/2015/02/d31308/).

15. Mikhail Volkov was sentenced to the term of 24 years for a series of racist attacks. Yury Tikhomirov was acquitted in the same case (in 2012, he was sentenced to ten years in prison for the murder of anti-fascist Ilya Dzhaparidze). More in: "The Verdict in the BORN case has been handed down" // SOVA Center. April 21, 2015 (http://www.sova-center.ru/racism-xenophobia/news/counteraction/2015/04/d31834/).

16. Ilya Goryachev receives a life sentence // SOVA Center. July 24,2015 (http://www.sova-center.ru/racism-xenophobia/news/counteraction/2015/07/d32496/).

17. Five people – under a combination of Arts. 282.1 (organizing an extremist community), 282, 116, 161 (robbery)
One person – under a combination of Arts. 116 and 282;
One person – under a combination of Arts. 282 and 359 (mercenary activity);
One person – under a combination of Arts. 280 and 318 (use of violence against a representative of the authorities);
One person – under a combination of Arts. 105 and 282 and 242.1 Part 2 of Criminal Code (demonstration of pornographic materials with images of minors);
Four people – under a combination of Arts. 205.2, 282, 213 and 150;
One person – under a combination of Arts. 282, 105, 111, 112, 214 and 243 (destruction or damage of monuments of history and culture);
One person – under a combination of Arts. 282, 105, 282.1 and 161;
One person – under a combination of Arts. 280, 282, 116 and 139 Part 1.

18. One person was convicted under a combination of Arts. 282, 244, 222 and 222.1;
Three people – under a combination of Arts. 282 and 354.1;
One person – under a combination of Arts. 282, 105, 111, 112, 214 and 243 (also included in the footnote above).

19. Not including the ones mentioned in the footnotes above.
Four people – under a combination of Arts. 282 and 222 (illegal storage of firearms);
Two people – under a combination of Arts. 280, 222 and 223;
One person – under a combination of Arts. 282 and 138.1 (illegal transfer of special hardware intended for private obtainment of information).

20. This was reflected in the sentence handed down in April in Nizhny Novgorod to 22-year-old citizen of Belarus Kirill Silivonchik for posting on his social media network page *photos and statements expressing his attitude toward the events in Ukraine, inciting to kill the Moskals, return the Crimea to Ukraine.* We doubt the appropriateness of this sentence. We also view his sentence of two years of settlement in a penal colony as excessive. For more information see: In Nizhny Novgorod, an Internet user was sentenced for incitement to terrorism // SOVA Center. April 15, 2015 (http://www.sova-center.ru/racism-xenophobia/news/counteraction/2015/04/d31796/).

21. On April 20, 2015, the Moscow District Military Court sentenced Boris Stomakhin under the Criminal Code Art. 205.2 to seven years in a penal colony. According to the prosecution, when kept in a pre-trial detention facility in Moscow, the journalist found out about the terror attacks in Volgograd and wrote the article "Or Blow Up a Couple of Railway Stations!," which was then posted in his blog on the portal lj.rossia.org. We view this sentence as excessive, not only because it was a punishment "for online publications," but also because the readership of Stomakhin's blog is known to be small. This was Stomakhin's third conviction.

22. A new criminal case against nationalist Nikolai Bondarik // SOVA Center. Dec. 30, 2015 (http://www.sova-center.ru/racism-xenophobia/news/counteraction/2015/12/d33583/).

23. S. Troitsky was convicted for two statements in the form of a single song – once for the concert and once for the video.

24. We do not include here clearly inappropriate sentences and verdicts against followers of Hizb ut-Tahrir, which will be covered in another report.

25. Participants "became acquainted with men of non-traditional sexual orientation" on the Internet, lured them to a meeting, and then beat up and tortured people, filmed their bullying on camera and posted it online. Altogether, they conducted 19 "actions." The officers of Center to Combat Extremism of the State Directorate of the Ministry of Internal Affairs of Russia in Sverdlovsk Province have found 11 people victimized by the actions. Four of them submitted statements in relation to five offenses. In November 2013, the leader of the organization, who was under recognizance not to leave, and another active member of the gang went into hiding, after which they were added to the federal wanted list. As a result, they were caught in Krasnodar Territory.

26. See An attack against Attack // SOVA Center. Oct. 30, 2014 (http://www.sova-center.ru/racism-xenophobia/news/counteraction/2014/10/d30556/).

27. The Attack Association case was returned to the prosecutor // SOVA Center. Dec. 25, 2015 (http://www.sova-center.ru/racism-xenophobia/news/counteraction/2015/12/d33543/).

28. A young man published materials about various activities of the club, such as meetings, marches, outings, etc. on a social media network page. Some of the published materials were xenophobic and contained images of Nazi symbols. He managed to recruit several residents of Kirov into the club.

29. FC Dynamo liquidated for extremism in Kirov // SOVA Center. July 5, 2013 (http://www.sova-center.ru/racism-xenophobia/news/counteraction/2013/07/d27476/).

30. His official title is "The chieftain of the 31st squadron of Cossack Forces "Horty Velesa," awarded the combat title of sub-yesaul."

31. The Ruling of the plenary meeting of the Supreme Court of the Russian Federation No. 1 "On Judicial Practice in Criminal Cases Regarding Crimes of Extremism" of June 28, 2011 // SOVA Center. June 29, 2011 (http://www.sova-center.ru/misuse/docs/2011/06/d21988/).

32. The list contains 3278 entries as of Feb. 13, 2016.

33. In March 2014, the Leninsky District Court banned virtually the entire library that was seized during the search at the Orenburg residence of Asylzhan Kelmukhambetov, who was convicted in June 2011 for the creation of a cell of banned Nurcular organization. The

Orenburg Province Court lifted the ban on some religious materials on Feb. 27, 2015. See: That's Enough Joking: the ban is lifted for 50 out of 68 religious materials deemed extremist in Orenburg // SOVA Center. Feb. 27, 2015 (http://www.sova-center.ru/misuse/news/persecution/2015/02/d31375/).

34. Videos "Angry Russia" (*Zlaya Rossiya*), "Cyborg – Glory of Russia" (*Kiborg – slava Rossii*), "Kolovrat – Our Country" (*Kolovrat – nasha strana*), "Instruction from Our Sisters" (*Nastavlenie sester*), the film *Russia with a Knife in Its Back 2* (*Rossiya s nozhom v spine – 2*), the Kavkaz-Jihad Web site, the book *History of the Prophets* (*Istoriya prorokov*) by Osman Nuri Topbaş, the book *The Red Kabbalah* (*Krasnaya Kabbala*) by Georgy Klimov.

35. See: Register of Banned Web Sites // Roskomsvoboda (http://reestr.rublacklist.net/).

36. See an updated list "Extremist resources in the Unified Register of Banned Web Sites // SOVA Center (http://www.sova-center.ru/racism-xenophobia/docs/2014/08/d30056/).

37. Full name: "On Amending the Federal Law 'On Information, Information Technologies and Protection of Information.'"

38. See: The updated list of resources in the register of Web sites blocked under the Lugovoi law // SOVA Center (http://www.sova-center.ru/racism-xenophobia/docs/2014/10/d30228/).

39. We view the provision of the Lugovoi law that demands blocking of information about activities conducted without permit as inappropriate, since the fact that the event is not permitted does not imply the grounds to ban information about it. The requirement to block posts on activities for which the authorities have not yet adopted any decision is even less legally appropriate.

40. Determination of the Constitutional Court of the Russian Federation to refuse to accept for consideration the complaint of the foreign organization Watchtower Bible and Tract Society of New York, Inc. against violation of constitutional rights and freedoms by Art. 1 Part 3 and Art. 13 of the Federal Law "On Countering Extremist Activities" as well as Art. 151 Part 5 Paragraph 2 of the Federal Law "On Information, Information Technologies and Information Protection" // Web site of the Constitutional Court of the Russian Federation. Dec. 22, 2015. (http://doc.ksrf.ru/decision/KSRFDecision221322.pdf).

Banning Organizations as Extremist

In 2016, 10 organizations were added to the Federal List of Extremist Organizations published on the Ministry of Justice Web site. This number is approximately the same as last year (when it was 11 organizations).

The following radical-right groups were added to the list in 2016: the TulaSkins Community Movement,[1] the "Russians" Ethno-Political Association,[2] the Russian National Union Attack,[3] the Community of Indigenous Russian People of Astrakhan, Astrakhan Province,[4] the *Volya* (Will) party, as well as its regional branches and other subdivisions.[5] For the first time in its existence, the list has come to contain a detailed description of an organization's flag and emblem (those of the Will Party). This was probably done in order to make it easier to invoke Art. 20.3 of the Code of Administrative Offenses, which concerns banned symbols.

Five religious organizations have been added to the list over the course of the year: Jehovah's Witnesses congregations in Stary Oskol, Belgorod,[6] Oryol,[7] and Elista,[8] and one Muslim organization, the "Mirmamed Mosque" prayer house.[9] The Mejlis of the Crimean Tatar People was also unlawfully banned (see below).

Aside from this, the list published on the FSB Web site of organizations recognized as terrorist has also been updated over the course of the year. Two international organizations have been added to it as entries No. 25 and 26: *Ajr of Allah subhanahu wa ta'ala SHAM* (The Blessing from Allah, Glory to Him, the Exalted SYRIA)[10] and the religious organization Aum Shinrikyo, AUM, Aleph.[11]

Criminal Prosecution

For Violence

In 2016, the number of convictions for violent hate crimes decreased compared to the previous year. In 2016, there were at least 19 convictions in

15 regions of Russia, where the courts recognized a hate motive (compared to 25 convictions in 19 regions in 2015). As a result of these court cases, 44 people were found guilty (compared to 61 people in 2015).

Art. 282 of the Criminal Code (incitement of hatred) figured in seven convictions for violent crimes (almost the same as last year). In all instances, this article was used in conjunction with other articles in large multiple-defendant trails or trials of members of ultra-right factions, such as members of the neo-Nazi gang 14/88 from Moscow or a Russian National Unity movement (*Russkoye Natsionalnoye Yedinstvo*, RNU) supporter in Omsk. In four cases, the incitement of hatred was invoked in connection with the calls for violence on the Internet that accompanied actual violence. In three cases, there were calls for xenophobic violence made during an attack in a public place.

The distributions of sentences in violent crime cases was as follows:

- One person was sentenced to 18 years' imprisonment;
- Two people were sentenced to up to 15 years' imprisonment;
- Seven people were sentenced to up to 10 years' imprisonment;
- Fourteen people were sentenced to up to five years' imprisonment;
- Nine people were sentenced to up to three years' imprisonment;
- Three people were sentenced to up to one year of imprisonment;
- Four people were given suspended sentences;
- Three people were sentenced to a fine;
- One person was released from punishment due to reconciliation with the victim.

Two people were additionally compelled to pay compensation for non-pecuniary damages. One of them was the neo-Nazi Andrei Malyugin, who received 18 years in prison for two hate-motivated murders. The court awarded compensation for non-pecuniary damages to the families of the victims: 1 million rubles to each family.

Of those convicted, 9% (four out of 44) received suspended sentences; this share is lower than a year earlier (44%). Three out of those who received suspended sentences were defendants in large group trials (some were minors). They include members of the aforementioned neo-Nazi group 14/88. Apparently, participation in the attacks could not be proved, or, perhaps, a deal had been made with the prosecution. The fourth case is that of a 17-year-old teenager who subjected a 15-year-old member of the "emo" subculture to battery in Vladimir.

Overall, the reduction in the number of suspended sentences for violent crimes is a positive trend. Our opinion, formed after many years of monitoring this sector, is that suspended sentences for violent racist attacks, in the overwhelming majority of cases, tend to engender a sense of impunity and do not stop ideologically motivated offenders from committing such acts in the future. For example, the aforementioned member of the Borovikov-Voyevodin group, Malyugin, was acquitted by a jury on June 14, 2011 (the case involved the entire gang). Soon after his release in August 2011, he was detained again because he almost immediately went on to commit two more murders. He was armed and resisted arrest.[12]

The majority of those convicted of violent offenses were still sentenced to various amounts of time in prison. Those who received prison sentences in 2016 included members of notable radical-right groups such as 14/88 and "Restruct!" (from Moscow), and the RNU (from Omsk).

For Crimes Against Property

In 2016, there were fewer convictions for ethno-religious and neo-Nazi motivated vandalism than a year earlier; the number of sentences proved to be the same as in 2014. We are aware of five sentencing decisions across five regions and six individual convicted offenders in 2016 (compared to eight sentencing decisions, seven regions and 14 offenders in 2015; four sentencing decisions, four regions and six offenders in 2014).

All four cases involved charges under Art. 214 of the Criminal Code (vandalism by reason of religious hatred). And only in one case, the case of adolescents from Vologda who defiled a mosque on Hitler's birthday, was Art. 282 of the Criminal Code invoked alongside Art. 214.

The two defilers of the mosque in Vologda were sentenced to corrective labor. Two more offenders were sentenced to restriction of liberty. These two were a vandal who cut down a wayside cross in Vyatskie Polyany, Kirov Region, and a resident of Vladimir who painted the emblem of the Azov Battalion (and wrote slogans) on a bridge across a river. Two more people were sent for compulsory medical treatment: a resident of Chelyabinsk Province who painted a swastika and symbols of the Azov Battalion on the monument to the Liberator Soldiers and a member of the Right Tatars society (*Pravye Tatary*) from Kazan, Emil Kamalov, who is accused of desecrating the church of the Savior Not Made by Hands and other acts of ideologically driven vandalism.

We do not wish to make judgements concerning the accuracy of the forensic and medical examinations conducted or draw conclusions about the mental state of the offenders. But we consider corrective labor and restriction of freedom quite adequate as punishment for the acts committed.

For Public Statements

The number of convictions for "speech of an extremist nature" (incitement to hatred, calls for extremist or terrorist activities, etc.) remained higher than the total number of all other extremism-related convictions. In 2016, no fewer than 181 such sentences were passed upon 198 people in 64 regions of the country. One may cautiously suggest that the number of convictions was still down on the year: In 2015, there were at least 204 such convictions, and 213 people were found guilty (plus one more person released due to remorseful actions) in 60 regions of the country. We are not counting the convictions that we consider unlawful, which are relatively few in number.

Interestingly, there were fewer public speech convictions in the second half of 2016, and their numbers dropped in the second half of the year compared to the first. (Also, notably fewer people were imprisoned for speech of an extremist nature.[13]) It is hard to tell what caused this drop in the activity of the law-enforcement agencies. The head of the international human rights organization "Agora" Pavel Chikov also noted that there has been a reduction in the number of politically motivated criminal cases. However, he points out that "one should not talk of an improvement, so much as of a slowing down of deterioration." He attributes this slowing down to the forthcoming presidential elections.[14] While we do not wish to make any judgements of a political nature, it is important to note that this is the first time since 2011 that our records have shown a year-on-year fall in convictions for public speech offenses. (Before 2011, there was also an overall upward trend, albeit with some year-on-year exceptions.)

It is possible that this slight drop did not reflect a real downward trend in such convictions but is rather an artefact of our incomplete data set. There is summary data[15] for combined convictions under Arts. 280, 280.1 (public calls for undermining the territorial integrity of the Russian Federation), 282, 282.1, 282.2 and 282.3 (financing of extremist activity) of the Criminal Code. Their number has grown compared to 2015 from 544 to 661 people.[16] Yet it is impossible to tell whether this growth is due to convictions for public speech offenses (Arts. 280, 280.1, 282 of the Criminal Code) or for participation in certain organizations and communities (Arts. 282.1, 282.2).

All the same, it may be asserted that the conviction rate for speech of an extremist nature has decreased or, at least, has not risen noticeably. This is in itself a contrast to the sharp increase in 2015 (up to 213 compared to 159 in 2014). Taking into account that the investigations in such cases usually last from six months to a year (and sometimes, of course, much longer), we can say that the slowdown in the launch of new criminal cases began back in the second half of 2015 and was clearly discernible by the first half of year 2016. It is likely that this is connected to the gradual relaxation of the general state of high alert triggered by the war in Ukraine and to the fact that the goals concerning the suppression of the ultra-right have largely been reached. One may also hope that the rising public outcry precipitated by the scale and nature of such recourse to criminal law has also played its role.

The majority of convictions (157 convictions, 173 offenders) were under Art. 282 of the Criminal Code. In 115 of the cases, this was the only article used in sentencing. In 22 convictions (of 22 offenders), only Art. 280 of the Criminal Code was used (public calls for extremist activity). In 16 cases, it was used in conjunction with Art. 282 of the Criminal Code.

In one case, the frequently used Art. 280 was combined with Art. 280.1 of the Criminal Code (public calls for undermining the territorial integrity of the Russian Federation). We are talking about the second sentencing of Andrei Bubeyev in Tver, which received considerable popular attention.

In one other case, Art. 354.1 Part 1 of the Criminal Code was called on (denial of facts established by the verdict of the International Military Tribunal for the trial and punishment of the major war criminals of the European Axis countries, approval of the crimes established by this verdict, as well as the dissemination of knowingly false information about the activities of the USSR during the years of World War II). In three cases, it was used in conjunction with Art. 282 of the Criminal Code; in one other case, with Arts. 282 and 280. So far, the new article seemed to have little impact on the severity of the punishment.

Arts. 282 and 280 of the Criminal Code may also have accompanied accusations under other articles, including those pertaining to acts of violence and vandalism (see sections Criminal Prosecution: For Violence and Criminal Prosecution: For Crimes Against Property).

In 10 sentencing decisions, Art. 205.2 of the Criminal Code was called on (public calls for terrorist activity). In two cases, Art. 205.2 was used on its own; in another six – in conjunction with Art. 282 of the Criminal Code; in two more, in conjunctions with Art. 280. As usual, in the majority of the cases (eight in total), this article was invoked in connection with radical Islamist statements, including statements pertaining to the war in Syria. Also similar to the previous year, there was one case where it was invoked in connection with anti-Russian statements connected to the events in Ukraine. The case involved a supporter of Right Sector.[17]

Some sentencing decisions warrant special consideration. Firstly, there is the sentence handed down in the case of one of the most notorious Russian nationalists, the de facto leader of the "Russians" movement and formerly the leader of the Movement Against Illegal Immigration (*Dvizhenie protiv nelegalnoi immigratsii*, MAII), Aleksandr Belov (Potkin). Belov was found guilty under Arts. 282, 280 and 282.1 of the Criminal Code, and Art. 174 (the legalization (laundering) of funds and other property acquired by other persons illegally). He was sentenced to a total of seven and a half years in a general-regime penal colony. Political activists and human rights activists reacted rather equivocally to Belov's case. In July 2015, the Union of Solidarity with Political Prisoners (*Soyuz solidarnosti s politzakliuchennymi*) recognized Belov as a political prisoner. At the same time, Belov was absent from the political prisoner list of the "Memorial" Human Rights Center. SOVA Center does not maintain any kind of a register of political prisoners; however, we do not believe that Belov may be considered a political prisoner for the reasons cited by the Union of Solidarity with Political Prisoners.[18] Yet, it seems fair to say that such a sentence is excessive for crimes of a non-violent nature. However, it seems that the bulk of Belov's prison term is not for xenophobic actions but for financial machinations,[19] a class of crimes typically punished by long sentences.

Another case that warrants attention is the sentencing of the schoolboy Kirill Benetsky by the Moscow District Military Court under Arts. 280 and 208 of the Criminal Code (aiding and abetting participation in an armed formation). While still a minor, the schoolboy made three social media posts containing calls for extremist action. On reaching majority, he travelled to Ukraine and joined. According to the investigators, Benetsky received general physical training, training in sabotage and ideological training, after which he joined the ranks of an illegal armed formation.[20] Fearing for his life, he fled Right Sector in April 2016 and was detained by law enforcement agencies in Bryansk Province on May 1. Benetsky was sentenced to six and a half years in a strict-regime penal colony. This was later commuted to six years and four months.

Another "aiding and abetting" sentence under Art. 208 of the Criminal Code (unaccompanied by any addition extremism-related charges) was imposed on the former member of NS/WP Nevograd, Kirill "Vegan" Prisiazhniuk. In December 2016, a court in Chechnya sentenced the former neo-Nazi to four years in prison. Earlier, in June 2014, he was sentenced to three years' imprisonment under Art. 33; Art. 105, Part 2, Paragraphs "a," "g" and "k"; Art. 282, Part 2, Paragraphs "1" and "c"; and Art. 213, Part 2 of the Criminal Code. He had been recruited by the Islamic State in the Kresty Prison, St. Petersburg. According to a cellmate who is the former leader of a neo-Nazi organization, Anton K., "He listened to music by Timur Mutsurayev, was inspired by fighters and so on.... He tattooed a Jihadi banner on his leg...."[21] When Prisiazhniuk left prison, he travelled to the Caucasus, where he married a Muslim woman and became a recruiter for the Islamic State. In particular, he helped one Larisa Abubakarova to travel to Syria. He later tried to travel to Syria himself but was apprehended at the border on Dec. 3, 2015.[22]

The distribution of sentences was as follows:

- Thirty-nine people received prison sentences;
- Eighty-two people received suspended sentences with no additional punishment;
- Twenty people were fined various amounts;
- Twelve people were sentenced to corrective labor;
- Thirty-seven people were sentenced to mandatory labor;
- Two people received suspended corrective labor sentences;
- Two people were sentenced to educational intervention;
- Two people were sent for compulsory treatment;
- Two people were released due to the statute of limitations.

The majority of the 39 people who had received prison sentences were convicted on multiple charges. Thus, in conjunction with public speech offenses, they would also have been charged under articles pertaining to violence, vandalism, theft, or drug possession and sentenced accordingly.

The prison terms may also have reflected earlier suspended sentences. Or, alternatively, the offender may already have been in prison and had his term increased.

Three people were convicted of repeat offenses involving "speech of an extremist nature," which substantially lengthens the prison term. Two had earlier convictions but had not yet started the prison terms they had been sentenced to. Among those who received repeat convictions was Andrei Bubeyev as well as a 30-year-old singer from Kostroma who was convicted under Art. 280 for the performance of a song that incited violence.

Heavier sentences were imposed under Art. 205.2 of the Criminal Code. These were all handed down for incitement of a radical Islamist nature: the publication of video clips or texts on the Internet calling for a "holy war" or prompting the reader/viewer to join the ranks of the jihadists. Five people from Syktyvkar, Maritime Territory, Sochi, Ust-Labinsk and Moscow were convicted in a joint case under Art. 205.2, Part 1 and Art. 282, Part 1. Their sentences ranged from 10 months to four and a half years in prison.

Five more people were convicted or sentenced without a jihadist context (or where such context is unknown to us). These sentences were imposed for the publication of the xenophobic audio and video clips "The Execution of a Tajik and a Dagestani" and "Argentine – Sex, Fight" and some unnamed materials containing calls for violence in Volgograd and Vladimir Province, Mari El Republic, and Altai Territory. All materials were published on the VKontakte social media network. To us, the sentences seem unreasonably harsh.

The share of suspended sentences, in comparison to the previous year, has risen to 41% (82 out of 198 offenders), 7% more than the year before (34%). More of those convicted (73 people) were sentenced to corrective, compulsory or educational labor or fines that do not involve imprisonment. It is unfortunate that the proportion of such sentences has fallen in comparison to 2015.

At least two sentences last year involved a ban on practicing a profession. These concerned a schoolteacher and an unarmed combat coach in a children's club. We consider these sentencing decisions justified, given that one involves racist statements made in the presence of minors, among whom may be children with various ethnic backgrounds. Such statements may provoke bullying or, in the case of a martial arts club, actual physical attacks.

In no fewer than ten cases, the offenders were banned from speaking in mass media, on the Internet, and during mass-participation public events.

Aside from this, we know of five more cases where the sentence involved a ban on Internet use for a given period of time. We see such a measure as, to say the least, strange. Firstly, the Internet may be necessary for work and everyday life. Secondly, it is far from clear how such a ban could be practically enforced.

Progressively more often we hear about confiscation of the "tools of crime," i.e., laptops, tablets, smart phones, etc. – devices used by the offenders to upload the "heretical" materials. These devices often cost far more than the total sum of all the fines imposed by the court. We see this measure as clearly excessive.

Similar to every year, the majority of convictions – 167 out of 198, or 84% (about the same as in 2014-2015) – relate to materials uploaded onto the Internet.

Such materials were found in:

- Social media – 152 cases (of which 102 were on VKontakte and 50 on other, unspecified social media – possibly also VKontakte);
- Internet forums – one;
- Internet-based mass media – one;
- Unspecified locations on the Internet – 13.

This trend has remained unchanged these past five years.[23]

We are talking about materials of the following types (several of which may coexist under one account or even on one page):

- Video clips – 70;
- Images (drawings, photographs, memes) – 59;
- Audio (songs) – 38;
- Texts (including republication of books) – 58;
- Quotes and comments (on social media and forums) – 15;
- Creation and administration of neo-Nazi groups – three;
- Unknown – 24.

Starting from 2012 and even more so from autumn 2014, the state has been actively prosecuting right-wing radicals for actionable speech offenses, even if sometimes on trivial grounds. In March 2016, the Kirovsky Court of St. Petersburg convicted Dina Garina, the leader of the ultra-right movement "Russians of St. Petersburg." She was given a suspended sentence for posting calls for violence against people from Dagestan on a social media network. In September 2016, a suspended sentence was imposed under Art. 282, Part 1 of the Criminal Code in Moscow upon the former leader of Russian Fascist Order Memory and the head of the Nation and Freedom Committee (*Komitet "Natsiya i svoboda"*, NFC) Moscow branch Vladimir (Ratnikov) Komarnitsky.

There were slightly more convictions for offline speech offenses than in the previous year (31). Their distribution is as follows:

- Delivering lectures – one;
- Reading a book aloud at a place of work – one;
- Directing a youth group (inflammatory speech) – two;
- Agitation in prison (appeals to cellmates) – one;
- Publication of books – two;
- Words shouted during an attack – three;
- Isolated inflammatory actions (exact nature unknown) carried out by leaders and members of ultra-right groups – two;
- Public insults in the street – two;
- Speech at a rally – one;
- Leafleting – five;
- Graffiti – six;
- Stickers – three;
- Writing of articles – one;
- Public performance of a song – one.

For Participation in Extremist and Banned Groups and Organizations

In 2016, prosecutions of the ultra-right under Art. 282.1 (organizing an extremist community) and 282.2 (organizing the activity of an extremist organization) of the Criminal Code were somewhat less of a feature than they were in 2015. We know of six such verdicts involving 19 people in six regions of the country[24] (compared to 10 verdicts involving 10 people in eight regions in 2015).

Art. 282.1 of the Criminal Code figured in three cases and was, quite justifiably, applied to the founders and members of ultra-right organizations.

In Orenburg Province, four young people from Orsk and Novotroitsk were sentenced to various prison terms under Art. 282.1, Parts 1 and 2;

Art. 282, Part 2, Paragraphs "a" and "c"; and Art. 111, Part 2, Paragraph "f." In 2010, two members of the ultra-right created a group in Orsk. The group was later joined by two more people from Orenburg Province. On Nov. 18, 2011, members of the group armed with a bat and a knife subjected a person of "non-Slavic appearance" to battery.

In Shadrinsk, Kurgan Province, five members of the White Wolves group (*Belye Volki*) were convicted. According to the investigators, a man from the city of Kurgan found "like-minded individuals" in Shadrinsk and created the White Wolves group in 2014. Between May and November 2014, the accused had drawn xenophobic graffiti on buildings, published calls for violence on social media, and, in August 2014, set fire to a cafe belonging to a man from Azerbaijan. The leader of the movement was convicted under Art. 282.1, Part 1 of the Criminal Code (alongside other articles) and given a suspended five-year prison term, along with restriction of liberty for one year, a probation term of two years and six months, a three-year ban on activities connected to setting up public organizations, and a one year ban on putting any materials whatsoever on the Internet or disseminating them via mass media, as well as on organizing public events. The others also received suspended prison sentences under various other articles.

In Moscow, the Zyuzino District Court passed a sentence under Art. 282.1, Part 2; Art. 282, Part 1; and Art. 222 of the Criminal Code (illegal acquisition, transfer, sale, storage, transportation, or bearing of firearms, their basic parts, ammunition, explosives, and explosive devices) on 10 members of Attack, a splinter group of the well-known neo-Nazi organization "Restruct!" They received suspended prison sentences.[25]

In the remaining three cases, Art. 282.2 of the Criminal Code was invoked (organizing the activity of an extremist organization).

In Omsk, a 59-year-old activist from RNU,[26] Aleksandr Krasnoperov, was convicted under Art. 105, Art. 280, Art. 282, and Art. 282.2, Part 1.1 of the Criminal Code. Krasnoperov was accused of the murder of another member of the ultra-right, the 19-year-old activist from Russian Runs and Sober Yards (*Trezvye Dvory*), Ilya Zhuravlev. Krasnoperov was the administrator of the RNU page on social media, where between 2009 and 2015 he had uploaded materials containing calls for racist violence and encouraging anyone who might be interested to join the RNU. He also conducted gatherings of RNU members at his flat. The court sentenced him to 10 years in a strict-regime penal colony.

In Nevinnomyssk, Stavropol Province, a student at an industrial college, Artyom Deykun, was convicted under Art. 282.2 of the Criminal Code. Between December 2015 and January 2016, Deykun had, in person and via his page on the social media network VKontakte, called on people to join the Misanthropic Division.[27] The court found Deykun guilty and sentenced him to a suspended three-year prison term and a further one year of restriction of liberty, with a three-year probationary period.

Finally, as has become traditional, Art. 282.2 of the Criminal Code was invoked in the conviction of yet another member of the neopagan organization the Spiritual and Tribal Rus Sovereignty. In February 2016, in the town of Yemanzhelinsk, Chelyabinsk Province, the court fined one of the members of this organization 50,000 rubles for writing letters to law-enforcement agencies and other official agencies containing information about the activities of his organization. This practice of "self-incrimination" is typical of the Spiritual and Tribal Rus Sovereignty.

Inappropriate Prosecution of Political and Civic Activists

The "Ukrainian Question"

The Russian authorities continue to use anti-extremist legislation against actions and statements related to the crisis in Ukraine. The specifics of the situation are not being taken into account. Anti-extremist legislation was written for use in peacetime – it is not adequate for a situation of military operations and does not take into account the intensity of emotion in Russian society, which painfully sensitive to the conflict with Ukraine, to which it has very close ties. In addition, some articles of the Criminal Code, such as Art. 280.1 on incitement to separatism, are used explicitly to pressure those critical of, for example, the annexation of the Crimea. As a result, the number of inappropriate prosecutions in connection with the "Ukrainian Question" remains high.

In March 2016, the Donetsk City Court of Rostov Province found Ukrainian pilot Nadezhda Savchenko guilty, including under Art. 105 Part 2 Paragraphs "a," "f," "g" and "k" of the Criminal Code (murder of two or more people committed by a group of people by previous agreement or an organized group, by a generally dangerous method, and based on hatred or enmity toward a social group) and sentenced her to a total of 22 years in a minimum-security colony and a fine of 30,000 rubles.[28] The indictment in Savchenko's case defined the social group toward whom hatred had supposedly motivated the pilot, as "the civilian population of Luhansk Province (Ukraine)" in connection with its "refusal to recognize the legitimacy of the current government in Ukraine and desire to create a separate territorial entity – the Luhansk People's Republic." The court accepted this qualification, but we believe that the actions that constituted the basis of charges against Savchenko took place under the military conditions, even though the war was not officially declared, and therefore they could be qualified only as a war crime, for which the provisions of Section VII of the Criminal Code, which pertain to peacetime conditions, are not applicable. Constructing an arbitrary social group, as was done in the indictment, transfers any war crime directed against civilians to the category of hate crimes; this is incorrect in principle.

The Kievsky District Court of Simferopol sentenced Ukrainian citizen Andrei Kolomiets to 10 years of imprisonment in a maximum-security colony in June 2016. Kolomiets was found guilty of committing crimes under Art. 30 Part 3 and Art. 105 Part 2 Paragraphs "a," "b," "f" and "j" (attempted murder of two people in connection with the discharge of their official duties, committed by a generally dangerous method, based on political or ideological hatred) and Art. 228 Part 2 (illegal acquisition, storage and transportation without the purpose of selling parts of plants containing narcotic drugs on a large scale). The court found Kolomiets guilty of the attempted murder of two employees of the Crimean Berkut Special Forces unit committed during clashes on Independence Square in Kiev in January 2014, when he attacked them with Molotov cocktails, being a member of the Ukrainian Insurgent Army (UPA), recognized in Russia as an extremist organization. In addition, he was involved in the storage and transportation of a narcotic plant on a large scale in Kabardino-Balkaria in 2015. In our opinion, Kolomiets's sentence under Art. 105 of the Criminal Code was imposed inappropriately. If a Ukrainian citizen actually threw Molotov cocktails on Ukrainian territory targeting other Ukrainian (at the time) citizens, Ukraine could have initiated a criminal case against him and asked the Russian authorities to facilitate the investigation. Acting on their own initiative, Russian law enforcement agencies have overstepped their jurisdiction.

Igor Stenin, the leader of the "Russians" of Astrakhan movement, was sentenced to two years in a penal colony under Art. 280 Part 2 of the Criminal Code in May 2016 (the verdict was upheld by the Astrakhan City

Court in July; Stenin subsequently filed a complaint with the ECHR). Stenin was found guilty of publishing an entry on the subject of the war in Ukraine on VKontakte; he also was charged for a comment left by another user. In our opinion, the short post cited in the court case, which called for the destruction of "the Kremlin invaders," can't be considered an incitement to extremist activity. The collective image of "the Kremlin invaders," used in the preceding years by disgruntled citizens to denote the authorities has obviously received even broader and less specific connotations in connection with the events in Ukraine. It is impossible to interpret this figure of speech as a direct call for violence against members of a particular social group, and previously the police had never prosecuted citizens for this popular slogan, not attaching much importance to it. Even if the statement is interpreted it as a call to action against the Russian authorities, it still pertains to activities outside Russian territory. The unjustified severity of Stenin's sentence – two years of real prison – should also be noted; he was soon transferred from a settlement colony to a minimum-security penal colony.

In the same month, the Zavolzhsky District Court of Tver sentenced local resident Andrei Bubeyev to two years in prison in a settlement colony. The criminal charges against him for public calls for extremist activity via the Internet (Art. 280 Part 2) and public calls for undermining the territorial integrity of the Russian Federation (Art. 280.1 Part 2) were brought in September 2015 for sharing on his VKontakte page Boris Stomakhin's article about the Crimea and an image of a hand that squeezes the toothpaste out of its tube with the caption "Squeeze Russia out of yourself," accompanied by the statement that the only possible form of protest had to involve the "active destruction" of Russia "as the Chechens did at one point, for example." The materials published by Bubeyev did indeed contain aggressive appeals, but we view the verdict against Bubeyev under Art. 280.1 as inappropriate, because criticism of Russia's new territorial acquisitions should not be equated to separatism. Bubeyev's defense appealed to the ECHR.

In February 2016, the Zheleznodorozhny District Court of Yekaterinburg found housewife Yekaterina Vologzheninova guilty of inciting hatred and enmity toward the authorities and "volunteers from Russia fighting on the side of the militias in Eastern Ukraine" (Art. 282 Part 1 of the Criminal Code) and sentenced her to 320 hours of mandatory labor with confiscation and destruction of her laptop and computer mouse. The prosecution was based on several posts shared via VKontakte social media network. Law enforcement based the charges on the following publications: *The Katsaps* poem by Anatoly Marushkevich, images styled to resemble World War II posters with the statements "Stop the Plague" and "Death to Muscovite Invaders," and three additional materials (texts exhibiting varying degrees of radicalism). The principal message of *The Katsaps* is that ethnic Russians living in Ukraine will defend it from Russia; the poem accuses the Russian authorities of attacking Ukraine but contains no aggressive appeals. As for the posters, they were obviously addressed to the Ukrainian citizens, urging them to defend their country from the occupation. From our point of view, the hostile feelings of the authors of such posts and probably of those sharing them, pertain to the activity of a certain group of citizens, rather than ethnic, religious, sexual or social affiliation of such a group, so these publications can't be qualified under Art. 282. In addition, we question the expediency of prosecuting a person for appeals addressed to citizens or authorities of another country.

Vyacheslav Kuteynikov, a retired sailor and a popular blogger, received a suspended two-year sentence and three years of probation under Art. 282 Part 1 in Rostov-on-Don in October 2016. The court found Kuteynikov guilty of publishing information aimed at inciting hatred against Russians on social media, specifically on LiveJournal. His verdict has entered into force. Kuteynikov had criticized, in harsh terms, the anti-Ukrainian propaganda campaign waged on Russian television. The context of the statements indicated that Kuteynikov applied his derogatory characteristics not to the Russian people overall, but to participants of the information war with Ukraine, and his invectives contained no incitement to violence.

In May 2016, the Sevastopol Investigation Department of the Russian Federation Investigative Committee opened a criminal case under Art. 282 Part 1 (incitement of hatred or hostility, and violation of human dignity) in relation to the substituted national anthem played at the opening meeting of the Public Expert Council under the Governor of Sevastopol on April 8, 2016. The attendees of the event heard a satirical version of the Russian national anthem, "Russia, Our Mad Nation." The organizers explained the incident as a mistake by the sound engineers, who had downloaded a wrong version from the Internet. Initially, the city authorities urged the community to avoid unnecessary dramatization of the situation and not to inflate the scandal around the occurrence. However, in their eagerness to utilize anti-extremist articles of the Criminal Code newly available to them, the Crimean law enforcement agencies could not resist and ignore even this minor comic incident. From our point of view, a criminal case under Art. 282 was unfounded in this instance, because the satirical version of the anthem contained no signs of inciting hatred toward anyone, and criticism of the state does not fall under Art. 282 or any other articles of the Russian legislation. We have no further information on the fate of this criminal investigation.

In March 2016, Minusinsk resident G. Nazimov was sentenced to 10 months of corrective labor under Art. 354.1 Part 3 of the Criminal Code (public desecration of the symbols of Russia's military glory) for posting on his VKontakte page a captioned image that was interpreted by law enforcement as an insult against the St. George ribbon. However, the offender obviously viewed the St. George ribbon as a symbol used by one of the sides of the Ukrainian conflict and not as a symbol of Soviet military glory of the Great Patriotic War.

Nationalist Vladimir Luzgin from Perm was fined 200,000 rubles by the province court in September 2016 under Part 1 of the same Art. 354.1 (denial of facts established by the verdict of the International Military Tribunal for the trial and punishment of the major war criminals of the European Axis countries, approval of the crimes established by this verdict, as well as the dissemination of knowingly false information about the activities of the USSR during the years of World War II) for sharing articles that contained a debatable interpretation of the Molotov-Ribbentrop Pact, as well as controversial statements relating to episodes of the history of the Bandera movement. The verdict was upheld by the Supreme Court of Russia, and Luzgin has appealed to the ECHR.

We know of at least five inappropriate court decisions handed down in 2016 under Art. 20.3 of the Code of Administrative Offenses for online display of Nazi symbols in the context of polemics related to the events in Ukraine. Since designating the opposite side of the conflict as "fascists" is quite common and was even encouraged by the official propaganda in Russia, social media network users actively utilize the Nazi symbols in order to vilify their ideological opponents. At the same time, Russian law enforcement agencies tend to punish any display of Nazi symbols regardless of the context. As a result, fines are issued to critics of Russian politics in Ukraine, to opponents of the Ukrainian authorities, and to supporters of the Donetsk and Luhansk republics (LPR/DPR). Nina Solovyova, an LGBT activist from Krasnodar, was sentenced to ten days of administrative detention for publishing the video of the song "This is Rashism, Baby" by

Boris Sevastyanov on social media. The video does show swastikas, since it includes a number of snippets from Third Reich newsreels.

In May, artist Pyotr Pavlensky was convicted under Art. 214 Part 2 of the Criminal Code (vandalism committed by a group of people by prior agreement) for his "Freedom" demonstration in St. Petersburg. He was sentenced to one year and four months of restriction of liberty but was released from punishment due to the statute of limitations for criminal responsibility. In February 2014, five participants of the "Freedom" demonstration in support of the Ukrainian Euromaidan unfurled a black flag and the state flag of Ukraine on Maly Konyushenny Bridge opposite the Church of the Savior on Blood; they also set on fire a number of automobile tires and banged on metal sheets with sticks. Despite the absence of a hate motive in the charges against Pavlensky, we believe that he was de facto sentenced for his ideological action, so we are discussing his case here and include it in our statistics. We consider his conviction inappropriate due to the absence of a crime in the act. First, the demonstration caused no property damage (the worst damage caused by the demonstrators consisted of some burn marks on the pavement), i.e., it did not meet the Criminal Code definition of vandalism. Additionally, Pavlensky had already faced administrative responsibility for the same offense, and double jeopardy is not acceptable.

In April 2016, the Supreme Court recognized the Mejlis of the Crimean Tatar People as an extremist organization and banned its activities. The Supreme Court of Russia upheld this decision in September. The request for the ban of the Mejlis was filed by the Crimean Prosecutor's Office in February 2016. The prosecutor's office cited a number of statements and actions by the leaders and members of the Mejlis as reasons for banning the Crimean Tatar organization, beginning with the adoption of the Declaration on the National Sovereignty of the Crimean Tatar people in 1991 and ending with participation in the transport blockade of Crimea. The majority of the actions with participation by Mejlis members mentioned by the prosecutor's office, took place before Crimea's transition to Russia and do not fall under the jurisdiction of the Russian court at all. The remarks of the Head of the Mejlis Refat Chubarov, which became the basis for a criminal case against him under separatism charges and were cited by the prosecutor's office as an argument in favor of eliminating the organization, contained no direct incitement to war for liberation of the peninsula as far as we could tell. The blockade of the Crimea from the Ukrainian side attributed to some members of the Mejlis was indeed an illegal action, but it was carried out on the territory of another state and was unrelated to the operation of the Mejlis as an organization on Crimean territory. Overall, the evidence of the organization's involvement in extremist activity presented by the prosecutor's office was not considered in detail or weighed by the court; the decision to close down the Mejlis was promptly pronounced because it was dictated not by the actual activities of the organization but by political motives openly stated by Crimean Prosecutor General Natalia Poklonskaya. In our opinion, this decision is not only inappropriate but also politically reckless since it could potentially provoke an aggravation of ethnic tensions on the peninsula.

In 2016, Russian law enforcement authorities continued to block Ukrainian resources (as well as Web sites that had relocated to Ukraine after the annexation of the Crimea and the beginning of the armed conflict) under the Lugovoi law. The reasons for limiting access to these resources are often quite obvious, since verbal activity in a situation of armed conflict typically contains appeals to destroy the enemy, but analytics or information materials have occasionally been blocked as well. In this regard, our position has remained the same – we consider such restrictions to be part of the ongoing information war between the two countries. We believe that evaluating them from the standpoint of following the rules of peacetime is pointless.

Other Cases of "Separatism"

In 2016, two new criminal cases unrelated to Ukraine were initiated without proper justification under the article on separatism.

In particular, it was reported in July that the Moscow FSB had opened a criminal case under Arts. 280.1 and 282 of the Criminal Code based on the post "A Bomb Ready to Explode" published by journalist Andrei Piontkovsky on his blog on the Echo of Moscow Web site in January 2016. According to the FSB, the article contained calls for "violation of the territorial integrity of Russia and actions aimed at inciting hatred and hostility based on ethnicity." We have no information whether Piontkovsky was ever charged as a defendant in this case. The publicist had left Russia even before the case was initiated. "A Bomb Ready to Explode" focused on the crisis in relations between the Russian and Chechen peoples. Originally, the text ended with the statement that, in order to avoid a catastrophe, Chechnya should be granted full independence, but these words were removed at some point after the publication of the text. In our view, calls for violent separatism are the only ones that merit prosecution, and Piontkovsky's post contained no such calls. Furthermore, we found the text to contain no statements inciting hatred on ethnic grounds. The case has never been solved.

For "Justification of Terrorism"

In December 2016, the visiting session of Privolzhsky District Military Court in Tyumen found blogger Aleksei Kungurov – a former member of Igor Strelkov's Committee of 25 – guilty of justifying terrorism (Art. 205.2 Part 1 of the Criminal Code). Kungurov faced responsibility for the text "Who Putin's Falcons Are Really Bombing," which was posted on his personal blog. According to Kungurov, the FSB objected to his allegations that Russia was actually helping the Islamic State rather than bombing it. We view Kungurov's verdict as inappropriate. The article "Who Putin's Falcons Are Really Bombing" contains an analysis of the situation in the Middle East and, in our opinion, includes no incitement to terrorism.

For Incitement of Hatred Toward Public Officials

We view criminal prosecution under Art. 282 of the Criminal Code on charges of inciting hatred toward the social group of public officials as inappropriate, since this social group can't be considered vulnerable and, in our opinion, anti-extremist articles should specifically protect vulnerable groups (such as people with disabilities, homeless people, sexual minorities, etc.), and this clarification needs to be included in the law so that its abuses, associated with an expanded interpretation of the nebulous term "social group," can be avoided.

A criminal case from this category was opened in April against Olga Li, a deputy of the Kursk Regional Duma. She was charged with incitement of hatred or hostility and violation of human dignity on the basis of membership in the social group "government representatives, particularly law enforcement officials and the judiciary" based on the text of her appeal to President Putin, which was publicly accessible on Li's page on VKontakte, and on videos of her speeches published elsewhere online. Li's statements contained harsh criticism of the authorities' foreign and domestic policies as well as accusations against certain government officials in Kursk Province of embezzlement and other offenses, but no dangerous incitement. In October, the investigation against Li under Art. 282 of the Criminal Code was dropped.

In February 2016, criminal charges under Art. 282 Part 2 Paragraph "b" (actions aimed at inciting hatred or hostility committed with the use of official position) were brought against well-known religious scholar Rais Suleimanov of Kazan. Law enforcement objected to the materials published by Suleimanov – an expert of the Institute of National Strategy – on VKontakte, Facebook and a number of other Web sites. The decision to open criminal proceedings stated that, from 2011 to 2016, the expert published materials testifying to "the alleged presence of underground radical Islamist gangs and active groups of ethnic separatists in the Republic of Tatarstan and the support shown to them by a large number of Muslims and Tatars and by the clergy and some officials of the republic" and also spoke of ongoing "mass persecution" against Russian residents of Tatarstan and the "propaganda of Tatar national exclusiveness" in the republic. We believe that estimating the popularity of the radical currents of Islam in Tatarstan or criticism against the ethnic policy of the republic's leadership in and of itself cannot be regarded as extremist statements, and prosecution based on expressing opinions on these topics can be regarded as an attack against freedom of speech. At the same time, as we noted earlier, certain statements by Suleimanov really have the potential to stir up hatred against peaceful representatives of "non-traditional" religious movements. In this regard, we find it difficult to assess the appropriateness of criminal prosecution against Suleimanov. In any case, the criminal case against him was dropped in July 2016.

Other Abuse of Criminalization of Incitement to Hatred

Several verdicts handed down by the Russian courts in 2016 for incitement of all kinds of hatred give us reasons to doubt the expedience of criminal prosecution in these cases. We readily concede that the share of such sentences among the verdicts handed down under Art. 282 of the Criminal Code in 2016 could be, in fact, much larger, and we simply lack the necessary information to assess the extent of their legitimacy. However, we have repeatedly said that the scale of prosecution against citizens under this article (and for public utterances overall) raises serious concerns.

The Zelenograd District Court in Moscow sentenced previously convicted 20-year-old Yevgeny Kort to a year of imprisonment in a settlement colony under Art. 282 Part 1 of the Criminal Code (incitement to ethnic hatred) in November 2016. Kort was charged with publishing a collage that included neo-Nazi Maksim "Tesak" Martsinkevich and a man resembling Aleksandr Pushkin on VKontakte. The image depicts Tesak pressing Pushkin against the wall; the action is accompanied by an offensive xenophobic comment. The investigation found that the image contained a "set of psychological and linguistic indicators of denigrating non-Russians." The defendant argued that he had not published the image but was merely keeping it in an album on his social media network page, but technically there is no difference between saving and posting. We view the criminal prosecution for publishing a single image, the content of which allows for various interpretations, as inappropriate, and the punishment as disproportionately harsh. Kort appealed the verdict, and the Moscow City Court softened the sentence to a fine of 200,000 rubles in January 2017.

In February, the Kirov District Court of Yekaterinburg found Semyon Tykman, a teacher in Or Avner Jewish Gymnasium, guilty of inciting hatred; the verdict was upheld by the Sverdlovsk Province Court in June. Tykman was sentenced to a fine of 200,000 rubles and released from punishment due to the statute of limitations. The case was opened based on claims filed with the Prosecutor's Office by the parents of two students in the school. According to the girls, in the winter of 2013, Tykman instructed them to spit in the direction of Orthodox churches when walking past them, as he was doing; he also argued that all the Germans should be annihilated for what they did to the Jews during World War II. During the trial, the only evidence against Tykman consisted of the records of FSB employees interviewing two minors – of questionable reliability, since the two texts were almost identical. Tykman has never admitted his guilt and expressed his readiness to appeal his sentence all the way up to the European Court of Human Rights.

In July, the Elista City Court of the Republic of Kalmykia handed down its verdict against Said Osmanov, who had desecrated a statue of Buddha. Osmanov was found guilty under Art. 148 Part 2 of the Criminal Code and Part 1 Art. 282 of the Criminal Code (incitement of ethnic hatred or enmity). The court gave him a suspended sentence of two years' imprisonment with a one-year probation. In spring 2016, Osmanov, a Dagestani athlete who arrived in Elista for a freestyle wrestling competition, entered a Buddhist temple at night along with teammates, urinated there and kicked a Buddha statue in the nose with his foot. Osmanov published a video recording of his vandalism on the Internet. We do not deny Osmanov's guilt; however, we doubt the appropriateness of the verdict with regard to incitement to ethnic hatred, since neither the media nor law enforcement in reports mention any statements made by Osmanov during his action in the Buddhist temple.

In early August, we learned about the verdict against Mukhidin Yusupov under Art. 280 Part 1 (public calls for extremist activity) and Art. 282 Part 1. Yusupov was sentenced to four years in a penal colony, with a two-year ban on serving in any public or political official position, for the crimes of inciting his inmates in a Moscow jail to participate in the religious struggle in Syria and making statements that incited hatred of the police. We consider Yusupov's verdict at least partially inappropriate. First, we don't view the police as a vulnerable population group in need of protection against acts of hatred under Art. 282 (this consideration is applicable to a number of other cases reported below), and next, we believe that Yusupov's statements in the presence of three fellow inmates can hardly be considered public.

In October, the Presnensky Court of Moscow found blogger and media manager Anton Nossik guilty under Art. 282 Part 1 of the Criminal Code (incitement of ethnic hatred) for publishing the post "Erase Syria from the Face of the Earth" on his LiveJournal blog in October 2015. Nossik was sentenced to a fine of 500,000 rubles; the defense appealed the verdict, and the Moscow State Court reduced the fine to 300,000 rubles in December. Nossik, however, continues to fight against the verdict, and he has filed an appeal with the European Court of Human Rights. In his post, Nossik called for the carpet-bombing of Syrian territory to the point of complete destruction of the civilian infrastructure of the country and praised the killing of civilians, including children, as well-deserved. We believe that Nossik's statements really contained the calls for gross violations of humanitarian law, in fact, for war crimes, as well as statements about the inferiority of Syrians, and therefore could incite hostility toward these people as a group. However, in our opinion, the criminal prosecution against the blogger was unnecessary, since his statements presented very little social danger – hostility toward Syrians is far from widespread in Russian society, and as for his calls for carpet-bombing, they were addressed to the governments of various countries, and Nossik's opinion has no effect on their decisions.

The Nakhimovsky District Court of Sevastopol handed down a 2-year suspended sentence to local resident Vitaly Slavikovsky under Art. 282 Part 1 in January. He was found guilty of incitement to hatred against members of particular ethnic groups as well as against fans of FC Spartak Moscow for posting materials on VKontakte. We view the charge as partially inappropriate – Spartak fans are not a vulnerable group in need of protection under anti-extremist legislation. This example clearly demonstrates that the vague notion of "social group" should be excluded from the anti-extremist articles of the Criminal Code.

The Dzerzhinsky District Court of Yaroslavl handed down a one-year suspended sentence with a probation period of one year to a local resident. He was found guilty under Art. 282 Part 1 for posting publicly accessible texts that incited hatred and hostility toward law enforcement officials and "the opponents of Fascism." On his VKontakte page in July 2015. We view this verdict as inappropriate, because anti-fascists do not belong to vulnerable population groups and law enforcement personnel are already protected by other Criminal Code articles.

For Extremist Symbols

In 2016, our records showed 17 cases of punishment for the display of Nazi or extremist symbols that obviously were not intended as dangerous propaganda – approximately half as many as a year earlier. Art. 20.3 of the Code of Administrative Offenses (propaganda or public display of Nazi attributes or symbols, as well as symbols of extremist organizations) was utilized to improperly fine and/or subject to administrative detention not only users of social media using Nazi symbols in the heat of controversy to expose opponents, but also antique dealers or even random citizens. Often, this article was used to exert pressure on activists who had fallen out of favor with the authorities. For example, in October, the Sortavala Town Court handed down a fine of 1,000 rubles to Vitaly Rystov, a local historian and the art director of the *Serdobol* anthology, under Part 1 Art. 20.3 of the Code of Administrative Offenses (public display of Nazi symbols). Rystov was charged with publishing three historical posters with swastikas on his VKontakte page. He denied his guilt, stating that he had saved the posters on his page for professional purposes and had not been aware that strangers could see them. Judging by the content of his account, Rystov adheres to leftist-patriotic views, and there are no reasons to suspect him of supporting Nazi ideology. On the other hand, the media reports a number of conflicts between Rystov and the city authorities in connection with his position on protecting Sortavala cultural heritage sites.

The Federal List of Extremist Materials

In 2016 the Federal List of Extremist Materials was updated 54 times, and 786 entries were added (compared to 668 the year before). Four entries were removed from the list without changing the numbering. The total number of entries grew from 3,229 to 4,015. Some of the entries list diverse materials of various types.

The new additions can be classified as follows:

- Xenophobic materials produced by modern Russian nationalists – 604;
- Materials produced by other nationalists – six;
- Materials considered the "classics" of racism – two;
- Materials produced by Islamist militants and other calls for violence issued by political Islamists – 69;
- Other Islamic materials (books by Said Nursi; materials produced by banned organizations including Hizb ut-Tahrir, etc.) – 18;
- Materials produced by Russian Orthodox fundamentalists – three;
- Other religious materials (materials produced by the Jehovah's Witnesses and others) – five;
- Particularly radical anti-Russian appeals from Ukraine (treated as a separate category from "other nationalists") – 11;
- Other materials from Ukraine's mass media and Internet – 13;
- Other materials containing incitements to violence and rioting – 27;
- Non-violent opposition materials – two;
- A large body of assorted texts blocked in its entirety – one;
- Parodies banned as serious statements – two;
- Materials banned clearly by mistake – two;
- Materials created by people who were, in our view, not in full possession of their faculties – two;
- Materials that cannot be identified – 18 (includes the four entries removed from the list).

As expected, the share of online materials on the list keeps increasing: At least 711 entries out of 786 refer to materials found on the Internet (compared to 594 entries out of 668 in the preceding year). A significant number of these are the various xenophobic materials from the social media network VKontakte. The offline materials include various xenophobic books

(predominantly published by Algoritm publishing house) and flyers; Islamic literature; Jehovah's Witnesses' brochures; the letters of the Spiritual and
Tribal Rus Sovereignty (for more information, see the section that deals
with persecution for the membership of various organizations); and the
banned graffiti from the bridge support in Vladimir.[29]

Sometimes, it is not entirely clear where the forbidden material was to
be found. Thus, for example, entry No. 3247 reads: "A depiction of a human
skull and bone with the caption 'Dead head... The head of all!!!' beneath
which is another caption: 'Death to Jews and people from the Caucasus
and Central Asia [derogatory Russian terms for both are used]; we'll give
you hell soon enough!!!' (ruling of the Yoshkar-Ola City Court, Mari El, of
Oct. 10, 2015)."

Four entries have been deleted from the list over the course of the year,
but this has hardly made a difference.

That said, the Prosecutor General's Office has attempted to improve the
situation by centralizing this kind of work. In November 2016, the text of a
Prosecutor General's Office Decree issued all the way back in March 2016
was made public. It rearranged the existing practices concerned with the
prohibition of extremist materials. However, the expansion of the Federal
List of Extremist Materials has only accelerated.

Some of the entries on the list look like quick notes jotted down for
one's own use or an organization's internal use – they are hard for ordinary
readers to understand. For example, entry No. 3393 reads: "graphic file
2sgfcP75YWU.jpg uploaded to the VKontakte social media network."
Other materials are only referred to by their URL, sometimes inaccurately
reproduced,[30] making the ban all the more pointless.

On other occasions, the reverse is true and the descriptions are needlessly
detailed. Take entry 3494: "A photo image containing a caption 'Pugachev,
Oryol is with you! All the Chechens out!' transferred onto a concrete fence
of the Krestitelskoye Cemetery, address: Oryol, Karachevskaya St., 97A.
Posted by A.A. Raevsky for public viewing on a VKontakte social media
network page, account of Anton Raevsky: www.vk.com/id137792260 (by
the ruling of Zavodskoy District Court, Oryol, March 9, 2016)." Despite
this extremely thorough description, it remains totally unclear whether it is
the inscription on the fence that is illegal or its image uploaded to the social
media network. Would a similar inscription on a different fence be equally
prohibited? Or a different photograph of the same inscription? Or the same
photograph but posted from a different account? Etc.

These are not idle questions. Take this example: In November 2016, the Novocheboksarsk City Court in the Chuvash Republic ruled that an administrative case had to be abandoned. The case was brought against Dmitry Pankov, a local activist of the People's Freedom Party (PARNAS), for sharing a photograph of Vitaly Milonov wearing a T-shirt with the banned slogan "Orthodoxy or death."[31] The court took into consideration the fact that, in the Federal List of Extremist Materials, this slogan ends with an exclamation mark. The phrase "Orthodoxy or death," as published by Pankov, has no exclamation mark.[32] Earlier, Chuvash opposition activist Dmitry Semenov had been fined for publishing a photograph of Milonov wearing a T-shirt with the same slogan.

The courts keep adding the same materials to the list as new entries. In August 2016, entry No. 3746 on the list was Dmitry Nesterov's book *Skyny: Rus probuzhdaetsia* (Skinheads: Rus Awakens), found to be extremist by Leninsky District Court in Yekaterinburg, Sverdlovsk Province, on March 22, 2016. The same book (also without any details regarding the publisher, the date of publication, etc.) had already been ruled to be extremist by the Leninsky District Court in Orenburg on July 26, 2010, and added to the Federal List of Extremist Materials as entry No. 1482. There was a similar story involving the "Iman Islam Namaz" brochure by Muhammad Saalih al-Munajjid (entries No. 3292 and 2073). What makes the Islamic brochure more notable still is that not only was it recognized as extremist twice in two years, but that both times were by the same court (the first time was in April 2013). Sometimes the same materials have multiple entries with different publishing data. For example, the film *The Eternal Jew* was added to the list in 2016 as no fewer than 10 separate entries, each with different bibliographic data (entries No. 3513-3522). And that, despite the fact that the same film was already on the list as at least five other separate entries. At least 15 such repeat entries were added to the list over the year.

Blocking of Online Resources and Internet Censorship

According to the data published on Roskomsvoboda[33] (only Roskomnadzor has access to the complete data set), in 2016, 486 Internet resources were added to the Unified Registry of Prohibited Web sites for extremism-related reasons by the decisions of various courts (compared to 283 in 2015).[34]

The additional registry stipulated under the Lugovoi law is growing extremely fast: In 2016, 923 new online resources were added to it (compared to 133 in 2015).[35] It is interesting that efforts to expand the registry picked up in earnest in the second half of the year. The bulk of the materials added were radical Islamist in nature (including video clips produced by the Islamic State).

The following online resources have been added to the registries over the course of the year:

- Xenophobic materials produced by contemporary Russian nationalists (this includes various video clips, songs by Kolovrat, Tsiklon B, Order and Argentina, poems by Aleksandr Kharchikov, Dmitry Nesterov's book *Skinheads: Rus Awakens*, incitements to join the Azov battalion posted on VKontakte, and much else);
- Investigations by journalists (e.g., Bill Buford's book *The English Disease*);
- Materials by the classic authors of fascism (books by Hitler, Mussolini, Himmler, etc.)
- Materials produced by Islamist militants and other calls for violence issued by political Islamists (including incitement to travel to Syria);
- Other Muslim materials (Said Nursi's books, materials produced be banned organizations, including Hizb ut-Tahrir, etc.);
- Video clips containing materials generated by the Ukrainian organizations and Web sites prohibited in Russia (clips by Right Sector);
- Other materials from Ukraine's mass media;
- Parodies banned as serious statements;
- Various other materials directed at undermining the government or inciting public disorder;
- Various materials produced by the peaceful opposition (e.g., calls to attend the march in memory of Boris Nemtsov in Nizhny Novgorod or the protest of the long-haul drivers);[36]
- Materials that cannot be identified.

All our objections concerning the efficacy and legality of such measures have been repeatedly voiced previously.[37] The situation has only worsened. Like the Federal List, the registers are ballooning in size. Both the human involvement and the component of critical analysis are steadily getting squeezed out of the system – hardly surprising, given the sheer size of it. In

2017, it came to be known that the keyword searches were done for the law-enforcement agencies by a special program called Laplace's Demon (*Demon Laplasa*). The program, which performs round-the-clock monitoring of social media, was developed by the Center for Research into the Legitimacy and Political Process, an autonomous non-commercial organization. The organization forwarded information about extremist content identified by the program to local law-enforcement agencies.[38]

Abuse of Blocking

We view unfounded restrictions on opposition materials and announcements of opposition demonstrations, as well as inappropriately banned religious materials, materials of nationalists, analysis of the Ukrainian situation and materials of a comic or satirical nature as inappropriate. We are also concerned about the mass blocking of any information related to the persecution of adherents of the radical Islamist party Hizb ut-Tahrir in Russia.

In addition, it is worth noting that, in 2016, Russian courts issued decisions to block dozens of anonymizing Web sites based on prosecutorial claims. As a rule, prosecutors justify their demands by the fact that, with the help of such services, Internet users can access extremist materials. However, the anonymizers, in and of themselves, contain no forbidden information. Meanwhile, access to prohibited materials can be achieved through other tools, including conventional search engines, since they can't be completely removed from the global network, but this possibility can't be used as a basis for cutting off access to search engines. Similarly, the fact that printing houses can theoretically print extremist materials can't be used as a basis for closing them down.

Selected Examples of Access Restrictions

Details on several noteworthy cases of bans and blocking of Web pages are provided below.

In early February 2016, Roskomnadzor added a YouTube page with Pavel Bardin's movie *Russia 88* to the list of banned Web sites, thus blocking it on the territory of Russia. This 2009 movie about neo-Nazis, anti-fascist in its ideology, was shown in Russia and received various cinematic prizes. The decision to block it was issued by the Naryan-Mar City Court of the Nenets Autonomous District based on a claim by the local prosecutor's office. The grounds for blocking were as follows: In 2012, the Leninsky District Court of Kemerovo banned the xenophobic video "Russia 88 (Babulka)" based on assembled scenes from Bardin's movie. The Naryan-Mar Prosecutor asked the court to block the banned video, which had been posted on YouTube and Yapfiles.ru as well as on VKontakte; the court also demanded that Bardin's movie be blocked as containing fragments of the extremist video. In accordance with the usual practice in such cases, the filmmakers were not involved in the trial, and the court granted the prosecutors' request. Responding to the ensuing media resonance, Roskomnadzor appealed to the Prosecutor General's Office, arguing that the Naryan-Mar Court decision was problematic; it was subsequently overturned. The mechanism used by the Prosecutor General's Office to allow Roskomnadzor not to execute the court decision is not known.

Also in February, the Russian-language information and analytical portal Voice of Islam (*Golos Islama*), based in Turkey, was blocked upon request of the Prosecutor General's Office. Lawyers representing the interests of the portal managed to prove that Roskomnadzor had violated the law, since, after blocking the site upon request of the Prosecutor General's Office, the agency failed to notify the editorial board specifically what materials should be removed for the restrictions to be lifted (also a common practice). The Prosecutor General's request to Roskomnadzor to block the Voice of Islam stated "The publications posted on the main newsfeed and in other sections of the Web site exhibit a biased presentation of the material and hostile attitude toward certain social groups, in particular toward representatives of law enforcement, government bodies and the leadership of the Russian Federation, and also toward Russia's foreign and domestic policies." Pro-Turkish material about the Kurds, an article criticizing Assad, and an article about the persecution of Muslims in Russia were cited as examples. Having identified the objectionable materials in the course of this court case, the editorial board deleted them from the pages of the portal, and it was unblocked in July.

In the same month of February, the hosting provider of the Roskom-svoboda project (rublacklist.net) received a notice from Roskomnadzor informing that one of Roskomvoboda's pages had been included in the Unified Registry of Banned Web Sites. The page on the Roskomsvoboda Web site that provided information on ways to bypass online access restrictions had been banned by decision of the Anapa City Court, which ruled that it could provide citizens with "access to prohibited materials, including extremist materials." The Krasnodar Territory Court upheld this decision. Information on ways to restore one's access to information is not legally prohibited for distribution in Russia, so the decision to block the Roskomvoboda Web page was inappropriate. The Roskomvoboda administrators decided to replace the contents of the banned page with the scanned report of the Ministry of Communications, which also lists the tools for circumventing the restrictions. Subsequently, official Roskomnadzor representative Vadim Ampelonsky said that the court decision was considered fulfilled, and the resource was taken off the Registry.

In March 2016, SOVA Center received two letters from Roskomnadzor which reported that, according to the decisions of the Leninsky District Court of Kirov and the Kumensky District Court of the Kirov Region, two pages of the SOVA Web site contain illegal information and should be deleted; otherwise, the site would be blocked. The information in question was a two-page reference book created back in 2008 as part of a joint project of SOVA Center and Swedish EXPO anti-racist research center and journal. The reference book was a Russian adaptation of *Far-Right Movements and Their Symbols*, a work by Swedish researcher Hakan Gestrin, published in Stockholm in the autumn of 2007, supplemented by the chapter on symbols used by Russian right-wing radicals. Like many similar reference books in other countries, this work is addressed primarily to teachers, police officers and other people who are facing ultra-right manifestations, primarily in the youth environment, and who need factual knowledge on this subject, including the symbols being used. The standardized Roskomnadzor missives provided no information on exactly what violations of the law the courts found in the reference book, but presumably these had to do with Nazi symbols prohibited by Russian law for any kind of display regardless of whether or not it was aimed at propaganda of Nazism. To avoid access restrictions, SOVA Center had to delete the reference material, leaving only a link to the page on another site that posted it.

Below, we would like to provide some examples of information related to public activities held without permits that was blocked under the Lugovoi law. We believe that the provision of the Lugovoi law on blocking information about public events clearly limits freedom of speech – the fact that the event has received no permit (or simply has not yet received its permit) gives no grounds for banning communication about it. Requests to block events that do not require official coordination are even more problematic.

In February 2016, upon request of the Prosecutor General's Office and Roskomnadzor, the Web site of the Open Russia movement deleted from its pages the article "Short Memory: City Administrations Refuse to Coordinate Demonstrations in Memory of Boris Nemtsov." According to the oversight agencies, the text contained "calls for mass riots, carrying out extremist activities and participation in mass (public) events conducted in violation of the established order." These claims were obviously related to the fact that the article focused on events in memory of Boris Nemtsov, who was murdered a year earlier in Moscow, and cited the words of the Nizhny Novgorod activists who were urging citizens to attend the memorial demonstration in the city center despite the absence of an official permit.

In October 2016, the social media network VKontakte blocked the page of the demonstration called "March against Hate-2016" at the request of the Prosecutor General's Office. It was reported earlier that the St. Petersburg authorities had refused the permit to hold another March against Hate in memory of Professor Nikolai Girenko, who was killed by neo-Nazis in 2004. Having received a refusal from the city authorities, the activists, via the channels available to them, expressed their intention to hold the event in the format of a walk.

NOTES

1. Found to be extremist by the Sovetsky District Court of Tula, July 6, 2015.
2. Found to be extremist by the Moscow City Court, Oct. 28, 2015.
3. Found to be extremist by the Moscow City Court, Aug. 11, 2015.
4. Found to be extremist by the Sovetsky District Court, Astrakhan, July 21, 2015.
5. Found to be extremist by the Supreme Court of the Russian Federation, Aug. 9, 2016.
6. Found to be extremist by the Belgorod Province Court, Feb. 10, 2016.
7. Found to be extremist by the Oryol Province Court, June 14, 2016.
8. Found to be extremist by the Supreme Court of the Kalmyk Republic, Feb. 25, 2016.
9. Found to be extremist by the Samara Province Court, July 22, 2016. It is discussed in: M. Kravchenko. Inappropriate Enforcement of Anti-Extremist Legislation in Russia in 2016...
10. Found to be a terrorist organization by the Moscow District Military Court, Dec. 28, 2015. Organization names based on the spellings given on the FSB Web site. Most probably, what is being referred to is the network that collects funds to provide humanitarian aid to jihadists – aid to prisoners, medical aid, etc.
11. Found to be a terrorist organization by the Supreme Court of the Russian federation, Sept. 10, 2016.
12. For more information see: Nationalist Malyugin gets 18 years of strict-regime penal colony // ZakS.Ru. 2016. 17 March (https://www.zaks.ru/new/archive/view/151187).

13. See: Who is in prison for "extremist crimes" that are not of a general criminal character. February 2017 // SOVA Center. Feb. 20, 2017 (http://www.sova-center.ru/racism-xenophobia/publications/2017/02/d36413/).

14. Pavel Chikov. The controlled thaw: What the repeat hearing of Dadin's and Chudnovets's case tells us // RBK. March 6, 2017 (http://www.rbc.ru/opinions/politics/06/03/2017/58bd186f9a7947c43c5ec254).

15. The main operation and statistical indicators of general-jurisdiction courts in 2016 // The official site of the Russian Federation's Supreme Court Justice Department. 2017 (February) (cdep.ru/userimages/sudebnaya_statistika/2017/Osnovnye_oper_pokazateli_2016.xlsx).

16. This is approximately two and a half times as many as we are aware of. According to SOVA Center, if one takes wrongful convictions into account, 261 people were convicted under Arts. 280, 280.1, 282, 282.1, 282.2. The difference in the statistics can be partly explained by the fact that we do not take the data for the North Caucasus into account. Besides, the prosecutor's offices do not always consider it necessary to report routine convictions. For example, we know that 817 criminal cases were initiated in 2016, but many have not yet reached the sentencing stage.

The data on "terrorist articles," as shown on the Supreme Court Web site, are also summary in nature: 182 people have been convicted under Arts. 205.1 (facilitating terrorist activity), 205.2, 205.3 (undergoing training for the purpose of carrying out terrorist activities), 205.4 (organizing a terrorist community and participation therein), 205.5 (organizing the activities of a terrorist organization and participation in the activities of the organization), and 206 (hostage-taking). The data are not for all "terrorist articles" other than 205.2; consequently, no direct comparisons with our data should be made.

17. For more information see: "Right Sector" supporter in Togliatti sentenced for materials uploaded on VKontakte // SOVA Center. June 14, 2016 (http://www.sova-center.ru/racism-xenophobia/news/counteraction/2016/06/d34789/).

18. For more information see: Is Aleksandr Belov a political prisoner? // SOVA Center. July 13, 2015 (http://www.sova-center.ru/racism-xenophobia/publications/2015/07/d32405/); V. Gefter. Being recognized as a political prisoner is not automatically praised // SOVA Center. July 21, 2015 (http://www.sova-center.ru/racism-xenophobia/publications/2015/07/d32467/); A. Verkhovsky. Incitement to hatred and political prisoner status // SOVA Center. July 28, 2015 (http://www.sova-center.ru/racism-xenophobia/publications/2015/07/d32511/).

19. For more information see: Aleksandr Belov sentenced to seven and a half years in a general-regime penal colony // SOVA Center. Aug. 24, 2016 (http://www.sova-center.ru/racism-xenophobia/news/counteraction/2016/08/d35264/).

20. Supreme Court lowers sentence for the Moscow schoolboy who joined Right Sector // RAPSI. Dec. 22, 2016 (http://www.rapsinews.ru/judicial_news/20161222/277423491.html).

21. Gleb Trifonov. Prominent Russian nationalist becomes ISIS recruiter // Life. Dec. 23, 2016 (https://life.ru/t/%D0%BD%D0%BE%D0%B2%D0%BE%D1%81%D1%82%D0%B8/951036/izviestnyi_russkii_nieonatsist_stal_vierbovshchikom_ighil).

22. For more details, see: Former NS/WP member sentenced for recruiting for ISIS // SOVA Center. Dec. 23, 2016 (http://www.sova-center.ru/racism-xenophobia/news/counteraction/2016/12/d36079/).

23. For example, see: N. Yudina. Anti-extremism in virtual Russia: 2014–2015 // SOVA Center. Aug. 24, 2016 (http://www.sova-center.ru/files/xeno/web14-15-eng.pdf).

24. Here we do not consider the sentences that are clearly inappropriate, or the sentences imposed on the members of Hizb ut-Tahrir al-Islami.

25. Two more men had been tried and convicted in connection with Attack earlier: one was given a suspended sentence of two years; the other, Vladimir Kudriashov, the founder of

Attack, who had been detained on the territory of the Luhansk People Republic at the request of the Russian Federation Investigative Committee and handed over to the Russian authorities, was sentenced to one year in a general-regime penal colony.

26. RNU Omsk branch was recognized as extremist by the decision of the Omsk Province Court in 2012.

27. Misanthropic Division was recognized as an extremist organization by the Krasnoyarsk Territory Court on June 17, 2015.

28. In May 2016, Nadezhda Savchenko was pardoned and released to Ukraine in exchange for two Russian citizens convicted in Ukraine for taking part in military operations in the Donbass.

29. For more information, see: Vladimir: for some reason, a court recognizes graffiti as extremist // SOVA Center. Dec. 20, 2016 (http://www.sova-center.ru/racism-xenophobia/news/counteraction/2015/12/d33425/).

30. We believe this is done on purpose, so as not to advertise the prohibited material.

31. This slogan was banned by the Cheremushkinsky District Court in 2010 and included on the Federal List of Extremist Materials under entry No. 865.

32. Court decides not to punish the Chuvash activist Pankov for re-posting a photograph of Milonov // SOVA Center. Nov. 22, 2016 (http://www.sova-center.ru/misuse/news/persecution/2016/11/d35873/).

33. See: Register of banned Web sites // Roskomsvoboda (http://reestr.rublacklist.net/).

34. See: Updated list: "Extremist resources" in the Unified Register of Prohibited Web Sites // SOVA Center (http://www.sova-center.ru/racism-xenophobia/docs/2016/04/d34421/).

35. See: Updated list: Resources Listed in the Register of Web Sites Blocked under the Lugovoi Law // SOVA Center (http://www.sova-center.ru/racism-xenophobia/docs/2017/01/d36203/).

36. Interestingly, but not a single Web page containing calls to attend the "Russian March" was blocked.

37. For example, see: N. Yudina Anti-extremism in virtual Russia…

38. Lawyer: Leader of the 'Instructions for survival' was called to center 'E' following the denunciation of an NGO that had allegedly developed the anti-extremist software for monitoring social media // Mediazone. Feb. 2, 2017 (https://zona.media/news/2017/08/02/demon_laplasa).

Banning Organizations as Extremist

In 2017, six organizations were added to the Federal List of Extremist Organizations published on the Web site of the Ministry of Justice, fewer than a year earlier (10 organizations). However, item 62, which was added in 2017, includes the inappropriately banned Administrative Center of the Jehovah's Witnesses in Russia and all of the Jehovah's Witnesses' 395 local organizations.

Of the ultra-right-wing organizations on the list, there was the organization "Frontier of the North," which was recognized as extremist by the decision of the Syktyvkar city court of the Komi Republic on Nov. 23, 2016,[1] and the T.O.Y.S. football fan organization (The Opposition Young Supporters), which was recognized as extremist by the decision of the Sovetsky District Court of Samara on April 11, 2017.[2]

Besides the ultra-right-wing organizations, in 2017 the Mejlis of the Crimean Tatar People[3] and the Naberezhnye Chelny division of the All-Tatar Social Center (ATSC)[4] were added to the list. Besides the gigantic aforementioned item 62, an already banned local organization of the Jehovah's Witnesses was added to the list – the Jehovah's Witnesses organization in Birobidzhan.[5] We believe all these decisions were inappropriate.

Besides this, the list of organizations recognized as terrorist published on the Web site of the Federal Security Service was updated. For the year, only one organization was added – Mujahideen of Jama'at al-Tawhid wal-Jihad (item 27).

Criminal Prosecution

For Violence

The number of sentences for violent crimes motivated by hatred significantly decreased compared to the preceding year. In 2017, at least 10 guilty verdicts in which courts recognized the motive of hatred were handed down in nine regions of Russia (there were 15 guilty verdicts in 19 regions in 2016). In these proceedings, 24 people were found guilty (compared to 43 people in 2016).

Racist violence was qualified under the following articles that contain the hate motive as an aggravating circumstance: murder, intentional infliction of minor injuries, hooliganism and beating. This set of articles has remained constant over the past five years. Art. 282 of the Criminal Code (incitement of hatred) in relation to violent crimes appeared in four convictions (compared to seven in 2016). In all cases, it was used for crime-related episodes of ultra-right propaganda (creating videos and uploading them online) and not for actual violence.

In two instances, this article was applied in well-known and resonant cases. The first was the verdict of the Babushkinsky District Court of Moscow against founder of the ultra-right movement "Restruct!" Maksim "Tesak" (Hatchet) Martsinkevich and his accomplices in the Occupy Drug Addiction[6] movement, who, in addition to beating up and mocking people they regarded as drug dealers, also posted reports about their actions on the Internet.

The second resonant sentence was handed down in Khabarovsk in the case of the infamous "Khabarovsk flesher-girls" – two young women and their male accomplice.[7] In addition to abusing animals and birds, one of the girls was posting on a social media network page the videos "with scenes of humiliation of the dignity of a young man***on the basis of belonging to a social group." However, we could not identify the specific group the court had in mind in this case – the "flesher-girls" posted videos that contained scenes of attacks against both LGBT and homeless people.

The motive of hatred toward the social group "homeless" was also taken into account in the verdict handed down by the Bryansk Province Court[8] against two supporters of the Straight Edge movement for killing Aleksandr Chizhikov, the vocalist of the rock band Otvet Chemberlenu (Response to Chamberlain); due to his drunkenness and untidy appearance, the attackers mistook him for a homeless person.

On the other hand, the hate motive was not taken into account in the verdict handed down in May in St. Petersburg for the murder of journalist Dmitry Tsilikin.[9] His murderer, Sergei Kosyrev, called himself a "cleaner" and his own life "a crusade against a certain social group" (referring to the LGBT), and characterized the feeling that made him kill Tsilikin as "not dislike, as the protocol says, but hatred." Civic activist Natalya Tsymbalova launched a petition, calling for the case to be reclassified as a hate crime, but Kosyrev was, nevertheless, convicted only of murder (Art. 105 Part 1 of the Criminal Code) and sentenced to eight and a half years in prison.[10]

Although SOVA Center finds using the notion "social group" in the context of anti-extremist legislation deeply problematic in principle,[11] there is no doubt that the homeless and the LGBT are, indeed, the kinds of "social groups" that need state protection, and legal regulations on hate crimes must protect them in one way or another.

Penalties for violent acts were distributed as follows:

- Two people received a prison sentence of up to 20 years;
- One person – up to 15 years;
- Four people – up to 10 years;
- Six people – up to five years;
- Six people – up to three years;
- Three people were sentenced to community service;
- One person received a suspended sentence;
- One person was referred for mandatory treatment.

We only know of six convicted offenders (including the already mentioned "Khabarovsk flesher-girls") who received additional punishment in the form of having to pay a compensation for material and moral harm to the victims.

We see that the number of suspended sentences for violent crimes decreased in 2017, which is generally a positive trend. Only one convicted offender – a native of Voronezh who beat up a native of Tajikistan and posted a video about it on the Internet – received a suspended sentence. Probably, the leniency was related to the fact that the victim's injuries were minor.

However, as can be seen from the above data, the majority of violent offenders were sentenced to various terms of incarceration – and this is certainly a positive trend.

For Crimes Against Property

Somewhat fewer sentences were handed down for crimes against property in 2017 than in the preceding year. We know of three sentences handed down in three regions against five people (compared to five sentences against six people in five regions in 2016).

In all three cases, the offenders were charged under Art. 214 Part 2 of the Criminal Code (vandalism committed on the basis of national or religious hatred). In one of the verdicts – for Nazi symbols on a monument to the soldiers who died in the Great Patriotic War – it was the only article applied. In another case, it was used in aggregation with Art. 282 of the Criminal Code, since, in addition to painting slogans on houses and fences, the young man had also posted images on the Internet. The third verdict was handed down in Lipetsk under Art. 115, Art. 105 Part 2 Paragraph "l," and Art. 214 Part 2 of the Criminal Code in the notorious case of attacks and murder motivated by ethnic hatred and arson of the baptismal font in the Lipetsk Diocesan Holy Dormition Monastery.

Three people were sentenced to restrictions of liberty, including the first two sentences listed in the previous paragraph; we view such punishments as adequate. The fact that the third verdict – handed down under aggregation of several articles, including Art. 105 of the Criminal Code (murder) – sentenced two out of the three offenders to long terms of imprisonment also does not raise any questions.

For Public Statements

The number of convictions handed down for "extremist statements" (incitement of hatred, calls for extremist or terrorist activity and so on) continued to exceed all other types of convictions for "extremist crimes" combined. In 2017, there were at least 213 convictions against 228 people in 65 regions. For 2016, we learned of 201 such convictions against 220 people in 66 regions.

In this section, we are not writing about the convictions that we think are inappropriate: In 2017, we considered 17 convictions of 17 people unjust (see below, not included in the numbers in this section).

Unfortunately, we can confirm that we found out about far from all of such convictions. According to statistics published on the Web site of the Supreme Court,[12] for statements (Parts 1 and 2 of Art. 148, Art. 205.2, Art. 280.1, Art. 282, and Art. 354.1 of the Criminal Code) only in the first half of 2017, there were 292 people convicted for whom these articles were main part of the accusation, and 82 people for whom these articles were supplementary, that is, between 292 and 374 people were convicted for "extremist statements."[13]

As usual, of the convictions we know about,[14] Art. 282 of the Criminal Code (incitement of hate and enmity) was applied in the majority of cases (in 199 convictions against 210 people). In the overwhelming majority of cases (136), this article was the only article applied in the conviction. In 13 convictions against 13 people, only Art. 280 of the Criminal Code (public calls for extremist activity) was applied. In another 29 cases, convictions were handed down according to both Arts. 280 and 282 of the Criminal Code.

The calculated number of convictions were handed down according to relatively recently adopted articles of the Criminal Code. In two convictions, Art. 280.1 of the Criminal Code (public calls for undermining the territorial integrity of the Russian Federation) was used. In one of these cases, the director of the Samara division of the Community of Indigenous Russian People, Viktor Permyakov, was also convicted according to Art. 282.[15]

In another two cases, Part 1 of Art. 354.1 of the Criminal Code (denial of facts established by the verdict of the International Military Tribunal for the trial and punishment of the major war criminals of the European Axis countries, approval of the crimes established by this verdict, as well as the dissemination of knowingly false information about the activities of the USSR during the years of World War II) was applied. In one case, this article was tried along with Art. 282, and in another, with Art. 282 and Art. 280. In both cases, this concerned publications on the Internet.

In all of these cases, the "new" articles did not entail harsh sentences. Those sentenced according to Art. 280.1 received conditional sentences; those convicted according to Art. 354.1 were fined.

Arts. 282 and 280 of the Criminal Code could be tried along with other articles, including for violent activity and vandalism.

Very little is known about convictions under Art. 205.2 of the Criminal Code (public calls for terrorist activity). It is often combined with other "extremist articles" including Arts. 282 and 280. This article was applied to radical Islamist statements, including those concerning the military conflict in Syria, and to supporters of banned Ukrainian organizations such as Right Sector,[16] the Ukrainian National Assembly-Ukrainian People's Self-Defense (UNA-UNSO), and the Misanthropic Division.[17] In addition, it was applied in the conviction against the head of the Union of Young Innovation Leaders in Tatarstan for homophobic statements justifying the mass murder at a gay night club in the United States.[18]

The punishments for those convicted for public statements were distributed as follows:

- Forty-seven people were sentenced to prison;
- One hundred fourteen received suspended prison sentences without any additional punishment;
- Thirty-one were convicted and fined in various amounts;
- Eight were sentenced to corrective labor;
- Twenty-two were sentenced to mandatory labor;
- One was sentenced to restrictions of freedom;
- Five were sent for forced treatment;
- One was released due to remorse.

As can be seen from the above data, the number of those sentenced to prison has risen (a year ago, we reported 36 people).

Thirteen of the 47 people sentenced to prison received terms in conjunction with other articles of prosecution (violence, arson, robbery, possession of narcotics).

Nine people were already in prison and their sentences were extended. The most well-known of such prisoners was the former leader of the MPPM and retired colonel of the Chief Intelligence Administration (GRU) Vladimir Kvachkov, who was sentenced to another 18 months in a maximum-security penal colony for the video "Kvachkov in IK 5 [Penal Colony #5] Mordovia."[19]

Six people were convicted for "extremist statements" for a second time, which greatly increases the risk of imprisonment. In this group, there was the leader of the Parabellum movement and activist in the People's Militia of Russia (formerly MPPM) Yury Yekishev, who received 18 months imprisonment for two anti-Semitic articles,[20] and the leader of the banned ultra-right-wing organization the People's Social Initiative (NSI), former leader of the Schulz 88 group Dmitry Bobrov, who received two years' imprisonment for the publication of the article, "The Racial Doctrine."[21]

Another two people were convicted earlier and already served their prison terms under articles on violence. Among them is the former participant in a band of Nazi skinheads from Chelyabinsk, Dmitry Shokhov (Gunther), who was sentenced to six months in prison for putting a xenophobic poster on the Internet.[22]

With account of the identity of accused, the former leader of the banned organizations "Russians," Slavic Union, and Slavic Force, Dmitry

Dyomushkin,[23] was sentenced to two and a half years in a minimum-security penal colony for two pictures posted on the social media network VKontakte.[24] This conviction was perhaps the most resonant in all of last year.

Predictably, the punishments were harsher for crimes committed as part of the anti-terrorism article, Art. 205.2 of the Criminal Code. Three people were sentenced to imprisonment for radical Islamist videos and publications posted on the Internet; four people (the aforementioned supporters of the banned Ukrainian organizations Right Sector, UNA-UNSO and Misanthropic Division) were imprisoned for radical publications connected with the events in Ukraine.

However, seven people received prison sentences without any of the aforementioned circumstances (or we did not know about any). This concerns convictions handed down in Bryansk, Krasnodar, Nizhnevartovsk, Saratov, Rostov-on-Don, Perm and Perm Territory for publications on the social media network VKontakte of various unnamed materials (video and audio clips, commentaries, etc.) including calls for violence. We consider these decisions unreasonably harsh. The situation has considerably deteriorated in comparison with last year (in 2016, we wrote about five such convictions), but did not reach the peak of 2015, when we counted 16 convictions for "extremist statements."

At the same time, the share of suspended sentences rose by eight percentage points in comparison with last year to 49% (114 of 228). A year ago, we wrote about 41% (82 of 198 convictions). The situation seems strange when suspended sentences are repeated. After all, this means that the previous sentence did not force the convict to think about his or her actions and did not stop him or her from committing the same crime. For instance, a conditional term for the publication of a xenophobic post on a social media network was received by the well-known St. Petersburg nationalist Nikolai Bondarik.[25] In April 2015, the court already gave him a suspended prison sentence of one and a half years for complicity in the preparation of a provocation on the holiday Eid al-Adha (two St. Petersburg residents said at the time that they had been victims of a xenophobic attack, however they then confessed that it had been staged).

In such cases, we feel that more appropriate punishments for such crimes would be fines or community service (mandatory or corrective labor). The share of such convicted people (62 people) who were sentenced to punishments not connected with real or suspended sentences of imprisonment has fallen in comparison to 2016. We have observed such a reduction for the second year in a row.

In the past year, in at least five verdicts, a ban on one's profession was applied. In one conviction in Vladimir Province, there was a ban on work with minors, and in the remaining four, there was a ban on work in mass media.

We know about at least 12 cases of bans on public statements on the Internet and bans on appearances on mass media, including a ban on attending the 2018 FIFA World Cup that was handed down to the leader of the T.O.Y.S. fan group, Yegeny (Gavr) Gavrilov.[26]

In addition, we know about seven cases where Internet access was taken away for a certain amount of time.

The overwhelming majority of verdicts were handed down for materials posted on the Internet, including various means of electronic communication – 205 of 213, which is 96%, about 10% more than in 2014-2016.

These materials were distributed via:

- Social media – 182 (including VKontakte – 138, unnamed social media networks – 38, which were probably also VKontakte, Odnoklassniki – four, and Facebook – two);
- Blogs (both on Live Journal) – two;
- One's own Web site – one;
- YouTube – two;
- Internet-based media – three (all three were comments on articles);
- Forums – one;
- Email lists – two (both of those convicted were supporters of the *Volya* party);
- Local network – one;
- Internet (not specified) – 11.

This ratio has remained virtually unchanged for the last six years.[27]

The convictions for sending files via email or for posting them on local networks are spurious. It is interesting that there have been no reports in the news on the number of recipients of emails or participants in these networks. We think that is important and necessary to repeat: nothing is being done to determine what size of the audience makes a statement "public." This aspect, no matter how important it is for the application of articles on propaganda, is still being ignored by courts. The Supreme Court, when it prepared its updated ruling on anti-extremism and anti-terrorism law enforcement in 2016,[28] also failed to discuss these issues.

This concerns the following types of materials (various materials can be posted on a single account and even on a single page):

- Video clips – 64;
- Images (drawings, de-motivational posters) – 36;
- Photographs – 22;
- Audio (songs) – 37;
- Texts (including republished books) – 59;
- Remarks, commentary (on social media and in forums) – 17;
- Web sites and groups created by convicts – three;
- Unknown – 31.

This ratio has also been stable over the past six years.

It is significant that most of the convictions were not for original posts, but for republications. Only in six cases could it be noted that the defendants themselves authored the materials in question; the remainder were simply posted by hitting the "share" button. It would be more effective if law enforcement officers found those who actually recorded the videos (how they found, for example, activists of the "Restruct!" movement filming their attacks), or those that wrote the texts (as in the case of Dmitry Bobrov, who wrote an article), or at the very least, those who initially posted the materials on the Internet, rather than taking in in someone among the myriad of reposters of such content.

Of course, one could say that remarks and comments on social media and in forums are "original texts," but we think that Internet chatter does not merit a criminal investigation in light of its locality and small audience.

Actually, it would be worthwhile to pay more attention to the creation of ultra-right-wing groups on social media that systematically propagate hate.

There were almost 75% fewer convictions for statements made offline than a year earlier: eight compared to 31 in 2016. They are distributed as follows:

- Public insults on streets – one;
- Leaflets, posters – three;
- Graffiti – two;
- Public performances of songs – two.

We do not object per se to the criminal prosecution of all such types of activities, and we have no doubts about the appropriateness of the verdicts. We note only that in these cases, it is necessary to take into account not only the content of these statements, but also other factors affecting the danger they pose for society, first and foremost the real size of the audience. That is, it is important to consider the degree of a statement's publicity (the number of attendees at a concert, for example).[29]

For Participation in Extremist and Banned Groups and Organizations

In 2017, the prosecution of ultra-right-wing groups according to Art. 282.1 (organizing an extremist community) and Art. 282.2 (organizing the activity of an extremist organization) of the Criminal Code was a good deal less notable than a year earlier. We learned about four such convictions and six individuals in four Russian regions[30] (in 2016, there were seven convictions against 20 people in seven regions).

According to our information, Art. 282.1 of the Criminal Code featured in the cases against the aforementioned leader of the T.O.Y.S. football fan group, Yevgeny (Gavr) Gavrilov from Samara. Charged in combination with Arts. 282 and 280, he was sentenced to a suspended prison sentence of six and a half years with four years of probation. Members of the group, soccer fans, committed "extremist" crimes and administrative offenses and posted Nazi symbols as well as calls for extremist activity on social media.[31]

In two cases, Art. 282.2 of the Criminal Code was applied on the continuation of the activities of an organization that had been banned as extremist.

In Barnaul, a resident of Zmeinogorsky District received a suspended prison sentence of two years with two years of probation for involvement in the activity of an unnamed extremist organization. The convicted man is "an adherent of nationalist ideas" who "persuaded his acquaintances to become involved in the activity of an extremist organization" and "propagated the ideas of racism, violence, separatist and revolutionary sentiments among youth."[32]

As usual, members of the neopagan organization the Spiritual and Tribal Rus Sovereignty were tried according to Art. 282.2 of the Criminal Code. Three activists of this banned organization from Krasnodar and Goryachy Klyuch came to the Starominsky district department of the bailiff service and began to promote the activity of Power of Rus. A criminal case was opened against all three for their activities at the department. The court found the defendants guilty and sentenced two to five months in prison and the third – due to his health – to suspended prison sentence of five months with one year of probation. This story is typical for the members of Rus Sovereignty, who actively attempt to promote their movement at government and law enforcement agencies. Granted, they rarely come in person to the government agencies, but instead simply send letters to officials. These same activists had earlier been repeatedly fined according to Art. 282.2 for such activities.[33]

We do not know anything about convictions made against right-wing radicals for organizing the activity of a terrorist organization (Art. 205.4) or for the organization of terrorist communities and participation in them (Art. 205.5), although some nationalist organizations had previously been banned as terrorist organizations.

Inappropriate Prosecution of Political and Civic Activists

The "Ukrainian Question"

As in previous years, in 2017, the Russian authorities continued to use anti-extremist legislation to address statements related to the conflict in Ukraine and dissemination of various Ukrainian materials. Here we would like to examine the cases of clearly inappropriate or disproportionate law enforcement reaction.

In June, the Meshchansky District Court of Moscow found Natalya Sharina, the former director of the Library of Ukrainian Literature, guilty under Art. 282 Part 2 Paragraph "b" of the Criminal Code (incitement of ethnic hatred or enmity with the use of official position) and Parts 3 and 4 of Art. 160 (embezzlement committed on a large or an especially large scale) and handed down a suspended sentence of four years followed by a four-year probation period. The prosecution was based on the fact of finding prohibited Ukrainian literature in the library as a result of a search conducted upon request of a local Ukrainophobic municipal deputy. Safekeeping and providing access to literature is the responsibility of librarians under the Law on Librarianship, which conflicts with the official requirement to vet the names of books from existing collections and new acquisitions against the constantly updated Federal List of Extremist Materials. Currently, this contradiction is managed at the level of procedural instructions. However, we view the criminal charges of engaging in a conscious propaganda act (deliberate distribution of materials that incite hatred) against a librarian for failing to withdraw materials from circulation as clearly inappropriate.

In the same month, the Kaluga District Court of Kaluga Province sentenced local resident Roman Grishin to 320 hours of mandatory labor, having found him guilty under Art. 282 Part 1 of the Criminal Code. He refused to comply and the court replaced the sentence with 40 days of imprisonment in a settlement colony. The charges of inciting ethnic hatred against Grishin were based on the video "A New Hit from Kharkov: This is Rashism, Baby" to a song by Boris Sevastyanov that Grishin shared on his VKontakte page in 2014. Sevastyanov's song contains sharp criticism of Russian state propaganda and foreign policy in connection with its actions in Ukraine (which, according to the author, are characteristic of totalitarian regimes), but includes no calls for aggression. The video contains images of Nazi symbols and emblems of the prohibited MAII, and its publication had already led to an arrest of activists from Krasnodar in 2015 under Art. 20.3 of the Code of Administrative Offenses (propaganda or display of Nazi symbols). However, in this case, as in many others, the display of Nazi symbols was not intended as propaganda of Nazi ideology, and certainly sharing this video did not correspond to the wording of Art. 282.

In February, a court in Saratov handed down a verdict under Part 1 of Art. 282 (incitement of hatred on the basis of belonging to a specific ethnicity and social group). Nineteen-year-old Aleksandr Gozenko was convicted for publishing on VKontakte in November 2015 four comments against ethnic Russians and *vatniks* [a derogatory nickname derived from a cheap cotton-filled winter coat]; one of the comments contained incitement to violence against the latter (as indicated in the court's decision, Gozenko called for "organizing a holocaust for *vata*"). We have had no access to the full text of his comments, so we do not know whether Gozenko made any statements that provoked ethnic enmity. As for the social group "vatnik" or "vata," it should be noted that such a group simply does not exist. Law enforcement agencies rephrased this term as "patriots of Russia," once again demonstrating that, in reality, it is not a social group, but adherents of a certain ideology. However, incitement of ideologically motivated hatred is not covered by Art. 282. Gozenko fully acknowledged his guilt, and the case was reviewed according to a special procedure. The court sentenced him to 160 hours of mandatory labor. It must also be noted that Gozenko was still a minor at the time he left the incriminating comments.

In November, the Petrogradsky District Court of St. Petersburg handed down a verdict under Art. 282 Part 1 of the Criminal Code to Anatoly Pleshanov. The court imposed a one-year suspended sentence. The charges against Pleshanov were based on statements he left in the "Konakovo and Konakovsky District" VKontakte group in the summer of 2014. The author expressed an extremely negative opinion with regard to Ukrainians who decided to move to Russia and spoke out against the annexation of Crimea. The author also made negative statements regarding migrants from Central Asia but was not found guilty of inciting hatred against them. According to the expert opinion, Pleshanov's statements were "aimed at humiliating the dignity of groups of individuals on the grounds of ethnicity and belonging to a social group" [residents of Ukraine]. As stated in the opinion, "the author writes that he is dissatisfied with the help Russia and Russian citizens provide to residents of Ukraine and demonstrates a negative attitude toward residents of Ukraine – Ukrainians. The author believes that the actual population of Russia receives no such help and support in their own country." At the same time, the experts found no "justification or rationalization of violence" or "calls for violent actions." Since Pleshanov's statements can only be regarded as a violation of dignity on the basis of nationality, we saw no need for criminal prosecution in this case.

In September, the Simferopol District Court handed down a verdict on the case of Ilmi Umerov, a Deputy Chairman of the Mejlis of the Crimean Tatar People. The court sentenced him to two years in a colony-settlement with a two-year ban on public activities, despite the fact that the prosecutor had asked for a suspended sentence. The criminal case under Art. 280.1 Part 2 of the Criminal Code (public calls for undermining the territorial integrity of the Russian Federation using media or the Internet) was opened in May 2016, after Umerov went live on the Ukrainian channel ATR in March and called for the return of the Crimea to Ukraine. However, in our opinion, this did not give grounds for criminal prosecution – it is impossible to accuse residents of the area who have never recognized Russia's annexation of the territory to begin with of separatism. In addition, the legality of Russia's annexation of the Crimea is questionable from the point of view of the international law, and the Crimean Tatars have the right to their point of view in this dispute. Umerov was sentenced to a real prison term despite his numerous health problems. However, in October, Ilmi Umerov, along with another Deputy Chairman, Akhtem Chyigoz, convicted on charges of organizing mass riots in the Crimea prior to the annexation of the peninsula, were released from custody and sent by plane to Turkey. According to media reports, they were pardoned by the president upon request of the mufti of Crimea, despite the fact that they had never applied for a pardon. Ukrainian President Petro Poroshenko said that the release of Umerov and Chyigoz happened due to agreements with Turkish President Recep Erdogan.

In December, the Astrakhan Province Court once again reviewed the case of Igor Stenin, the leader of the "Russians" of Astrakhan movement and upheld his conviction handed down by the Sovetsky District Court of Astrakhan in May 2016. At that time, the nationalist was sentenced under Art. 280 Part 2 of the Criminal Code (public calls for extremist activities via the Internet) to two years in a settlement colony. We would like to remind readers that in 2016 the lower court found Stenin guilty of publishing a post on VKontakte on the subject of the war in Ukraine, in which he made public calls for liquidation of the "Kremlin invaders." He was also held responsible for a comment made by another user that the investigation mistook for a post shared by Stenin). The appellate court (the Astrakhan Province Court) approved this decision. Then, already in 2017, by the order of the Supreme Court, the verdict was reviewed by the appellate court and overturned for lack of corpus delicti. Stenin was released from the penal colony where he was serving his sentence. We must admit that we know of no other such cases in the practice of anti-extremist law enforcement. However, in November, the Supreme Court of the Russian Federation unexpectedly granted the appeal of the Prosecutor General's Office and returned Stenin's case to the appellate court for a new consideration, where, once again, he was found guilty.[34]

It was reported in June that the Investigative Committee in Ulyanovsk had dropped the criminal case under Art. 280 Part 1 and Art. 282 Part 1 of the Criminal Code against Danila Alferiev, an activist of the Left Bloc, for lack of corpus delicti. The case against Alferiev was opened in the summer of 2016, when he was charged with inciting hatred against the social group "representatives of the authorities that currently govern Russia," based on a speech he delivered at a communist rally on Nov. 7, 2014. The activist talked about "the fifth column sitting in the State Duma, which caused the Maidan to flare up in Ukraine and which must be cleaned out," about the betrayal by

"United Russia, Medvedev and Putin" and about his own readiness to take part in the Donbass conflict and "cleanse Russia from the occupation," if given the corresponding order by Zyuganov. As Alferiev explained later, his speech was a "political performance-art piece" – a parody of the speech by Andrei Kovalenko, the leader of the Eurasian Youth Union Moscow branch, which gained some popularity online. We saw no grounds for prosecuting Alferiev.

The Oktyabrsky District Court of St. Petersburg banned five materials in 2017 from Ukrainian Web sites (one video, three articles and a de-motivating poster were added to the Federal List of Extremist Materials) containing statements about the involvement of Russian special services in terrorist attacks that took place in Russia since the late 1990s, as well as in the terrorist attacks that took place on Ukrainian territory since the development of the military conflict there. The court relied on the provision of the law "On Combating Extremist Activity," according to which public false accusations of this activity (and terrorism, in particular) against state officials constitute extremist activities. However, in our opinion, the trial failed to prove convincingly that the authors of the materials or the commentators whose opinion they cited were putting forward "knowingly false" propositions, that is, propositions in which they themselves had no reason to believe. This provision of the law is problematic per se. It can be assumed that libelously accusing high-ranking officials of serious crimes can lead to destabilization, and therefore the legislator classified them as extremist activity, but it is not clear why some such accusations, say, of ideologically-motivated murders are considered a form of extremist activity, while others – for example, accusations of other criminal murders – are not. We believe that such a provision has no place in the law on extremist activity – accusations of any kind of crimes put forward by one person against another can be examined in court in defamation suits (the question of what code should contain the article on defamation needs a separate discussion).

In 2017, as in the preceding year, Russian law enforcement agencies continued to block Ukrainian resources as well as Web sites that relocated to Ukraine after the annexation of the Crimea under the Lugovoi law. The reasons for restricting access to these resources are often quite obvious, since journalism during an armed conflict tends to use aggressive rhetoric, but the restrictions often affect analytical, informational or satirical materials as well.

The Fight Against Nationalist Activists in Federation Regions

Demonstrations by activists of nationalist movements in the constituent republics of the Russian Federation frequently attract attention of law enforcement agencies. In 2017, a number of sentences were handed down in cases initiated earlier, while tense discussions about the official languages in the republics led to new instances of pressure against local nationalists.

In April, the Oktyabrsky District Court of Ulan-Ude found Buryat activist and blogger Vladimir Khagdayev guilty of public calls for separatism (Art. 280.1 Part 2 of the Criminal Code) and of storing narcotic drugs on a large scale without the purpose of sale (Art. 228 Part 2 of the Criminal Code) and handed down a suspended sentence of three years with a three-year probationary period. We doubt that Khagdayev's statements merited criminal prosecution. According to the investigation, "having personal convictions in favor of uniting the Mongolian peoples in a single state," Khagdayev published a post and two comments that contained calls for actions toward separation of Buryatia from Russia, on VKontakte under the pseudonym "Genghis Bulgadaev" in 2014 and 2015. The incriminating social media network post is an image showing a quote from an interview with journalist Aleksandra Garmazhapova in which she was critical of the Russian nationalists and mentioned separation of Buryatia from Russia as a hypothetical scenario; this post definitely contained no separatist appeals. In his two comments, Khagdayev called for a "major geopolitical shift" and reshaping of the world and Russia, and also asked a rhetorical question "When will it be possible to take up weapons and go assimilate a Russian lieutenant-colonel neighbor?" Despite the radical nature of Khagdayev's comments, it should be recognized that they contained no specific suggestions and were left on a post that attracted almost no attention, so they hardly presented a significant public danger.

In May, the Vysokogorsky District Court of Tatarstan sentenced the Tatar nationalist Ayrat Shakirov to pay a fine of 100,000 rubles under Art. 282 Part 1 of the Criminal Code for publishing the banned video "08.02.2013 Rally in Makhachkala" on VKontakte but released him from punishment due to the statute of limitations. Shakirov denied ever posting this particular video or a number of other videos he found on his page. The video, which provides the basis for the current prosecution against the activist, is on the Federal List of Extremist Materials. It contains a recording of a speech by Gadzhimagomed Makhmudov, representative of the Ahlus

Sunnah organization, during the rally against the abuse of power by the *siloviki* (Russia's military-security establishment), conducted with official permission in Makhachkala on Feb. 8, 2013. Makhmudov's emotional speech reflected his outrage at the difficult situation of Muslims in Russia, but it contained no dangerous appeals, and, in our opinion, provided no grounds for a ban. It's not entirely clear who was implied as the object of hatred allegedly incited by Shakirov, but in any case the video does not substantiate such charges.

In October, the Leninsky District Court of Ufa sentenced Sagit Ismagilov, an activist of the Bashkir national movement, to a fine of 320,000 rubles under Art. 282 Part 1 of the Criminal Code (the Supreme Court of Bashkortostan reduced the fine to 100,000 rubles in December). Ismagilov was found guilty of sharing a text on VKontakte on the closing down of the Humanitarian Research Institute in Ufa, in which the author blamed the Tatars for the collapse of the Bashkir culture. The text was accompanied by a photograph of a book page with a fragment from a 16th-century poem containing invectives against the Tatars of the Golden Horde. In our opinion, works of past centuries should not be evaluated for compliance with modern ideas of tolerance and, particularly, with legislation on extremism. Here we are in agreement with the relevant clarification recently issued by the Constitutional Court.[35] The combination of the two texts can indeed be regarded as a statement aimed at violation of dignity on the basis of ethnicity. However, we believe that violation of dignity should be decriminalized as an act that does not pose a significant danger to society.

In August, the Vakhitovsky District Court of Kazan sentenced Danis Safargali, the leader of the Tatar Patriotic Front Altyn Urda [the Golden Horde] to three years of imprisonment in a minimum-security penal colony on charges of deliberately causing minor health damage (Art. 115 of the Criminal Code), beating (Art. 116), hooliganism (Art. 213) and inciting hatred (Art. 282).[36] The verdict was approved by the Supreme Court of Tatarstan In November. We consider Safargali's sentence under Art. 282 (handed down for 15 publications on VKontakte) at least partially inappropriate. Among other offenses, Safargali was charged with the humiliation of the Russian president, government agencies and the media, but none of the above categories should be considered a vulnerable social group protected by anti-extremist legislation. The charges against Safargali of incitement to ethnic hatred (mostly with regard to politically motivated posts) and of incitement to religious hatred (for the publication of a video to the song of the band Ensemble of Christ the Savior and Crude Mother Earth that was critical of the Russian Orthodox Church and Orthodox radicals) also did not appear very convincing.

In October, the same Vakhitovsky District Court of Kazan discontinued the case of writer Aidar Khalim, who was charged with inciting ethnic hatred. The charges against Khalim were based on his emotional statements about Russians, including references to Russian President Vladimir Putin, made on Oct. 11, 2014, during his address at the meeting dedicated to the Day of Memory of the Defenders of Kazan Killed in 1552. In his speech, Khalim reportedly reiterated the thesis of his own book *Ubit Imperiyu* (To Kill an Empire; later recognized as extremist) about the "biological death" of the Russian people and said that Russians could only be saved after "getting rid of Putin." Apparently, despite Khalim's adherence to rather radical nationalist views, the abovementioned speech contained no calls for aggressive actions toward Russians but merely expressed his opinions on the policy of the Russian authorities and on the imperial mindset. Nevertheless, we assume that the writer was not convicted solely due to his venerable age and prominence in the republic.

In May, the Naberezhnye Chelny City Court granted the request of the Republic of Tatarstan Prosecutor's Office to liquidate the Naberezhnye Chelny branch of the ATSC and ban it as an extremist organization. The organization, formerly headed by Rafis Kashapov (convicted for incitement to separatism), was banned despite its change of leadership.

In August, it became known that a criminal case had been opened in Kazan under Art. 282 against unidentified people based on the fact of the activity of ATSC's flagship organization. According to the Center, the case was triggered by a picket and a conference conducted by the Center that focused on the fate of the Tatar language as the second state language in Tatarstan. During these events, critical statements were made about the language policy in the republic that cited the fact that Tatar is almost never used as an official language and proposed various measures to maintain its status.

In mid-October, Tatarstan Prosecutor General Ildus Nafikov issued a warning to the ATSC regarding the impermissibility of violating legislation on combating extremism. The Prosecutor's Office gave the organization two months to address the violation, which consisted of "carrying out its activities and issuing its decisions in the Tatar language only." The Prosecutor's Office stated that, according to the Federal Law on the State Language of the Russian Federation, Russian as the state language "is mandatory for use in the activities of organizations of all forms of ownership." In addition, the prosecutors found "signs of information aimed at inciting hatred on the basis of 'relation toward language' " in the January speech "Save the Tatar language" by the ATSC presidium to deputies of different levels and political and public organizations of the republic, which proposed discussing the idea of granting Tatar the status of the only state language in the republic in order to counteract its gradual displacement. The Prosecutor's Office regarded this suggestion as a discriminatory statement and declared that the ATSC was seeking to "limit the rights and legitimate interests of Russian-speaking citizens." It should be noted that violations of the Law on Language are not covered under anti-extremist legislation. As for discussions regarding the status of a particular language, in our opinion, they do not violate the law, and ATSC made no calls for discrimination on the basis of one's linguistic identity.

For Calls to Extremist Activities and Incitement of Hatred Toward Public Officials

Prosecution for various statements "against the authorities" presents a separate direction of law enforcement agencies' fight against "extremism." In our opinion, such prosecution is appropriate only when dealing with dangerous incitement to specific violent actions; otherwise, it only fuels discontent in society. We would like to remind readers that the Supreme Court of the Russian Federation, in its Ruling No. 11 of the plenary meeting "On Judicial Practice in Criminal Cases Regarding Crimes of Extremism," of June 28, 2011, pointed out that the limits of permissible criticism against officials should be wider than in the case of ordinary citizens, and that criticism of political beliefs or organizations per se should not be seen as an act aimed at inciting hatred or enmity;[37] this position was confirmed in 2016.[38]

In August, the Tverskoi District Court of Moscow handed down a verdict against members of the Initiative Group of the Referendum "For Responsible Power" (*Za otvetstvennuiu vlast*, FRP), Yury Mukhin, Valery Parfyonov, Aleksandr Sokolov and Kirill Barabash, who were found guilty under Part 1 of Art. 282.2 of the Criminal Code for continuing the activities of an organization recognized as extremist, namely the banned Army of People's Will (*Armiya Voli Naroda*, APW). Mukhin received a suspended sentence of four years followed by one year of restrictions on freedom and four years of probation; Sokolov was sentenced to three years and six months in a minimum-security penal colony; Parfyonov and Barabash – to four years in a penal colony each. Barabash was also stripped of his military rank of lieutenant colonel of the Air Force Reserve. The Moscow City Court considered an appeal in the case in December and reduced the prison terms for Barabash and Parfyonov from four years to three years and ten months in a minimum-security colony due to extenuating circumstances – the court took into account Parfyonov's health and the fact that Barabash was a combat veteran. We believe that the APW, an organization of the Stalinist-nationalist kind repeatedly implicated in xenophobic propaganda, was banned inappropriately. The decision to recognize it as extremist was based solely on the ban of the leaflet *You have elected – You are to judge!* (*Ty izbral – tebe sudit*), which contained a proposal to hold a nationwide referendum and adopt a new article of the Constitution and the corresponding law, according to which the president and members of parliament would be criminally responsible for the deteriorating quality of life of the population; it was also suggested that any attempts to evade punishment should put them outside the law. The call to conduct any kind of referendum, in our opinion, should not be regarded as extremist, therefore we considered the ban of the organization to be unfounded,[39] and accordingly we also view prosecution for continuing the activities of the APW as inappropriate.

In September, the Novocheboksarsk City Court in Chuvashia sentenced Aleksei Mironov, a volunteer of Aleksei Navalny's Cheboksary headquarters, to two years three months in a settlement colony. Mironov was found guilty under Art. 280 Part 2 of the Criminal Code (public calls for extremist activities via the Internet) and Art. 282 of the Criminal Code (incitement to ethnic hatred) for his VKontakte posts. We do not consider the charge under Art. 282 inappropriate, although, in our opinion, the offense didn't deserve a real prison sentence. Meanwhile, Mironov's conviction under Art. 280 was based on the fact that he had posted an image on his VKontakte page of an identity card of a citizen subject to military conscription, accompanied by the caption in English: "God bless the USA. Keep calm and f*** Russia" and with the text "I officially call for a violent change of government" placed on top of the image. In our opinion, such an anti-government statement of a general nature made by an ordinary citizen poses no danger to the state, especially since the audience of this post was minimal.

In November, the Krasnogvardeysky District Court of St. Petersburg handed down a verdict in the case of Russian nationalist Vladimir Timoshenko, finding him guilty of inciting hatred toward the social group "employees of agencies and institutions of the state" (Art. 282 Part 1 of the Criminal Code), and sentenced him to two years in a maximum-security penal colony. The defense intends to appeal the verdict. Timoshenko was previously convicted in 2010 in the Novgorod Province for an attempt to prepare a terrorist attack (according to the investigation, he intended to blow up the wall of the Novgorod Kremlin to draw attention to the problems of "Russia and the Russian people,") as well as in Kislovodsk, in 2011, for illegal manufacture and trafficking of weapons. In January 2015, while in a penal colony in the Novgorod Province, Timoshenko dictated a text over the telephone to his fiancée which she then published on his behalf in the "Slavic Force – Nord West Peterburg" community on VKontakte. The text was dedicated to the "fight" against "the anti-national regime of Putin and his power base, the punitive-repressive apparatus" and contained a call to "deliver a crushing blow" against this apparatus. We believe that the verdict against Timoshenko was inappropriate – the published text (unlike other personal notes seized from him), contained a call only for an abstract "crushing blow," not for any specific actions.

In December, the Miass City Court in the Chelyabinsk Province found Aidar Kuchukov guilty of incitement to ethnic hatred (Art. 282 Part 1) and handed down a 2-year suspended sentence with a 2-year probationary period. Kuchukov is a former investigator in the Miass police department and a former lawyer, who was deprived of his status for significant violations of his client's interests in a criminal case. His political views are oppositional. He was found guilty on the basis of his 2016 publications on the social media network Moi Mir, in which he "imposed provocative topics, unrelated to those being discussed, on the conversation participants, and posted messages grounded in ethnic hatred" as well as used insulting language with respect to Russians. We do not know whether Kuchukov made hateful xenophobic statements that incited hatred. However, from the report by the prosecutors, we know that Kuchukov was also charged for leaving comments under the news posted by various media outlets; in particular, he commented "about the inevitability of imminent defeat of the Russian Armed Forces in Syria, about the vulnerability of our weapons, about the anti-national regime of Vladimir Putin and the rapid growth of popular protest aimed at changing the government" and "about illegal activities of the FSB in the Crimea, the anti-national annexation of the peninsula, and the deterioration of quality of life in Russia because of it." Such statements of opinion on political issues are not covered under Art. 282 of the Criminal Code.

It is worth noting that at least one person had such charges against him dropped in 2017. In November, the Gryazovetsky District Court in the Vologda Province acquitted civic activist Yevgeny Domozhirov, who had been charged under Part 1 of Art. 282 for inciting hatred toward the social group of "Vologda police officers." Domozhirov posted on his Web site a material, in which he, in harsh terms, described the local police officers who had arrived to conduct a search at his house and then damaged his mother's hand in the ensuing squabble. He was found guilty of insulting a police officer (Art. 319 of the Criminal Code) and sentenced to 90 hours of mandatory labor.[40]

In March, the Federal List of Extremist Materials came to include two images banned in 2016 by the Central District Court of Tver. One of them is the de-motivating poster (No. 4071 on the list), described by the court as follows: "A poster depicting a man who resembles President of the Russian Federation V.V. Putin with makeup on his face – painted eyelashes and lips – this, according to the author(s) of the poster, was intended as a hint regarding the supposedly non-standard sexual orientation of the Russian president. The text under the image (reproduced with original spelling and punctuation but with the obscenities removed): 'Putin's voters are like***there seem to be many of them, but among my acquaintances there are none.' " The de-motivating poster does not contain calls for incitement of hatred on any of the grounds listed in the law "On Combating Extremist Activity," and, therefore, its prohibition was obviously inappropriate.[41] The same can be said about the image included on the list as No. 4072 ("a poster-collage depicting three people, two of them (in the uniform of the Third Reich soldiers) resemble President V.V. Putin and Prime Minister D.A. Medvedev; a photograph of Kirill, Patriarch of Moscow and All Russia, with the caption 'The invaders are in Moscow already' is on the right"). In our opinion, this collage is an tool of political polemics and, in and of itself, does not call for any unlawful actions. However, the court found that both images insult the dignity of citizens on the basis of belonging to a social group, although in both cases it is impossible to establish the specific social group is implied by the decisions.

Banning the image of the President in makeup was perceived as a funny oddity and actively discussed online, leading to quite serious consequences. In June, the Yelets City Court ordered local activist Gennady Makarov detained for five days under Art. 20.29 of the Code of Administrative Offenses for distribution of the controversial image. Makarov's post on

VKontakte actually discussed the fact that the image had been recognized as extremist. The publication cited the corresponding item of the Federal List and criticized the court's decision; the caption was not displayed. Makarov appealed the decision of the court in the ECHR; his complaint has been communicated.

Other Abuse of Criminalization of Incitement to Hatred

We regard several other sentences handed down by the Russian courts in 2017 for the incitement of various kinds of hatred to be inappropriate or insufficiently justified. It can be assumed that the percentage of such sentences, among those delivered in 2017 under Art. 282, is, in fact, much higher, but, in most cases, we simply have no information to assess the degree of appropriateness of verdicts under Art. 282. We can only repeat that the very scale of prosecution against citizens under this article (and for public utterances overall) raises serious concerns.

As noted above, in our opinion, anti-extremist articles should protect only particularly vulnerable groups of the population. However, law enforcement agencies bring people to responsibility for inciting hatred to a wide variety of social groups.

Rapper David "Ptakha" Nuriyev was fined 200,000 rubles in Moscow in March 2017 for inciting hatred against "a group of people united on the basis of 'assisting law enforcement agencies in search and detention of criminals' and being representatives of the public organization Antidealer." The prosecution was based on Ptakha's speech in the 16 Tons nightclub in September 2015 on the subject of the Antidealer movement, which contained insults against the movement's activists and calls for unlawful actions (damaging their property), but no incitement to violence.

Mikhail Pokalchuk, a resident of Gorokhovets in Vladimir Province, received a suspended prison sentence with a one-year probation period under Part 1 of Art. 282 in February. He was found guilty of inciting hatred toward the social group "anti-fascists" by publishing a video on VKontakte. There was at least one new similar case – against a 28-year-old resident of Novgorod who published on the same social media network an image "expressing his negative assessment of representatives of the social group antifa, which advocates the fight against fascism" – in 2015.

We were informed in November about newly initiated criminal pro-ceedings under Art. 282 Part 1 of the Criminal Code against Valery Bolshakov – the chairman of the Union of Workers of Sevastopol. He was charged with "giving a deliberate negative assessment of the social group 'Terek Cossacks' acting on the basis of political and ideological hatred and enmity." In addition to the fact that the Terek Cossacks can hardly be considered a vulnerable social group, it should also be noted that the incitement of political and ideological hatred is not covered by Art. 282.[42]

In mid-March, an English language instructor from Vladivostok received a suspended sentence of two years for "using phrases and idioms" that violated the dignity of Russians during a volleyball game on an embankment court. Since his statements were heard not by numerous passers-by on the embankment but only by the conflicting parties on the court, they should not have been considered public. In addition, we also believe that violation of dignity should be removed from Art. 282, since it does not pose a serious public danger.

In May in Cheboksary, 61-year-old local resident Vladimir Avdeyev received a suspended sentence of two and a half years for publishing three compositions by the Ensemble of Christ the Savior and Crude Mother Earth that have been put on the Federal List of Extremist Materials (No. 3011): "Breaking the Crescent," "Heart Takes No Orders," and "Crucify All These Deputies." Avdeyev claimed that he had shared someone else's post on his social media network page about the fact that the songs had been added to the Federal List, and that post had the audio recordings of the banned songs as an attachment, but this circumstance had no effect on the court decision. The song "Heart Takes No Orders" comically extols Hitler; the song "Crucify All These Deputies" talks about the parliamentarians wallowing in vice; the song "Breaking the Crescent" is about migrants from the Caucasus as internal enemies who are blamed for all ills. The texts of the latter two songs clearly express hostility or disrespect toward groups of citizens (note, however, that the law does not prohibit offensive statements about groups of politicians) and include direct calls for reprisals against representatives of such groups. At the same time, the lyrics of the song about the deputies come across as grotesque, while the song "Breaking the Crescent" has a pronounced xenophobic character and could be taken seriously by the audience. Nevertheless, taking into account that the Ensemble verbally recommends perceiving their texts as satirical, the prosecution for the dissemination of their texts – and they are increasingly appearing in criminal and administrative cases – appears insufficiently justified. It is worth noting that two more comic songs by the Ensemble ("Kill the Cosmonauts" and

"The Collider"), banned for no reason whatsoever, were recognized as extremist in 2017.

Meanwhile, one notorious case under Art. 282 was closed in 2017. In early August, the Maikop City Court closed a criminal case against ecologist Valery Brinikh for lack of corpus delicti; he had been charged with contributing to incitement to ethnic hatred (Art. 33 Part 5 and Art. 282 Part 1 of the Criminal Code) for publishing an article on environmental pollution caused by a large pig farm. The investigation believed that the material "foments ethnic hatred and sows enmity," and "calls for carrying out extremist activities." In his article "The Silence of the Lambs" the author accused the residents of the Adygean district where the polluting enterprise was located of subservience to the authorities and failure to actively defend their interests. The text was recognized as extremist in 2014. However, now, in connection with the termination of the case against Brinikh, the ban was lifted in September 2017 – notably, on the initiative of the Adygea Republic Prosecutor's Office.

For "Rehabilitation of Nazism"

In March, a criminal case under Art. 354.1 was opened in Magadan against 62-year-old zoologist Igor Dorogoi. The charges were based on Dorogoi's publications on the social media network Odnoklassniki, in which he expressed negative opinions of Georgy Zhukov, Mikhail Tukhachevsky, Aleksandr Marinesko and Roman Rudenko as people involved in the mass death of people, and of Meliton Kantaria as a tool of Soviet propaganda. The investigation inappropriately interpreted these statements as "dissemination of information expressing obvious disrespect to society with regard to the days of military glory and the memorable dates of Russia associated with defending the Fatherland" (Art. 354.1 Part 3). Dorogoi also faced responsibility for some of the comments left by his readers, which were interpreted as an assertion that the USSR "started the war" in 1939, despite the fact that the comments contained no such statements. In addition, the investigation interpreted a photograph taken in Western Ukraine of a poster featuring Stepan Bandera and the caption "National Heroes of Ukraine: Hero of Ukraine Stepan Bandera" as an endorsement of the crimes established by the verdict of the International Military Tribunal (Art. 354.1 Part 1), although the verdict of the Tribunal never mentioned Bandera's activity. We see this case as an attempt to restrict the right to a historical discussion, which is definitely outside the scope of the article on justification of Nazism even in its current problematic wording. In 2021, Igor Dorogoi died and was never sentenced.

In March, the Leninsky District Court of St. Petersburg recognized "Bandera and Banderites: Who They Really Were," an article by historian Kirill Aleksandrov, as extremist material, and the St. Petersburg City Court upheld this ban in December. The decision of the Leninsky District Court was based on an opinion authored by an expert from St. Petersburg State University that found that Aleksandrov's article contained denial of the acts and the approval of the crimes established by the International Military Tribunal and libel against the actions of the USSR during World War II – that is, it fell under the formula of Art. 354.1 of the Criminal Code. Having read Aleksandrov's article, we found no denial of the crimes of the Nazis and their allies and no dissemination of any information about the actions of the USSR except for what is already well-known. In addition, it is important to note that the fact that a text corresponds to the formula of a Criminal Code article does not necessarily entail that it should be considered extremist. First, a court must establish that the text in question corresponds to Art. 1 Part 3 of the Law on Combating Extremist Activity, according to which extremist materials are defined as "calling for extremist activity to be carried out or substantiating or justifying the necessity of carrying out such activity, including works by leaders of the National Socialist German Workers' Party, the Fascist party of Italy, publications substantiating or justifying ethnic and/or racial superiority or justifying the practice of committing war crimes or other crimes aimed at the full or partial destruction of any ethnic, social, racial, national or religious group."

In August, the Moskovsky District Court of St. Petersburg recognized the book *Vostochnye Razmyshleniya* (Oriental Reflections) by Polish publicist Jan Nowak-Jeziorański as information prohibited for distribution in Russia both in the paper layout and in the electronic copy published online.[43] In making this decision, the court relied primarily on the prosecutorial assertion that the distribution of the book violated Art. 354.1, because the book contained false information about the activities of the USSR during World War II. The experts brought in by the prosecutor's office to examine the text, for example, regarded the author's treatment of events that traditionally caused controversy – the Warsaw Uprising, the Volyn Massacre and the Katyn Massacre – as a "distortion" of history. In our opinion, this decision explicitly restricts historical debate and constitutes unreasonable interference with the right to freedom of speech using a tool provided to law enforcement by the wording of Art. 354.1, which criminalizes the public dissemination of knowingly false information about the activities of the USSR during World War II.

For Extremist Symbols

According to the statistics of the Judicial Department of the Supreme Court, in the first half of 2017 alone, 910 people faced responsibility under Art. 20.3 of the Code of Administrative Offenses (propaganda and public display of Nazi attributes or symbols, as well as symbols of extremist organizations),[44] but only for some of these administrative cases we have the details and can judge the extent of their legitimacy. In the course of the year, our records showed 46 episodes of prosecution for public display of Nazi symbols or symbols of banned organizations that were obviously not aimed at dangerous propaganda – an approximately 250% increase over the preceding year. Increasingly, this article is being used to exert pressure against activists seen as undesirable by the authorities.

As an illustration, let us review the chain of punishments that were imposed on activists in Krasnodar Territory. In June, Natalia Kudeyeva – a supporter of Vyacheslav Maltsev and a coordinator of the *Artpodgotovka* [Preparatory Artillery Fire] movement protest walks in Krasnodar – was sentenced to 14 days detention under Art. 20.3 of the Code of Administrative Offenses (the term of her detention was reduced to 10 days on appeal) for publishing a collage with a swastika and a portrait of Putin on VKontakte. Such de-motivating posters aimed at criticizing Russia's political course gained significant online popularity in 2014. Local blogger Leonid Kudinov created and posted on the Internet a number of videos telling the story of Kudeyeva's detention and of other prosecutions under Art. 20.3, in which he noted in particular, that "patriotic" citizens regularly published images with swastikas without facing any consequences and cited corresponding examples. As a result, he was brought to responsibility for posting the videos not once but three times – he was fined twice and detained for a day once. In October, activist Raisa Pogodayeva from Goryachy Klyuch in Krasnodar Territory was detained for 10 days for sharing one of Kudinov's videos. The story didn't end there either. "Throughout December, everyone was writing me personal messages. I have 1,400 VKontakte friends. Everyone wanted to know why I had been incarcerated. Well, I got tired of answering everyone separately and decided to post the information on my wall, so everyone could see," said Pogodayeva. She attached the link leading to Kudinov's video for the post about the reasons for her detention. Since the video was played on her page, she was sentenced for 10 days under detention once again in January 2018. "The prosecutor told me later that I was supposed to remove the video, leaving only the hyperlink," the activist explained.[45]

Publishing images of historical objects is also punishable under Art. 20.3. This frequently affects antique dealers if they post online ads regarding the sale of items from the Third Reich accompanied by photographs.

Amateur history connoisseurs also face responsibility under Art. 20.3. Thus, in November, the Krasnoarmeysky District Court of Volgograd fined Sergei Demidov, a senior operator of the Kaustik plant, for posting images of the Third Reich flag and details of the uniforms of Nazi military units on his VKontakte page. Demidov is interested in the history of the Great Patriotic War – particularly the Battle of Stalingrad – and participates in excavations of the battlegrounds in the Volgograd Region; on his VKontakte page, he published the photographs of his finds and various materials about the Wehrmacht, the Red Army, the course of military operations and military equipment; his intentions were clearly unrelated to propaganda of Nazism.

The Federal List of Extremist Materials

In 2017, the Federal List of Extremist Materials was updated 33 times (a year earlier it was updated 54 times), 330 items were added to it (a year ago there were 786 items), and it grew from 4,015 to 4,345 entries.[46] However, there are actually more materials: Some entries may include several materials at once. We should also note that in 2017, item No. 4175 was excluded from the list after being added earlier that year, as were items No. 3452-3455, which had been added in 2016.

The Justice Ministry has changed the procedure for announcing changes to the Federal List of Extremist Materials. Since December 2017, the Ministry of Justice has not only added to the list, but has also posted a dated news article about the updates. However, this information is now published with a delay. For instance, certain new items appeared on the list on Jan. 10 while in the news, the respective update was reported on Dec. 29.

The list was less intensively updated than a year earlier – obviously due to the new procedure for banning materials for extremism. The corresponding regulation of the Prosecutor General's Office adopted in the spring of 2016 only began to impact judicial decisions by 2017.

Additions to the list are distributed across the following topics:

- Xenophobic materials of modern Russian nationalists – 212;
- Materials of other nationalists – 27;
- Materials of Islamic militants and other calls by political Islamists for violence – 30;
- Other Islamic materials – 13;
- Materials of Eastern Orthodox fundamentalists – two;
- Other religious materials – seven;
- Extremely radical anti-Russian speeches from Ukraine (we distinguish them from "other nationalists") – six;
- Other materials from the Ukrainian media and Internet – six;
- Other materials calling for disorder and violence – three;
- Fiction and historians' texts – two;
- Anti-religious materials – eight;
- Peaceful opposition materials – three;
- Parody materials taken seriously – five;
- Christian anti-Islamic materials – one;
- Materials that were clearly banned by mistake – two;
- Materials that were created, in our opinion, by people in an altered state of consciousness – one;
- Unidentifiable materials – two.

The share of online materials on the list is unsurprisingly growing: At least 304 items of 330 are materials from the Internet, including those sent through messengers (a year ago it was 711 items of 785). The majority are various xenophobic materials from VKontakte. Offline materials in 2017 included various types of ethno-xenophobic literature, books by Eastern Orthodox fundamentalists, Muslims, Jehovah's Witnesses and Yehowist-Ilyinites, as well as leaflets.

Sometimes it is not completely clear where precisely a piece of banned material was posted: Thus, for example, item 4,028 was only described through its title without any additional publication data.

However, the case is often otherwise: The same material published and posted at different Web addresses appears on the list several times. Thus, a drawing "in the form of a pig dressed in jeans, tennis shoes and a jacket, in the hands of which is an object that resembles a knife" with a xenophobic text is repeated with various Web addresses from item 4,228 to 4,232. Duplicates posted on different pages were repeatedly added to the list in 2017.

Unfortunately, the slowdown in the growth of the list has not improved the quality of the description of items, and the number of carelessly described materials is growing. Thus, how can we, for example, interpret the material from item 4,299: "leaflet *Agent of German espionage rules Russia!*, author and place of publication unknown, on four pages"?! At least a dozen leaflets with such a headline, which were published between 1918 and the 1920s, can be found in major libraries.

Furthermore, it is already regular protocol that some materials continue to inappropriately be deemed extremist. In 2017, at least 38 of such materials were added to the list (materials of Jehovah's Witnesses, brochures of the Yehowist-Ilyinites, Muslim materials, opposition materials from Ukrainian Web sites and some others).

Blocking of Online Resources and Internet Censorship

Based on the data of the Roskomsvoboda Web site,[47] we believe that 297 resources have ended up on the Unified Register of Banned Web Sites "for extremism" following a court decision compared to 486 a year earlier.[48]

The following types of resources were on the Unified Register during the year:

- Xenophobic materials of Russian nationalists – 180;
- Nazi symbols independent of ties with Russian nationalists – three;
- Materials of radical Islamic militants and other calls by political Islamists for violence – 31;
- Peaceful Muslim materials – 40;
- Banned Islamic symbols on their own, apart from connections with radical Islamists – one;
- Anti-Islamic materials – one;
- Materials of the Jehovah's Witnesses – two;
- Inflammatory anti-government materials (including Boris Stomakhin's article) – two;
- Extremely radical statements from Ukraine and symbols of banned organizations – nine;

244 | RUSSIA'S ANTI-EXTREMISM LAW ENFORCEMENT

- Other materials from the Ukrainian media and Internet – six;
- Materials by Fascist ideologists – nine;
- Large, varied masses of texts that were blocked as a whole – one;
- Peaceful materials criticizing the Russian Orthodox Church – five;
- Peaceful opposition materials – three;
- Materials that were clearly banned by mistake – one;
- Unknown – three.

The Unified Register is supplemented with the separate register according to the Lugovoi law.[49] While the Unified Register expanded more slowly last year than earlier, the Lugovoi register is growing rapidly: In 2017, 1,247 resources were added to it (in 2016, 923 were added).[50] In total, according to our calculations, 2,495 resources blocked "for extremism" have been added to the Lugovoi register.

The following types of resources were added to the Lugovoi register:

- Materials of radical Islamic militants and other calls by political Islamists for violence (including ISIS videos and calls to go to Syria) – 488;
- Materials of Hizb ut-Tahrir Islamist party – 442;
- Materials of Ukrainian nationalist organizations and the Web sites of Ukrainian organizations banned in Russia – 141;
- Other materials of Ukrainian media – 61;
- Materials of Russian nationalists – 35;
- Calls to participate in the rallies of Russian nationalists (including the calls of Vyacheslav Maltsev for revolution on Nov. 5) – 14;
- Calls to attend opposition rallies – four;
- Calls for violence (real and parodies) unrelated to the above categories – 25;
- Materials of Russian separatists and about them – seven;
- Other calls to participate in local demonstrations – three;
- Anti-religious materials – 11;
- Web sites of undesirable organizations – eight;
- Anti-Ukrainian Web sites – one;
- Resources with compromising materials – one (the Web site of UtroNews);
- Various religious materials – one (the video where Takeshi Kitano listens to Shoko Asahara in an old Japanese TV show);[51]

- Fiction – one (the book *Islamic Breakthrough* by Muslim Dmitry Akhtyamov);
- Parody Russophobic materials – one;
- Online games – one (the game "Russian Terrorists");
- Web sites on Armenian-Azerbaijani themes – one (the article "Grey wolves in Derbent. From whence do the roots of a mass shooting of tourists grow?" by Nadzhmudin Aliev, which was published on Kavkaz-Press);
- Unidentifiable materials – one.

Pages that were created for the mobilization of mass demonstrations (resources with calls for revolution by Vyacheslav Maltsev), that is, precisely those which might explain the adoption of the Lugovoi law, despite multiple blockings, remain freely accessible until now. Many materials that are the same (or practically the same) as those that were blocked are currently completely available, and during the preparation for a demonstration, all information on the Internet reaches its intended recipients almost instantaneously.

On the list, there are also links to banned Ukrainian Web sites and to pages of organizations considered undesirable, and this is a clear example of political bias. Besides this, the number of links to blocked opposition Web sites and calls to attend opposition rallies on the list is rising. These examples show that extrajudicial blocking carried out only on the basis of suspicion inevitably leads to arbitrariness and abuse by the authorities.

NOTES

1. Nationalist movement "Frontier of the North" liquidated in Syktyvkar // SOVA Center. Nov. 25, 2017 (http://www.sova-center.ru/racism-xenophobia/news/counteraction/2016/11/d35899/).

2. T.O.Y.S. group banned in Samara // SOVA Center. April 26, 2017 (http://www.sova-center.ru/racism-xenophobia/news/counteraction/2017/04/d37256/).

3. Recognized as extremist by the Supreme Court of the Republic of Crimea on April 2, 2016. For more information, see: Mejlis of the Crimean Tatar People recognized as an extremist organization // SOVA Center. April 26, 2016 (http://www.sova-center.ru/misuse/news/persecution/2016/04/d34413/).

4. City Court of Naberezhnye Chelny liquidates Rafis Kashapov's organization // SOVA Center. May 11, 2017 (http://www.sova-center.ru/misuse/news/persecution/2017/05/d37014/).

5. Recognized as extremist by the Court of the Jewish Autonomous Region on Oct. 3, 2016.

6. Moscow: Maksim "Tesak" Martsinkevich and his accomplices convicted // SOVA Center. June 27, 2017 (http://www.sova-center.ru/racism-xenophobia/news/counteraction/2017/06/d37365/).

7. Verdict rendered in the Khabarovsk flesher-girls case // SOVA Center. Aug. 25, 2017 (http://www.sova-center.ru/racism-xenophobia/news/counteraction/2017/08/d37747/).

8. Verdict rendered in the case related to murder of the leader of Otvet Chamberlenu band // SOVA Center. Aug. 28, 2017 (http://www.sova-center.ru/racism-xenophobia/news/counteraction/2017/08/d37762/).

9. St. Petersburg: Verdict rendered in the case related to murder of journalist Dmitry Tsilikin // SOVA Center. May 30, 2017 (http://www.sova-center.ru/racism-xenophobia/news/counteraction/2017/05/d37195/).

10. Recognize Tsilikin's murder as a hate crime // Change.org. Sept. 19, 2016 (https://www.change.org/p/признать-убийство-циликина-преступлением-на-почве-ненависти).

11. See for example: Verkhovsky, A., Kozhevnikova, Galina. Inappropriate Enforcement of Anti-Extremist Legislation in Russia in 2008 // SOVA Center. April 21, 2009 (http://www.sova-center.ru/en/misuse/reports-analyses/2009/04/d15800/).

12. Total statistical figures about the activity of federal courts of general jurisdiction and magistrates' courts for the first six months of 2017 // Official Web site of the Supreme Court of the Russian Federation (http://www.cdep.ru/userimages/sudebnaya_statistika/2017/F1-svod_1-2017.xls).

13. According to data posted on the Supreme Court's Web site, Parts 1 and 2 of Art. 148 were the main article of accusation for three people, and two had an additional article; Art. 205.2 – 33 and six, respectively; Art. 280 – 49 and 26; Art. 280.1 – one and two; Art. 282 – 205 and 45; Art. 354.1 – one and one. These articles may be combined both with one another and with other articles (see below in this presentation), so the real number of those convicted for statements remains between the sum of the first figures and the sum of the first and second.

14. Furthermore, all calculations are made based specifically on convictions we know about, despite the fact that judging by Supreme Court data there are at least two and a half times more, perhaps even three times more, convictions. However, according to the amount of data we possess, it is possible to suppose that the observed regularities and proportions will be accurate for the entire volume of convictions.

15. Togliatti: Conviction made in the case of the leader of the Community of Indigenous Russian People // SOVA Center. Dec. 21, 2017 (http://www.sova-center.ru/racism-xenophobia/news/counteraction/2017/12/d38543/).

16. Magnitogorsk: conviction made for publications on social media // SOVA Center. April 27, 2017 (http://www.sova-center.ru/racism-xenophobia/news/counteraction/2017/04/d36916/).

17. In Moscow, participants of the Misanthropic Division movement were convicted // SOVA Center. June 20, 2017 (http://www.sova-center.ru/racism-xenophobia/news/counteraction/2017/06/d37326/).

18. Kazan: director of the Union of Young Innovation Leaders convicted // SOVA Center. February 1, 2017 (http://www.sova-center.ru/racism-xenophobia/news/counteraction/2017/02/d36294/).

19. Leader of NOMP, colonel Kvachkov, receives another 18 months in strict-regime prison // SOVA Center. Aug. 23, 2017 (http://www.sova-center.ru/racism-xenophobia/news/counteraction/2017/08/d37714/).

20. Moscow: conviction made in case against Yury Yekishev // SOVA Center. May 3, 2017 (http://www.sova-center.ru/racism-xenophobia/news/counteraction/2017/05/d36967/).

21. For the announcement of the verdict, D. Bobrov did not appear and fled from the investigation. For more details see: Leader of the NSI receives two years in prison // SOVA Center. Sept. 12, 2017 (http://www.sova-center.ru/racism-xenophobia/news/counteraction/2017/09/d37860/).

22. Chelyabinsk: Conviction under Art. 282 made against former member of skinhead group // SOVA Center. May 12, 2017 (http://www.sova-center.ru/racism-xenophobia/news/counteraction/2017/05/d37036/).

23. Dmitry Dyomushkin has repeatedly become a figure in criminal and administrative cases and has violated his travel restrictions. However, he had never been convicted before.

24. Dyomushkin receives two and a half years in a minimum-security penal colony // SOVA Center. April 25, 2017 (http://www.sova-center.ru/racism-xenophobia/news/counteraction/2017/04/d36897/).

25. Nationalist Nikolai Bondarik sentenced in St. Petersburg // SOVA Center. Jan. 9, 2017 (http://www.sova-center.ru/racism-xenophobia/news/counteraction/2017/01/d36141/).

26. Leader of T.O.Y.S. convicted in Samara // SOVA Center. Nov. 24, 2017 (http://www.sova-center.ru/racism-xenophobia/news/counteraction/2017/11/d38350/).

27. See, for example, Yudina, N. Anti-Extremism in Virtual Russia in 2014-2015 // SOVA Center. Aug. 24, 2016 (http://www.sova-center.ru/files/xeno/web14-15-eng.pdf).

28. Ruling of the Plenary Meeting of the Supreme Court of the Russian Federation No. 41 on issues of judicial practice in criminal cases of terrorist and extremist nature // SOVA Center. Nov. 28, 2016 (http://www.sova-center.ru/racism-xenophobia/docs/2016/11/d35905/).

29. About approaches to law enforcement in this field, see: Rabat Plan of Action on the prohibition of advocacy of national, racial or religious hatred that constitutes incitement to discrimination, hostility or violence // Office of the United Nations High Comissioner for Human Rights. 2013 (http://www.ohchr.org/EN/Issues/FreedomReligion/Pages/RabatPlanOfAction.aspx).

30. Here we do not look into convictions that were clearly unjustified, and also do not go into the convictions against members of Hizb ut-Tahrir al-Islami.

31. In the city of Samara, a resident was ruled to be guilty of terrorist crimes // Official Web site of the Russian Federation Investigative Committee Department for the Samara region. Nov. 21, 2017 (http://samara.sledcom.ru/news/item/1182233/).

32. A suspended sentence of two years handed down for involvement in the activity of an extremist organization // SOVA Center. Sept. 29, 2017 (http://www.sova-center.ru/racism-xenophobia/news/counteraction/2017/09/d37965/).

33. For more details, see: In the Krasnodar territory, conviction made in case against members of the Spiritual and Tribal Rus // SOVA Center. Dec. 27, 2017 (http://www.sova-center.ru/racism-xenophobia/news/counteraction/2017/12/d38580/).

34. It was reported in February 2018 that Stenin left Russia with his wife and son. He explained that he had decided to leave fearing the pressure on his family by security officials but that he still intends to pursue the overturning of his verdict and compensation for unreasonable prosecution.

35. The Constitutional Court Ruled on a Complaint Regarding Prohibition to Recognize the Content of the Sacred Texts of the Major World Religions as Extremist // SOVA Center. May 29, 2017 (http://www.sova-center.ru/misuse/news/lawmaking/2017/05/d37184/).

36. Safargali was sentenced for violent actions following his clash with representatives of the company from which he and his wife were renting a space for a student hostel in a building in the Kazan city center.

37. Ruling of the Plenary meeting of the Supreme Court No. 11 "On Judicial Practice in Criminal Cases Regarding Crimes of Extremism" // SOVA Center. June 29, 2011 (http://www.sova-center.ru/misuse/docs/2011/06/d21988/).

38. Ruling of the Plenary Meeting of the Supreme Court of the Russian Federation No. 41 "On Issues of Judicial Practice in Criminal Cases of Terrorist and Extremist Nature" // SOVA Center. Nov. 28, 2016 (http://www.sova-center.ru/racism-xenophobia/docs/2016/11/d35905/).

39. If we consider the calls by the APW from the point of view of Art. 17 of the European Convention for the Protection of Human Rights and Fundamental Freedoms, which states that the Convention does not protect actions aimed at excessive limitation of human rights recognized by it, it can be said that the APW called for such a limitation. However, the proposed limitation can hardly be considered so radical, as to justify the need to ban the organization.

40. The Vologda Province Court upheld this sentence in January 2018.

41. It is worth noting that this de-motivator is indisputably homophobic; nevertheless, it cannot be regarded as inciting hatred toward gays.

42. In early 2018, Bolshakov also faced charges for his other posts as well as for his one-man picket (under Art. 280).

43. This decision was upheld by the St. Petersburg City Court in January 2018.

44. Consolidated Statistical Data on the Activities of Federal Courts of General Jurisdiction and Magistrates' Courts for the First Half of 2017 // Judicial Department at the Supreme Court of the Russian Federation. 2017 (http://www.cdep.ru/index.php?id=79&item=4151).

45. A retiree from Krasnodar Territory was Arrested Twice for a VKontakte Video // OVD-Info. February 5, 2018 (https://ovdinfo.org/express-news/2018/02/05/pensionerku-iz-krasnodarskogo-kraya-dvazhdy-arestovali-za-rolik-vo-vkontakte).

46. As at Feb. 15, 2018, this list consists of 4,382 items.

47. See: The Unified Register of Banned Web Sites // Roskomsvoboda (http://reestr.rublacklist.net/).

48. See the updated list: "Extremist resources" on the Unified Register of Banned Web Sites // SOVA Center (http://www.sova-center.ru/racism-xenophobia/docs/2016/04/d34421/).

49. Full name: "On Amending the Federal Law 'On Information, Information Technologies and Protection of Information.' "

50. See the updated list: Resources on the register of Web sites blocked according to the Lugovoi law // SOVA Center (http://www.sova-center.ru/racism-xenophobia/docs/2017/10/d38006/).

51. Only the first part of this show is banned, the second part is not.

Banning Organizations as Extremist

In 2018, seven organizations were added to the list of extremist organizations published on the Web site of the Ministry of Justice, which is slightly higher than in the previous year, when six organizations were added.

Over the year, the following radical organizations banned in December 2017 were added to the list:

- The neo-Nazi group Schtolz (Schtolz Khabarovsk, Schtolz Far East, Schtolz-Iugent),[1] whose members attacked representatives of liberal and left-wing movements and youth subcultures, as well as LGBT people. Officials first noticed this group in April 2017 after Anton Konev, a 17-year-old group member, attacked people in an FSB receiving room, leading to the death of two people in the building and the attacker himself.

- Two soccer "firms": Sector 16, a group of soccer fans from Bugulma Municipal District in the Republic of Tatarstan (S-16 or Bugulma Ultras)[2] and a Tula-based fan group, which was incomprehensibly described in the list as "the organization of soccer fans *Firma* of soccer fans of *Pokolenie* [Generation]."[3]

- *Nezavisimost* (Independence), a regional non-governmental organization for the promotion of national self-determination of the peoples of the world, founded by members of ultra-right organizations but apparently inactive, which was apparently added to the list because one of its founders was on the "Rosfinmonitoring list" (list of organizations and people involved in terrorist or extremist activities).[4]

The right-wing populist Interregional Grassroots Movement *Artpodgotovka*,[5] which formed around the Saratov-based blogger Vyacheslav Maltsev, was also added to the list.

In addition, the list included two recently banned organizations. The first is a religious group titled "In Honor of the Icon of the Majestic Mother of God" [*Bogomater Derzhavnaya*, the name of the icon] in Novomoskovsk, Tula Oblast,[6] which is in fact a convent for women followers of the fundamentalist priest Father Vasily Novikov, who died in 2010, some of whose sermons were banned for promoting ethnic and religious enmity.

The second organization is the Karelian regional branch of the inter-regional youth charity public organization Youth Human Rights Group (YHRG),[7] which was liquidated because its founder was listed as Maksim Yefimov, who is on the "Rosfinmonitoring list." We believe that the case against Yefimov was wrongfully initiated and that the inclusion of YHRG on the list of extremist organizations contravenes the law, since a court shut it down but never deemed it extremist.[8]

Besides this, the list of organizations deemed terrorist, which is published on the FSB's Web site, was also updated in 2018. For the year, two organizations were added – Chistopol Jamaat[9] (entry 28) and *Rokhname ba sui davlati islomi* (Travel Guide to the Islamic State)[10] (entry 29).

Criminal Prosecution

For Violence

In 2018, the number of people convicted of violent hate crimes was higher than in the preceding year. In 2018, at least 11 convictions, in which the courts recognized a hate motive were handed down in 11 regions of Russia (compared to 10 sentences in nine regions in 2017).[11] In these proceedings, 45 people were found guilty (compared to 24 people in 2017).

Art. 282 of the Criminal Code (incitement to hatred) in relation to violent crimes appeared in five convictions (compared to seven in 2017), and in four cases it was used for specific instances of ultra-right propaganda (videotaping violence and publishing it on the Internet), and not for violence per se. In the last case, Aleksandr Zenin, who had been on the federal wanted list for 12 years on suspicion of complicity in the murder of Timur Kacharava on Nov. 13, 2005,[12] was convicted under Art. 282 Part 2 Paragraph "a" of the Criminal Code (incitement to hatred with the use of violence). The Smolninsky District Court of St. Petersburg sentenced Zenin to one and a half years of imprisonment,[13] since Art. 105 of the Criminal Code (murder) was dropped from the charges. The appropriateness of this sentence is questionable,[14] given that the victims and the investigation considered Zenin to be the organizer of the group attack (even if he did not specifically plan a murder), and given the fact that, taking into account his pre-trial detention (one day in pre-trial detention counts for one and a half days in prison) and the subsequent month for filing an appeal, the offender most likely will never go to a penal colony.

The verdict of the Babushkinsky court of Moscow against Maksim "Tesak" (Hatchet) Martsinkevich – the leader of the ultra-right social movement "Restruct!" – is also worth mentioning, although the hate motive was not taken into account. Martsinkevich was sentenced to 10 years in a penal colony under Art. 162 Part 2 of the Criminal Code (robbery committed by a group of people) and Art. 213 Part 2 of the Criminal Code (hooliganism committed by a group of people) in a court case related to attacks conducted under the pretext of combating drug trafficking as part of the Occupy Drug Addiction project. The other defendants in the case were sentenced to prison terms ranging from two years and 11 months to nine years in a penal colony. The court released one person from custody due to the completion of punishment.[15]

We know that in at least one case, the motive of hatred toward a "social group" was imputed. In addition to the exotic social groups of the past years, such as "Chinese Communists,"[16] "rock music fans,"[17] "Russian military,"[18] "volunteer police assistants,"[19] "psychiatrists,"[20] "men,"[21] "thugs" (*gopniki*),[22] etc., a new social group – "anime" – was discovered in 2018. This puzzling social group appeared in June 2018 in the verdict of the Central District Court of Novosibirsk in the case of the attack against an 18-year-old student by ultra-right teenagers. Law enforcement agencies qualified this case as group hooliganism with the motive of hatred toward the social group "anime" (Art. 213 Part 2 of the Criminal Code). The court found both young people guilty. One of them received a suspended sentence of two and a half years with a subsequent two-and-a-half-year probation period; the other one received a suspended sentence of one and a half years with a subsequent 2-year probation period.[23]

Penalties for violent acts were distributed as follows:

- One person was sentenced to life imprisonment;
- Three people were sentenced to 15-20 years in prison;
- One person – to 10-15 years;
- Six people – to 5-10 years;

- Twelve people – to 3-5 years;
- Four people – to up to three years;
- Nine people received a suspended sentence;
- Two people were sentenced to fines;
- Two people – to corrective labor;
- One person – to community service;
- Two people – to restrictions on freedom;
- Two people were found guilty but released from punishment due to the expiration of the statute of limitations;
- One person was acquitted.

We only know of one convicted offender who received an additional punishment in the form of having to pay compensation to his victims for material and moral harm. It is possible that other decisions on additional compensation were issued, but the official sources seldom report on them.

We also know of other additional penalties: one ban on the use of the Internet, and three additional fines.

As demonstrated by the above data, 20% of convicted offenders (nine out of 45) received suspended sentences in 2018, significantly exceeding the corresponding numbers for 2016 and 2017.

Six individuals who received suspended sentences were defendants in large group trials (including members of the Misanthropic Division from Chelyabinsk). Perhaps, their direct participation in the violent actions could not be proved, or they made a plea bargain.

The suspended sentences for the above-mentioned teenagers from Novosibirsk who had attacked an anime fan were apparently related to their age (they were minors) and the fact that the student did not suffer serious injuries.

The suspended sentence imposed on the ultra-right activists in Rostov-on-Don for attacking journalist Vladimir Ryazantsev from *Kavkazsky Uzel* (Caucasian Knot) is probably explained by the fact that the attack was qualified under the "light" Art. 116 of the Criminal Code (battery), which does not entail severe punishment.

However, a suspended sentence to a resident of Kalmykia for attacking a 46-year-old Chechen woman, whom he had "grabbed by the hair, hit in the face with his knee, broke her nose, knocked out her teeth and kept beating with his fists and feet,"[24] seems to be incongruent with his crime.

More than half (26 of 45) of those convicted for violence were sentenced to various terms of imprisonment. One person in Chita was sentenced to life imprisonment for a series of crimes, including the murder of eight people motivated by hatred on the basis of nationality.

For Crimes Against Property

Somewhat fewer sentences were handed down for crimes against property in 2018 than in the preceding year. We know of two sentences handed down in two regions against six people (compared to three sentences against five people in three regions in 2017).

In one of the sentences, destruction of a few dozen gravesite memorials at a cemetery in Smolensk was qualified under Art. 244 Part 2 Paragraphs "a" and "b" of the Criminal Code (desecration of burial places motivated by hooliganism and by ideological hatred). For all four convicted offenders, the article related to property damage was not the only one and not the main one among their charges. The defendants were sentenced to various terms of imprisonment in conjunction with other Criminal Code articles – Art. 35 Part 1, Art. 116 (battery by an organized group motivated by national hatred), and Art. 161 Part 2 Paragraph "d" (robbery committed with the use of coercion). This sentence was also reported in our Criminal Prosecution: For Violence section.

Art. 214 Part 2 of the Criminal Code (vandalism committed by reason of ideological hatred) was the principal and the only article in the sentence handed down in Yekaterinburg against Igor Shchuka, an activist of the Other Russia and a citizen of Belarus. The court sentenced him to a year of corrective labor for trying to set fire to the Boris Yeltsin monument.

In addition, we know of at least two more sentences handed down for apparently ideologically motivated vandalism in which the court sentence did not take the hate motive into account (both cases utilized Art. 214 Part 1 of the Criminal Code).

For Public Statements

In 2018, the number of convictions passed down for "extremist statements" (incitement of hatred, calls for extremist and terrorist activity, and so on) continued to dominate in comparison to all other convictions for "extremist crimes" combined. However, the annual increase in such convictions has stopped. SOVA Center knows of 183 convictions against 192 people[25] in 65 regions of the country.[26] This is slightly less than in 2017, when we learned about 197 such convictions against 253 people in 70 regions of the country. These numbers do not include convictions we consider wrongful, but there were also fewer of these: In 2018, we considered six convictions against seven people wrongful, and these convictions will not be further considered in this report.

These statistics do not include clearing of criminal responsibility with payment of a court fine. This kind of outcome appeared in Russian law (Art. 76.2 of the Criminal Code) in 2016. As far as we know, cases on "extremist statements" ended in this way twice in 2017 and ten times in 2018. We can only welcome the appearance of this alternative to a criminal conviction "for words."

In 2018, we changed our system of conviction classification. It has become more detailed.

We deem appropriate only those convictions where we can assess with certainty the content of the statements and where we believe that courts handed down convictions in accordance with the norms of the law, at least in respect of the actual content of the statement (although failure to account for other criteria may make some of these convictions wrongful overall). We know of 55 such appropriate convictions against 65 people.

In the vast majority of cases – labeled as "Unknown" (109 convictions against 109 people) – we know nothing or too little about the content of the publications or republications to be able to assess the appropriateness of these decisions. However, people whose prosecutions we can assume were appropriate on the basis of circumstantial evidence have also fallen into this category. This would include, for example, people who were previously part of an ultra-right group, people previously prosecuted under "extremist" administrative or even criminal articles, and those noted in the publications of law enforcement agencies for having called for violent actions. But since we could not access the text of the publications, we had to acknowledge that we could not fully assess the appropriateness of these prosecutions. After all, there have been cases when high-profile nationalist activists have been prosecuted for entirely innocent publications.

Convictions that we had trouble assessing fell into the category of "Uncertain" (five convictions against five people), for example, cases where we are inclined to treat one of the charges as appropriate and another as wrongful.

Similarly, our category "Other" (13 convictions against 13 people) is topped off by individuals convicted, probably appropriately, under extremist articles of the Criminal Code, but whose prosecution cannot be classified as combating nationalism and xenophobia. These would include, for example, supporters of the *Artpodgotovka* movement or anarchists calling for attacks on officials at government agencies.

Speaking about the statistics overall, unfortunately, we know of far from all convictions. According to data posted on the Supreme Court's Web site,[27] during just the first six months of 2018 alone, Parts 1 and 2 of Art. 148, Art. 205.2 Art. 280, Art. 280.1, Art. 282, Art. 354.1 of the Criminal Code were the main articles of accusation of "extremist statements" for 283 people and additional articles of accusation for 81 people. Thus, between 283 and 364 people were convicted for "extremist statements."[28] And these Supreme Court figures are slightly lower than for the same period of the previous year.

The ever-popular Art. 282 of the Criminal Code (incitement of hatred or enmity) was used in 155 convictions of 161 people that we know of.[29] In the overwhelming majority of cases (108), this article was the only article listed in the conviction.

Only Art. 280 of the Criminal Code (public calls for extremist activity) was used in 15 convictions of 15 people. In another 22 cases, it was combined with Art. 282.

Art. 280.1 of the Criminal Code (public calls for undermining the territorial integrity of the Russian Federation) was applied in one conviction. As in the previous year,[30] a suspended sentence under this article was handed down to a member of the Community of Indigenous Russian People (*Obshchina korennogo russkogo naroda*, CIRP). This time, Ivan Kolotilkin, the leader of the Ulyanovsk branch of the CIRP, was punished.[31] In his case, as in the case of last year's CIRP leader from Samara, Art. 280.1 was applied in conjunction with Art. 282.

Art. 354.1 of the Criminal Code (denial of facts established by the verdict of the International Military Tribunal for the trial and punishment of the major war criminals of the European Axis countries, approval of the crimes established by this verdict, as well as the dissemination of knowingly false information about the activities of the USSR during the years of World War II) was applied in three convictions. It was the sole article in only one case: in Stavropol Territory, a 20-year-old local resident was sentenced to 150 hours community service for a photograph "with a raised hand in the form of a gesture similar to the Nazi salute" near the memorial "To Soldiers who Perished in the Great Patriotic War," which was published on a social media network page.[32]

The most recent case, against the Perm-based activist Roman Yushkov, ended in an unusual manner. He was convicted under Art. 282 and Part 1 of Art. 354.1 of the Criminal Code for posting links on his Facebook page to the article "Jews! Pay the Germans Back the Money for Fraud with the 'Holocaust six millions Jews!' " [sic; the author used English as quoted]. However, Art. 354.1 of the Criminal Code allows for appeal to a jury, which Yushkov took advantage of, and he was acquitted by the jury.[33]

Naturally, articles concerning "extremist statements" can be combined with totally different articles, usually those concerning crimes against people or property.

For example, the case of Vladimir Dyachenko, the leader of the Stavropol cell of Russian National Unity (RNE) and an ideologue of the neo-pagan religious group Children of Perun, featured, along with the illegal possession of weapons and drugs, voice recordings of conversations in which Dyachenko spoke about killing "non-Slavs" by hitting them on the head with an armature and slitting their throats.[34]

In Chuvashia, the republic's Supreme Court convicted Sergei Ilyin, a former volunteer for the battalion of the Organization of Ukrainian Nationalists (OUN, banned in Russia), under Part 3 of Art. 359 (participation of a mercenary in an armed conflict), Parts 1 and 3 of Art. 354.1, Part 1 of Art. 282, and Part 2 of Art. 280 of the Criminal Code. In addition to participating in military actions, Ilyin was accused of posting certain materials to social media. In total, he was given a prison sentence of three-and-a-half years and fined 50,000 rubles.[35]

It is worth taking separate note of convictions under Art. 205.2 of the Criminal Code (public calls for terrorist activity), which became noticeably more popular in 2017 and 2018. According to data from the Supreme Court, this article was the main article of accusation for 39 people and an additional article of accusation for 11 people in the first half of the year.

SOVA Center is aware of 24 convictions handed down against 25 people under Art. 205.2 of the Criminal Code (that is, one-quarter of the actual convicted people). In eight cases, it was the only article in the conviction. In four of the eight convictions, it was applied in cases of calls for military jihad and support of ISIS.[36] Four of the other convicted people included a supporter of Misanthropic Division,[37] a former member of RNU, an anarchist, and a cadet at the military medical academy who called for attacks on members of the authorities.

Art. 205.2 was also combined with other "extremist articles," for example, with Art. 280 (in two cases), Art. 282 (in six cases), and both of these articles (in three cases). In almost of all these "integrated" cases, it was applied for radical Islamic statements. The exception was the conviction handed down by the Far Eastern Military District Court under Part 2 of Art. 280, Part 1 of Art. 282, and Part 2 of Art. 205.2 in relation to two residents of Altai Territory for creating a social media group where calls for violence against Muslims and members of "peoples of the Caucasus and Central Asia" were posted.[38]

In the remaining cases, this article was combined with other general crime articles of the Criminal Code, including threat of murder, distribution of narcotics, and illegal acquisition and possession of weapons (Art. 222 of the Criminal Code). At various times, members of the group The Russian Republic of the Rus (*Russkaya Respublika Rus*) were convicted of weapons possession and terrorist propaganda:[39] Velsk resident Vasily Pivkozak was sentenced to three years in a general regime penal colony for explosives found in his home and some posts on the social media network VKontakte,[40] and Severodvinsk resident Aleksei Lebedev was sentenced to six years in a general regime penal colony for similar actions[41] (Igor Byzov of Arkhangelsk was only convicted under Arts. 282 and 280 and was sentenced to a two-year suspended sentence).[42]

We do not know the content of most of the incriminating statements, particularly of alleged calls for military jihad, but we cannot rule out the possibility that parts of these criminal cases were fabricated.[43]

The punishments for those convicted for public statements were distributed as follows:

- Forty-nine people were sentenced to prison terms;
- Ninety-three received suspended prison sentences without any additional punishment;
- Twenty-seven were convicted and fined in various amounts;
- Eight were sentenced to corrective labor;
- Six were sentenced to community service;
- Five were referred for forced treatment;
- Four were released due to expiration of the statute of limitations;
- One was given disciplinary measures;
- One was acquitted.

The number of people sentenced to prison rose slightly compared to the previous year (a year ago we reported 47 people).

Twenty-three of the 49 people sentenced to prison received terms in conjunction with charges not related to statements (violence, arson, robbery, possession of narcotics).

Predictably, the punishments were harsher for crimes committed as part of Art. 205.2 of the Criminal Code. Twelve people were sentenced to imprisonment for radical Islamist videos and publications posted on the Internet, as well as for radical publications connected with events in Ukraine (the aforementioned supporters of Misanthropic Division and OUN).

Nine people were already in prison and their terms were extended.

Five people were convicted for "extremist statements" for a second time, which greatly increases the risk of imprisonment. As in the previous year, this group included the leader of the Parabellum movement and activist in Kvachkov's People's Militia of Russia (the former MPPM) Yury Yekishev, who received two years' imprisonment for publishing a notorious antisemitic caricature from the early 20th century with the inscription "We will drive out this vile beast with the Russian twig so that this vermin does not defecate on us anymore" [the original rhymes].[44]

However, 12 people received prison sentences without the circumstances stated above (or we are not aware of them in certain cases). We are talking about sentences imposed in Perm, Syktyvkar, Tula Province, Perm Territory, Ufa and some other regions for publishing various materials on the social media network VKontakte (video and audio clips, comments, etc.), including calls for violence. We do not know anything about who these people were and what the content was of the publications for which they were convicted, but this is why we can assume that most of them did not carry out large-scale campaigns, and therefore these sentences are most likely unjustifiably harsh.

The situation has deteriorated in comparison with the previous year: We reported on seven such convictions in 2017.[45]

The share of suspended sentences has remained virtually unchanged at 48.5% (93 out of 192) instead of the 49% (113 out of 228) of 2017. The share of those convicted (41 people) sentenced to punishments not connected with real or suspended sentences of imprisonment but instead to mandatory and corrective labor or fines continued falling for the third year. People punished in this way included Vladimir Ratnikov (Komarnitsky), who was given 160 hours of community service for publishing songs by the groups Kolovrat and

Bandy Moskvy (Gangs of Moscow) on his VKontakte page,[46] and the ultra-right activist Dina Garina, who was sentenced by a St. Petersburg court to 120 hours of community service for insulting representatives of authorities.[47]

Of the additional punishments in 2018, we know of the following: bans on holding senior positions (two cases), engaging in social activism (two cases), working in the media (three cases), organizing public events (two cases), and operating a means of transportation (one case). Beyond this, there is an entire array of additional punishments connected with Internet use. And while we can understand measures like bans on public statements on the Internet (12 cases) or moderating and administering social media or Web sites on the Internet (four cases), total bans on using the Internet (four cases) appear strange and excessive.

As usual, the overwhelming majority of verdicts were made for materials posted on the Internet – 172 of 183, or 94% (as compared to 96% in 2017).

These materials were posted on:

- Social media – 155 (including VKontakte – 98, unnamed social media networks which were most likely also VKontakte – 55, Odnoklassniki – two);
- YouTube – one;
- Internet-based media – two (comments on articles);
- Radio stations – one;
- Forums – one;
- Online (not specified) – 12.

These concern the following types of materials (various types of materials can be posted to a single account or even a single page):

- Video clips – 49;
- Images (drawings) – 31;
- Photographs – 22;
- Audio (songs) – 36;
- Texts (including republished books) – 32;
- Remarks, commentary (on social media and in forums) – 15;
- Unknown – 17.

As usual, the overwhelming majority of these materials were republications. It was only noted three times that the convicted people themselves prepared the materials that became the subject of court proceedings.

By the year's end, judges had started to take into account the ruling on extremist crimes made by the Plenum of the Supreme Court and adopted on Sept. 20, 2018.[48] For example, in October, a criminal case under Art. 282 of the Criminal Code against a 35-year-old local resident of Krasnoyarsk Territory accused of publishing xenophobic images on VKontakte was closed for lack of a corpus delicti.[49] The investigation found that the accuser's actions were of little significance and, following the Supreme Court's recommendation, deemed that the overall content of the page was not aimed at promoting hate and that the publication did not attract broad attention from the public.

Convictions for statements made offline were slightly higher than in the previous year: 11 compared to eight in 2017. They are distributed as follows:

- Raised voices during an attack – one;
- Leaflets – five;[50]
- Graffiti – two;
- Preparation and distribution of brochures – one;
- Members of ultra-right groups for unknown episodes of propaganda – two.

For Participation in Extremist and Banned Groups and Organizations

We are not aware that there were any convictions in 2018 under Art. 282.1 of the Criminal Code (organizing an extremist community, even though there were three in the first six months. According to the Supreme Court's data), and prosecutions of ultra-right groups occurred more under Art. 282.2 (organizing the activity of an extremist organization) were approximately the same amount as the previous year.[51] We know of three such convictions against six people in three regions of the country[52] (in 2017 we were aware of four convictions against six people in four regions), and all three related to Ukrainian organizations.

The first two cases concerned the ultra-right Ukrainian movement Right Sector, which is banned in Russia.

In Bryansk Province, the Sevsk District Court sentenced 28-year-old Ukrainian citizen Aleksandr Shumkov to four years in a general regime correctional facility. According to the investigation, Shumkov was the personal bodyguard of Dmitry Yarosh, the leader of Right Sector, and participated in the blockade of Crimea. Shumkov served in a military unit in the village of Chornobaivka, Bilozerka District, Kherson Province and was detained in August 2017 while attempting to enter Russia. In addition, Shumkov took part in a number of actions "intended to intimidate residents of Kherson Province who were demonstrating against the blockade of the Crimea and calling for the restoration of economic and political ties with Russia."[53] In other words, all the incriminating actions took place outside of Russia.

Meanwhile, the Pervomaysk District Court in Rostov-on-Don sentenced 42-year-old Ukrainian citizen and member of Right Sector Roman Ternovsky to two years and three months in a general regime facility. Ternovsky served in command positions in the Ukrainian Volunteer Corps of the Border Guard Service, but, according to the investigation, he came to Russia in December 2016 and published "materials intended to draw attention to the activities of the extremist organization Right Sector" for general access on Facebook.[54]

The last case concerned a different banned ultra-right movement: the Misanthropic Division. In Rostov-on-Don, a conviction was handed down in a case against four activists of this group: Aleksandr Vishnyakov, Sergei Konev, Andrei Bezuglov, and Ruslan Pavlyuk. According to the investigation, Pavlyuk got Bezuglov and Konev involved. On Jan. 10, 2017, these three people and Vishnyakov attacked Vladislav Ryazantsev, a journalist from the human rights publication *Caucasian Knot*, and beat him. According to Ryazantsev, "One of the attackers mentioned in his testimony that the cause of the attack was that *Caucasian Knot* was distributing false information about nationalist movements." The court found all four young people guilty in proportion to each one's participation under Art. 116 (battery), Part 2 of Art. 282.2, and Part 1.1 of Art. 282.2 of the Criminal Code (involvement in the activities of an extremist organization) and sentenced them to various terms of imprisonment.[55]

Inappropriate Prosecution of Political and Civic Activists

For Incitement to Extremist Activities

In June, the Toropets District Court of Tver Province handed down a verdict in the case of local resident Vladimir Yegorov, who was charged with public calls for extremist activities via the Internet (Art. 280 Part 2 of the Criminal Code). The opposition activist was found guilty and received a suspended sentence of two years followed by a three-year probation period and the ban on moderating Web sites. The court also ordered the CPU to be removed from his personal computer. Yegorov filed an appeal with the ECHR. The prosecution was based on Egorov's post in the VKontakte public group "Toropets Citizens," of which he had been a moderator. The post contained a photo of Putin and a text stating that intelligence services-directed propaganda worked to exonerate the head of state while shifting the blame for all government blunders to other officials. The author urged readers "not to be led astray" by such propaganda tricks and declared that "the chief Kremlin rat with his friends and partners in crime should be brought down." Such abstract, albeit aggressive, anti-government statements by ordinary citizens pose no significant danger since they cannot be implemented by the author's audience. In our opinion, criminal prosecution in such cases is inappropriate – removal of a provocative post is quite sufficient.

In the summer, the media reported on a case opened under Part 2 of Art. 280 of the Criminal Code (public calls for extremist activities on the Internet) against Abakan resident Lydia Bainova. Bainova, known in the republic as a popularizer of Khakass culture, was brought to trial in Abakan. She was prosecuted for her post of July 2017 on VKontakte. According to Bainova, she created the post on the social media network after, at the entrance to the playroom in one of the city cafes, the children said to her and her daughter: "Only Russians can come in here." In her post, Bainova expressed her protest against the fact that people "to whom this land belongs" were not respected in Khakassia and characterized the degree of her indignation, adding: "In such moments, it feels like we need to arrange a revolution, a takeover! Return power and land to our people! Take it back in a fight!" However, the regional FSB department terminated the case against Bainova in November, having found in her actions no intent to incite extremism. The Prosecutor's Office of the republic later apologized to her for the damage caused by the unfounded prosecution. Indeed, Bainova's post was emotionally charged and therefore abrasive, but such statements should not be regarded as calls for extremist activity representing a significant danger for society and meriting criminal prosecution.

For Calls to Separatism

In April, the Severomorsky District Court of Murmansk Province handed down a suspended sentence of one and a half years with a probation period of one and a half years to local resident P. under Art. 280.1 Part 2 of the Criminal Code (public calls for undermining the territorial integrity of the Russian Federation via the Internet). P. was prosecuted for comments he left on the news post "Barque *Sedov* will no longer belong to Murmansk," on VKontakte. His comments were as follows: "Murmansk Province should be separated from Russia altogether. The entire periodic table is underground in the region. We need to hold a referendum, and all the money would remain in the region," "I am in favor of the referendum. To each resident of Murmansk Province – 10,000 euros on their personal account," and "To secede from Russia." It was reported that "at the court hearing, P. fully admitted his guilt, repented of his deed, and actively assisted the preliminary investigative agencies in the detection and investigation of the crime." In our opinion, calls for a referendum should not be prosecuted; punishment is appropriate only against calls for violent actions with secessionist goals. Art. 280.1, which does not limit prosecution in this manner, unreasonably restricts the discussion of the territorial composition of the Russian Federation.

In November, a court in Ulyanovsk handed down a suspended sentence of two years with the ban on leading any public organizations to Ivan Kolotilkin, an activist of the CIRP. He was found guilty under Art. 282 Part 1 and Art. 280.1 Part 1 of the Criminal Code. The prosecution against Kolotilkin was based on the fact of his handing out leaflets, which contained ethno-xenophobic (probably anti-Semitic) propaganda and called for creating a new (ethnically) Russian state of on the territory of Russia. We doubt the appropriateness of the charges related to the calls to violate territorial integrity of the Russian Federation, since the known materials of the Ulyanovsk CIRP contain no calls for violent separatism.

For Incitement of Hatred Toward Public Officials and Other Anti-Government Statements

In November, the Magassky District Court of Ingushetia sentenced the opposition activist Magomed Khazbiev to two years and 11 months of imprisonment in a settlement colony and a fine of 50,000 rubles after convicting him of illegal possession of weapons and explosives (Art. 222 Part 1 and Art. 222.1 Part 1 of the Criminal Code), insulting a representative of the authorities (Art. 319 Part 1 of the Criminal Code) and inciting hatred against head of the Republic of Ingushetia Yunus-Bek Evkurov, as well as against "representatives of the judicial system, law enforcement agencies, the government, and the authorities of the Republic of Ingushetia as a whole" (Art. 282 Part 1 of the Criminal Code). The latter charge was related to an interview of Khazbiev in which he criticized the republic's authorities and called for their replacement. We regard this part of the verdict as inappropriate, since a call for changing the government, as long as it doesn't involve any calls for unlawful actions, belongs to the area of public debate, not of criminal law enforcement. In addition, as explained by the Supreme Court, the criticism of officials "in and of itself, should not be viewed in all cases as an act aimed at violation of the dignity of a person or a group of people, since the limits of permissible criticism of officials and professional politicians are wider than regarding ordinary citizens."

The verdict imposed in May under Art. 282 Part 1 by the Balaklavsky District Court of Sevastopol on local resident I. Stukalo also gives reasons for doubt; he received a suspended sentence of two years with an eight-month probation period. According to law enforcement, the Balaklava resident published an image on his social media network page with a caption intended "to incite hatred and hostility toward law enforcement agencies of the Russian Federation." We have no information on the image in question and do not know whether the caption contained calls for violence. However, overall, we believe that law enforcement officers do not constitute a vulnerable social group in need of protection under Art. 282. On the contrary, they belong to the category of officials who should not be overly sensitive to harsh criticism.

A criminal case under Art. 282 of the Criminal Code was initiated in Saratov in August against local resident Natalia Kovalyova. She was charged with inciting hatred toward the social group "judiciary" for publishing a number of videos on her own YouTube channel with satirical songs and appeals to the authorities in which she denounced the "corruption, nepotism and gatekeeping" practiced, in her opinion, by the Saratov judiciary. The case was opened as a result of an inspection following the complaint by the Saratov Province Court. The head of this court was the prime target of Kovalyova's criticism in the incriminating materials. We believe that the prosecution against Kovalyova under Art. 282 was inappropriate. Judges are protected by other legal regulations and need no special protection from the manifestations of hatred as a vulnerable social group; moreover, Kovalyova's publications were not directed against the entire judicial community – they were targeting only a small number of its representatives. In addition, her videos contained no aggressive appeals that would merit criminal prosecution due to their social danger. Once the plenary meeting of the Supreme Court of Russia adopted amendments to the ruling on the procedure for dealing with extremist cases in September, the prosecution against Kovalyova under Art. 282 was discontinued. The investigation stated that it did not find an intent to incite hatred in her actions. Kovalyova even managed to win 15,000 rubles in compensation in court for illegal criminal prosecution under this article, but she was charged with contempt of court and libel against the judge.

In 2018, activists faced ongoing prosecution under Art. 20.29 of the Code of Administrative Offenses for distribution of inappropriately prohibited materials. Members of the political opposition were brought to court for distributing Aleksei Navalny's video about unfulfilled promises of the United Russia party "Let's Remind Crooks and Thieves about Their Manifesto-2002" (*Napomnim zhulikam i voram ikh manifest-2002*), videos about alleged involvement by Putin and the FSB in the terrorist attacks of the late 2000s, photos of conservative deputy Vitaly Milonov in a T-shirt with the banned slogan "Orthodoxy or Death," satirical songs of the band The Ensemble of Christ the Savior and the Crude Mother Earth (an anarchist from Sevastopol spent 11 days under detention just for sharing the latter, although fines were the punishment of choice in other known cases), and so on.

The "Ukrainian Question"

Our records showed a number of cases in 2018 of law enforcement using anti-extremist legislation with respect to statements on the conflict in Ukraine, and their reaction was incommensurate or clearly disproportionate to the actual content of the statements.

In January, the Voskresensk City Court in Moscow Province found Valentin Sokolov guilty under Art. 282 Part 1 and sentenced him to a real prison term. An activist from Kolomna, Sokolov was nominated for election as a candidate to the Moscow Province Duma from the *Rodina* (Motherland) Party in 2016. The prosecution was based on his Facebook posts (several videos accompanied by xenophobic remarks calling, in particular, for violence against black people) and on a post of his on Odnoklassniki – an image containing the text that was interpreted as inciting hatred toward Russians. We consider this sentence inappropriate in the part pertaining to the Odnoklassniki post. The screenshots show that Sokolov shared an image accompanied by a pro-Ukrainian text that included a call for killing Russians, along with the following comment: "How crazy does one have to be to spout such heresy. Or it is a deliberate incitement. Scary to read." However, the fact that Sokolov republished the text not for the purpose of propaganda of the ideas contained in it, but, on the contrary, in order to discredit them, was not reflected in the case record. The investigation only paid attention to the fact that the text was preserved without comment in the "Miscellaneous" folder on Sokolov's page (the Odnoklassniki social media network saves all published images in this folder automatically). In March, the Moscow Province Court reduced Sokolov's sentence from one and a half years to eight months of incarceration.

In Velikiye Luki in Pskov Province, 21-year-old gamer Mikhail Larionov received a 2-year suspended sentence under Art. 282 Part 1 of the Criminal Code. In January, Larionov posted a clip from a live stream of the multiplayer game World of Tanks on Twitch.com. In this video titled "Disrespect toward the Ukrainian people!" he "incited the public to aggressive actions against Russians." Larionov's statements should be interpreted in the context of the game and the communication style typical among players. The principal audience of game streams recognizes even aggressive statements as humorous rather than inflammatory. It is unlikely that Larionov intended to provoke national hatred; more likely, he wanted to taunt the other player. If law enforcement believed that Internet users outside of the gamer community could misinterpret the players' conversation, then warning Larionov and asking him to close public access to the video would have been sufficient.

In April, a court in Kromy in Oryol Province handed down a verdict in a case against local poet Aleksandr Byvshev pertaining to the publication of his poem "On the Independence of Ukraine." The poet was sentenced under Art. 282 of the Criminal Code to 330 hours of community service with a three-year ban on teaching. However, the province court revised this decision in June and increased the punishment to 400 hours of community service – at the same time, crediting Byvshev 300 hours of community service he had already served in accordance with his 2015 sentence for another poem on the same topic. Thus, the actual community service requirement came down to 100 hours. "On the Independence of Ukraine" contained statements that can be interpreted as humiliating for residents of Russia, but the poem's intent was political rather than xenophobic. In addition, as SOVA Center has repeatedly pointed out, violation of dignity is an act that does not present significant social danger and should not be subject to criminal prosecution.

In the same month, yet another case against Aleksandr Byvshev was opened under Art. 282 Part 1. He was charged for publishing on the site orlec.ru his poems "The Russian spirit" and "A Mighty Pile," which, according to law enforcement, contained "statements derogatory in character against a particular ethnic group." Byvshev published these poems in September 2017 in the comments on an article about a garbage pile in a building courtyard in Oryol. The author mocks Russians' disinclination toward cleanliness and order and speaks of his fellow citizens in unflattering terms, but, nevertheless, both poems contain nothing that could serve as the basis for criminal prosecution for incitement of hatred.

Evidently having decided not to rest on their laurels, law enforcement agencies opened another case against the poet in July – this time under Part 2 of Art. 280 (public calls for extremist activity committed with the use of the Internet). The case is based on the fact of publication of his poem "Dedicated to Expansion of NATO to the East." We doubt the appropriateness of the charges. Despite his bellicose rhetoric, the author calls for the expansion of NATO's borders as part of a containment strategy, not for a war with Russia. In addition, leaders of NATO or of the NATO countries are not among Byvshev's audience; therefore, it is hard to envision his calls posing an actual threat.

In 2018, the Federal List of Extremist Materials came to include a number of disparate Ukrainian materials seized from the Library of Ukrainian Literature[56] in Moscow and banned in 2015 by the Meshchansky District Court. We had no opportunity to get acquainted with most of them and cannot assess the validity of their prohibition; the only obvious fact is that not all of them are nationalist. Surprisingly, the set of banned materials also includes two editions of the book *The Empire of the Kremlin* by well-known Sovietologist and publicist Abdurakhman Avtorkhanov (1908-1997), first published in Germany in 1988. The arguments of the court are unknown to us. *The Empire of the Kremlin* deals with the Soviet period of Russian history, which the author views through the prism of the "colonial policy" of the leadership toward the peoples of the USSR, revealing the chauvinistic attitudes of the Soviet leaders. The book contains neither nationalist rhetoric, nor aggressive appeals based on the author's ideology, nor statements justifying Nazism. Perhaps the issues with the book were related to Avtorkhanov's interpretation of the Molotov-Ribbentrop Pact or the history of the Bandera movement – the prosecutors and the court could have interpreted it as spreading false information about the activities of the USSR during the war. However, the signs of potentially being liable under Art. 354.1 of the Criminal Code do not provide a formal basis for recognizing a material as extremist. We would also like to remind readers that, in our opinion, the clause in Art. 354.1 Part 1 that provides punishment for spreading false information about the activities of the Soviet government during World War II should be excluded from the article as excessively restricting the discussion on historical subjects and thus violating the right to freedom of expression.

Other Abuse of Criminalization of Incitement to Hatred

We view several additional cases of prosecution for incitement of various kinds of hatred unrelated to criticism of the government as inappropriate or insufficiently justified.

On May 24, activists of the Sudak "Anticorruption Bureau" Dmitry Dzhigalov and Oleg Semenov were sentenced under Art. 282 to fines of 300,000 and 50,000 rubles respectively (Semenov was issued a smaller fine taking into account the six months he spent in pre-trial detention). They were found guilty of violating the dignity of Bulgarians. The prosecution was based on a published video, in which Semenov rebuked Bulgarians for failing to invite the Russian delegation for the celebration of the anniversary of the country's liberation from the Ottoman yoke during the Russian-Turkish war of 1877-1878. Semenov accused them of ingratitude toward Russians, and also made some statements about the deportation of Crimean Bulgarians under Stalin. Obviously, the real reason behind the prosecution against Dzhigalov and Semenov had to do with their public fight against landfills and illegal construction, which had annoyed local authorities. We have doubts regarding the proportionality of the criminal prosecution against Dzhigalov and Semenov. They were charged with violation of dignity, which is an act of small gravity. In addition, Semenov and Dzhigalov were not previously known to engage in xenophobic propaganda. In any case, the Supreme Court of the Crimea overturned the activists' sentence in February 2019 in connection with the partial decriminalization of Art. 282 Part 1.

A criminal case opened in September under Art. 282 Part 1 against Lyubov Kalugina, a feminist activist from Omsk, attracted media and public attention. The activist was charged with inciting hatred toward men on a social media network. The statements in her posts that law enforcement found objectionable varied in their aggressiveness, ranging from crude humor to ones which could be seen as insulting dignity and inciting violence. However, we believe that the risk to the public stemming from aggressive statements made by radical feminists is small, since their rhetoric is not related to actual violent practices; thus, there was no need for criminal prosecution against Kalugina. Her case was terminated by the investigators in February 2019, also as a result of the reform of Art. 282

In December 2018, the Moscow City Court overturned the sentence in the case of Yevgeny Kort, convicted in 2016 under Art. 282 Part 1 of the Criminal Code (incitement to national hatred), and sent the case to the Zelenogradsky District Court for a re-trial. Kort had been sentenced to a year in a settlement colony (incarceration was later replaced with a fine) for sharing an image on VKontakte. The image was a racist collage from the account of well-known ultra-right activist Maksim "Tesak" Martsinkevich. It depicted Tesak pressing Pushkin against the wall, accompanying this action with a xenophobic insult. Kort's appeal was delivered to the Moscow City Court by Vladimir Davydov, the Deputy Chairman of the Supreme Court of Russia. Davydov pointed out that the verdict failed to provide evidence that Kort had acted with direct intent to violate the dignity of a group of people on the basis of nationality, and that a conviction should not be "based on assumptions." The sentence had served as the basis for filing a complaint with the Constitutional Court regarding application of Art. 282 of the Criminal Code; however, this case had not been accepted for consideration. The Supreme Court initially rejected the appeal against the verdict as well but changed its position after the adoption of the new ruling on the procedures in extremism-related cases. In 2019, the proceedings in the Kort case were closed due to the decriminalization of his act.

In September, the Chelyabinsk Province Court handed down a verdict against Aleksandr Gir, a participant in the pogrom at the Tornado rock festival in 2010, who had been hiding from the investigation and the court. Let's recall that, at that time, locals injured several dozen guests at the festival and were later brought to responsibility. Gir was found guilty not only of the organization of mass riots accompanied by violence, but also under Art. 282 Part 2 Paragraph "a" (publicly committed actions aimed at inciting hatred, as well as at the violation of dignity on the grounds of affiliation with a particular social group, with the application of violence). We view the charge of inciting hatred, brought up against Gir and several other pogrom participants, as inappropriate. They were accused of inciting hatred toward rock music fans, who can hardly be considered a separate social group. In addition, the main reason for the attack was not an ideological confrontation, but an ordinary conflict between the defendants and guests of the festival that took place the day before the pogrom.

For Extremist Symbols

According to the statistics of the Judicial Department at the Supreme Court, in 2018, 963 people faced responsibility under Art. 20.3 of the Code of Administrative Offenses (propaganda and public display of Nazi attributes or symbols, as well as symbols of extremist organizations),[57] but we have the details only for some of these administrative cases and can judge the extent of their legitimacy. In the course of the year, our records showed 29 instances of prosecution for public display of Nazi symbols or symbols of banned organizations obviously not aimed at dangerous propaganda, which represents a significant decrease from the preceding year (46 instances).

As before, this article is often improperly used to exert pressure against activists disfavored by the authorities. Thus, in August, Dmitry Teterin, an activist of Navalny's headquarters in Naberezhnye Chelny and one of the organizers of a rally against pension reform, was fined 2,000 rubles for publishing an image on VKontakte that depicts Russian President Vladimir Putin in Nazi uniform with the caption "Führer of the Fourth Reich." We believe that Teterin was penalized inappropriately, because he used Nazi symbols as a means of political polemics and did not promote the ideology of Nazism.

Historical photographs published without any political connotations also attract law enforcement attention. In August, the Kyzyl Town Court of the Republic of Tuva fined local activist Oyumaa Dongak 1,000 rubles. Law enforcement objected to several of her VKontakte posts. One of them contained an excerpt from a present-day interview with a German woman who had participated in the activities of the Nazi League of German Girls and a link to the interview itself. The post was illustrated by an archival photograph in which girls were waving swastika-decorated flags. The second publication included a photograph of Hitler sitting and holding a newspaper accompanied by the information that the leader of Nazi Germany had once been named "man of the year" by *Time* magazine. The third post showed a famous 1936 photograph from a Hamburg shipyard where, in the crowd cheering for Hitler, one man was clearly not raising his hand. The fourth image illustrated the material on the creation of the atomic bomb in Germany. The court did not consider it relevant that Dongak's posts condemned Nazism, assessing only the formal side of her action. The Supreme Court of the Republic upheld this decision.

However, in some cases, the courts took the defendants' side. For example, in February 2018, the Arkhangelsk Province Court overturned a decision by the Isakogorsky District Court, which a month earlier had fined Mikhail Listov, a volunteer of the Arkhangelsk headquarters of Aleksei Navalny, for two VKontakte publications: a famous 1945 photo of Soviet soldiers throwing Nazi banners to the ground near Lenin's Mausoleum on Red Square during the Victory Parade, and a still from a controversial dance show on the Russia 1 TV channel in which one of the participants was wearing a Nazi uniform. Listov's posts were obviously not intended to promote Nazism, and his case was widely publicized via a flash mob launched in his support by Aleksei Navalny in which social media users were sharing the photo with the Nazi banners published by Listov. Possibly, it was the resonance of this case that led to the introduction of the draft bill to amend Art. 20.3 in the State Duma.

The Federal List of Extremist Materials

In 2018, the Federal List of Extremist Materials was updated 38 times (a year earlier it was updated 33 times), 466 entries were added to it (a year ago 330 items were added), and it grew from 4,345 to 4,811 entries.[58]

Thus, additions to the list again intensified, wiping out the 2017 decline driven by an order of the Prosecutor General issued in the spring of 2016 that largely centralized the procedure for banning materials due to extremism.[59]

Additions to the list are distributed across the following topics:

- Xenophobic materials of Russian nationalists – 250;
- Materials of other nationalists – 22;
- Materials of Islamic militants and other calls by Islamists for violence – 43;

- Other Islamic materials – 40;
- Materials of Hizb ut-Tahrir – 21;
- Other religious materials (materials of Jehovah's Witnesses) – 39;
- Extremely radical anti-Russian speeches from Ukraine (we distinguish them from "other nationalists") – four;
- Other materials from the Ukrainian media and Internet – six;
- Anti-government materials calling for disorder and violence – six;
- Materials with works of fascist and neo-fascist classic authors – three;
- History books and other historical texts – five;
- Large heterogeneous selections of texts banned in their entirety – one;
- Parody materials – 16;
- Peaceful opposition Web sites – four;
- Radical anti-Christian Web sites – two;
- Fiction – one;
- Anti-Islamic materials – two;
- Unidentifiable materials – 21.

At a minimum, 402 of the 486 items are materials from the Internet (a year ago it was 304 of 330 items) including various types of video and audio recordings and pictures, mainly from social media. Offline materials included books by nationalists, classic Nazis, Orthodox fundamentalists, Jehovah's Witnesses, and Islamic authors, as well as newspapers and leaflets.

Sometimes it is not completely clear where precisely a piece of banned material was posted. For example, item 4,591 is described as a "graphic illustration of soldiers carrying out an attack with the text 'They fought for the homeland! And you hand it out to the black asses without a fight' " without any source information. And in terms of item 4,721 – "Informational Material – the article 'French March,' " not just the place of the material's publication is unclear, but also everything about the article in general, since articles with the same name and widely varying content can be found absolutely anywhere.

Blocking of Online Resources and Internet Censorship

Based on the data of the Roskomsvoboda Web site,[60] we believe that 611 resources have ended up on the Unified Register of Banned Web Sites "for extremism" following a court decision in 2018 compared to 296 a year earlier.[61] After comparing the data of Roskomsvoboda with the data of Roskomnadzor, we believe that in reality there are actually many more court decisions on the blocking of specifically "extremist content."

According to our observations, the lion's share of the resources that ended up in the Unified Register over the year were materials from various types of Russian nationalists ranging from xenophobic songs to the books of well-known nationalist authors (76%) to the materials of Islamist fighters (from ISIS videos to Timur Mutsurayev's songs) (8%) and non-violent Muslim materials (5%). A noticeable percentage of resources were connected with Ukraine (from radical to non-violent publications of the Ukrainian media, 2% each), while less than 2% accounted for blocked Russian opposition resources and 1.5% were links to the classics of fascism. The remainder of blocked resources (less than 4%) were comprised of materials from other nationalists and Jehovah's Witnesses, seditious anti-government materials, materials critical of the Russian Orthodox Church, parody materials banned as serious and radical anti-Christianity Web sites (with the exception of neo-pagan nationalists).

The quality of these blockings continues to raise eyebrows and sometimes outright sarcasm. A good example is the resource marked as "list of audio compositions found for the query '*Pechki-Lavochki*' [translates as 'this and that, nothing in particular', or 'idle, friendly chat']." The highest-ranking response given for the query "*Pechki-Lavochki*" on Yandex is a song by the Belarussian folklore ensemble Syabry that was popular in Soviet times. What is probably being referred to, however, is the song "Pechki-Lavochki" performed by the ultra-right artist The Czech, which was deemed extremist by the Rtishchevo District Court, Saratov Oblast on June 22, 2017, and was added to the Federal List of Extremist Materials under entry No. 4202,[62] but this is impossible to understand from the descriptions in the register.

The number of obviously wrongful blockings is rising. For example, in 2018, materials of Jehovah's Witnesses and non-violent Muslim materials were again found in the Unified Register. These resources were blocked simply due to lack of understanding.

The separate register based on the Lugovoi law,[63] is growing rapidly. It is impossible to give even an approximate count of the resources in the register.

According to Roskomnadzor,[64] a total of 51,892 resources were blocked for extremism over the first three quarters of 2018. Almost all of these are not the Web sites themselves for which a query was received from the Prosecutor General's Office (there are almost 400 of these) but a "mirror" of these Web sites found by Roskomnadzor itself. And, judging by their number, these are not necessarily "mirrors" in the exact sense, but different Web sites with the same or very similar materials.

In its reports, Roskomnadzor itself identifies the following types of resources:

- Materials with ISIS propaganda – over 17,000;
- Materials of Hizb ut-Tahrir – almost 17,000;
- Materials of banned organizations from Ukraine (Right Sector, UNA-UNSO, UPA, Stepan Bandera's Trident, Brotherhood, Azov) – almost 5,000;
- Calls for "mass unrest, extremist activity, participation in mass (public) events conducted in violation of the established order" – 728.

Roskomnadzor did not identify the other 12,000 resources.

On the other hand, this agency did report that illegal information was removed from 32,235 resources in the first three quarters of 2018, and that the blockings were lifted (it is possible that some of these were blocked previously). Thus, this register grew over this time period to reach approximately 20,000 entries.

The scale of the blockings is shocking, and it is not at all clear which specific resources the agency had in mind or how dangerous the propaganda was. It also remains unclear why these resources needed to be blocked so urgently that they required extrajudicial blocking. The number of wrongful punishments in this register is also growing. Given such a large scale, it is inevitable that there will be resources blocked by mistake. It is telling that we know the least of all about blocked resources with calls for mass unrest created for mobilization of mass actions, since the Lugovoi law was apparently adopted specifically because of the need for such blockings.

Every year, the situation changes only for the worse. These registers are swelling, and, unlike the Federal List, they are not published anywhere officially, which complicates public monitoring of this work. As a result, the system for blocking is a cause for a great deal of criticism and leads inevitably to political arbitrariness, the pursuit of accountability, and restrictions in freedom of speech on the Internet.

NOTES

1. Deemed extremist by the Central District Court of Khabarovsk in December 2017. See: Schtolz group Deemed Extremist in Khabarovsk // SOVA Center. Dec. 6, 2017 (https://www.sova-center.ru/racism-xenophobia/news/counteraction/2017/12/d38434/).

2. Deemed extremist by the Bugulma City Court of the Republic of Tatarstan on May 28, 2018. See: Bugulma: Group of Soccer Fans Sector 16 Deemed Extremist // SOVA Center. Aug. 9, 2018 (https://www.sova-center.ru/racism-xenophobia/news/counteraction/2018/08/d39816/).

3. Deemed extremist by the Proletarsky District Court of Tula on June 14, 2018.

4. Deemed extremist by the Moscow City Court on Dec. 1, 2017. Moscow City Court Bans Activities of Nezavisimost Foundation // SOVA Center. Aug. 29, 2018 (https://www.sova-center.ru/racism-xenophobia/news/counteraction/2018/08/d39930/).

5. Deemed extremist by the Krasnoyarsk Territory Court on Oct. 26, 2017, and confirmed by the Supreme Court in February 2018. See: *Artpodgotovka* Movement Deemed Extremist // SOVA Center. Oct. 26, 2017 (https://www.sova-center.ru/racism-xenophobia/news/counteraction/2017/10/d38151/).

6. Deemed extremist by the Tula Oblast Court on July 25, 2016. See: In Tula Oblast, Followers of Priest Vasily Novikov Deemed Extremist Organization // SOVA Center. July 26, 2016 (https://www.sova-center.ru/religion/news/harassment/refusal/2016/07/d35086/).

7. Liquidated by the decision of the Supreme Court of the Republic of Karelia of Dec. 18, 2014. See: YHRG of Karelia Liquidated // SOVA Center. Jan. 26, 2015 (https://www.sova-center.ru/misuse/news/persecution/2015/01/d31110/).

8. YHRG Karelia Added to the List of Extremist Organizations // SOVA Center. Nov. 11, 2018 (https://www.sova-center.ru/misuse/news/persecution/2018/11/d40252/).

9. For more on this organization, see: Case of Chistopol Jamaat Closed // Radio Svoboda. March 23, 2017 (https://www.idelreal.org/a/28386294.html).

10. See: FSB Exposes Large Tajik Online Community of IS Recruiters // Nastoyashchee vremya. Aug. 11, 2016 (https://www.currenttime.tv/a/27914349.html).

11. Only the sentences that we consider appropriate are included in this count.

12. Murder of an antifascist musician in Moscow // SOVA Center. Nov 14, 2005 (https://www.sova-center.ru/racism-xenophobia/news/racism-nationalism/2005/11/d6326/).

13. St. Petersburg: an accomplice in the murder of Timur Kacharava was punished with one and a half years in a penal colony // SOVA Center. Dec. 20, 2018 (https://www.sova-center.ru/racism-xenophobia/news/counteraction/2018/02/d38904/).

14. Olga Tseitlina and Stefania Kulaeva comment on the Aleksandr Zenin case // SOVA Center. September 14, 2018 (https://www.sova-center.ru/racism-xenophobia/publications/2018/09/d40002/).

15. This was a re-trial of Martsinkevich's criminal case. In June 2017, the Babushkinsky District Court sentenced him to the same prison term, having added a nine-year sentence in the case of the "Restruct!" movement to one unserved year in his previous sentence. Moscow: The verdict was delivered to Maksim Martsinkevich and his accomplices // SOVA Center. Dec. 29, 2018 (https://www.sova-center.ru/racism-xenophobia/news/counteraction/2017/06/d37365/).

16. Ali Yakupov was acquitted again // SOVA Center. Nov. 27, 2017 (https://www.sova-center.ru/misuse/news/persecution/2017/11/d38357/).

17. Rock music fans as a social group // SOVA Center. July 26, 2011 (https://www.sova-center.ru/misuse/news/other-actions/2011/07/d22208/).

18. The trial of the Yury Budanov murder case has begun // SOVA Center. Nov. 16, 2012 (https://www.sova-center.ru/misuse/news/persecution/2012/11/d25822/).

19. Rapper Ptakha was fined under Art. 282 // SOVA Center. March 16, 2017 (https://www.sova-center.ru/misuse/news/persecution/2017/03/d36599/).

20. A St. Petersburg court did not recognize materials on human rights violations in psychiatry as extremist // SOVA Center. Aug. 14, 2018 (https://www.sova-center.ru/misuse/news/counteraction/2012/07/d24792/).

21. Rozhana, the man-hater // SOVA Center. Oct. 13, 2013 (https://www.sova-center.ru/misuse/news/persecution/2013/10/d28230/).

22. Verdict delivered in Kazan in the case of an attack against the natives of Tajikistan // SOVA Center. March 18, 2011 (https://www.sova-center.ru/racism-xenophobia/news/counteraction/2011/03/d21193/).

23. Novosibirsk: Verdict delivered in the case of hooliganism with the motive of hatred toward the social group "anime" // SOVA Center. July 2, 2018 (https://www.sova-center.ru/racism-xenophobia/news/counteraction/2018/07/d39640/).

24. Kalmykia: A suspended sentence for beating and an attempt to set a vehicle on fire // SOVA Center. 2018 (https://www.sova-center.ru/racism-xenophobia/news/counteraction/2018/12/d40435/)

25. One more person was acquitted.

26. Data as of Feb. 18, 2019.

27. Aggregated statistical data about the activity of federal courts of general jurisdiction and magistrate courts for the first six months of 2018 // Official Web site of the Supreme Court of the Russian Federation (http://www.cdep.ru/userimages/sudebnaya_statistika/2018/k3-svod_vse_sudy-1-2018.xls).

28. According to data posted on the Supreme Court's Web site, there were none for whom Parts 1 and 2 of Art. 148 were the main article of accusation; it was an additional article for 6 people. Art. 205.2 was the main and additional article for 39 and 11 people, respectively. Art. 280 was the main and additional article for 32 and 25 people, respectively. Art. 280.1 was the main and additional article for three people each. Art. 282 was the main and additional article for 209 and 40 people, respectively, and Art. 354.1 was the main and additional article for zero and two people, respectively. These articles may be combined with each other or with other articles (see below), so the actual number of people convicted for statements is somewhere between the sum of the first numbers and the sum and the first and second numbers.

29. From here on, all calculations are made using convictions known to us, even though, judging by the Supreme Court's data, there are approximately three times as many convictions. But, given the amount of data we possess, we can assert that the observed patterns and proportions will be true for the entire number of convictions.

30. Togliatti: Verdict handed down in the Case of Leader of the Community of Indigenous Russian People // SOVA Center. Dec. 21, 2017 (http://www.sova-center.ru/racism-xenophobia/news/counteraction/2017/12/d38543/).

31. Ulyanovsk: Court Sentences Activist from Community of Indigenous Russian People to Two-Year Suspended Sentence // SOVA Center. Nov. 8, 2018 (https://www.sova-center.ru/racism-xenophobia/news/counteraction/2018/11/d40261/).

32. Izobilny: Community Service for a Photo with a Nazi Salute in Front of a Memorial to Soviet Soldiers // SOVA Center. Oct. 24, 2018 (https://www.sova-center.ru/racism-xenophobia/news/counteraction/2018/10/d40190/).

33. Perm: Roman Yushkov Acquitted in Third Criminal Case. Prosecutor's Office Demands Quashing of Conviction // SOVA Center. Sept. 5, 2018 (https://www.sova-center.ru/racism-xenophobia/news/counteraction/2018/09/d39970/).

34. Yessentuki: Court Sends Local Ultra-Right Pagan Vladimir Dyachenko to Forced Treatment // SOVA Center. Aug. 13, 2018 (https://www.sova-center.ru/racism-xenophobia/news/counteraction/2018/08/d39836/).

35. Cheboksary: Court hands down Sentence Against Former Marksman of the Organization of Ukrainian Nationalists Battalion // SOVA Center. Nov. 28, 2018 (https://www.sova-center.ru/racism-xenophobia/news/counteraction/2018/11/d40332/).

36. In another case, the content of statements on social media was unknown, although it is highly likely that this was also Islamist propaganda, since the person convicted was from Uzbekistan.

37. Supreme Court Upholds Conviction of Kaliningrad Resident Convicted of Calls for Terrorism on Social Media // SOVA Center. June 27, 2018 (https://www.sova-center.ru/racism-xenophobia/news/counteraction/2018/07/d39732/).

38. Residents of Altai Territory Convicted for Calls for Violence Against Muslims and Natives of the Caucasus and Central Asia Posted to Social Media // SOVA Center. June 22, 2018 (https://www.sova-center.ru/racism-xenophobia/news/counteraction/2018/06/d39595/).

39. The name of this organization is similar to the name Russkaya Respublika, which gained notoriety after the publication of a "death sentence" for Nikolai Girenko in 2005.

40. Supporter of Russkaya Respublika Rus Convicted // SOVA Center. March 6, 2018 (https://www.sova-center.ru/racism-xenophobia/news/counteraction/2018/03/d38966/).

41. Third supporter of Russkaya Respublika Rus Convicted // SOVA Center. April 16, 2018 (https://www.sova-center.ru/racism-xenophobia/news/counteraction/2018/04/d39219/).

42. Arkhangelsk: One More Supporter of Russkaya Respublika Rus Convicted // SOVA Center. March 14, 2018 (https://www.sova-center.ru/racism-xenophobia/news/counteraction/2018/03/d39001/).

43. Kostromina, Darya. "Pro-terrorist Statements." Cycle of Surveys "Criminal Prosecution for Terrorism in Russia and Abuse by the Government // HRC Memorial. Feb. 11, 2019 (https://memohrc.org/sites/default/files/presledovaniya-za-proterroristicheskie-vyskazyvaniya-2019-02-08.pdf).

44. Yury Yekishev Sentenced to Two Years' Imprisonment and Released in the Courtroom // SOVA Center. Jan. 26, 2018 (https://www.sova-center.ru/racism-xenophobia/news/counteraction/2017/11/d38333/).

45. Who has been Imprisoned for Extremist Crimes not of a General Criminal Nature // SOVA Center. Dec. 24, 2013 (http://www.sova-center.ru/racism-xenophobia/publications/2013/12/d28691/).

46. Conviction in the Case of Publication of Racist Songs on Social Media by Leader of the Cherny Blok Movement Enters into Force // SOVA Center. March 12, 2018 (https://www.sova-center.ru/racism-xenophobia/news/counteraction/2018/03/d38984/).

47. However, Dina Garina was released from serving her punishment because the statute of limitations had expired. See St. Petersburg: Court Hands Down Conviction in Case against Dina Garina // SOVA Center. Dec. 12, 2018 (https://www.sova-center.ru/racism-xenophobia/news/counteraction/2018/12/d40438/).

48. Ruling of the Plenum of the RF Supreme Court of September 20, 2018, "On Judicial Practice in Criminal Cases Regarding Crimes of Extremism" // SOVA Center. Sept. 20, 2018 (https://www.sova-center.ru/misuse/docs/2018/09/d40044/).

See also SOVA's commentary on the Ruling on extremist crimes // SOVA Center. Sept. 25, 2018 (https://www.sova-center.ru/misuse/publications/2018/09/d40054/).

49. Krasnoyarsk Territory: Case Under Art. 282 Closed for Absence of Crime Event // SOVA Center. Oct. 4, 2018 (https://www.sova-center.ru/racism-xenophobia/news/counteraction/2018/10/d40098/).

50. Supporters of *Volya* party distributed both leaflets.

51. These numbers do not include prosecutions that we consider wrongful: In 2018, we deemed 10 convictions against 27 people wrongful.

52. Here we do not look at convictions that were obviously wrongful or convictions of members of Hizb ut-Tahrir al-Islami.

53. Conviction in the Case against Dmitry Yarosh's Personal Bodyguard Handed Down in Sevsk // SOVA Center. June 5, 2018 (https://www.sova-center.ru/racism-xenophobia/news/counteraction/2018/06/d39498/).

54. Rostov-on-Don: Participant of Right Sector Sentenced to Four Years' Imprisonment // SOVA Center. June 8, 2018 (https://www.sova-center.ru/racism-xenophobia/news/counteraction/2018/06/d39527/).

55. Rostov-on-Don: Verdict handed down in Case of Participants in Attack on *Caucasian Knot* Journalist. // SOVA Center. March 26, 2018 (https://www.sova-center.ru/racism-xenophobia/news/counteraction/2018/03/d39074/).

56. See: Criminal case initiated against the Director of the Library of Ukrainian Literature // SOVA Center. Oct. 29, 2015 (https://www.sova-center.ru/misuse/news/persecution/2015/10/d33129/).

57. Consolidated Statistical Data on the Activities of Federal Courts of General Jurisdiction and Magistrates' Courts for the First Half of 2018 // Judicial Department at the Supreme Court of the Russian Federation. 2018 (http://www.cdep.ru/index.php?id=79&item=4758).

58. As of Feb. 15, 2019, the list had 4,847 entries.

59. For more information see: Kravchenko, M. Misuse of Anti-Extremism in November 2016 // SOVA Center. Dec. 13, 2016 (https://www.sova-center.ru/en/misuse/news-releases/2016/12/d35994/).

60. See: The Unified Register of Banned Web Sites // Roskomsvoboda (http://reestr.rublacklist.net/) [name plays on "Roskomnadzor," the banning entity, and *svobóda*, freedom].

61. See the updated list: 'Extremist Resources' in the Unified Register of Banned Web Sites // SOVA Center (https://www.sova-center.ru/racism-xenophobia/docs/2019/01/d40512/).

62. Federal List of Extremist Materials Grows to Entry 4,202 // SOVA Center. Aug. 30, 2017 (https://www.sova-center.ru/racism-xenophobia/news/counteraction/2017/08/d37779/).

63. Full name: "On Amending the Federal Law 'On Information, Information Technologies and Protection of Information.'"

64. Reports on the activities of Roskomnadzor // Official Web site of the Federal Service for Supervision in Communications, Information Technologies and Mass Communications (http://www.rkn.gov.ru/plan-and-reports/reports/p449/).

Banning Organizations as Extremist

In 2019, four organizations were added to the Federal List of Extremist Organizations published on the Web site of the Ministry of Justice (compared with seven in 2018). They are all very different.

- FC Kamaz Fans Association Autograd Crew (a.k.a. Kamaz Ultras, Blue White Crew).[1] The association was formed in Naberezhnye Chelny in 2008 and had between 15 and 20 active participants and approximately 200 ultra-right supporters; some of the members have convictions for administrative and criminal offenses.

- Public association Path of Truth and Unity (Russian nationwide movement *Kursom Pravdy i Yedinenia*, All-Russian political party *Kursom Pravdy i Yedinenia*, political party *Kursom Pravdy i Yedinenia*).[2] Path of Truth and Unity unites the followers of the leader of the Conceptual Party "Unity" (*Yedinenie*) General Konstantin Petrov, whose party was founded upon the para-religious Concept of Public Security "Dead Water," which has a rather radical nationalist component.[3] (Interestingly, the list provides a detailed description of the organization's flag and emblem. A detailed description of symbols has only been given once before, for the *Volya* party.)

- Public association Union of Slavic Forces of Rus (a.k.a. "The Union of Soviet Socialist Republics," "USSR").[4] This exotic organization, created by Sergei Taraskin, a dentist, is based on a phantasmagoric ideology, a mix of references to the Bible (with quite a peculiar interpretation) and a discourse on space, the Universe, etc. The USSR employs antisemitic rhetoric and promotes the idea of an international Jewish conspiracy that is allegedly leading humanity to ruin by various means, including by manufacturing genetically modified foods and wireless and mobile communications radiation.

Several USSR activists have been prosecuted for administrative and criminal offenses.

- Pagan religious association Karakol Initiative Group (a.k.a. "Ak Dyan," "Jany Altai"-Movement," "Ak Jan," "Altai Ak Jan," "White Faith," "Altai Dyan Ak Dyan," "Altai Faith White Faith").[5] According to the Prosecutor's office, the goal of the movement's followers is to "convert all the Altaians to their faith, eliminate all Buddhist organizations, reduce the number of Orthodox churches, chapels, and roadside crosses, and, as an ultimate ideal, to completely cleanse the Altai Republic of them."

Furthermore, the list of terrorist organizations published on the Web site of the FSB was updated in 2019 with two organizations – Network (*Set*)[6] (entry 30) and Katiba Tawhid wal-Jihad[7] (entry 31) (in the previous year, similarly, two organizations were added).

Criminal Prosecution

For Violence

The number of those convicted of violent hate crimes was lower in 2019 than in the previous year. In the past year, in St. Petersburg, Omsk, and Khabarovsk Territory, at least four guilty verdicts were handed down in which the hate motive was officially recognized.[8] 10 defendants were found guilty in these trials[9] compared to 11 (in 11 regions) in 2018.

Worthy of note is the guilty verdict in the Zheleznodorozhny District Court of Barnaul for a xenophobic attack and insults targeting "natives of the Caucasus" that occurred in one of the city's shopping malls. During the investigation, the attacker justified his actions by saying that he was "outraged by the behavior of foreign nationals who came [to Russia] from other countries." Despite that fact, the criminal case was initiated without recognizing the hate motive under Art. 116.1 of the Criminal Code (battery committed by a subject of administrative penalty) and later terminated due to the reconciliation of the parties.

In other guilty verdicts, racist violence was categorized under the following articles containing a hate motive as a categorizing attribute: "infliction of light bodily harm," "battery," and "involvement of a minor in a criminal group." The first two articles are applied virtually every year. Three convictions for violent crimes (compared to five in 2018) were based on Art. 282 of the Criminal Code (incitement of hatred), namely, Paragraphs "a" and "c" of Art. 282 Part 2 of the Criminal Code (incitement of hatred or enmity with the use of violence or with the threat of its use, or by an organized group). Art. 280 of the Criminal Code (public calls for extremist activity) was similarly invoked in three guilty verdicts. In two of them, it was used in conjunction with Art. 282 of the Criminal Code and was added to other charges against the co-defendants in joint trials and against the members of ultra-right groups such as the Omsk group[10] and the founder and member of the group known as Schtolz Khabarovsk.[11]

Penalties for violent acts were distributed as follows:

- One person was sentenced to more than 20 years in prison;
- Two people were sentenced to 10 to 20 years in prison;
- Two people were sentenced to five to 10 years;
- Three people received suspended sentences;
- One person was sentenced to compulsory community service;
- One person was relieved from punishment due to the expiration of the statute of limitations.

We are aware of just one case of additional punishment, given to the above-mentioned Schtolz group leader,[12] who was barred from leading and participating in public organizations for eight years and from publishing appeals and any materials in public information and telecommunications networks, including the Internet, for two years.

As is evident from the above data, half of those convicted for violence (five out of 10) have received prison time of various lengths. However, the share of suspended sentences is on the rise for the second consecutive year, having reached 30% in 2019 (three out of 10), as compared to 20% (nine out of 45) in 2018.

We question the appropriateness of the suspended sentence given to the resident of Omsk for two attacks, a beating of a passerby suspected of being a drug user and a beating of a person of "non-Slavic appearance."[13] The sentences received by two adolescents from St. Petersburg for the perpetration of a "white subway car" attack – moderate suspended sentences – also seem far too lenient to us,[14] even though the convicted were minors when they committed the crime.

For Crimes Against Property

We are not aware of any sentences for crimes against property where a hate motive was cited in 2019. (In 2018, two such sentences were handed down in two regions against six individuals, and in 2017 there were three sentences in three regions against five individuals.)

For Public Statements

According to our data, incomplete as it may be, the number of convictions for "extremist statements" (incitement to hatred, incitement to extremism or terrorism, etc.) decreased by one-half compared with 2018. SOVA Center has information about 98 convictions against 103 individuals in 47 regions of the country.[15] In 2018, we had information about 206 such convictions against 218 people in 65 regions. These numbers do not include the convictions that we find inappropriate, but numbers of those are falling: In 2019, we found five convictions against five individuals inappropriate (these convictions are not included in this report).

For the second year, we are using a more detailed approach to classifying convictions. Whereas prior to 2018, we divided convictions for statements into "inappropriate" and "all other," in the past two years we have been using more detailed classification.

We have information about 12 lawful convictions against 16 individuals.

In our assessment of appropriateness and lawfulness, we apply the Rabat Plan of Action on the prohibition of advocacy of national, racial or religious hatred that constitutes incitement to discrimination, hostility or violence, which was developed by the UN.[16] The Rabat Plan of Action contains a six-part test to assist courts in making decisions on incitement cases: It recommends that courts take into consideration not only the content of the expression but also its context, extent of publicity, social status of the speaker, intent of the speaker to incite hatred and likelihood of causing harm. This test is supported almost in its entirety by the Russian Supreme Court.

An example of an appropriate conviction is the court decision issued in Vladivostok in the case of Anna Skripko, a paramilitary security guard at a Pacific Fleet facility of the Russian Navy. She published a video titled "Colonel Kvachkov's Comments on the Situation of Russian Nationalists in Prisons" on her page on the VKontakte social media network and distributed this video personally and via messengers "among civilian personnel of the paramilitary guard." Skripko received a suspended sentence of two years of imprisonment with deprivation of the right to engage in activities related to public organizations under Art. 280 Part 2 of the Criminal Code. The sentence took into account the content of the statement (ex-colonel Kvachkov's republished speech contains explicit calls for armed violence), Skripko's audience was wide enough, and, given that the propaganda was disseminated among armed personnel, among whom colonel Kvachkov and his supporters enjoy a certain degree of popularity, these calls presented considerable public danger.

In the vast majority of cases – marked as "Unknown" (67 convictions against 68 people) – we are not familiar with the exact content of the materials and therefore cannot assess the appropriateness of the court decisions.

Convictions that we find difficult to assess fall under the category of "Uncertain" (five convictions against five people); for example, we find one of the charges appropriate but not the other.

Our statistics in the "Other" category (15 convictions against 15 people) included individuals who called for attacks on government officials and those who were convicted under extremism articles of the Criminal Code more appropriately than not but whose prosecution cannot be classified as counteraction to nationalism and xenophobia.

Speaking about the overall statistics, our information about convictions is, regretfully, far from complete. According to the data posted on the Supreme Court Web site,[17] just in the first half of 2019, Arts. 282, 280, 280.1, 205.2, 354.1, and Art. 148, Parts 1 and 2 of the Criminal Code were the main charges against 115 people convicted of extremist statements.[18] This is lower than the 230 reported by the Supreme Court in 2018.[19]

The first half of 2019 was marked by the annulment of sentences and reviewing of cases as a result of the partial decriminalization of Art. 282 of the Criminal Code.[20] We have information about ten convictions (in addition to the eight deemed inappropriate) that were annulled due to the decriminalization,[21] including the conviction against former leader of the Black Bloc ultra-right movement Vladimir Ratnikov, who was found guilty of publishing neo-Nazi songs on the social media network VKontakte and sentenced to 160 hours of mandatory labor in March 2018. At least 15 other cases (two of them partially and five entirely unlawful) were dismissed at the preliminary investigation stage,[22] including the case of Aleksei Kas-yan, a researcher of the Institute of Linguistics of the Russian Academy of Sciences, who was charged with incitement to national and religious hatred for three xenophobic posts on LiveJournal. Seventeen cases were discontinued by the courts[23] "due to the absence of corpus delicti," including the criminal proceedings against the leader of Guerillas' Guerrilla Truth Aleksei Menyailov and his wife Slatana Menyailova, who were charged with creating and publishing videos against women.[24]

As a result of the decriminalization of Art. 282, the terms for those who were serving sentences for multiple offenses have been reduced. Some convicts were released early in 2019. Some of the most famous of these were editor-in-chief of the *Radical Politics* periodical Boris Stomakhin and the former leaders of banned organizations Dmitry (Schulz) Bobrov of the National-Socialist Initiative (NSI), Dmitry Dyomushkin of the "Russians" and Slavic Union movements, and Vladimir Kvachkov of the MPPM.

Art. 280 of the Criminal Code (public calls for extremist activity) partially replaced Art. 282 of the Criminal Code and was applied in the vast majority of the verdicts known to us,[25] that is, in 68 verdicts against 69 people. In 61 of these convictions, this was the only charge.

Art. 282 was applied in four convictions known to us, namely, Paragraphs "a" and "c" of Art. 282 Part 2 of the Criminal Code (incitement of hatred or enmity with the use of violence or with the threat of its use, or by an organized group).

We have information about one conviction under the updated Art. 282 Part 1 of the Criminal Code: A resident of Vladikavkaz, Republic of North Ossetia, who had previously been fined under Art. 20.3.1 of the Code of Administrative Offenses (incitement of hatred) for publishing materials targeting the Ukrainians and later had again published posts aimed at the natives of Tajikistan and Uzbekistan, Roma, and other ethnic groups in social media, received a three year suspended sentence.

We have information on one conviction under Art. 280.1 of the Criminal Code (public calls for undermining the territorial integrity of the Russian Federation). In the town of Sibai, the Republic of Bashkortostan, a 55-year-old local resident received a one-and-a-half-year suspended sentence for publishing a post calling on residents of Bashkiria, Tatarstan, Udmurtia, Mordovia, Mari El, and Chuvashia to secede from the Russian Federation. He did not rule out the use of force to achieve that goal and called for a war against "Moskals" (an ethnic slur for Russians).

We are considering convictions under Art. 205.2 of the Criminal Code (public calls for terrorist activity or public justification of terrorism) separately. According to the Supreme Court data, in the first half of 2019, it was the main article in 45 convictions; in 11 convictions, it was applied along with other articles.[26] SOVA Center is aware of 30 sentences handed down to 31 people (this is about one-third of the total number of those convicted under it). In 15 cases, this was the only article applied in the conviction. In six other cases, it was applied in combination with Art. 280.

Art. 205.2 of the Criminal Code must be mentioned separately because, in the vast majority of the verdicts known to us, it was applied in convictions for radical Islamic propaganda and calls to go to Syria and join ISIS. Two guilty verdicts were handed down against the anarchists who called for the overthrow of the government and justified the actions of a young comrade who set off a bomb inside a Federal Security Service's office, killing himself in the blast. In another case, Arkady Markov, a municipal deputy of the town of Ostrov in Pskov Province and a "citizen of the USSR,"[27] was punished for publishing an excerpt from the Russian TV series *Igra: Revanche* (Game: Revenge) on his VKontakte page and on the Web site titled Platform for Social Journalism. In the excerpt, the main character kills an FSB colonel, accusing him of violating the military oath of the USSR. In his comments, Markov suggested his readers take a page from that book and insisted that "the protection of the socialist Fatherland is a sacred duty of every citizen of the USSR." At least five of those punished for incitement to terrorism were sentenced while already imprisoned.

In some instances, this article was applied in combination with other criminal articles, including murder, making explosives, involving a minor in terrorism, etc.

Those who were convicted of public statements received the following sentences:

- Fifty people were sentenced to imprisonment;
- Forty-six received suspended sentences without any additional measures;
- Four were sentenced to various fines;
- One was sentenced to mandatory labor;
- One was referred to mandatory treatment.

The number of those sentenced to imprisonment was slightly higher than in the previous year (in 2018, we reported 49 prison sentences).

Some received prison terms in conjunction with charges other than statements (robbery, violence, arson, or drug possession) or based on outstanding sentences. Five individuals were charged with repeat offenses, which always significantly heightens the risk of prison time. Five others were already serving prison time, and their terms were increased. Penalties under Art. 205.2 of the Criminal Code were predictably harsher since it deals with terrorism.[28]

Seven individuals, however, received prison terms in the absence of any of the abovementioned circumstances (or, perhaps, in some cases, we just do not know about them). Only one publication that was the subject of criminal investigation is available for our assessment. Blogger Vladislav Sinitsa's tweet became widely known and drew the attention of the public. Asked by a Twitter user why someone would reveal the identity of law enforcement and special forces officers, Sinitsa warned "courageous law enforcement officers" that one day, "instead of their child ... they will receive a package with a CD with snuff video in the mail" from townsfolk angered by the tough crackdown on protests. The court has deemed this comment an incitement to social hatred with the threat of the use of violence; on Sept. 3, Sinitsa was sentenced under Art. 282 Part 2 to five years in a penal colony.[29] While the tweet is undoubtedly aggressive, we find the sentence far too harsh.

As for the materials published by other offenders, we are not familiar with their contents; the only source available to us is general statements in press releases from the prosecutor's offices and investigative committees ("calls for extremist activity against representatives of the regions of Caucasus and Central Asia"). We can only assume that neither were the majority of the convicted widely known public figures, nor did they conduct mass propaganda, and thus imprisonment was, in some cases, an unjustifiably harsh and cruel punishment.

In 2019, the proportion of suspended sentences (44%, or 46 out of 103) was a bit lower compared with 48.6% (93 out of 192) in 2018. The share of the convicts whose sentences did not involve prison time (actual or suspended), i.e., those sentenced to fines or mandatory labor, has also been continuously declining for four years.

In terms of additional punishments, in 2019 we have information about the following bans: on holding leadership positions (two cases), holding positions in state and local governments (three), participation in the activities of public organizations (four), engaging in public activism (two). Some additional penalties were related to the Internet, such as bans on posting materials in public telecommunications networks, including the Internet (three), bans on administering Internet sites (15), and bans on Internet use (eight).

As usual, the vast majority of sentences – 85 out of 98, or 86%, in 2019 (94% in 2018) – were handed down for materials posted on the Internet. Thus, the overall decrease in the number of sentences did not impact offline statements.

These materials were posted on:

- Social media – 64 (41 on VKontakte; two on Twitter; one on Instagram; two on Odnoklassniki; and 19 on unidentified social media networks[30]);
- Messengers – three (one of them on Telegram);
- Video channels (probably YouTube) – one;
- Online news media – two (comments on articles in online media);
- Unspecified online resources – 14.

The types of content are as follows (different types of content may have been posted in the same account or even on the same page):

- Video – 28;
- Images (drawings) – 12;
- Photographs – five;
- Audio (songs) – nine;
- Texts – 22;
- Comments (on social media and forums) – eight;
- Administration of ultra-right online communities – two;
- Unspecified – 15.

Both breakdowns have remained virtually the same in the past eight years.[31]

The number of convictions for offline statements (13) turned out to be slightly higher than the 11 in the previous year's records. They were distributed as follows:

- Shouts during an attack – three;
- Shouts during a football match – one;
- Graffiti – three;
- Distribution by mail – one;[32]
- Convicted of engaging in propaganda in prison – five.

We have doubts about the lawfulness of only those sentences for terrorist propaganda given to those who are already in prison where we are not familiar with the actual content of the charges (it is easier to fabricate evidence in a colony or prison). There are certainly quite a lot of individuals prone to violence among the prison population; therefore, any promotion of hatred in prison is undoubtedly dangerous. However, it is not clear whether the key parameter in the articles of law applicable to statements – the audience size – has been taken into account; in most cases, the audience size is not reported. In some instances, the audience was definitely extremely small: Propaganda was conducted in a prison cell where only a few inmates were held.[33]

In 2019, for the first time in several years, we encountered criminal prosecution for mailing a letter. At the end of February 2019, Andery Zlokazov, a supporter of the Union of Slavic Forces of Rus (for more details, see the Banning Organizations as Extremist section of this chapter) and "Governor of Sverdlovsk Oblast of the RSFSR," sent an "order" to the leadership of the military units of the Ministry of Defense and the National Guard (Rosgvardia) containing "calls for revolution" from "Commander of the Armed Forces of Sverdlovsk Oblast." This letter raised serious doubts about the mental capacity of the "citizen of the USSR," and he was sent to mandatory treatment.

For Participation in Extremist and Banned Groups and Organizations

In 2019, we have information about six individuals convicted under Art. 282.1 of the Criminal Code (organizing an extremist community) and three under Art. 282.2 (organizing the activity of an extremist organization); these numbers do not include inappropriate convictions, the numbers of which have increased significantly compared to the previous year. Twelve verdicts against 40 people have been deemed inappropriate, whereas in 2018, we reported six verdicts against 14 people under Arts. 282.1 and 282.2.

In 2019, in all the sentences known to us, Art. 282.1 was applied to the founders and members of ultra-right groups and nationalist organizations.

In Perm, members of the PNZS group (Perm Nazi Squad) received two sentences for drawing graffiti on the building of the Prosecutor's office of Perm Territory and for setting fire to the building which housed the United

Russia party office (by mistake, the perpetrators set fire to the State Institute for the Development of Education of Perm Territory, which was located in the same building). Based on the combined effect of Arts. 282.1 and 167 of the Criminal Code, they were sentenced to various terms of imprisonment.

In the Far East, the founder and a member of the Schtolz group have both been found guilty.[34] Two of the group members received extended sentences based on the combined effect of Art. 282.1 and a whole range of other articles, including Art. 105 of the Criminal Code (murder).

In Moscow, political consultant and Moscow City Duma nominee from the Communist Party Pyotr Miloserdov was sentenced to two and a half years in a penal colony under Art. 282.1 of the Criminal Code. He was charged with membership in a Kazakhstan extremist community founded by Aleksandr Belov, the former leader of two banned ultra-right organizations, the Movement Against Illegal Immigration and the "Russians."[35] The criminal case on the creation of this community involved, among other things, a meeting with the representatives of the local Cossacks, a workshop held at a sanatorium on Kirgiz Issyk-Kul Lake, and preparations for a "Russian March" to be held in Kazakhstan; however, Miloserdov's role in all this remains unclear.

Just as a year earlier, supporters of Ukrainian organizations were charged under Art. 282.2. A Stavropol court sentenced two alleged activists of the banned ultra-right organization Misanthropic Division[36] to prison; they were also found guilty of planning assassinations of law enforcement officers. A Samara court sentenced a football fan for two years and one month in a penal colony for calls (both in person and posted in VKontakte) to join him and go to Ukraine to fight for the Right Sector movement, banned in Russia.[37] He was previously charged under Arts. 213 (hooliganism) and 116 (battery) of the Criminal Code.

Some nationalist organizations were previously banned as terrorist organizations. But we do not know anything about convictions made against right-wing radicals in 2019 for organizing and participating in the activity of a terrorist organization (Art. 205.4), and also for organizing and participating in terrorist communities (Art. 205.5).

On the whole, however, according to the Supreme Court data, in the first half of 2019 alone, articles related to participation in extremist or terrorist communities and continuation of activities of the organizations that have been banned as extremist or terrorist (Arts. 282.1, 282.2, 205.4, 205.5) were used in verdicts against 100 people. And since the total figure obtained by adding the data from this report and those on the inappropriate enforcement of anti-extremism legislation is much lower, we cannot rule out the possibility of the presence of radical nationalists among those convicted under these articles, probably most of all under Art. 282.2.

Inappropriate Prosecution of Political and Civic Activists

In 2019, after partial decriminalization of Art. 282 of the Criminal Code on incitement to hatred, which had been often used to prosecute people for expressing political views, the courts more frequently prosecuted ideological opponents of the authorities under other articles of the Criminal Code, as well as under Art. 20.3.1 of the Code of Administrative Offenses, which is similar in wording to Art. 282 Part 1 of the Criminal Code. Nearly fifty cases of prosecution under new parts of Art. 20.1 of the Code of Administrative Offenses for disrespect for the authorities and society on the Internet are also worth noting. Overall, it can be stated that online opposition activity remains the focus of attention for law enforcement agencies and is often the basis for unjustified persecution.

For "Rehabilitation of Nazism"

In March, the Volgograd Province Court fined Aleksei Volkov – coordinator of Aleksei Navalny's headquarters in Volgograd in 2017 – 200,000 rubles under Art. 354.1 of the Criminal Code (rehabilitation of Nazism) Part 3 (public desecration of the symbols of Russia's military glory). He was charged for publishing in the Volgograd VKontakte community of Navalny's supporters a collage of the Motherland Calls statue covered with green dye. This post was made following the green dye attack against Navalny during his "pre-election" visit to Barnaul. The creators and distributors of the collage obviously did not intend to express disrespect for the monument and contribute to the rehabilitation of Nazism – on the contrary, they likened the clearly unlawful attack on Navalny to an attack on the famous sculpture. Distribution of such an image can hardly be considered a desecration of the monument. In addition, the legislation never defines the concept of "symbols of Russia's military glory" used in the wording of Art. 354.1 Part 3 of the Criminal Code, so it is unclear what exactly should be regarded as such.

In December, the jury and then the Supreme Court of Chuvashia found opposition blogger Konstantin Ishutov guilty under Art. 354.1 Part 1 of the Criminal Code (rehabilitation of Nazism) and Art. 242.1 Part 2 Paragraph "d" of the Criminal Code (dissemination of child pornography on the Internet). Ishutov was sentenced to three and a half years in a penal colony and a fine of 150,000 rubles. We consider Ishutov's sentence inappropriate in its part related to the rehabilitation of Nazism. The verdict was based on two of his publications on social media. In 2010, Ishutov wrote on LiveJournal that the Chuvash authorities had never recognized the fact that the region was a burial place for thousands of German POWs who had worked at the peat plant in Zavolzhye, and no funds were allocated to care for the mass grave. The blogger noted that, on the contrary, it was customary in Germany to look after mass graves, memorials and monuments. Neither the text of his post nor the discussion that followed contained any statements to justify the actions of the Nazis. The blogger was also charged for his 2018 Facebook post containing a photograph of a 1941 German leaflet addressed to citizens of the Soviet Union and the Red Army soldiers and officers in which the Nazis promised to transfer household plots into private ownership and to restore freedom of religion in the USSR. Ishutov accompanied the publication with a comment, "When the Third Reich cares for the Soviet people more than Putin does for the Russian people." From our point of view, neither episode provided sufficient grounds for criminal prosecution, because Ishutov's intent was obviously not to justify the crimes of the Third Reich but to criticize the policies of the Russian authorities.

For Incitement to Extremist Activities

In December, the Kuntsevsky District Court of Moscow found Yegor Zhukov, a student at the Higher School of Economics and a video blogger, guilty of incitement to extremist activity on the Internet under Art. 280 Part 2 of the Criminal Code. Zhukov received a three-year suspended sentence and a two-year ban on administering a Web site or engaging in similar activities. According to the investigation, four videos from Zhukov's YouTube channel contained "calls for extremist activities motivated by political hatred and enmity, including calls for forcibly changing the constitutional system, rioting and obstructing the lawful activity of law enforcement officials," and the court agreed with this assessment. In these videos, Zhukov called on the opposition to engage in a more active and well-thought-out struggle against the current system of government in Russia, but he advocated exclusively non-violent methods of resistance and, moreover, argued that violent methods were unacceptable. In our opinion, the methods of political struggle listed by Zhukov do not fall within the definition of extremist activity provided in the corresponding law.

For Other Anti-Government Statements

In 2019, we became aware of 31 cases of responsibility under Art. 20.29 of the Code of Administrative Offenses in various regions of Russia for distributing the banned video about unfulfilled campaign promises of the United Russia party, "Let's Remind the Crooks and Thieves about Their Manifesto-2002," created by supporters of Aleksei Navalny. Belgorod Province, where at least 18 people faced responsibility for the video, is a clear leader here.[38] Courts put the offenders under administrative detention in two cases and levied fines in 28 cases; the outcome of one case is unknown. We can assume that law enforcement agencies have chosen this video because it can be easily found on social media and thus allows for imposing "preventive measures" in the form of administrative punishments against opposition-minded Internet users without much effort. In Belgorod Province, it has obviously become the favorite tool of the operatives of the local Center for Combating Extremism – fans of quota-based policing who utilize the video to improve their statistics in the fight against extremism. We would like to remind readers that the content of the notorious video, recognized as extremist in 2013, merely lists a number of unfulfilled campaign promises from the 2002 United Russia party manifesto and calls for voting for any party other than the ruling party. We view the prohibition of this video and punishment for its distribution as inappropriate.

At least 11 cases of filing baseless charges against opposition activists under Art. 20.3 of the Code of Administrative Offenses (display of banned symbols) were reported to us in 2019. One case was dismissed; three cases led to administrative detentions and seven more to fines. The cases in question involve the use of forbidden symbols with no intent to promote the corresponding ideology – for example, the use of swastikas in opposition memes.

Thus, in November, the Sverdlovsk District Court of Irkutsk punished political strategist and public figure Igor Madasov with two days of administrative detention for his Facebook post depicting two badges – one of the Russian police patrol service and the other one of the Third Reich Department of Finance (featuring an eagle holding a Nazi swastika) – with the caption, "POLICE everything old is new again."

In August, Aleksandr Kruglov, the chairman of the organizing committee of the All-Russian Communist Party (Bolsheviks) (VKP(b)), was fined 1,000 rubles in Samara after three images depicting Vladimir Putin and Nazi symbols were found on his VKontakte page. Obviously, Kruglov did not pursue the aim of advocating Nazi ideology by posting these images; on the contrary, he used the swastika as a means of political criticism. The province court rescinded the fine due to procedural violations committed by a lower court.

In 2019, citizens were held responsible at least 56 times under Art. 20.1 Parts 3-5 of the Code of Administrative Offenses for dissemination of online information expressing disrespect for society and the state in indecent form. Fines were imposed in 32 cases (two people were fined twice), proceedings were discontinued in 18 cases (four of these cases were attempts to penalize previously punished offenders for their new statements); the outcome of six cases is unknown. In addition, we know of four cases in which the police rejected the informants' complaints and refused to report the incidents. Almost all cases under Art. 20.1 Parts 3-5 of the Code of Administrative Offenses pertained to disrespect for the authorities – most often to obscene statements about the president, but also to statements targeting local officials, judges and law enforcement officers. The offenders include local activists, journalists and bloggers, as well as ordinary Internet users dissatisfied with the authorities. It is worth noting that the first court decisions under Art. 20.1 Part 3 of the Code of Administrative Offenses were handed down in the spring, the majority of the punishments were imposed in the summer, and the flow of cases decreased in the fall. In addition, lawyers from Agora International Human Rights Group, who provide legal support in such cases, were increasingly successful in getting them dismissed.[39]

For Anti-Government Group Initiatives

In June, it became known that Chelyabinsk activists Oksana Yeremina and Yury Vashurin were charged under Art. 213 Part 2 of the Criminal Code (hooliganism motivated by political hatred committed by an organized group). In the course of the protest rally "He is Not Our Tsar" on May 5, 2018, in Chelyabinsk, protesters broke through the police cordon. According to the investigation, the participants in the unauthorized rally filled the intersection and the area around the Alyi Shopping Center, "using their numerical advantage to obstruct the customary flow of people" and creating a threat of their accidental exit onto the roadway. According to the indictment, Yeremina was calling on protesters to break through the cordon and then started an "active forward movement" and broke through the cordon along with other protesters; Vashurin also participated in this break, linking his arms with other rally participants. Thus, according to the investigation, the defendants grossly violated public order and expressed obvious disrespect for society, "in order to express their political will and political opinion, as well as to protest the current Head of State, President of the Russian Federation V.V. Putin, and to express their disagreement with results of the 2018 elections for President of the Russian Federation." The case was dismissed with respect to Boris Zolotarevsky, the former coordinator of Aleksei Navalny's Chelyabinsk headquarters, who had previously been a suspect as well; the investigation concluded that, although Zolotarevsky was the action's organizer, he was not involved in the crime since he had been detained before the rally began. In our opinion, breaking through a cordon and filling a square or an intersection with participants in a mass event might be considered a violation of the procedure for holding a mass event, but not hooliganism committed on the basis of political hatred. Yeremina and Vashurin were acquitted in January 2021.

In December, a criminal case on alleged organizing of an extremist community was opened against Ingush opposition members who had participated in organizing protests against changes to the Ingushetia-Chechnya border in March 2019. Malsag Uzhakhov, Akhmed Barakhoyev and Musa Malsagov were charged under Art. 282.1 Part 1 of the Criminal Code for creating the Ingush Committee of National Unity (*Ingushsky Komitet Natsionalnogo Yedinstva*, ICNU); Barakh Chemurziev, Zarifa Sautieva, Ismail Nalgiev, Bagaudin Khautiev and Akhmed Pogorov – under Art. 282.1 Part 2 of the Criminal Code for participating in the Committee. The activists were previously charged under Art. 33 Part 3 and Art. 318 Part 2 of the Criminal Code with organizing violence motivated by political hostility against representatives of the authorities in connection with the discharge of their official duties, endangering their lives or health.

The charges stemmed from the events of March 27, 2019, which took place on the square near the Ingushetia National Television and Radio Company in Magas, where the protest rally turned into clashes with the National Guard. Uzhakhov was also charged under Art. 239 Parts 2 and 3 of the Criminal Code (operating a public association involving individuals in commitment of illegal acts). According to the investigators, Uzhakhov, Barakhoyev and Malsagov, united by their political hostility toward Ingushetia's president Yunus-Bek Yevkurov, created an extremist community, namely the ICNU chaired by Malsagov. ICNU activists disseminated calls for participation in non-permitted protests via mass media and social media and also organized such demonstrations. They declared that the rally on March 27 would last indefinitely until the protesters' demands were met, thereby "psychologically motivating and enticing" the rally participants to disobey government officials and use violence against them; this stance led to clashes. At the same time, the above-listed activists were not charged with using violence or threatening to use it. Allegedly, the ICNU members deliberately encouraged the protesters to use violence against government officials motivated by political hostility, when, "manipulating ethnic customs" and "provocatively invoking male dignity and national unity," they urged protesters to protect elders and women by any means necessary.

We view the charges brought against the Ingush activists, both under Art. 282.1 and Art. 318 of the Criminal Code, as inappropriate. The investigation has provided no convincing arguments either that the activists had planned in advance to provoke violence (and got together for this very purpose), or that their calls (whether planned or voiced spontaneously) were intended to motivate the audience to violence. Thus, firstly, it is impossible to regard this association of activists as an extremist community – that is, as a group created in order to plan extremist crimes – and secondly, the calls described in the indictment cannot be viewed as actions intended to organize the use of violence.

Abuse of Criminalization of Incitement to Hatred

Due to partial decriminalization of Art. 282 of the Criminal Code, a number of criminal cases under this article regarded by us as inappropriate or problematic were terminated in 2019.

- The overturn of the verdict against Sagit Ismagilov, an activist of the Bashkir national movement, who had been fined for inciting ethnic hatred for his statement about the Tatars of the Golden Horde.[40]

- The overturn of the verdict against Dmitry Dzhigalov and Oleg Semenov, activists of the "Anti-Corruption Bureau of Crimea" in Sudak, who had been sentenced to pay fines under Art. 282 for the violation of dignity of the Bulgarians.[41]

- The overturn of the verdict against Ingush activist Sarazhdin Sultygov, who had been fined for inciting hatred toward the Ossetians.[42]

- The overturn of the verdict against Arkadia Akopian from Prokhladny (Kabardino-Balkaria), who had been fined for distribution of prohibited Jehovah's Witnesses brochures viewed as incitement to religious hatred.[43]

- The reduction by three months – as a result of dropping the charges of inciting hostility toward Yunus-Bek Yevkurov – of the sentence against Magomed Khazbiev, an Ingush opposition activist, who had been sentenced under several criminal articles to two years and 11 months in an open prison.[44]

- The reduction of the sentence against Danis Safargali, the leader of the Tatar Patriotic Front Altyn Urda (the Golden Horde) due to termination of his prosecution under Art. 282 of the Criminal Code;[45] in 2017, he was sentenced to three years of imprisonment on several criminal charges, including for posting statements targeting representatives of certain ethnic and religious groups, the president of Russia, the authorities and the mass media.

- The expunging of the conviction of St. Petersburg nationalist Vladimir Timoshenko, who had served a two-year sentence in a maximum-security penal colony for inciting hatred toward the social group "employees of government institutions and agencies."[46]

- The release of the blogger Ruslan Sokolovsky from punishment under Art. 282 Part 1 of the Criminal Code, under which (in aggregation with Art. 148 Part 1 and Art. 138.1 of the Criminal Code (illegal sale or acquisition of special devices intended for secretly obtaining information)) he had received a suspended sentence. The blogger was charged for publishing videos which the court found, among other issues, to violate dignity on the grounds of nationality, religion and belonging to a social group.[47]

In addition, we would like to note the following cases that we regarded as inappropriate or doubtful, and for which prosecutions under Art. 282 of the Criminal Code were discontinued:

- Ending the prosecution against student Daniel Markin from Barnaul, who was charged with violating the dignity of Christians by posting atheistic memes.[48]

- Dropping the prosecution under Art. 282 of the Criminal Code (but not under Art. 280 of the Criminal Code, under which he has also been charged) against Yury Zalipayev, a Jehovah's Witness from the city of Maisky (Kabardino-Balkaria), for distributing prohibited Jehovah's Witnesses brochures.[49]

- Terminating the case of feminist Lyubov Kalugina in the Omsk Region, who was charged with inciting hatred against men on a social media network.[50]

- Ending the prosecution of Amin Shayakhmetov, who was charged with inciting hatred and violation of dignity on the grounds of ethnicity, language and attitude toward religion for posting texts on a Web site belonging to the Shura of Muslims of the Republic of Bashkortostan; the criminal case against him had been terminated with imposition of a court fine.[51]

- Terminating the prosecution against Valery Bolshakov, the former Chairman of the Sevastopol Workers Union and the secretary of the Sevastopol branch of the Russian United Labor Front Party (ROT FRONT) charged for his negative assessments of the Terek Cossacks made on a social media network. Bolshakov was sentenced only under Art. 280 Parts 1 and 2 of the Criminal Code for his calls for overthrowing the regime; then this verdict was overturned by the appellate court.[52]

- Ending the prosecution against poet Aleksandr Byvshev for incitement of hatred against Russians in connection with the online distribution of his poems; later, the charges under Art. 280 Part 2 and Art. 294 Part 1 of the Criminal Code (obstruction of justice) were also dropped due to the absence of corpus delicti.[53]

According to our information, nine people were inappropriately held liable under new Art. 20.3.1 of the Code of Administrative Offenses, which was introduced as a result of decriminalization of Art. 282 Part 1 of the Criminal Code. Six of them were fined, one received 15 days detention, one case was closed; and for one we don't know the outcome.

The Privolzhsky District Court of Kazan fined left-wing activist D. Valiev 10,000 rubles for answering a question about the intellectual abilities and tolerance of Russians on the Internet portal Ask.FM. In his answer, the activist accused Russians of intolerance and cowardice. Valiev is a supporter of anti-fascist ideology, and his remark was dictated by his rejection of certain views that are common in Russian society rather than by his desire to humiliate Russians on ethnic grounds.

The Laishevsky District Court of Tatarstan fined I. Sirazetdinov 10,000 rubles. Sirazetdinov posted the video "Foreign Fascist Dictatorship in the Country" on a VKontakte public page, which consisted of a recorded meeting of the Academy for Geopolitical Problems chaired by the head of this organization, Leonid Ivashov. During the meeting, Ivashov described to the audience his vision of the social, economic and political situation in Russia and criticized the authorities for their clannishness, exploitation of natural resources and the population, the country's economic decline, the low standard of living for the majority and so on. Only once did he resort to his habitual nationalist rhetoric and express his suspicions concerning the Jews and the Han Chinese and their desire for world domination. This statement, however, was far removed not only from inciting hatred, but also from violation of dignity. They can be classified as an insignificant case of hate speech, which, in our opinion, does not deserve punishment. We also reiterate our belief that authors rather than distributors of inflammatory statements should face primary responsibility for them.

The Norilsk City Court twice dismissed the case of Eva Repina, a citizen of Uzbekistan and a Norilsk resident, in respect of whom a report under Art. 20.3.1 of the Code of Administrative Offenses was compiled based on the fact that she created the "Online Idiots" album on VKontakte, where she kept screenshots of posts and comments containing xenophobic remarks against non-Muslims and Russians – in order to submit complaints, according to her. The court concluded that Repina's actions were not intended either to incite hatred or hostility against a group of people on the basis of their religion, or to violate the dignity of a group of people on the basis of their ethnicity. This did not stop the FSB from issuing to Repina a ban on entering the country until the end of 2038 (even prior to the case review), followed by the cancellation of her temporary residence permit. Repina lost her appeal against this decision. We see no reason to prohibit Repina from living in Russia – it is evident that she had no intention of inciting hatred toward Russians and non-Muslims by collecting xenophobic comments in her album, and removal of the album from public access would have been a sufficient measure to prevent online conflicts. A twenty-year ban on entering the country based on evidence of an administrative offense is an obviously disproportionate response.

The Aldansky District Court of the Republic of Sakha (Yakutia) sentenced assembly line operator N. Filippov to 15 days under detention. While reading information on the ethnic conflict on the "Criminal Yakutia" Instagram page, Filippov found a comment on the post that was "extremist in its nature and incited Yakuts to unite against Russians" and forwarded it to a certain girl "just for laughs." Despite the fact that this commentary apparently called for xenophobic violence, we doubt the appropriateness of Filippov's sentence, since a statement forwarded to a single person cannot be considered a public statement, and Art. 20.3.1 punishes for public statements.

FC CSKA fan Yevgeny Ogurtsov from Novocheboksarsk (Chuvashia) was fined 10,000 rubles for publishing a collection of his own poetry and advertising it on VKontakte. A number of his poems contained unflattering expressions targeting the players and fans of FC Spartak. We had no opportunity to review Ogurtsov's poems. However, in our opinion, the players and fans of FC Spartak do not form a vulnerable social group in need of special protection against manifestations of hatred, and, unless Ogurtsov had called for violent actions against them, there was no reason for charges.

In Ust-Ilimsk in the Irkutsk Province, a case under Art. 20.3.1 of the Code of Administrative Offenses was opened against Vladimir Ivaschenko, the former head of the local branch of the Young Guard of United Russia, who characterized his fellow town residents as a "narrow-minded herd" and "cattle" for choosing Anna Schekina, a candidate from the LDPR, as the town mayor; he also made some unflattering comments about her personally. We believe that the town residents should not be classified as a particularly vulnerable group of people who require protection from incitement of hatred. We generally advocate for excluding the term "social group" from Art. 282 of the Criminal Code and Art. 20.3.1 of the Code of Administrative Offenses, since the presence of such a vague term is fraught with abuse. In any event, the Prosecutor's Office in its decision to initiate a case stated that resolving the question of whether Ivaschenko's statements violated the dignity of Ust-Ilimsk residents and whether these residents form a social group required "conducting an administrative investigation including analysis and expert examination." Apparently, the case has never reached court.

We also object to punishment imposed in charges of inciting hatred (violation of dignity) against government officials, since they do not constitute a social group that needs special protection from hate. Thus, we view charges under Art. 20.3.1 of the Code of Administrative Offenses for harsh statements addressed to officials as inappropriate. Our records showed three such cases in 2019.

The Mendeleyevsky District Court of Tatarstan fined Radislav Fedorov 10,000 rubles for posting two videos on VKontakte, one of which we have never had a chance to review. The second one, "Dimon: Who Are You?" is an animated video in which Aleksei Navalny and Leonid Volkov escort rapping prime minister Dmitry Medvedev to an electric chair; in our opinion, it does not provide a sufficient reason for sanctions.

The Promyshlennovsky District Court in Kemerovo fined Igor Molchanov 10,000 rubles for posting on his VKontakte page a text "containing a negative and insulting assessment of representatives of various official bodies and law enforcement agencies in order to incite hostility and violate their dignity."

The Zlatoust City Court of the Chelyabinsk Province fined Mikhail Gorin 10,000 rubles for inciting hatred against the social group "law enforcement agencies." The charges were based on the fact that in 2018, Gorin posted a comment in the VKontakte group "Cops out of Control." In his post, he spoke rudely about policemen and their friends who were posting information in a local online group on traffic accidents, and about the group's administrators, who, according to Gorin, were artificially creating a positive image of police officers in order to whitewash their illegal activities. In the commentary, Gorin expressed support for the administrator of the Cops out of Control and called not only for the dismissal of "such creatures in uniform" from the Internal Affairs agencies, but also for them to be burned alive at the stake as witches were burned during the Inquisition. In our opinion, many arguments from the ECHR's decision in the case of Savva Terentyev, convicted under Art. 282 Part 1 of the Criminal Code for his call for burning the "infidel cops" on town squares, apply in this case; the European Court of Human Rights ruled that Terentyev's verdict violated the Convention on Human Rights.[54]

For Extremist Symbols

While the State Duma was considering amendments to the legislation on the public display of prohibited symbols, law enforcement agencies continued to actively apply Art. 20.3 of the Code of Administrative Offenses, with its usual downsides.

According to statistics provided by the Judicial Department of the Supreme Court, 1,388 people[55] were punished under Art. 20.3 just in the first half of 2019, compared to 1,652 cases for the entirety of 2018[56] – that is, we have observed a sharp increase in the application of this article despite its recognized shortcomings that caused the authorities to engage in its reform. Only in some of these incidents do we know the details of the corresponding administrative cases and can assess their appropriateness. In the course of the year, we noted 31 cases of responsibility for public display of Nazi symbols or symbols of banned organizations not aimed at dangerous propaganda (compared to 29 in 2018). In all cases, the charges were brought against individuals, including opposition activists, representatives of small business, or ordinary social media users. According to our information, fines were imposed in 26 cases, administrative detention in three cases, and five out of 31 cases were dismissed.

In June, the Omsk Province Court overturned the decision of the Pervomaisky District Court of Omsk, which had fined designer Ilya Frishman 1,000 rubles in April under Part 1 of Art. 20.3 of the Code of Administrative Offenses. The proceedings in his case have been discontinued. Frishman was fined for posting videos with Nazi symbols on VKontakte, namely a spoof of the movie *Seventeen Moments of Spring* created by the Channel 1 TV show *Big Difference* and three humorous videos based on a popular scene from the movie *The Bunker*. Frishman stated in court that he had never intended to advocate Nazi ideology, and that he was an ethnic Jew and an Israeli citizen whose ancestors had died at the hands of the Nazis, but the court did not take his arguments into account. However, the district prosecutor spoke in his defense, demanding that the Frishman case be discontinued due to the absence of corpus delicti. Representatives of the Ministry of Internal Affairs, in turn, opposed the elimination of the fine, stating that the episodes from *The Bunker*, modified and taken out of context, did not condemn fascism, but, on the contrary, represented it as "something funny and amusing." They further argued that displaying Nazi paraphernalia in such videos not only failed to cause abhorrence among young people but, instead, was making those symbols fashionable. The province court canceled the fine based on the results of an expert examination.

However, it is not always possible to bring absurd cases to an end. Thus, Elena Kurkina, the head of a circus box office, was fined 1,000 rubles in September in Volgograd. In 2016, Kurkina posted a photo on a social media network that depicted actors involved in a play about the Great Patriotic War and wearing Third Reich uniforms.

Yury Vladykin from Glazov (Udmurtia) was fined 1,000 rubles in December for the fact that, over four years earlier, he set up a display of antiques on an open cabinet shelf of the shoe repair shop where he works, which included, among other items, an envelope depicting Hitler and a swastika. In court, Vladykin explained that he had "committed an offense due to ignorance and misunderstanding." However, the court indicated that "the content of Art. 20.3 Part 1 of the Code of Administrative Offenses of the Russian Federation does not stipulate the intent of the person in respect of whom the administrative case is being conducted as a necessary criterion for being charged with an administrative offense, since one's guilt can also be expressed in reckless actions."

An absurd episode took place in the city of Samara in November. A solemn post-reconstruction opening of a memorial complex dedicated to the participants of the Great Patriotic War took place in the village of Upravlencheskoye in November. During the ceremony, it turned out that the monument, originally erected in 1975, no longer features the image of the swastika, split apart by a sword. The district administration said that they had not reinstalled the swastika due to the fact that its use was prohibited by Art. 6 of the Federal Law "On Immortalization of the Victory of the Soviet people in the Great Patriotic War of 1941-1945," and its display was punishable under Art. 20.3 of the Code of Administrative Offenses.

The practice of punishing the use of Nazi symbols as a visual tool in Internet posts that are critical of the Russian authorities has also continued (see above).

The Federal List of Extremist Materials

In 2019, the Federal List of Extremist Materials expanded much more slowly than in 2018: It was updated 26 times (compared to 38 times in 2018) with 193 new entries (466 in 2018), and the total entries grew from 4,811 to 5,004.[57]

Thus, though the expansion of the Federal List has slowed down in 2019; working with it is impossible due to its sheer size.

New entries added to the list in 2019 fall into the following categories:

- Xenophobic materials of contemporary Russian nationalists – 120;
- Materials of other nationalists – seven;
- Materials of Islamic militants and other calls for violence by political Islamists – 16;
- Other Islamic materials – three;
- Other peaceful worshippers – one;
- Other materials from the Ukrainian media and Internet – four;
- Anti-government materials inciting riots and violence (including pieces by Boris Stomakhin) – six;
- Materials citing works by classic fascist and neo-fascist authors – eight;
- Homophobic materials – nine;
- Banned parody – one;
- Peaceful opposition Web sites – two;
- Radical anti-Christian Web sites – one;
- Materials created, in our opinion, in an altered state of consciousness – four;
- Unidentified materials – 11.

At least 157 entries out of 193 refer to online content (in 2018, it was 402 out of 466). They include various kinds of video and audio clips and images, mostly from social media. Offline sources include newspapers and books by nationalists, classic authors of fascism, and Muslim authors.

In addition to poor descriptions abundant with typos and mistakes, new entries refer to materials that have already been listed, albeit with different output data or online sources. By the end of 2019, there was a total of 246 such duplicate entries in the list.

And as before, the classification of materials as extremist is obviously inappropriate. Records showed at least five such instances in 2019.

Blocking of Online Resources and Internet Censorship

The judicial mechanism of blocking access to banned or other, allegedly dangerous, materials by means of their inclusion in the Single Register of

Prohibited Web Sites is being executed with increasing frequency. We cannot estimate the number of resources added to the Register specifically for extremism in 2019; without a doubt, it constitutes but a small share of the many tens of thousands of resources blocked in the past year. Only Roskomnadzor has complete information. Some information is published on the Roskomsvoboda Web site,[58] and the analysis of their data for the period between January and April has revealed about 900 such resources[59] (compared to a little more than 600 for all of 2018; however, as happens every year, we cannot be sure whether we have identified each and every resource blocked "for extremism").

Judging by these 900, the ideological spectrum of the resources added to the Single Register "for extremism" in 2019 has not changed much. The majority (78%) are Russian nationalists' materials, from xenophobic songs to works by popular nationalist authors; 7% are Islamist militants' materials, from ISIS videos to Timur Mutsurayev's songs; peaceful Islamic materials constitute 4%. Apart from these, there are a small number of references to the works by the classic authors of fascism (3%) and Ukraine-related resources, from the ultra-radical (less than 2%) to peaceful publications by the Ukrainian mass media (1.5%); and banned parody (2%). The share of other materials – those of other nationalists and Orthodox fundamentalists, provocative Web sites and non-radical opposition Web sites – was about 2.5%.

The number of obviously inappropriate blockings in this category is also high. We are unable to provide a quantitative assessment, but the materials blocked in 2019 include those of Jehovah's Witnesses and Falun Dafa, peaceful Islamic materials, and other resources that clearly present no public danger. The mass blocking of Hizb ut-Tahrir party materials also remains a cause for serious concern: While the party has been banned and some of its materials may well be illegal, the history of law enforcement against it suggests an assumption that the majority of its materials do not contain any dangerous calls and are being blocked merely based on affiliation with the banned organization, although such an approach is not based on law.

A separate register, based on the Lugovoi law,[60] provides for extra-judicial blocking of Web sites that disseminate calls for extremist activities, mass riots and many other activities. The number of blockings in this register conducted by the Prosecutor's office is growing at a much faster pace than that of the Single Register; we no longer have any means of obtaining even an approximate number of "extremist resources" in the Lugovoi Register.

For the second consecutive year, we have been working only with the data published on the Roskomnadzor Web site.

According to Roskomnadzor,[61] in the first nine months of 2019, 97,040 resources were blocked "for extremism" (the data for the whole year are not available yet; in the same period in 2018, 51,892 Web sites were blocked). According to reports, these are not the original Web sites ordered by the Prosecutor-General's office (their number is a mere 369) but mirror Web sites "identified" by Roskomnadzor itself. Judging by the numbers though, we believe that these are not all mirror Web sites in the exact sense but also other Web sites with identical or very similar content.

In its reports, Roskomnadzor identifies the following types of resources:

- ISIS propaganda – more than 20,700 materials (more than 17,000 in 2018);
- Hizb ut-Tahrir – more than 14,700 materials (more than 17,000 in 2018);
- Banned Ukrainian organizations (Right Sector, UNA-UNSO, Ukrainian Insurgent Army, Stepan Bandera's Trident, Brotherhood and Azov) – more than 12,100 materials (about 5,000 in 2018);
- Calls for mass riots, extremist activities and participation in un-sanctioned mass public events violating the established order – 122; 96 of them in the 3rd quarter (728 in 2018).

This amounts to about 47,600 resources in total. Roskomnadzor did not specify the remaining 49,400.

As the Federal Service reported, in the first three quarters of 2019, "illegal information" was deleted from 194,325 resources and they were unblocked (it is possible that some of them were blocked earlier).

What is striking in these reports is the number of extra-judicial blockings growing year after year. Interestingly, the combined number of blocked ISIS and Hizb-ut-Tahrir materials has not changed that much compared to the previous year's data for the same period, while the amount of banned Ukrainian organizations' blocked materials has more than doubled. What is remarkable, by the way, is how few resources that disseminate calls for mass riots get blocked, while they are those very resources whose threat led to the adoption of the Lugovoi legislation in the first place: In 2019, their number was several times lower than in 2018. Unfortunately, it remains completely unclear what is behind these high numbers, what resources are affected, how dangerous the materials are, and whether immediate, extrajudicial blocking is justifiable. Our suspicion is well-founded that at this scale of numbers, mistakes and arbitrary actions are simply inevitable.

Unfortunately, official data on blockages for 2020 were not published, so we are limited to the data for 2019.

NOTES

1. Designated as extremist by the Naberezhnye Chelny city court of the Republic of Tatarstan on Feb. 6, 2019. See: Tatarstan: Autograd Crew Football Fans Association designated as extremist // SOVA Center. Feb. 6, 2019 (https://www.sova-center.ru/racism-xenophobia/news/counteraction/2019/02/d40618/).

2. Designated as extremist by the Maikop District Court of the Republic of Adygea on May 7, 2018, and by an appeal ruling by the Judicial Board on administrative cases of the Supreme Court of the Republic of Adygea of Oct 16, 2018. See: One more organization added to the Federal List of Extremist Organizations // SOVA Center. Feb. 16, 2019 (https://www.sova-center.ru/racism-xenophobia/news/counteraction/2019/02/d40640/).

3. Yevgeny Moroz, Pagan Stalinists or "Conceptual Party 'Yedinenie' " // SOVA Center. Nov. 24, 2003 (https://www.sova-center.ru/religion/publications/2003/11/d1377/).

4. Designated as extremist by the Supreme Court of the Komi Republic on July 11, 2019. See: The Komi Republic: USSR banned by court // SOVA Center. July 8, 2019 (https://www.sova-center.ru/racism-xenophobia/news/counteraction/2019/07/d41233/).

5. Designated as extremist by the Onguday District Court of the Altai Republic on Dec. 11, 2018. See: In the Altai Republic, a court bans the activity of the Ak Tyan movement // SOVA Center. Dec. 18, 2018 (https://www.sova-center.ru/religion/news/harassment/refusal/2018/12/d40429/).

6. Designated as terrorist by the Moscow district military court on January 17, 2019, came into force on March 14, 2019. We are not covering the Network case in more detail in this report as it definitely does not relate to the topic of countering nationalism and xenophobia.

7. Designated as terrorist by the Moscow district military court on June 5, 2019, came into force on July 5, 2019.

8. Only the verdicts in which the hate motive was officially recognized and which we consider appropriate are included in this count.

9. One relieved from punishment due to the expiration of the statute of limitations.

10. Omsk: guilty verdict for the local ultra-right group members remains unchanged // SOVA Center. Oct. 4, 2019 (https://www.sova-center.ru/racism-xenophobia/news/counteraction/2018/10/d40102/).

11. The group was designated extremist in December 2017.

12. In the Far East, the leader and a member of the "Schtolz" group are convicted // SOVA Center. June 26, 2019 (https://www.sova-center.ru/racism-xenophobia/news/counteraction/2019/06/d41188/).

13. Omsk. Sentence delivered in the case of xenophobic attacks // SOVA Center. Oct. 7, 2019 (https://www.sova-center.ru/racism-xenophobia/news/counteraction/2019/10/d41549/).

14. St. Petersburg. "White subway car" attack perpetrators receive suspended sentences // SOVA Center. Sept. 3, 2019 (https://www.sova-center.ru/racism-xenophobia/news/counteraction/2018/09/d39950/).

15. Data as of Feb. 24, 2020.

16. Rabat Plan of Action on the prohibition of advocacy of national, racial or religious hatred that constitutes incitement to discrimination, hostility or violence // SOVA Center. Nov. 7, 2014 (https://www.sova-center.ru/racism-xenophobia/publications/2014/11/d30593/).

17. Consolidated statistics on the activity of federal courts of general jurisdiction and magistrate courts for the first half of 2019 // Official Web site of the Supreme Court of the Russian Federation (http://www.cdep.ru/userimages/sudebnaya_statistika/2019/k4-svod_vse_sudy-1-2019.xls) (further – Consolidated statistics of the Supreme Court for the first half of 2019).

18. According to the data posted on the Supreme Court Web site, the highest number of criminal convictions (62) were handed down under Art. 280 of the Criminal Code, and in 53 of them this article was the main charge. It is followed by Art. 205.2 of the Criminal Code with 56 convicted; for 45 of them this being the main charge. No convictions were handed down under Art. 280.1 of the Criminal Code. Only one individual was convicted under Art. 354.1 (rehabilitation of Nazism). One individual was convicted under Art. 148 Part 2 of the Criminal Code (no convictions under Part 1 of this article, insulting of religious believers' feelings). Art. 282 of the Criminal Code was used to convict 27 people, for 15 of them this was the main charge; 21 were sentenced under the decriminalized Part 1, i.e., for a repeat offense in one year, and only six under the more grave Part 2.

For more information, see: Official statistics of the Judicial Department of the Supreme Court on the fight against extremism for the first half of 2019 // SOVA Center. Oct. 22, 2019 (https://www.sova-center.ru/racism-xenophobia/news/counteraction/2019/10/d41613/).

19. Consolidated statistics on the activity of federal courts of general jurisdiction and magistrate courts for the first half of 2018 // Official Web site of the Supreme Court of the Russian Federation (http://www.cdep.ru/userimages/sudebnaya_statistika/2018/k3-svod_vse_sudy-1-2018.xls).

20. Putin signs law partially decriminalizing Art. 282 of the Criminal Code // SOVA Center. Dec. 28, 2018 (https://www.sova-center.ru/misuse/news/lawmaking/2018/12/d40472/).

21. Sentences overturned due to partial decriminalization of Art. 282 // SOVA Center. Sept. 30, 2019 (https://www.sova-center.ru/racism-xenophobia/news/counteraction/2019/03/d40730/).

22. Criminal cases discontinued as a result of partial decriminalization of Art. 282 of the Criminal Code // SOVA Center. April 22, 2019 (https://www.sova-center.ru/racism-xenophobia/news/counteraction/2019/03/d40720/).

23. Criminal cases discontinued as a result of partial decriminalization of Art. 282 of the Criminal Code // SOVA Center. Nov. 1, 2019 (https://www.sova-center.ru/racism-xenophobia/news/counteraction/2019/03/d40721/).

24. Suvorov: case against "Guerillas' Guerrilla Truth" leader Aleksei Menyailov and his wife Slatana terminated // SOVA Center. Jan. 25, 2019 (https://www.sova-center.ru/racism-xenophobia/news/counteraction/2019/01/d40580/).

25. All further numbers reflect the convictions known to us, although, judging from the Supreme Court data, the actual numbers are much higher. But given the volume of available data, it can be assumed that the observed patterns and proportions will hold true for the total number of verdicts.

26. A year earlier, according to the Supreme Court data for the same period, Art. 205.2 was the main article in convictions against 39 people; in 11 convictions, it was applied along with other articles.

27. "Citizens of the USSR" is a community that denies the collapse of the Soviet Union and insists on implementing Soviet laws. In their opinion, the Russian Federation does not exist.

28. Another reason to exclude those who received prison time "for words only" under Art. 205.2 from our totals is because too little information is available about the cases under

this article. Besides, we have observed that the vast majority of sentences under Art. 205.2 have nothing to do with countering incitement to hatred.

29. Suspect in the Moscow Case Vladislav Sinitsa sentenced to five years in penal colony. He tweeted about the children of law enforcement officials // Meduza. Sept. 3, 2019 (https://meduza.io/feature/2019/09/03/sud-prigovoril-figuranta-moskovskogo-dela-vladislava-sinitsu-k-pyati-godam-kolonii-on-napisal-tvit-o-detyah-sotrudnikov-pravoohranitelnyh-organov).

30. Most probably, VKontakte.

31. See: N. Yudina. Anti-Extremism in Virtual Russia, 2014–2015 // SOVA Center. Aug. 24, 2016 (https://www.sova-center.ru/en/xenophobia/reports-analyses/2016/08/d35262/).

32. For more information, see Yekaterinburg: a supporter of the Union of Slavic Forces of Rus referred to mandatory treatment // SOVA Center. April 29, 2019 (https://www.sova-center.ru/racism-xenophobia/news/counteraction/2019/04/d40955/).

33. See: Cases of terrorist propaganda in pre-trial detention centers and places of detention // SOVA Center. April 15, 2019 (https://www.sova-center.ru/misuse/news/persecution/2019/04/d40881/).

34. Movement designated as extremist in December 2017. See: The Schtolz group designated as extremist in Khabarovsk // SOVA Center. Dec. 6, 2017 (https://www.sova-center.ru/racism-xenophobia/news/counteraction/2017/12/d38434/).

35. Aleksandr Belov gets seven and a half years in penal colony // SOVA Center. Aug. 24, 2016 (https://www.sova-center.ru/racism-xenophobia/news/counteraction/2016/08/d35264/).

36. Misanthropic Division is a group of radical neo-Nazi pagans that gained notoriety in connection with the events in southeast Ukraine and is supporting the current Kiev government. In 2015, the group was designated as extremist by the Krasnoyarsk District Court. For more details see: Misanthropic Division movement declared extremist // SOVA Center. Aug. 27, 2015 (https://www.sova-center.ru/racism-xenophobia/news/counteraction/2015/08/d32663/).

37. Five organizations added to the Federal List of Extremist Materials // SOVA Center. Jan. 28, 2015 (https://www.sova-center.ru/racism-xenophobia/news/counteraction/2015/01/d31141/).

38. See: Belgorod Province: Administrative sanctions for the distribution of the video "Let's Remind the Crooks and Thieves about Their Manifesto-2002" // SOVA Center. Oct. 23, 2019 (https://www.sova-center.ru/misuse/news/persecution/2019/10/d41616/).

39. See: Sanctions against citizens for online insults against the state and society // SOVA Center. 2019 (https://www.sova-center.ru/misuse/news/persecution/2019/04/d40942/).

40. Bashkir activist Ismagilov exempted from criminal responsibility // SOVA Center. Feb. 20, 2019 (https://www.sova-center.ru/misuse/news/persecution/2019/02/d40680/).

41. The Supreme Court of the Crimea overturns the verdict against activists of the Anti-Corruption Bureau // SOVA Center. Feb. 8, 2019 (https://www.sova-center.ru/misuse/news/persecution/2019/02/d40638/).

42. Sentence against co-chair of Mehk-Khel Movement overturned // SOVA Center. Sept. 30, 2019 (https://www.sova-center.ru/misuse/news/persecution/2019/09/d41518/).

43. The case under Art. 282 of the Criminal Code against a follower of Jehovah's Witnesses convicted in Kabardino-Balkaria has been closed // SOVA Center. March 1, 2019 (https://www.sova-center.ru/misuse/news/persecution/2019/03/d40726/).

44. Charges of inciting hostility toward local authorities against an Ingush opposition activist dropped // SOVA Center. Feb. 28, 2019 (https://www.sova-center.ru/misuse/news/persecution/2019/02/d40712/).

45. The court releases Danis Safargali from punishment under Art. 282 of the Criminal Code // SOVA Center. Feb. 14, 2019 (https://www.sova-center.ru/misuse/news/persecution/2019/02/d40658/).

46. Vladimir Timoshenko's criminal record for inciting hatred against civil servants expunged // SOVA Center. May 20, 2019 (https://www.sova-center.ru/misuse/news/persecution/2019/05/d41034/).

47. Blogger Sokolovsky released from punishment under Art. 282 of the Criminal Code due to its decriminalization // SOVA Center. May 8, 2019 (https://www.sova-center.ru/misuse/news/persecution/2019/05/d40988/).

48. A Barnaul court terminates the proceedings in the case of Daniil Markin // SOVA Center. Jan. 21, 2019 (https://www.sova-center.ru/misuse/news/persecution/2019/01/d40538/).

49. The Supreme Court of Kabardino-Balkaria recognizes Yury Zalipaev's right to rehabilitation // SOVA Center. March 15, 2019 (https://www.sova-center.ru/misuse/news/persecution/2019/03/d40772/).

50. Criminal prosecution of Omsk feminist Kalugina discontinued // SOVA Center. Feb. 5, 2019 (https://www.sova-center.ru/misuse/news/persecution/2019/02/d40611/).

51. Criminal prosecution for posts on the Shura of Muslims of the Republic of Bashkortostan Web site dropped in Ufa // SOVA Center. Feb. 7, 2019 (https://www.sova-center.ru/misuse/news/persecution/2019/02/d40626/).

52. Valery Bolshakov's sentence revoked // SOVA Center. Aug. 26, 2019 (https://www.sova-center.ru/misuse/news/persecution/2019/08/d41387/).

53. Aleksandr Byvshev's case discontinued // SOVA Center. Oct. 30, 2019 (https://www.sova-center.ru/misuse/news/persecution/2019/10/d41649/).

54. See: The ECHR found violation of the Convention on Human Rights in the case of Savva Terentyev // SOVA Center. Aug. 28, 2019 (https://www.sova-center.ru/misuse/news/counteraction/2018/08/d39919/).

55. Consolidated statistical data on the activities of federal courts of general jurisdiction and magistrates' courts for the first half of 2019 // Judicial Department at the Supreme Court of the Russian Federation. 2019 (http://www.cdep.ru/index.php?id=79&item=5083).

56. Consolidated statistical data on the activities of federal courts of general jurisdiction and magistrates' courts for 2018 // Judicial Department at the Supreme Court of the Russian Federation. 2019 (http://www.cdep.ru/index.php?id=79&item=4891).

57. As of Feb. 21, 2020, the list has 5,008 entries.

58. See: List of blocked Web Sites // Roskomsvoboda (http://reestr.rublacklist.net/).

59. "Extremist resources" in the Single Register of Prohibited Web Sites // SOVA Center (https://www.sova-center.ru/racism-xenophobia/docs/2019/12/d41805/).

60. Full name: "On Amending the Federal Law 'On Information, Information Technologies and Protection of Information.' "

61. Reports on activities of Roskomnadzor // Official Web site of the Federal Service for Supervision of Communications, Information Technology and Mass Media (http://www.rkn.gov.ru/plan-and-reports/reports/p449/).

Banning Organizations as Extremist

In 2020, five organizations were added to the Federal List of Extremist Organizations published on the Web site of the Ministry of Justice (compared with four in 2019).

Among right-wing organizations, Russian Republic of Rus, recognized as extremist by the Moscow City Court on May 20, 2020, joined the list as entry 77. Russian Republic was founded in 2003 and gained notoriety in June 2005, after its Web site published an announcement sentencing human rights expert Nikolai Girenko to execution; Girenko was shot two weeks later.[1] Following the conflict between the organization's leader, Supreme Leader Vladimir Popov (a neo-Nazi well-known in the 1990s), and the head of its Executive Committee Viktor Krivov (who started his "career" back in the 1980s in *Pamyat* [Memory]), Russian Republic of Rus broke away from the organization[2] and united 22 "Communities of Indigenous Russian People." Members of Russian Republic of Rus appeared as defendants in criminal cases more than once.[3] Two of the "Communities of Indigenous Russian People," one in Astrakhan and the other in the Shchyolkovsky District of Moscow Province, were previously recognized as extremist and added to the Federal List of Extremist Organizations.[4]

The list also includes the Bashkir nationalist organization Bashkort, which was recognized as extremist by the Supreme Court of Bashkortostan on May 22, 2020. This organization, headed by Fail Alchinov[5] and Ilnar Galin, is one of the most active organizations of local nationalists. Bashkort has existed since 2014 and, according to its declaration, "carries out various events aimed at protecting the Bashkir language, culture, history, and traditions***protects the constitutional rights of the Bashkir people, their inalienable right to self-determination, and the sovereignty of the republic." The prosecutor's office demanded the organization be banned on the grounds that its "elders" included individuals convicted of extremism: Sagit Ismagilov, Fanzil Akhmetshin, and Ayrat Dilmukhametov. Bashkort claimed that Dilmukhametov was never among its members, and that Sagit Ismagilov and Fanzil Akhmetshin were not involved in the management of the organization. According to the other claim of the prosecutor's office, the speeches of the leaders and members of the organization contained slogans "inciting hatred toward non-Bashkirs and "representatives of the authorities." In the organization's materials published on its official page in VKontakte, "statements that bear the signs of calling for the violation of the territorial integrity of the Russian Federation and the creation of a single Islamic state" were found.[6]

We consider unlawful the banning of the religious group Allya-Ayat (the name varies depending on the transliteration of the Kazakh original: Al Ayat, Allya Ayat, Elleh Ayat, Allah Ayat, Elleh Ayat, and others), recognized as extremist by the Samara Province Court on May 28, 2019, and added to the list under entry 75, as in this case the anti-extremism legislation was not applied for its intended purpose. Allya-Ayat was already banned in Kazakhstan and some Russian regions. The adherents of this teaching, founded in the early 1990s by Farhat Abdullayev, preach a cure for all diseases by applying the magazine *Selennaya Star* to the body, pronouncing a certain "formula of life," consumption of special tea, and prolonged contemplation of the sun. As a result, several seriously ill residents of the region who had become followers of Allya-Ayat refused medical help and died.[7]

In October, an entire subculture, the Prisoners' Criminal Unity (*Arestantskoye Ugolovnoye Yedinstvo*, PCU) joined the list; it was recognized as extremist by the Supreme Court on Aug. 17, 2020.[8] The Prosecutor General's Office indicated that "the PCU is a well-structured and managed organization," whose members "are involved, among other things, in organizing mass riots," and the ideology "poses a real threat to the life and health of citizens, society and the state." In our opinion, the decision to ban the PCU as an extremist organization was not entirely justified. First, we do not agree that the PCU is a single structure. Next, although the ideology of the underworld (and the PCU subculture) is focused on illegal activities and conceptually incompatible with respect for the constitutional rights of citizens, this ideology is not political and is not aimed at changing the constitutional order. Therefore, we believe that the activity of promoting this ideology should not be subject to anti-extremist legal regulation, although it can be criminalized in principle. Perhaps a new criminal norm should have been created for the organizers of structures that exploit criminality and incite violence close in the wording of Art. 239 Part 1 of the

Criminal Code (creation of a public association whose activity is fraught with violence against individuals).

Recognizing the PCU as an extremist organization gave the authorities the opportunity to prosecute for the dissemination of the PCU ideology and symbols under anti-extremist articles – Art. 282.2 of the Criminal Code and Art. 20.3 of the Code of Administrative Offenses. The first case of application of Art. 282.2 of the Criminal Code was only reported to us in 2021. But Art. 20.3 was utilized against the PCU followers probably hundreds of times throughout 2020 for online dissemination of criminal symbols as well as, for example, for tattoos with the corresponding images. We view such persecution as unreasonable, since these actions, in reality, do not signify support of any structure, but rather belonging to a criminal subculture – unfortunately, a very popular one in Russia due to the fact that a large number of its citizens have passed through the penitentiary system. The effectiveness of such punishments also raises doubts, since it obviously drives the criminal subculture underground, exacerbating the isolation of its followers from society while they need help in resocialization and adaptation.

And finally, in 2020, the charity care home Ak Umut (Bright Hope), recognized as extremist by the Kirovsky District Court of Kazan on Sept. 25, 2014, was added to the list. The Muslim care home was recognized as extremist (in our opinion, without proper grounds) due to the fact that in 2013 and 2014, Islamic books from the Federal List of Extremist Materials were found in its library and classrooms.

In July 2020, the Krasnoyarsk Territory Court banned the activities of the far-right Nation and Freedom Committee (*Komitet "Natsiya i Svoboda,"* NFC). The Committee was created in September 2014 as part of the "Russians" association and, after the latter was banned a year later, became one of the main contenders to be the successor of the association. The founder and leader of the NFC is Vladimir Basmanov (Potkin), who has been in exile for a long time. The NFC systematically opposed the "Russian Spring" in eastern Ukraine. According to the prosecutor's office, the reason for the ban was a prosecutor's review, during which "instances of mass distribution of extremist materials and incitement of hostility and hatred toward representatives of various social groups were revealed."[9] The Committee was added to the list of extremist organizations in February 2021. Meanwhile, on the basis of the NFC and its ally the Popular Resistance Association (*Assotsiatsiya narodnogo soprotivleniya,* ANS), a new association – the Movement of Nationalists – was created.

Thus, as of Feb. 28, 2021, the list includes 81 organizations[10] whose activity is banned by court order and continuation of activity is punishable by Art. 282.2 of the Criminal Code (organizing the activity of an extremist organization).

The list of terrorist organizations published on the Web site of the FSB was not updated in 2020. As of the beginning of 2021, there were 33 organizations on the list. But on April 6, 2020, the US State Department declared the Russian ultra-Orthodox pro-monarchist Russian Imperial Movement (RIM) a terrorist organization. This was the first time that the US had labeled a far-right organization as terrorist. The US also named the leaders, Stanislav Vorobyov, the head of the military-patriotic club *Imperial Region* and the leader of the *Partisan* courses Denis Gariev, and the former coordinator of the organization Nikolai Trushchalov "specially designated global terrorists." The participation of RIM's members in the war in the Donbass and contacts with the organizers of a series of bombings in the Swedish city of Gothenburg in 2016-2017 attracted the attention of the US authorities.[11] On Feb. 3, 2021, Canada also labeled RIM as a terrorist organization.[12]

Criminal Prosecution

For Violence

In 2020, the number of those convicted of violent hate crimes was practically the same as a year before. In 2020, in Moscow, St. Petersburg, Novosibirsk Province, and Stavropol Territory saw at least five guilty verdicts in which the hate motive was officially recognized.[13] Eight defendants were found guilty in these trials (nine in 2019).

Racist violence was categorized under the following articles containing a hate motive as a categorizing attribute: "murder" (Art. 105 Part 2 Paragraph "k" of the Criminal Code), "hooliganism" (Art. 213 Part 1 Paragraphs "b" and "c" of the Criminal Code), and "battery" (Art. 116 of the Criminal Code). This is a standard set of articles used in the past five years. One conviction for violent crimes was based on Art. 282 of the Criminal Code (incitement of hatred) (compared to three in 2019). In June 2019 in the city of Nevinnomyssk in Stavropol Territory, a 25-year-old local resident punched an unfamiliar 37-year-old woman in the face while shouting racial slurs and calls for violence "against representatives of her ethnic group." The next day, the suspect attacked a 30-year-old man in a similar manner. He was convicted under Art. 282 Part 2 Paragraph "a" of the Criminal Code (incitement to hatred with the use of violence). We believe that in this case it would be more appropriate to apply another article with the categorizing attribute, perhaps Art. 116, 115, or 112 of the Criminal Code (depending on the severity of the inflicted injuries). However, this application of Art. 282 is also possible: Ruling No. 11 of the Plenum of the Supreme Court of the Russian Federation of June 28, 2011, "On Judicial Practice in Criminal Cases Regarding Crimes of Extremism" clarifies that Art. 282 of the Criminal Code may be applied to violent crimes if they are aimed at inciting hatred in third parties, for example, in the case of a public and demonstrative ideologically motivated attack.

Penalties for violent acts were distributed as follows:

- Two people were sentenced to six years in prison;
- One person was sentenced to four years in prison;
- One person received a suspended sentence;
- Four people were sentenced to pay fines.

We have doubts about the suspended sentence that a resident of Novosibirsk received for attacking a native of Buryatia on a regional train. The leniency of the sentence is perhaps explained by the fact that the attacker pleaded guilty and repented, and the victim's injuries were not serious (other passengers on the train stepped in to protect him, stopped the attack, and handed the attacker over to the police). However, we do not believe a suspended sentence for an ideologically motivated attack is an adequate punishment: Often, this provides aggressive young men with a sense of impunity and fails to prevent them from carrying out similar attacks in the future.

The fines handed down to four far-right activists in St. Petersburg for attacking a man they thought was an anti-Fascist can also be explained by the sincere remorse of the perpetrators and their status as minors. On the other hand, "spraying gas in the face," threatening with knives and "shooting in the face with an aerosol pistol" should have resulted in a more severe sentence than the fines between 10,000 and 40,000 rubles. Especially keeping in mind that one of the suspects in this case was Dmitry Nedugov, a member of the well-known neo-Nazi group NS/WP; in the end, he was not charged in this case.

The others convicted in 2020 were sentenced to terms between four and six years, which seems to be quite proportionate for their crimes.

We should mention separately the sentences that we believe were given for xenophobic violence even though the motive of hatred was not included in the charges or we are not aware of it. Characteristically, all the attackers received suspended sentences or were sentenced to restriction of freedom.

On Aug. 7, two people received suspended sentences under Art. 213 Part 2 of the Criminal Code for an attack on Nigerian nationals on the subway. In August, Artyom Vlasov received a one-year suspended sentence under the same article for participating in an attack on an anti-fascist concert at the "Tsokol" club on Sept. 2, 2018. On Feb. 6, 2020, the Basmanny District Court of Moscow sentenced Anton Berezhny to one year and 11 months of restriction of freedom for an attack on a gay couple in June 2019. Berezhnoy attacked the young men with a knife while shouting homophobic slurs. One of the victims, Roman Yedalov, died on the spot, the other, Yevgeny Yefimov, received a non-life-threatening wound. Berezhny was charged with murder (Art. 105 Part 1 of the Criminal Code) and battery (Art. 116 of the Criminal Code), but the jury, while finding him guilty of attacking Yefimov, found him not guilty of murder. We do not understand how this could have happened. All we know is that during the trial, Berezhnoy admitted his guilt in the attack but denied his guilt in the murder and said that Yedalov "fell on the knife."[14]

At the end of the year, news of 2003-2007 homicide investigations came out completely unexpectedly.

In October 2020, the investigators reported that the first suspects had been identified in the case of the brutal double murder of Shamil Odamanov (Udamanov) from Dagestan and a native of Central Asia. The video showing the decapitation of Odamanov by the far-right against the background of a swastika flag and the shooting of the second victim at point-blank range appeared on the Internet in the summer of 2007.[15] The video was initially alleged to be a fake, but the father of the deceased Odamanov identified the victim in the video as his son.[16] The video was widely distributed on the Internet; every year the prosecutor's office reported punishments of ordinary social media users who published this video, while nothing was heard about the murder investigation. Suddenly, in October 2020 – 13 years later! – it was reported that neo-Nazi Sergei Marshakov, who is serving a sentence for shooting at FSB officers, and former member of Format-18 Maksim Aristarkhov, who is also serving time in jail, were charged in this case. It is also reported that before his death, Maksim "Tesak" Martsinkevich confessed to this murder and his involvement together with members of nationalist organizations in other murders of people of "non-Slavic appearance" carried out between 2002 and 2006.[17]

In late December, other members of well-known Nazi gangs were also detained in Moscow, Sochi, and Tyumen: Semyon (Bus) Tokmakov, one of the most famous leaders of the Moscow skinheads of the late 1990s, previously the leader of the Nazi skinhead brigade Russian Goal and the youth organization of the far-right People's National Party (*Narodnaya Natsionalnaya Partiya*, PNP), Andrei Kail, the successor of Bus in the PNP, Aleksandr Lysenkov, also a member of the PNP, Maksim Khotulev, Pavel Khrulev (Myshkin) and Aleksei Gudilin. They are accused of involvement in a series of "particularly serious crimes including the murders of Central Asian nationals" committed in the early 2000s. The Investigative Committee reported that the crimes surfaced as part of the investigation of the abovementioned double murder.[18]

For Crimes Against Property

In 2020, we are aware of just one sentence for crimes against property where a hate motive was cited. (In 2019, we had no information about such sentences; in 2018, we wrote about two sentences against six people in two regions.)

In Volgograd, a local resident received a one-and-a-half-year suspended sentence under Art. 214 Part 2 of the Criminal Code (vandalism motivated by national hatred) and Art. 280 (public calls for extremist activity) combined with a 2-year ban on the right to engage in activities related to the administration of Web sites on the Internet. We find this punishment proportionate to the offense of drawing several swastikas and a target sign and writing an anti-Semitic slur on a monument in the summer of 2018 at the memorial complex "The front line of the defense of Stalingrad in November 1942, the troops of the 62nd and 64th armies." Although compulsory, unpaid community work to be done in their free time would have been an even more appropriate sentence.

Exactly such punishment was imposed on another anti-Semitic graffiti artist in the Vologda region. On Feb. 10, 2020, the magistrate's court for the 42nd judicial district of the Oktyabrsky court district sentenced Vyacheslav Kotenko to 280 hours of compulsory community work for drawing a yellow cross on the monument to Holocaust victims, installed in 2018 with the support of the Russian Jewish Congress in the village of Aksay as part of the project "To Restore Dignity."[19] In this case, the sentence was given under

Part 1 of Art. 214 of the Criminal Code, and the motive of hatred was not included in the charge.

For Public Statements

According to our incomplete data, the number of convictions for "extremist statements" (incitement to hatred, incitement to extremism or terrorism, etc.) increased slightly in 2020 compared to a year earlier. SOVA Center has information about 99 convictions against 111 people in 49 regions of the country.[20] In 2019, we had information about 73 such convictions against 79 people in 47 regions. These numbers do not include the convictions that we find inappropriate: In 2020, we found 13 convictions against 19 people inappropriate. Acquittals are also excluded from our statistics (there was one such verdict in 2020). We record separately and do not include in the statistics instances of release from criminal responsibility with payment of court fines, an alternative introduced in Russian law in 2016. In 2020, our records showed two instances of such releases from responsibility with payment of court fines. We have no information about any instances of this alternative being applied in anti-extremism law enforcement in 2019; in 2018 we had information about 11 such releases from responsibility in cases concerning "extremist statements."

As for the overall statistics, our information about convictions is, regretfully, far from complete. According to the data posted on the Supreme Court Web site,[21] just in the first half of 2020, 132 people were convicted of extremist statements (Arts. 282, 280, 280.1, 205.2, 354.1, Parts 1 and 2 of Art. 148 of the Criminal Code), including those for whom this was the main charge.[22] This is higher than the 115 such sentences reported in 2019.[23] We used our data in the report, since the data of the Supreme Court does not permit a meaningful analysis to be carried out.

This is the third year that we are using a more detailed approach to conviction classification.[24]

We deem appropriate those convictions where we have seen the statements or are at least familiar with their contents and believe that the courts have passed convictions in accordance with the law.

In 2020, we considered four convictions against five individuals lawful. An example of such a lawful conviction is the verdict the Presnensky District Court of Moscow in the case of the two writers well-known in ultra-right circles: Oleg Platonov, the author of the banned books *The*

Mystery of the Zion Protocols, The Zion Protocols in World Politics and many other similar works, and Valery Yerchak, Co-Chair of the Union of the Russian People and the Belarusian branch of the Union of Orthodox Brotherhoods. They were convicted under Art. 282 Part 2 Paragraph "c" of the Criminal Code (incitement to national hatred by an organized group) for publishing the anti-Semitic book by Yerchak titled *Word and Deed of Ivan the Terrible* (entry #1381 of the Federal List of Extremist Materials).[25]

In the vast majority of cases – marked as "Unknown" (64 convictions against 70 people) – we are not familiar with the exact content of the materials and therefore cannot assess the appropriateness of the court decisions.

Convictions that we find difficult to assess fall under the category of "Uncertain" (seven convictions against eight people): For example, we find one of the charges appropriate but not the other.

Our statistics in the "Other" category (24 convictions against 28 people) included individuals who called for attacks on government officials and those whose convictions under extremism articles of the Criminal Code were mostly appropriate but whose prosecution cannot be classified as counteraction to nationalism and xenophobia.

According to our data, Art. 280 of the Criminal Code (public calls for extremist activity) was applied in the vast majority of the verdicts,[26] that is, in 66 verdicts against 75 people. In 52 of these convictions (53 people), this was the only charge. In some instances, it was combined with other charges, for example, with Art. 214 of the Criminal Code (vandalism).

To our knowledge, Art. 282 was applied in 10 convictions against 15 people. In addition to the anti-Semitic writers mentioned above, others (with the exception of the two PCU supporters, see below) were charged for similar offenses under Art. 20.3.1 of the Code of Administrative Offenses (incitement of national hatred) earlier in the year and were charged with a criminal repeat offense within a year after that.

We have information about one conviction under Art. 280.1 of the Criminal Code (public calls for undermining the territorial integrity of the Russian Federation). The Supreme Court of the occupied Crimea sentenced in absentia the Crimean Tatar businessman, former Deputy Prime Minister of the Crimean government and owner of the ATR TV channel Lenur Islyamov to 19 years of imprisonment in a high-security colony and to the restriction of freedom for one year under a combination of Art. 280 with Part 1 of Art. 208 of the Criminal Code (organization of an illegal armed formation) and Art. 281 Part 2 Paragraphs "a" and "b" of the

Criminal Code (sabotage committed by an organized group and entailing grave consequences). According to the court, Islyamov planned to blow up power transmission towers in Kherson Province in November 2015; for this purpose, he "created and headed the illegal armed formation Noman Celebijikhan Crimean Tatar Volunteer Battalion." In addition, Islyamov was accused of repeatedly calling in the media for the return of the Crimea to Ukraine. Unfortunately, the Prosecutor General's Office did not specify the statements in question and whether they contained calls for armed struggle, so we refrain from assessment of the verdict under Art. 280.1.[27]

Art. 354.1 of the Criminal Code (denial of facts established by the verdict of the International Military Tribunal for the trial and punishment of the major war criminals of the European Axis countries, approval of the crimes established by this verdict, as well as the dissemination of knowingly false information about the activities of the USSR during the years of World War II) was cited in three verdicts against three individuals (for two of them, it was the one and only charge). All three court decisions punished those who published statements and comments on VKontakte containing "approval of Nazi actions, denial of facts established by the verdict of the International Military Tribunal for the trial and punishment of the major war criminals ," including, in one case, the approval of the Holocaust.

Art. 205.2 of the Criminal Code (public calls to carry out terrorist activities) has, in recent years, gained popularity among law enforcement officers. According to Supreme Court data, in the first half of 2020, a total of 53 people were charged under this article, for 43 of them, this was the main charge.[28] SOVA Center is aware of 31 sentences under Art. 205.2 of the Criminal Code handed down to 35 people (not including wrongful convictions). In 23 instances, this was the only article applied in the conviction. In six other cases, it was applied in combination with Art. 280.

In previous years, the majority of the sentences under this article were applied in convictions for radical Islamic propaganda (as far as SOVA Center is aware), whereas in 2020, the scope of its application turned out to be more diverse.

As before, some were charged with calls to join ISIL or other radical Islamic organizations or to travel to war zones and fight, a total of eight sentences. In at least five such cases, the calls were carried out by convicts in penal colonies.

Two sentences were handed down for calling for the violent overthrow of the government. In six cases, the sentences were handed down for justifying the actions of Mikhail Zhlobitsky, who committed a terrorist attack in the FSB's building in the Arkhangelsk region, and calling for the repetition of such acts.

Six sentences were handed down for justifying the terrorist attack on Christchurch mosques (New Zealand) committed on March 15, 2019.

Three sentences were handed down for calls for radical far-right violence, including endorsing the actions of one of the leaders of the National Socialist Society, Maksim (Adolf) Bazylev, and the neo-Nazi Militant Terrorist Organization.

In some instances, this article was applied in combination with other anti-terrorism articles of the Criminal Code, including Art. 205.4 Parts 1 and 2 of the Criminal Code (creation of and participation in a terrorist group), Art. 30 Part 1, Art. 205 Part 2 Paragraph "a" (preparation for carrying out of a terrorist act by carrying out an explosion), etc.

Penalties for public statements were distributed as follows:

- Thirty-nine people were sentenced to imprisonment;
- Fifty received suspended sentences without any additional measures;
- Twenty were sentenced to various fines;
- One was sentenced to the restriction of liberty;
- One's penalty was unknown.

The number of those sentenced to imprisonment was significantly lower than in the previous year (in 2019, we reported 50 prison sentences).

Fifteen received prison terms in conjunction with charges other than statements, including participation in extremist and terrorist groups and organizations. Eleven were already serving prison time, and their terms were increased. Eight people were charged under the "terrorist" Art. 205.2 of the Criminal Code (see more below). One person was convicted twice in the course of the year under an administrative article; he was sentenced to a fine for a criminal repeat offense but refused to pay it and was eventually sentenced to a penal colony.

Four individuals, however, received prison terms in the absence of any of the abovementioned circumstances (or, perhaps, in some cases, we just do not know about them). One received a prison sentence for calling for knife attacks on police officers in Facebook comments. Another, 59-year-old Ravil Tukhvatullin, convicted in Ufa under Part 2 of Art. 280 of the Criminal Code, according to law enforcement agencies, heads an unregistered public organization Association of the Indigenous Peoples of Rus of Ufa Gubernia and recognizes himself as a citizen of the USSR[29] and a deputy of the long-defunct Supreme Soviet of the USSR. It is reported that from February to October 2018, Tukhvatullin published videos on his page in Vkontakte in which he called for the violent overthrow of state power, mass riots and revolution. The court sentenced him to one and a half years in a penal colony. We are not familiar with the materials published by him.

Even less is known about the other two cases: One person was jailed for posting certain "extremist" material on Instagram, and the other for "has called for violence against representatives of certain ethnic groups" on Vkontakte. We do not know who these people are, but if they were not widely known and did not carry out systematic propaganda, real imprisonment seems to us to be an excessive punishment.

In comparison with the previous year, the situation has improved: In 2019, we reported seven convictions "for words only," i.e., without the listed aggravating circumstances, 12 in 2018, seven in 2017, five in 2016, 16 (the highest number) in 2015, and only two in each of the years 2013 and 2014.[30] If we were to look at the share of prison sentences "for words only" (without any of the abovementioned "aggravating circumstances") among the total number of those convicted of statements in these years (leaving out the obviously unlawful sentences), we would see that the share of such convictions was 3.6% in 2020; 6.8% in 2019, 5.5% in 2018, 2.8% in 2017, 2% in 2016, 6.5% in 2015, and slightly higher than 1% in years 2013 and 2014.

As in previous reports, we have excluded Art. 205.2 of the Criminal Code from our calculations (above) of those convicted "for words only," because, firstly, the penalties under the "terrorist" article are predictably harsher, and, secondly, our awareness is insufficient of the specific content of cases under this article. In addition, up until 2018, the vast majority of sentences under Art. 205.2 of the Criminal Code had nothing to do with countering incitement to hatred. However, law enforcement under this article is expanding (see above), and it is often applied together with Art. 280 of the Criminal Code.

In 2020, eight people were sentenced to imprisonment under this article (without the circumstances listed above), four of them under the combination of Art. 205.2 with Art. 280, one person in combination with Art. 319 of the Criminal Code (insulting a representative of the authorities). If one is to believe the reports of the prosecutor's office, these people truly called for the commission of terrorist acts in an aggressive form, but it is not clear how large their audience was, and we do not know the specific content of their publications.

In 2020, the proportion of suspended sentences has remained virtually the same at 45% (50 out of 111) compared to 44% of the previous year. The share of the convicts whose sentences did not involve prison time (actual or suspended), i.e., those sentenced to fines or mandatory labor, has been continuously declining for four years. And it is a pity, because these punishments, we believe, would be more effective than suspended sentences, both for convinced propagandists of hatred and for ordinary reposters on social media.

In terms of additional punishments, in 2020 we have information about the following bans: on public speeches (four), on activities related to media appearances (seven), on administering Internet Web sites (nine), and on Internet use in general (12). These data are probably incomplete.

As usual, the vast majority of sentences were imposed for materials posted on the Internet – 87 out of 99, or 87%, compared with 86% in 2019.

These materials were posted on:

- Social media – 84 (36 on VKontakte, two on Facebook; three on Instagram; one on Odnoklassniki, 42 on unidentified social media networks[31]);
- Messengers – two (one of them on WhatsApp);
- YouTube – two;
- Blogs – one;
- Unspecified online resources – 12.

The types of content are as follows (different types of content may have been posted in the same account or even on the same page):

- Comments and remarks (on social media and forums) – 27;
- Other texts – 28;
- Videos – 16;
- Images (drawings) – 11;
- Audio (songs) – nine;
- Administration of groups and communities – five;
- Photographs – two;
- Selling items on the Internet – one;
- Unspecified – 12.

While the breakdown reflected in the first list has remained roughly the same for the past nine years (see previous annual reports on this topic),[32] the second list reflects major changes: Video materials have definitely lost their leading position in favor of various text formats, including comments on social media. So far, we have been unable to explain this fact.

It is interesting to see whom all these public statements were targeting. Where possible, as we became familiar with the materials or at least the descriptions of the prosecutor's offices and investigative committees,[33] we have identified the following targets of hostility in the sentences passed in 2020 (some of the materials expressed hostility to several groups):

- Ethnic enemies overall – 41 (natives of the Caucasus – eight, natives of Central Asia – three, Jews – seven, non-Slavs in general – five, unspecified – 18);
- Law enforcement officers – 22 (six of these contained approval of the actions of Mikhail Zhlobitsky);
- Muslims – 14;
- Russian Orthodox – four;
- "Infidels" (calls for armed jihad, romanticizing militants, calls to join ISIS) – five;
- Covid-19 positive – one;
- Subculture groups – one (rappers);
- Unknown – 14.

For all its imperfection, we believe that this classification more or less reflects the trends in law enforcement and correlates with our understanding of the situation: The majority of sentences are imposed for ethno-xenophobia, and the second place is divided between statements against the authorities (and even specifically against their repressive apparatus) and statements motivated by religious or anti-religious xenophobia.

The number of convictions for offline statements (12 for 20 people) turned out to be roughly the same as in 2019 (13). They were distributed as follows:

- Writing and publishing a book – two (four people);
- Graffiti – two;[34]
- Flyers – one;
- Engaging in propaganda in prison – six (10 people);
- Unspecified episodes of propaganda by members of far-right gangs – one (three people).

We may consider prosecution for publishing books and putting up leaflets proportionate (depending on their content of course), but we doubt the need for criminal prosecution for individual graffiti on buildings.

We have doubts about the lawfulness of the sentences for terrorist propaganda given to those who are already in prison.

For Participation in Extremist and Banned Groups and Organizations

In 2020, we have information about 12 verdicts against 34 offenders under Arts. 282.1 (organizing an extremist community), 282.2 (organizing the activity of an extremist organization), 205.5 (participation in the activities of a terrorist organization), and 205.4 of the Criminal Code (participation in the activities of a terrorist group), which is slightly more than in 2019, when we wrote about 10 sentences against 28 people. These numbers do not include inappropriate convictions, whose number in the past year was much higher than other categories: we have deemed 44 sentences against 91 people inappropriate.

In 2020, Art. 282.1 of the Criminal Code was cited in six verdicts against 20 people. As is customary, it was primarily applied against members of ultra-right groups.

Three members of the unregistered monarchist neo-Nazi organization Baltic Vanguard of the Russian Resistance (*Baltiiskii avangard russkogo soprpotivleniya*) were convicted in Kaliningrad. Aleksandr Orshulevich was sentenced to eight years in a general regime penal colony, Aleksandr Mamaev (a hieromonk of one of the alternative Orthodox churches) and Igor Ivanov each got six years in a penal colony.[35] According to the case file, Orshulevich created this small group with the aim of "forcibly seizing power in Kaliningrad Province by committing a number of extremist crimes, including those aimed at the Kaliningrad region's secession from the Russian Federation and its sovereign existence within the European Union." In March 2011, he drew a swastika on a memorial plaque "In the Memory of the Genocide of People of Jewish Nationality during Kristallnacht in 1939" and wrote an anti-Semitic slogan on the Internet. Orshulevich, Ivanov and Mamaev were allegedly preparing for another propaganda campaign, for which they made stencils for writing xenophobic texts in public places in Kaliningrad.

Three far-right activists were convicted in Astrakhan. Two young men were convicted under a combination of Art. 282.1, Art. 222.1 Part 3 of the

Criminal Code (illegal acquisition and storage of explosives), Art. 223.1 Part 3 of the Criminal Code (illegal manufacture of weapons); the third man was convicted under Art. 282.1 and Art. 280 Part 2 of the Criminal Code. The only adult at the time of the crime was sentenced to five and a half years in prison, and the other two – to five years in prison and fines of 15,000 rubles each. The young men promoted neo-Nazi ideology, recruited new members into the group, conducted trainings using military equipment, built explosive and incendiary devices and planned to commit violent crimes. During the searches, home-made explosives and "extremist literature" were found and seized.

In the Tomsk region, the court sentenced the members of Vesna Crew group under a combination of Art. 282.1, Art. 280 Part 1 and Art. 282 Part 2 Paragraphs "a" and "c" of the Criminal Code. The group organizer was sentenced to four years in a general regime penal colony, one of the members – to three and a half years in a penal colony, and the other two received suspended prison sentences. According to the investigation, the young people published videos on the Internet where they boasted of "acts of vandalism against the property of people of non-Slavic appearance" and attacks on "these people and representatives of certain social groups, including with the use of improvised weapons."

In Yekaterinburg, the garrison military court sentenced three administrators of VKontakte public pages who promoted the PCU (see https://en.wikipedia.org/wiki/A.U.E.), depending on their roles to terms ranging from four years of probation to seven years in a penal colony under a combination of Art. 282.1, Art. 280 Part 2, and Art. 282 Part 2 of the Criminal Code. According to the central office of the FSB, which was involved in the investigation, spouses Nikolai and Natalia Babarika administered the public page of the PCU.[36] Their friend Artyom Zuev administered the Internet community, organized the work of the printing shop Absolut, and, together with Nikolai and Natalia, sold items decorated in the style inspired by a thief's lifestyle through social media. Natalia was also accused of publishing 14 posts calling for attacks on police officers and the FSB. We question the legality and justification of conviction under anti-extremism articles in this case.[37]

In addition to those mentioned, a verdict was passed in Moscow in the infamous case of New Greatness,[38] whose leader and one of the members had a nationalist background. However, no elements of racism and nationalism have been found in the activity of New Greatness. The group was infiltrated by several provocateurs at once; nonetheless, none of the group members were charged with any "crimes of an extremist nature," which calls into question the application of Art. 282.1 of the Criminal Code.

Art. 282.2 of the Criminal Code was invoked in three sentences against three people.

Just as a year earlier, supporters of the banned Ukrainian Right Sector movement were charged with this article. In Adygea, a prisoner of a local penal colony was sentenced to five years in prison under Art. 282.2 Parts 1.1 and 2 of the Criminal Code (recruitment into an extremist organization and participation in it). The defendant had created a Right Sector cell in the colony and persuaded other convicts to join it. In Stavropol Territory, the Pyatigorsk city Court found Aleksandr Atamanov guilty under Art. 282.2 Part 1.1 of the Criminal Code and Art. 228 Part 2 of the Criminal Code (large-scale possession of narcotic substances) and sentenced him to five years in a penal colony. Atamanov was detained on March 23, 2019. During the search, three packages with drugs and 25 Right Sector leaflets were found. According to law enforcement agencies, on Dec. 23, 2018, Atamanov "by means of persuasion, requests, proposals and proclaiming slogans" was involving three persons in the activities of Right Sector and distributing leaflets with its symbols.

The third offender convicted under Art. 282.2 of the Criminal Code was a 62-year-old supporter of the banned Union of Slavic Forces of Russia (USSR) Leonid Yanushkovsky. A court in Ulyanovsk sentenced him to five years of probation. According to investigators, between September 2019 and February 2020, Yanushkovsky "held, according to the organization's hierarchy, the position of Acting Head of Ulyanovsk Province of the RSFSR [an abbreviation for Russia from the Soviet era]" and "held meetings***campaigned and called on people to join the movement."

In 2020, Art. 205.4 was applied in convictions of nine people. In previous reports, we wrote that this article was applied almost exclusively to radical Islamists, but in 2020, it was used to convict other kinds of offenders.

Thus, in Moscow, the 2nd Western District Military Court handed down a verdict in the case of three supporters of the banned movement *Artpodgotovka*,[39] Andrei Tolkachev, Yury Korny, and Andrei Keptya were found guilty under Art. 205.4 Part 2 and Art 205 Part 2 Paragraph "a" in combination with Art. 30 Part 1 of Criminal Code (preparation of a terrorist attack by a group of people) and were sentenced to terms ranging from six to 13 years in a high-security penal colony. *Artpodgotovka* supporters, together with three other young men, were detained in the early morning of Oct. 12 on Manezh Square, where they came to set fire to pallets of hay left there after a city fair. In our opinion, imprisonment under the articles on terrorism and participation in a terrorist group for a thwarted attempt to set fire to hay in an empty square at 5 a.m. is an excessively harsh measure.

Mikhail Ustyantsev was convicted under a combination of Art. 205.4 Part 1, Art. 205.5 Part 1, and Art. 239 Part 1 of the Criminal Code (the founding of a religious association whose activities involve violence against citizens or other harm to their health) in Rostov-on-Don. He was sentenced to 15 years in prison in a high-security penal colony. According to the court, in 2010, Ustyantsev established and headed a branch of Aum Shinrikyo and disseminated the teachings of this organization among the residents of Moscow, St. Petersburg, and Volgograd. We cannot assess the lawfulness of the verdict, as we are not aware of the details of this case.

The rest of the sentences known to us under Arts. 205.4 and 205.5 were, as usual, associated with radical Islamism. In November, the 2nd Western District Military Court sentenced five prisoners of the penal colony in Voronezh Province under Art. 205.4 Parts 1 and 2, Art. 30 Part 1, and Art. 205 Part 2 Paragraph "a" of the Criminal Code (preparation of a terrorist act by carrying out an explosion), Art. 205.2 Part 1, Art. 205.1 Part 1.1 (inducing a person to commit a criminal terrorist act), and Art. 280 Part 1 of the Criminal Code.[40] According to the investigation, from September to November 2018, the accused showed other convicts videos and images that, according to the expert's opinion, promote and justify terrorism. They were planning to commit a terrorist act in Voronezh and attack law enforcement and special service officers after their release. The prisoners were sentenced to terms ranging from six to 24 years in prison.

A 19-year-old resident of Minusink, Krasnoyarsk Territory was found guilty under Art. 205.2 Part 2, Art. 30 Part 1, and Art. 205.5 Part 2 of the Criminal Code. According to the investigation, she posted several comments on social media justifying terrorism and also planned to join ISIS. She was sentenced to three and a half years in a penal colony.

According to the Supreme Court data, in the first half of 2020, articles related to participation in extremist or terrorist groups and continuation of the activities of organizations that have been banned as extremist or terrorist (Arts. 282.1, 282.2, 205.4, 205.5) were used in verdicts against 97 people,[41] which means there were about 200 such verdicts in the whole year.

We have information about just over a half of these cases: Having summed up the data from this report and the report on incidents of inappropriate enforcement of anti-extremism legislation, we get the total of 122 convicted in 2020.

Inappropriate Prosecution of Political and Civic Activists

It should be noted that almost all cases of prosecution under criminal articles related to speech or administrative anti-extremist articles reported in 2020, which we regard as inappropriate, were, in fact, punishment for expression of political views, primarily for harsh statements against the authorities. Most of these statements were made online; as it has been the case in recent years, online opposition activity attracts the attention of law enforcement agencies and often provokes unjustified and disproportionate reactions.

For Calls to Extremist Activities and Incitement of Hatred

In late October, the Nakhimovsky District Court of Sevastopol retried the case of Valery Bolshakov – the former head of the Sevastopol Workers Union and the secretary of the Sevastopol branch of the Russian United Labor Front Party (ROT FRONT) – and handed down a suspended sentence of two and a half years with a two-year ban on holding leadership positions under Art. 280 Parts 1 and 2 of the Criminal Code (public calls for extremist activity including those committed on the Internet). The verdict was upheld by the Sevastopol City Court in December. The charges against Bolshakov under Art. 280 Part 2 were based on his social media network posts that included offensive characteristics of the Terek Cossacks and called for "kicking them out to Novorossiya"; the posts also contained accusations against the Russian authorities of "genocide against the people of Russia," Lenin quotes and calls for "establishing the dictatorship of the proletariat by violent means." The charge under Art. 280 Part 1 was based on a speech made by Bolshakov during his one-man picket with the placard "Down with Putin's Police State."

The court found that the placard as well as Bolshakov's speech (in which he wished for the imminent demise of "Putin's dictatorship" and the "police state" and the subsequent establishment of the dictatorship of the proletariat) contained calls for "the elimination of the officially acting government." We are inclined to believe that the calls for revolution and for the proletariat to take power, which are often heard from activists on the left, are, in most cases, not capable of instigating real violent anti-government actions and are more accurately interpreted as a figure of speech employed to convey dissatisfaction with the current authorities. Bolshakov's statements about the Cossacks, however, can indeed be understood as a call for their deportation; at the same time, the court should have taken into account the vanishingly small likelihood for such calls to be implemented in the modern political context. Earlier, in June 2019, Bolshakov was sentenced on the same charges to the same punishment, but then the sentence was canceled and the case was returned to the prosecutor's office.

It became known in January that former police officer Aleksei Dymovsky had been charged under Art. 280 Part 2 of the Criminal Code (public calls for extremist activities via the Internet) in connection with his YouTube video "Aleksei Dymovsky: Thought of Killing Putin" recorded in October 2019. It is worth recalling that Dymovsky gained notoriety in 2009 when he publicly addressed Russian officers and Prime Minister Vladimir Putin with a story about the *palochnaya sistema* ("quota system," implying that the number of cases filed and solved by the police should meet the quasi-plans of the authorities) and corruption in the Ministry of Internal Affairs system. After that, he was dismissed from the police, and a case of fraud with the use of official position was opened against him; it was later terminated. Dymovsky's statement was a notable event in the public discussion preceding the reform of the Ministry of Internal Affairs.

The 2019 video shows Dymovsky in a taxi going through Novorossiysk to the police department in order to voluntarily surrender the explosives he found, which the police failed to pick up at his signal. Meanwhile, Dymovsky explains that he used to keep TNT at home for several years because he "wanted to use this TNT against Putin, Vladimir Vladimirovich," but eventually gave up these thoughts because he came to the conclusion that Putin was a "mentally ill person." In the video, Dymovsky also calls on all honest people to unite and invites them to a rally. After the video recording, Dymovsky's car was stopped by traffic police, he decided to voluntarily surrender his TNT to them and was subsequently questioned by the police. However, several days later, he was detained and charged with illegal storage and transportation of explosives (Art. 222.1 Part 1 of the Criminal Code). We view the charge under Art. 280 of the Criminal Code as inappropriate, since the latter contains no calls for violence against the president or other officials, and the call for all honest people to unite is peaceful in its character.

In August, the Oktyabrsky District Court of Novorossiysk returned Dymovsky's case to the prosecutor; according to his lawyer, it was due to the fact that some materials that the defense intended to use as evidence of Dymovsky's innocence had disappeared from his file – in particular, the interrogation record of the taxi driver and the video operator, and the disk with the video itself, on which he announced his intention to voluntarily surrender the explosives.

Statements directed against the authorities occasionally lead to punishment under Art. 20.3.1 of the Code of Administrative Offenses (incitement to hatred, enmity and violation of human dignity on group grounds), introduced into the Code of Administrative Offenses as a result of partial decriminalization of Art. 282 of the Criminal Code. Based on our information on the application of this legal regulation in 2020, we view ten people as having been subjected to inappropriate punishment, one of whom was punished three times. A fine was imposed in six cases, community service in two, and detention for a period of five to 11 days in three cases.

The vast majority of these punishments were triggered by crude but not violent statements by social media users against law enforcement or the authorities. We regard punishment for such statements as inappropriate. Law enforcement officials should not be considered a vulnerable social group protected by anti-extremist legislation. The European Court of Human Rights has repeatedly noted that law enforcement agencies should be extremely tolerant of criticism unless it involves a real threat of violence. With regard to officials, the Supreme Court of the Russian Federation, in the Ruling "On Judicial Practice in Criminal Cases Regarding Crimes of Extremism" of June 28, 2011,[42] emphasized that the permissible threshold of criticism against them is higher than for private individuals.

In December, the court placed Natalia Podolyak, a resident of Krasnoyarsk, under detention for 10 days under Art. 20.3.1 of the Code of Administrative Offenses (incitement to hatred). She left a comment on Facebook under the post about citizens being detained for violating the quarantine in which she made rude statements about police officers and the state in general and also wrote, "People and their right to freedom of movement should never be so disrespected." Obviously, there were no calls for violence against the police in Podolyak's comment, so we regard the punishment against her as inappropriate.

The Voskresensk City Court in Moscow Province placed activist Aleksei Kholkin under detention for five days. The Moscow Province Court upheld this decision. The administrative case against Kholkin was based on a link to the video "Everyone Comes Out to Protest. The Government Should Resign," which he posted on his Facebook page intending, in law enforcement's opinion, to "incite hatred of government officials." The video features a number of activists, including Vladimir Filin, Elena Rokhlina, Angelica Latsis and Kirill Myamlin – members of the Permanent Council of the National Patriotic Forces of Russia – who criticize the policy of the Russian authorities and call for joining a protest rally. The video contains no calls for xenophobic or anti-state violence.

In August, the Taganrog City Court of Rostov Province fined local resident Vladislav Shulga the amount of 10,000 rubles. An ex-employee of G.M. Beriev Aircraft Plant, Shulga is a defendant in a case related to the 2017 thallium poisoning of plant employees. He had left the following emotional comment on a local Taganrog portal: "It is not the laws that are stupid, but those who are set to enforce them are criminals! Scum are our judges, scoundrels are our policemen, and swindlers are our prosecutors." This comment was deemed a violation of the human dignity of the government officials. Stanislav Tkachev, who left the comment "All cops are bastards, especially the First Department and investigator R." on the same Web site, faced the same punishment.

In September, local video blogger Mikhail Alferov from Kemerovo was punished under Art. 20.3.1 of the Code of Administrative Offenses three times for having published three videos that the court recognized as insulting to police officers. The court sentenced him to a fine of 15,000 rubles, 96 hours of community service and 11 days of administrative detention.

Over the summer, courts in Tatarstan punished three Tatar nationalists under Art. 20.3.1 who, addressed a rally on Oct. 12, 2019, in memory of the Kazan defenders who died during the capture of the city by the troops of Ivan the Terrible. Fauzia Bayramova, the chair of the Ittifaq party, was fined 10,000 rubles in June; Imam Ayrat Shakirov received 40 hours of community service in August, and 81-year-old Galishan Nuriakhmet, the deputy chairman of the ATSC, was fined 5,000 rubles. The punishments were based on statements made by the three rally participants, which differed but generally amounted to pointing out Russia's colonial policy and the need to fight colonial oppression. Law enforcement agencies and the court regarded these statements as inciting hostility toward Russians.

We do not agree with this position: In and of itself, a public expression of disagreement with the "colonial" policy of the federal and republican authorities is not the same as inciting hatred toward ethnic Russians.

Within the same paradigm of countering "anti-colonialists," the Supreme Court of Tatarstan recognized *The Hidden History of the Tatars: The National Liberation Struggle of the Tatar People in the 16th-18th Centuries for the Establishment of an Independent State*, a book by the writer and journalist Vakhit Imamov published in 1994, as extremist in July. Imamov's book is a popular retelling of events from the history of the uprisings of the peoples of the Volga region that took place from the 16th through 18th centuries; according to its annotation, the work is intended "primarily for students at schools and gymnasiums of Tatarstan as an additional textbook on the history of their native land." The book, written in 1991, does, in fact, contain a positive assessment of the Tatars' struggle for independence and national rights and against the "colonial oppression" of Tsarist Russia. At the end of Imamov's work, he says that "the struggle to create a state independent of Moscow's dictate, which began 440 years ago, continues today." This statement accurately reflects the situation in the early 1990s, when the new status of the republics of the former USSR was being determined. All this, in our opinion, did not provide any grounds for banning the book as extremist today.

It should be noted, however, that the expression of a diametrically opposite opinion can also lead to punishment. Thus, in July, Mikhail Scheglov, the chairman of the Russian Culture Society, was fined 10,000 rubles; the Supreme Court of Tatarstan upheld this decision in August. He made the statements for which Scheglov was punished in an open letter to Rustam Minnikhanov, the head of Tatarstan. Opposing church closures related to the coronavirus, Scheglov noted that such a ban on the part of the authorities looks "not like concern for people's health, but like a form of theomachy and new persecution of Christians" taking place "in the very center of Orthodox Russia," which is "deeply symbolic for a 'national' republic with its definite numerical preponderance of the non-Orthodox officials." In essence, Scheglov's words constitute criticism of the actions of the authorities that he regarded as unfair with respect toward Orthodox believers. Even if we interpret these statements as creating a negative image of the Muslims who are allegedly abusing their dominant position in the government of Tatarstan, they can only be qualified as a mild case of hate speech, which, in our opinion, does not present sufficient grounds for punishment.

One such case, opened in 2019, was discontinued in February; it had been filed under Art. 20.3.1 of the Code of Administrative Offenses against video blogger Pavel Sychev. He was charged for publishing a video back in 2019 about the "Let's Regain the Right to Vote" rally that took place in August. The video discussed violence by the National Guard of Russia against the demonstrators and the fact that the security forces were not wearing their identity badges. Sychev used harsh characterizations with respect to law enforcement officers but did not call for violence against them. A linguistic examination conducted by experts at the Voronezh Regional Center for Forensic Examination of the Ministry of Justice concluded that "the National Guardsmen of the Russian Federation are not a social group," and that "there are no linguistic and psychological signs of humiliation or incitement to enmity" in Sychev's video.

For Incitement to Separatism

As we indicated above, we view punishment imposed for calls for the separation of a particular territory from Russia as inappropriate unless the calls are for violent separatism. We also would like to note that, in accordance with the amendments made to legislation in December 2020, Art. 280.1 applies only to calls made again within a year after being held accountable for an administrative offense. Therefore, criminal cases under this article that were in court at the time the amendment was adopted are subject to closure, and prior sentences made under it must be reviewed. In addition, convictions under it must be expunged unless they expire by December 2020.

In August, the Central District Military Court in Samara sentenced Ayrat Dilmukhametov, an activist of the Bashkir national movement, to nine years in a maximum-security penal colony with a three-year ban on administering Web sites. The verdict, which we consider inappropriate, was handed down under Art. 280.1 Part 2 of the Criminal Code for publication of calls for the violation of the territorial integrity of the Russian Federation on the Internet. The charges of separatism were based on Dilmukhametov's video speech in which he announced his intention to win elections for the head of Bashkortostan and then initiate the renegotiation of a federal agreement between the subjects of the Russian Federation on new conditions. Dilmukhametov did not speak about secession from Russia, his plans looked rather abstract, and he proposed or made no specific steps to implement his program, let alone any calls for achieving it by violent methods. Nevertheless, he was found guilty not only under the article on separatism, but also under Art. 282.3 Part 1 (financing of extremist activities); the court found that Dilmukhametov was trying to collect funds via the Internet "to support the struggle for the new 4th Bashkir Republic."

In January, a criminal case under Art. 280.1 of the Criminal Code was opened against Rashid Maisigov, an Ingush activist and a former editor of the FortangaORG portal. Maisigov was charged for an Instagram post made in February of 2019 in which he called for the population of Ingushetia to secede from Russia and join Georgia, and for the Georgian leadership and the world community to support such a step. In addition, the investigation claimed that he had also posted leaflets in Nazran and Magas that called on other states to issue passports to all residents of the republic. The charge was dropped in January 2021 due to the abovementioned change in legislation.

In September, a citizen of Ukraine born in 1998 was detained in the Crimea for distributing leaflets in the cities of the peninsula with calls "to take actions aimed at violating the territorial integrity of the Russian Federation." The young man was detained as a defendant under Art. 280.1 Part 1 of the Criminal Code; leaflets with the indicated content were confiscated from him. According to the investigators, the young man was a member of the "Ukrainian Resistance in the Crimea" VKontakte community, which shared various materials criticizing the annexation of the Crimea to Russia and calling for its return to Ukraine. We found no calls for violent actions among the community's posts that we were able to access.

For "Justification of Terrorism"

We classify as inappropriate a number of sentences passed by Russian courts in 2020 under Art. 205.2 of the Criminal Code, which covers propaganda of terrorism. Several of them are associated, once again, with harsh anti-government rhetoric.

The 2nd Western District Military Court in Kursk found Sergei Lavrov guilty under Art. 205.2 Part 2 of the Criminal Code (public calls for terrorism on the Internet) in May and sentenced him to five years in a minimum-security penal colony with loss of the right to administer Web sites for two and a half years. In addition, Lavrov was ordered to undergo involuntary mental health treatment. The investigation argued, and the court agreed, that Lavrov had called for "carrying out terrorist activities by forcibly seizing power" on his VKontakte page. He was charged for eight posts, one of which talked about a military coup, and the other seven criticized the "anti-national" and "occupation" government, "unfair elections," and the president of Russia. One of them called for a "military tribunal over the anti-national Putin regime." In several of these texts, Lavrov expressed confidence that a "people's revolution" was inevitable in Russia. In our opinion, only the first post we mentioned could be viewed as a direct call for violent activity. The rest of his publications contained no signs of justifying terrorism or calls for it. Although law enforcement agencies had a formal reason to prosecute Lavrov, we consider the punishment imposed on him disproportionately severe. Moreover, we do not consider criminal prosecution against Lavrov necessary; more lenient measures could have been sufficient, given the insignificant audience of his page and publications.

In October, the same Court handed down a sentence against Mikhail Sharygin, a resident of Nizhny Novgorod. The ex-candidate for the city Duma from Yabloko was found guilty of public calls for terrorism committed on the Internet and sentenced to a fine of 400,000 rubles. Sharygin published a comment on NN.ru in which he suggested blowing up the fence around a construction site. The fence inconvenienced local residents, and the guards on the construction site prevented ambulances from passing through to the houses, but the developer never dismantled the fence, ignoring an official order. The court, based on the expert opinion, decided that Sharygin, in his commentary, was setting the local residents against the city authorities as two sides of a socio-political conflict, and that he also outlined the way to influence the authorities (by blowing up the fence) – that is, he called for a terrorist attack. We believe that this categorization is incorrect. On the one hand, the objective side of terrorist attack as a crime is characterized by the intent to intimidate the population – but we have no reason to assume that such an explosion would have frightened the population. On the other hand, the socio-political motivation for such an action is also far from obvious since the situation can be more appropriately characterized as a local economic dispute. Accordingly, the unauthorized demolition of the fence, if it ever took place, would have to be qualified under Art. 167 of the Criminal Code (intentional destruction or damage to property) or Art. 330 of the Criminal Code (arrogation of authority), and calling for it should have been qualified as incitement to destruction of property or as arrogation, but not a call to perform a terrorist attack.

In July 2020, at a visiting session in the Pskov Province Court, a three-judge panel of the 2nd Western District Military Court found journalist Svetlana Prokopieva guilty of justifying terrorism via mass media under Art. 205.2 Part 2 of the Criminal Code and sentenced her to a fine of 500,000 rubles as well as the costs of expert examinations and confiscation of her mobile phone and laptop. In February 2021, this decision was upheld by the Military Court of Appeal and entered into force. The prosecution was based on Prokopieva's radio show, "A Minute of Enlightenment," aired in the fall of 2018 on the Echo of Moscow in Pskov radio station and focused on the causes of the explosion at the FSB office lobby in Arkhangelsk on Oct. 31, 2018. Analyzing this incident, Prokopieva argued that the actions of a young man, who had committed the explosion, stemmed from the repressive policies of the state, and that young people growing up in the atmosphere of state-sanctioned brutality were at risk of responding to the state in the same manner. The show contained no statements to indicate that the ideology or practice of terrorism was correct and deserved to be imitated and never claimed that it was attractive or appropriate.

One new case should be pointed out – a charge under Art. 205.2 Part 1 of the Criminal Code was brought against Darya Polyudova, an activist of the Left Resistance (*Levoe Soprotivlenie*) movement, based on a video recording saved on Polyudova's phone. In the video, in a conversation with a fellow activist, she commented on the armed attack against the FSB building on Lubyanka Street in Moscow organized by Yevgeny Manyurov on Dec. 19, 2019. According to the investigation, Polyudova's statements in approval of Manyurov's actions could be heard by people around her. It must be taken into consideration, however, that the objective aspect of the crime under Art. 205.2 of the Criminal Code implies that the statements are made publicly, that is, addressed to a group or an indefinitely wide circle of people. However, in this case, it is unclear whether anyone except for her conversation partner heard or could have heard Polyudova's words. Even if someone did hear them, such people were obviously few in number. The subjective aspect of the crime, meanwhile, is characterized by a direct intention. If the conversation in question was private, not intended for prying ears, then it follows that Polyudova had no criminal intent in this case. It is worth noting that, even prior to facing this charge, in January 2020, she was put in pre-trial detention as a defendant on charges under Arts. 280.1 Part 1 and Art. 205.2 Part 2 of the Criminal Code based on her video interview and social media posts with calls for separatism, including armed separatism.[43]

We have serious doubts about the legality of a verdict for publications that cannot be said to have a direct anti-government character. The verdict was handed down by the 2nd Western District Military Court in June under Art. 205.2 Part 2 of the Criminal Code. Aitakhaji Khalimov, a 27-year-old resident of Kaliningrad, was sentenced to three and a half years of imprisonment in a minimum-security penal colony. The prosecution was based on the fact that Khalimov had shared three clips about the First Chechen War on his VKontakte page. We doubt the appropriateness of the verdict against Khalimov. In our opinion, the videos do, in fact, positively evaluate and romanticize the actions of the militants, specifically their military actions, but they say nothing about terrorist attacks. At the same time, these materials contain no calls for continuation of armed separatist activities in Chechnya. It should also be borne in mind that the First Chechen War ended with the signing of peace agreements, and the separatists were not held legally accountable for their actions; therefore, it is not clear why the justification of those already historical events as a separatist rebellion should be equated with justification or propaganda of terrorism and fall under Art. 205.2 of the Criminal Code. If law enforcement agencies view glorification of the First Chechen War as dangerous, they should have chosen appropriate arguments and categorized Khalimov's actions accordingly. In addition, we regard a real prison term of three and a half years in a minimum-security penal colony as an excessively severe punishment for speech.

For Other Anti-Government Statements

In 2020, we became aware of 34 cases of responsibility under Art. 20.29 of the Code of Administrative Offenses in various regions of Russia for distributing the banned video about unfulfilled campaign promises of the United Russia party "Let's Remind the Crooks and Thieves about Their Manifesto-2002," created by supporters of Aleksei Navalny (our records showed 31 such cases in 2019). The courts issued fines ranging from one to 3,000 rubles. Belgorod Province is still in the lead with 13 people sanctioned.[44] Law enforcement agencies actively monitor the distribution of this video, because it can be easily found on social media, and "preventive measures" in the form of administrative punishments can be imposed against opposition-minded Internet users without much effort. We would like to remind readers that the content of the notorious video, recognized

as extremist in 2013, merely lists a number of unfulfilled campaign promises from the 2002 United Russia party manifesto and calls to vote for
any party other than the ruling party. We view the prohibition of this video
and punishment for its distribution as inappropriate.

We know about inappropriate punishments against eight activists across
the political spectrum under Art. 20.3 of the Code of Administrative Offenses
for using the swastika as a means of political criticism in opposition posts;
one activist faced charges on three separate occasions. Five activists were
punished with administrative detentions; fines were levied in four cases.

In August, the Vologda City Court fined Yevgeny Domozhirov, a known
local activist, 2,000 rubles. The sanction was based on a video "They Destroy:
The Real Fascists," which Domozhirov posted on his personal VKontakte
page in May. In the video, the activist complained about the clearing of a
park in which the trees had been planted by World War II veterans and
stated that the local authorities behaved "like the real fascists both with
respect to the veterans and to this memory." The video featured images of
Governor Oleg Kuvshinnikov and Mayor Sergei Voropanov, edited to add
Nazi caps to their heads. In this case, as in many similar ones, the swastika
was used as a visual means of criticizing the authorities – as a symbol of a
"criminal regime."

Activist Liana Timerkhanova from Kazan was fined 2,000 rubles for
posting an image on VKontakte, which depicted Artyom Khokhorin, the
head of the Ministry of Internal Affairs in Tatarstan, as Adolf Hitler with
the Nazi armband.

Activist Albert Gerasimov, a member of the United Communist Party
from Penza, was fined 2,000 rubles for a post on VKontakte in which he
wrote that Black American runner Jesse Owens was admitted to the Berlin
Olympics in 1936, while, in modern Russia, Aleksei Navalny was deprived
of the opportunity to participate in the presidential election. The post was
accompanied by a photo of Hitler with a swastika on his sleeve. A month
later, Gerasimov was brought to court again for failure to delete his post.
A fine was imposed but not upheld by the province court. Meanwhile,
however, Gerasimov was once again brought to responsibility for the same
publication, placed under detention for 10 days, and the province court
upheld this decision.

Local opposition activist Grigory Severin was put under detention for
12 days in Voronezh. The case was based on five images with Nazi symbols
published on VKontakte between January 2014 and May 2020. These in-

cluded a photo of a 1939 badge depicting the swastika, which symbolized the friendship of Germany and the USSR, and a cartoon depicting President Vladimir Putin as a Nazi. Severin stated in court that he considered himself an anti-fascist and did not want Russia to look like Nazi Germany.

In Vladivostok, the court placed the activist Gia (Georgy) Kakabadze under detention for seven days for posting collages with Vladimir Putin in a Nazi uniform on Instagram.

All these cases clearly illustrate that the note on exceptions added to Art. 20.3 of the Code of Administrative Offenses in March 2020 has failed to prevent all the instances of its misuse; there are still many of them.

In 2020, citizens were brought to responsibility at least 30 times under Art. 20.1 Parts 3-5 of the Code of Administrative Offenses for dissemination of online information expressing disrespect for society and the state in indecent form. A year earlier, there were at least 56 such cases, i.e., the trend that was observed in the second half of 2019 remained – the regulation has been applied less frequently. Fines were imposed in 21 cases (one person was fined three times; another person was fined twice), detention – in one case (repeated offense), proceedings were discontinued in five cases, the outcome of two cases is unknown, and one fine was imposed outside of our review period in early 2021. Almost all cases pertained to disrespect for the authorities – most often directed against the president, but also against officials, police officers, or judges. It is worth noting that, although the regulation initially was supposed to apply specifically to obscene statements, in fact it is increasingly used when Internet users simply make rude or harsh statements, for example, by calling Vladimir Putin a fascist or a thief.[45]

For Anti-Government Group Initiatives

In August–September, the Leninsky District Court of Chelyabinsk found two eighteen-year-old activists of the Other Russia party guilty of involvement in the activities of the banned National Bolshevik Party (NBP). Artyom Golubev was handed down a four-year suspended sentence with a four-year probationary period under Art. 282.2 Parts 1 and 1.1 of the Criminal Code (organizing the activities of an extremist organization and recruitment into it). Mikhail Prosvirnin received a three-year suspended sentence and Aleksandr Kryshka – a suspended sentence of two and a half years, both under Art. 282.2 Part 2 (participating in the activities of an extremist organization). According to the investigation, in April 2020, these three members of the Other Russia attacked a monument to the Czechoslovak Legion soldiers in Chelyabinsk, on which the defendants inflicted several blows with a sledgehammer, while unfurling the banner "You Shall Pay for Konev!" This action, as well as their alleged attempt to set fire to the Leninsky District Police Department of Chelyabinsk in protest against the beating and rape of a detainee that took place there in May, was interpreted as a continuation of the NBP's activities. We consider inappropriate both the ban against the NBP and prosecutions against activists for participating in it, and believe the actions attributed to the activists should have been qualified under other articles.

Also in August, the Leninsky District Court of Perm found Aleksandr Shabarchin and Danila Vasilyev guilty of hooliganism committed by an organized group (Art. 213 Part 2 of the Criminal Code); the third defendant, Aleksandr Etkin (Kotov), was acquitted. In November, the Perm Province Court of Appeals mitigated the punishment for Aleksandr Shabarchin to a two-year suspended sentence instead of two years in a minimum-security colony. Danila Vasilyev was handed down a one-year suspended sentence by a lower court. The case was initiated in connection with a public action conducted in November 2018 – a dummy appeared on a Perm street representing Putin dressed in a prison uniform emblazoned with the words "liar" and "war criminal Pynya V.V." In a video that was subsequently posted on the "Groza Permi" YouTube channel, people in camouflage uniforms escorted a man in a Putin mask through the Perm city center and then tied a dummy with the president's photograph for a face to a post near the local central department store. The initial charge included the motive of hatred against Putin's supporters as a social group. However, the court excluded the social hatred motive from the charges – in our opinion, quite appropriately. We believe that in order to avoid such nonsensical cases, the concept of a social group, which has no precise definition, should be excluded from the legislative regulations. Overall, we believe that the investigation did not have sufficient grounds to qualify the tying of the dummy to the post as hooliganism, that is, a gross violation of public order.

In mid-June, the Tverskoy District Court of Moscow handed down a two-year suspended sentence with three years of probation and additional restriction of freedom for six months in the case of Vyacheslav Gorbaty. The retiree from Chernogolovka in Moscow Province was an activist of the Initiative Group of the Referendum "For Responsible Power" (FRP). The verdict was approved by the Moscow City Court in August. Gorbaty was found guilty of participating in the activities of the extremist organization APW under Art. 282.2 Part 2 of the Criminal Code. In 2016, the materials of the case were separated from the case of Yury Mukhin (the ideologist of the APW and FRP) and his associates Aleksandr Sokolov and Valery Parfyonov. The investigation claimed that Gorbaty had served as the leader of a cell of the banned organization in Moscow Province and had collected 143,000 rubles for its activities, but the charge under Art. 282.3 of the Criminal Code for financing of extremist activities was dropped in February due to expiry of the limitation period. The case under Art. 282.2 of the Criminal Code went to court in October 2018 and was initially returned to the prosecutor, but, in May 2019, Gorbaty was charged anew. Army of People's Will – an organization of the Stalinist-nationalist kind repeatedly implicated in xenophobic propaganda – was recognized as extremist in 2010. We view this decision as inappropriate, since it was based solely on the ban of the leaflet *You have elected – You are to judge!* (*Ty izbral – tebe sudit*), which we consider unfounded. Accordingly, we also view sentences under Art. 282.2 against the activists of FRP (as the APW's successor) as inappropriate.

For "Rehabilitation of Nazism"

Beginning in May 2020, a series of criminal cases were initiated under Art. 354.1 Parts 1 and 3 of the Criminal Code, which covers the rehabilitation of Nazism (denial of the facts established by the International Military Tribunal, or approval of Nazi crimes and dissemination of information expressing obvious disrespect to society about the days and symbols of Russia's military glory) for attempts to upload photographs of the Third Reich leaders or famous collaborators (in particular, Adolf Hitler and Andrei Vlasov, but under different names) to the Web sites of the Immortal Regiment movement on the eve of May 9, Victory Day. Apparently, in all cases the offense consisted only of submitting photographs; the images did not, in fact, get onto the Web sites, since they were filtered out during pre-moderation. We believe that the actions of the Internet users were qualified incorrectly.

An action such as uploading photographs of Nazi leaders to a Web site, even on the commemorative day of May 9, in and of itself, constitutes neither a public endorsement of Nazi crimes nor dissemination of any information about a day of Russia's military glory. Apparently, these photographs were not accompanied by any statements approving or denying Nazi crimes.

According to the Investigative Committee, the majority of the users involved in such attempts turned out to be foreigners, but over ten people were residents of various regions of Russia. As we were informed, at least 12 such criminal cases were initiated in 2020 against the following people: Andrei Shabanov from Samara, Denis Vorontsov from Volgograd, Vyacheslav Kruglov from Ulyanovsk, Muhammad El-Ayyubi from Kazan, Daniil Shestakov, Daniil Simanov and Maksim Gusev from Perm, Dmitry Borodaenko from Kemerovo, Yevgeny Akhmylov from Chita, a resident of Tula, a resident of Nyurbinsky District of Yakutia and Aleksandr Khoroshiltsev from Voronezh.

Verdicts were handed down in six such cases:

- In September, the Perm Province Court found 19-year-old student Daniil Simanov guilty based on the fact that, on May 4, 2020, Simanov, using a social media network application, sent a photo of Andrei Vlasov to the Memory Bank Web site to be included in the "Immortal Regiment Online" action. He was sentenced under Art. 354.1 Part 3 to 200 hours of community service with the confiscation of his computer.

- Also in September, the Ulyanovsk Province Court sentenced local resident Vyacheslav Kruglov under Art. 30 Part 3 and Art. 354.1 Part 1 of the Criminal Code for an attempt to post a photo of Hitler on the Memory Bank Web site to pay a fine of 120,000 rubles on a 12-month installment plan.

- In October, the Zabaikalsky Territory Court fined Yevgeny Akhmylov, a teacher at Chita Polytechnic College, 150,000 rubles under Art. 354.1 Part 3 of the Criminal Code for an attempt to upload a photograph of Ataman Pyotr Krasnov to the Immortal Regiment Web site.

- In November, the Perm Province Court found Daniil Shestakov guilty under Art. 354.1 Part 3 of the Criminal Code and sentenced him to nine months of community service for submitting photos of Andrei Vlasov as a part of the Immortal Regiment Online Campaign.

- In December, the Supreme Court of Tatarstan found Muhammed El-Ayyubi, a 21-year-old student from Kazan, guilty under Art. 354.1 Part 1 and Art. 228 Part 1 (illegal possession of narcotic substances) of the Criminal Code; he received a suspended sentence of one year of imprisonment and had to pay a 150,000-ruble fine. El-Ayyubi submitted Hitler's photo to the Memory Bank Web site (in 2021, this sentence was overturned; the case was sent for a new trial).

- Kemerovo resident Dmitry Borodaenko was sentenced in the same month by the Kemerovo Province Court under Art. 30 Part 3 and Art. 354.1 Part 1 to pay a fine of 120,000 rubles – also for submitting the photo of Hitler to the Memory Bank Web site.

Yet another case on disseminating information about the days of Russia's military glory and memorable dates that expressed clear disrespect toward society was opened in January and closed in June 2020. It was the case of blogger Nikolai Gorelov from Kaliningrad (writing under pen name Kirichenko), who, on May 9, 2018, published a text of his own composition on his VKontakte page, in which fictional representatives of different countries and social strata as well as real historical characters "thanked" the Red Army in observance of Victory Day. Some characters talked about their suffering inflicted either directly by or with the assistance of the Red Army; others tell how, thanks to the Red Army, they succeeded in committing atrocities. The text is obviously political and partly satirical; it suggests that readers take a critical look at the military operations of the Soviet Union, but never condoned Nazism.

In addition, a case under Art. 354.1 Part 3 of the Criminal Code (public desecration of the symbols of Russia's military glory) was opened in July against blogger Mikhail Alferov from Kemerovo based on a video posted by Alferov on YouTube on May 9, 2020. In the video, Alferov criticized, in harsh terms, the opulent decoration of the city for Victory Day, which contrasted with the unsatisfactory condition of residential buildings. The blogger also expressed his dissatisfaction with the use of St. George ribbon and demanded that police officers remove it from their uniform. In our opinion, statements about certain symbols, even if regarded as offensive, should not be equated with desecrating the symbol itself (by the way, the very concept of "symbols of military glory" is not clarified in Russian legislation).

A criminal case under the same part of the same article was opened in mid-September against an activist of the Citizens of the USSR movement from Krasnoyarsk, who posted on his VKontakte page "a swastika photoshopped from a St. George ribbon" with the caption "the flag worthy of the state." By publishing this image, the Krasnoyarsk resident obviously did not seek to justify the Nazi ideology or to desecrate the St. George ribbon as a symbol of military glory – most likely, the publication was intended as a critical statement about the politics of modern Russia.

For Extremist Symbols

According to statistics provided by the Judicial Department of the Supreme Court, there were 1,052 cases of punishment under Art. 20.3 in the first half of 2020, compared to 2,388 cases for all of 2019.[46] These numbers indicate that the total for this year might be lower than the year before, but a sharp decrease in the application of this article is unlikely.

As usual, we know the details of the corresponding administrative cases and can assess their appropriateness only for some of these incidents. Our records showed more cases of inappropriate persecution in 2020 than in 2019. People faced punishment without proper grounds on at least 44 occasions according to our information (we counted 31 such cases in 2019), with 43 cases pertaining to individuals and one to a legal entity; the defendants included activists, representatives of small businesses, and ordinary social media users. A fine is known to be imposed in 27 cases, administrative detention in 10, six out of 44 were dismissed, and the outcome of the remaining two is unknown to us. Evidently, the introduction of a note to Art. 20.3 stating that the article does not apply to cases in which a negative attitude toward the ideology of Nazism and extremism is being formed and there are no signs of propaganda or justification of Nazi or extremist ideology could not fundamentally improve the situation and reduce the application of punishment only to cases in which banned symbols were actually displayed in order to promote a dangerous ideology. Past enforcement problems persist, and the 2020 cases differ little from those of the preceding year.

The punishment against antique dealers under Art. 20.3 for advertising Third Reich items with Nazi symbols continue; we became aware of six such cases in 2020. We believe that this article should be applied primarily not to antique dealers, but to modern manufacturers of items with Nazi and neo-Nazi symbols (badges, clothing, copies of weapons, etc.) and distributors of such products. In addition, in our opinion, the confiscation of goods is unjustified in such cases, since for the seller antiques are objects of material value and not a propaganda tool.

The Petropavlovsk-Kamchatsky City Court sentenced local resident Yevgeny Barkov, to a fine of 1,000 rubles twice. Barkov posted two advertisements on Avito for the sale of two German objects from the Third Reich period – a medal and a badge. These artifacts contained Nazi symbols and, according to the court orders, were subject to confiscation as tools of an administrative offense. Barkov filed complaints against the rulings with the Kamchatka Territory Court indicating that he had posted ads with photos of Nazi paraphernalia not for the purpose of propagating Nazism but with the intention of selling it. However, the court upheld the earlier rulings. In one of the decisions, the territory court came to the conclusion that Barkov's lack of propaganda intent did not give grounds for his release from responsibility, since any actions that make attributes and symbols "accessible for observation by other people, including by publishing them in the media – the category to which the Avito Web site certainly belongs" may be defined as an offense; the court also referred to the position of the Constitutional Court stated in 2014 that the use of Nazi paraphernalia, regardless of its genesis, could cause suffering to people whose relatives died during the Great Patriotic War. In its decision on Barkov's second complaint, the court noted that his actions did not fit any of the exceptions established by law, since the announcement did not contain "explanations that would form a negative attitude toward the ideology of Nazism."

As before, several left-wing activists who consistently adhere to anti-fascist views became victims of persecution under Art. 20.3 of the Code of Administrative Offenses in 2020. Thus, Lev Burlakov, the administrator of the "Levomarginal" public page on VKontakte, was placed under detention for 10 days in Naberzhnye Chelny. The incriminating materials included three posts of his authorship (a meme with an NSDAP congress photo ridiculing the dogmatic perception of Marxism, an image with Nazi symbols shared from the community "These Funny Offended Rightists," and a critical post with a photo from the Russian March in Yekaterinburg) as well as five comments from other users. In Tatarstan, the Naberezhnye Chelny City Court has sentenced Denis Belov, a member of the Marxists Union, to 14 days of administrative detention based on several posts on his VKontakte page. Some of his anti-fascist posts contained Nazi symbols and a series of images with black and red anarcho-communist symbols (which law enforcement and the court may have misinterpreted as symbols of the banned Right Sector).

The sanctions for the use of the swastika in a satirical or historical context, or in informational materials, still continues as well.

We learned in December that in Dankov of the Lipetsk Region, Sergei Korablin was fined 1,000 rubles under Art. 20.3 Part 1 of the Code of

Administrative Offenses for posting an episode from the South Park animated series on his VKontakte page back in 2010 in which one of the characters comes to school on Halloween in a Hitler costume with the swastika on his shoulder; the horrified teacher tries to rectify the situation by dressing the boy as a ghost, but the outfit ends up looking like a Ku Klux Klan robe.

Lipetsk resident Artyom Barsukovsky was fined the same amount for a comment in a local VKontakte community he left on a news story about the introduction of a mask regime in shops in the Lipetsk region. The commentary contained a video of Hitler's speech, which was overlaid with an audio recording of Ramzan Tutayev, the deputy imam of one of Chechnya's mosques, imploring people not to go outside without masks and gloves (in the spring of 2020, the video with Tutayev's appeal gained viral popularity and spawned a number of memes). The swastika is visible on Hitler's sleeve in the video. Barsukovsky said in court that he posted the video "in order to ridicule the current situation in the region in connection with the epidemiological situation with the coronavirus," and therefore, in his case, it would be appropriate to apply the note to Art. 20.3, but the court decided that this argument was based on a misinterpretation of the law.

In some cases, however, the note to Art. 20.3 of the Code of Administrative Offenses does get taken into account. In the Alikovsky District of the Chuvash Republic, the police refused to open an administrative case under Art. 20.3 against Galina Ivanova, a teacher in the Bolshevylskoye village Secondary School. A participant in an amateur play about World War II, Ivanova posted a photo on a social media network of her in a scout costume standing next to another participant who was playing a HiPo member and wearing a Nazi swastika on his sleeve. A photo was reported to the police by lawyer and former Deputy Grigory Mikhailov, who was in conflict with the school principal (a chairman of the Deputies' Assembly). However, the police found no offense in the actions of the teacher, who, nevertheless, has deleted the image from her page.

The Russian courts have no consistent tactics in applying the amendment. A court in Novokuznetsk in Kemerovo Province imposed a fine of 1,000 rubles upon Yevgeny Zabelin, a member of the Essence of Time (*Sut vremeni*) movement, who posted a photograph with Nazi symbols on his VKontakte page in the fall of 2014. The image in question was an illustration to a LiveJournal post focused on the connection between philosopher Aleksandr Dugin and Golden Dawn, a far-right party in Greece. The post characterized this connection as reprehensible. The punishments were based on the fact that one of the Golden Dawn propaganda materials mentioned in the post contained a photo of Rudolf Hess with a swastika-decorated armband. Zabelin tried to appeal this decision, but the Kemerovo Province Court approved the fine. Meanwhile, Pavel Guryanov, a former activist of the same movement from Perm, was able to successfully invoke the amendment to Art. 20.3 of the Code of Administrative Offenses. A report was compiled against him based on his 2016 LiveJournal post about the visit by a *Foreign Policy* journalist to the Azov Regiment training camp in Ukraine; the material was illustrated with photos featuring Azov insignia such as the Wolfsangel symbol formerly used by the Nazis. Guryanov said that he did not pursue the goal of advocating Nazism – on the contrary, his publication was anti-fascist in its intent. The district court agreed with him and ruled to dismiss his case.

It is worth noting that the courts made decisions to terminate proceedings in absurd cases of displaying the swastika both before and after the clarifying note was added to Art. 20.3 in March 2020.

In the summer, the case of a 16-year-old teenager was terminated in Voronezh. The charges, filed in February, were based on materials shared on his VKontakte page, including a Tom and Jerry meme (where they personify the Third Reich and the USSR in World War II, and the characters are labeled with the corresponding Soviet and Nazi insignia), an amateur video of Rammstein's song "Heute Nacht," and a fragment from Quentin Tarantino's movie *Inglourious Basterds*, in which Hitler hits the table and shouts "Nein, nein, nein!" The case filed against Irina Shumilova, a 19-year-old activist of the Left Block, for sharing the same Tom and Jerry video in March, was also dropped in the summer. In February, that is, before the amendments were adopted, the courts overturned previously imposed punishments in two cases of publishing the Tom and Jerry videos on VKontakte – the case of Vladislav Shenets in Kaliningrad and of minor Stepan L. in Kursk.

The note to Art. 20.3 could well be applied to the cases of demonstrating the so-called Svarog square reported to us in 2020. This neo-pagan symbol was previously used by Northern Brotherhood, a nationalist organization appropriately declared extremist in 2012. Accordingly, the demonstration of the Svarog square became punishable under Art. 20.3. Now, the history of the Northern Brotherhood is unlikely to be widely known, while the Svarog square is a rather popular symbol in nationalist and neo-pagan circles; it is not hard to find people displaying it. In Moscow, the court fined TV anchor

Yevgeny Kolesov 1,000 rubles and Power of the Law (*Sila zakona*) – the public organization engaged in the fight against swindlers, of which Kolesov is one of the founders – 10,000 rubles for using the Svarog square in the logo on the organization's Web site. Kolesov stated that he used this sign because he views it as an ancient Slavic amulet, but the court was not convinced. We found no evidence of the propaganda of the Northern Brotherhood ideology in the activities of Kolesov or his organization; most likely, he knew nothing about the existence of such an organization, its symbols, or the ban against it. The same can be said about Khabarovsk activist Rostislav Smolensky, the owner of a well-known campaign car covered with slogans in support of Sergei Furgal, the jailed former governor of the Khabarovsk Territory. Smolensky was placed under detention for 10 days in Vladivostok, because, during his live Instagram broadcast from his Furgalomobile, the camera showed the rear-view mirror decorated with a cross and two neo-pagan amulets, one of them in the shape of a Svarog square. We believe that in both of the above cases the courts should have taken into account that the symbols were displayed without any intent to promote a banned organization.

The Federal List of Extremist Materials

In 2020, the Federal List of Extremist Materials expanded somewhat slower than in 2010: Exactly as a year before, it was updated 26 times, but with 139 new entries (193 in 2019). Thus, the total entries grew from 5,004 to 5,143.[47]

The new entries fall into the following categories:

- Xenophobic materials of contemporary Russian nationalists – 71;
- Materials of other nationalists – eight;
- Materials of Islamic militants and other calls for violence by political Islamists – 154;
- Other Islamic materials – one;
- Materials of Orthodox fundamentalists – seven;
- Materials by other peaceful worshippers (the writings of the Pentecostal minister William Branham) – 21;
- Materials from the Ukrainian media and Internet – one;
- Anti-government materials inciting riots and violence – five;

- Works by classic fascist and neo-fascist authors – two;
- Parody banned as serious materials – two;
- Peaceful opposition materials – one;
- Radical anti-Christian materials – one;
- Anti-Islamic articles – one;
- Works of art with aggressive content – two;[48]
- Unidentified materials – four.

The breakdown of this list is roughly the same as in 2019.

At least 90 entries out of 139 refer to online content, mostly on social media. This includes video and audio clips, long texts, and images. Offline sources include books and brochures by Russian and other nationalists, classic authors of fascism, Pentecostals, pagans and Muslim authors.

However, often the description of the materials makes their sources indeterminable. For example, entry 5017 is described as "the text of the information material: an article titled 'The question is not in everyday human hostility***The cult of Devil worship in modern Jewry' (begins with the words 'World Jewry is the only population among the cultured peoples of the earth whose secret morality***' and ends with the words '***For the sake of this moment we live, for the sake of this moment all our deeds are done')." No information is provided on the exact location of the text described in such detail.

In entry 5027, on the contrary, the location is specified to the page: "An image consisting of two parts located on p. 153 of the book *Simferopol: Say what you may, but we need the truth!* (popular science publication edited and compiled by A. Shilko. Simferopol, Tverbest, 2016. – 296 pages), and depicting a man in the uniform of a special combat unit of the Nazi SS troops with the Russian tricolor on his sleeve and on his helmet; first he threatens a peasant with a gun, then the peasant cuts off his head with a saber; the caption reads THE BEAUTY OF A DEBT IS IN ITS PAYMENT 'In the morning, a Moskal [Russian] said to the peasants, "Hats off!" In the night, his helmet was taken by the partisans, together with his head.' "

Not only does entry reproduce the banned material on the Web site of the Ministry of Justice, but it also illustrates the problem that has not been solved in all the years of the list's existence, that is, if an identical image is printed in another book, will it be considered as already banned or will it have to be designated as extremist again? There are no clear instructions for law enforcement regarding this. In practice, we see that from year to year the same materials with different output data or published at different Internet addresses are added to the list.

Thus, in 2020, the song "Shamil is Leading the Platoon" by Timur Mutsu-rayev ("the recording begins with words 'The houses are burning, volley after volley***' and ends with '***Shamil is leading the platoon home...' "), recognized as extremist by the Sovetsky District Court of Bryansk in September 2020, was added as entry 5142. However, the same song is already on the list: It was already recognized as extremist in February 2014 (entry 2330). The difference between entries 2330 and 5142 is that in the former, the song title is recorded in the Latin alphabet (*Shamil_vedet_otryad.mp3*). But, for those who cannot read Latin letters, entry 2330 contains a clarification that the recording begins with words "The houses are burning, volley after volley...."

By the end of 2020, there were a total of 264 such duplicate entries in the list.

All the problems with the descriptions in the list, which we have re-peatedly reported in previous years, were still there in 2020. In this huge register, materials are entered with an endless number of spelling, grammatical, and bibliographic errors.

Also added to the list are materials that are obviously unlawfully rec-ognized as extremist: In 2020, records showed at least 25 such entries.

As you can see, the replenishment of the list as a whole has been slowing down since the Prosecutor General's Office adopted the instruction in 2016 centralizing this process. It is also easy to see what a huge share the materials of Russian nationalists have in this annual replenishment. But it is also true that this share has decreased markedly – from about three quarters in 2016 to about half in 2020.

The contribution to the list of Ukrainian materials is also rapidly de-creasing, as the hot phase of the war is now growing distant, as well as that of radical Islamist materials. Other types of materials do not show such a stable trend, so their total share has now clearly increased compared to 2016.

NOTES

1. Russian Republic claims responsibility for the murder of Nikolai Girenko // SOVA Center. June 26, 2004 (https://www.sova-center.ru/racism-xenophobia/news/racism-nationalism/2004/06/d6533/).

2. In 2003, after the first Constituent Assembly, the UN, the government and the Presidential Administration of the Russian Federation were notified of the creation of the Russian Republic. The Constituent Assembly elected Vladimir Popov as Supreme Leader. After the meeting, Popov disappeared with the constituent documents of Russian Republic; the documents were later recovered, and the head of the executive committee of the State Council, Viktor Krivov, headed and created Russian Republic of Rus. Popov is still referred to as Supreme Leader on the Web site of the old Russian Republic, which Krivov calls one of its "imitation organizations." Supreme Leader Popov issued a decree dismissing Krivov "for exceeding his authority." See Anna Kozkina. Outsiders. How veteran leader of *Pamyat* (Memory) Krivov re-established Rus in the image and likeness of Tatarstan // Mediazona. Aug. 25, 2017 (https://zona.media/article/2017/08/25/outsiders-5-rusreprus).

3. Russian Republic of Rus added to the Federal List of Extremist Organizations // SOVA Center. Sept. 2, 2020 (https://www.sova-center.ru/racism-xenophobia/news/counteraction/2020/09/d42839/).

4. The Community of Indigenous Russian People of the Shchyolkovsky District of Moscow Province was recognized as extremist by the Shchyolkovsky City Court of Moscow Province of Feb. 25, 2014 and was added to the list as entry 36. The Community of Indigenous Russian People of Astrakhan, Astrakhan Province, was recognized as extremist by the Soviet District Court of the city of Astrakhan on July 21, 2016 and was added to the list as entry 55.

5. Previously, he was among the leaders of another local nationalist organization, Kuk Bure.

6. In Bashkiria, the local nationalist organization Bashkort is recognized as extremist // SOVA Center. May 22, 2020 (https://www.sova-center.ru/racism-xenophobia/news/counteraction/2020/05/d42447/).

7. Samara Province court declares the religious group Allya-Ayat extremist // SOVA Center. May 28, 2019 (https://www.sova-center.ru/misuse/news/persecution/2019/05/d41067/).

8. For more information, see: The PCU movement is recognized as extremist // SOVA Center. Aug. 17, 2020 (https://www.sova-center.ru/misuse/news/persecution/2020/08/d42774/).

9. The Nation and Freedom Committee is recognized as an extremist organization // SOVA Center. July 29, 2021 (https://www.sova-center.ru/racism-xenophobia/news/counteraction/2020/07/d42712/).

10. Not counting the 395 local organizations of Jehovah's Witnesses that were banned along with their Management Center and listed in the same paragraph.

11. US State Department Designates the Russian Imperial Movement as Terrorist Organization // SOVA Center. April 7, 2020 (https://www.sova-center.ru/en/xenophobia/news-releases/2020/04/d42276/).

12. Currently Listed Terrorist Entities // Public Safety Canada. Feb. 3, 2021. (https://www.publicsafety.gc.ca/cnt/ntnl-scrt/cntr-trrrsm/lstd-ntts/crrnt-lstd-ntts-en.aspx#511); Government of Canada lists 13 new groups as terrorist entities and completes review of seven others // Government of Canada. Feb. 3, 2021. (https://www.canada.ca/en/public-safety-canada/news/2021/02/government-of-canada-lists-13-new-groups-as-terrorist-entities-and-completes-review-of-seven-others.html).

13. Only the verdicts in which the hate motive was officially recognized and which we consider appropriate are included in this count.

14. "He Fell on the Knife": Person involved in the murder of a gay male acquitted // SOVA Center. Feb. 26, 2020 (https://www.sova-center.ru/en/xenophobia/news-releases/2020/02/d42138/).

15. In Adygea, a student who posted a neo-Nazi video on the Internet is charged under Art. 282 of the Criminal Code // SOVA Center. Oct. 19, 2007 (https://www.sova-center.ru/racism-xenophobia/news/counteraction/against-cyberhate/2007/10/d11796/).

16. Relatives of the missing Dagestani native recognize him in a neo-Nazi video posted on the Internet // SOVA Center. June 4, 2008 (https://www.sova-center.ru/racism-xenophobia/news/counteraction/2008/06/d13503/).

17. Suspects announced in the double neo-Nazi murder committed in the 2000s // SOVA Center. Oct. 21, 2020 (https://www.sova-center.ru/racism-xenophobia/news/counteraction/2020/10/d43089/).

18. Suspects arrested in a series of racist murders // SOVA Center. Dec. 25, 2020 (https://www.sova-center.ru/en/xenophobia/news-releases/2020/12/d43443/).

19. Sentence imposed for desecration of the monument to Holocaust victims in Volgograd Province// SOVA Center. Feb. 12, 2020 (https://www.sova-center.ru/racism-xenophobia/news/counteraction/2020/02/d42077/).

20. Data as of Feb. 17, 2021.

21. Consolidated statistics on the activity of federal courts of general jurisdiction and magistrate courts for the first half of 2020 // Official Web site of the Supreme Court of the Russian Federation (http://cdep.ru/index.php?id=79&item=5460) (further – Consolidated statistics of the Supreme Court for the first half of 2020).

22. According to the data posted on the Supreme Court Web site, the highest number of criminal convictions were handed down under Art. 280 of the Criminal Code (public calls for extremist activity): In the first 6 months of 2020, 80 people were charged (for 68 of them, this was the main charge). It is followed by Art. 205.2 of the Criminal Code (propaganda of terrorism) with 73 convicted in the first half of 2020 (for 58 it was main charge). The number of convicted people under other articles is much lower: One person was convicted under Art. 280.1 (calls for separatism), three were convicted under Art. 354.1 (rehabilitation of Nazism), one – under Part 1 of Art. 148 (insulting of religious believers' feelings), three – under Art. 282 (incitement to hatred).

It should be noted that the total number of the convicted under all these articles as the main and additional charges results in a greater number than the actual number of those convicted for statements, since a significant fraction of them had more than one article in their sentences. Thus, 132 is an incomplete number of people convicted of statements for the first half of the year, but if we add the 29 for whom these articles constitute extra charges, we get the total of 161, which is higher than the real number of those convicted of statements.

For more information, see: Official statistics of the Judicial Department of the Supreme Court on the fight against extremism for the first half of 2020 // SOVA Center. Oct. 18, 2019 (https://www.sova-center.ru/racism-xenophobia/news/counteraction/2020/10/d43072/).

23. Consolidated statistics on the activity of federal courts of general jurisdiction and magistrate courts for the first half of 2019 // Official Web site of the Supreme Court of the Russian Federation (http://cdep.ru/index.php?id=79&item=5460xls).

24. Prior to 2018, convictions for statements were divided into "inappropriate" and "all other."

25. Oleg Platonov and Valery Yerchak sentenced in Moscow // SOVA Center. Dec. 23, 2020 (https://www.sova-center.ru/racism-xenophobia/news/counteraction/2020/12/d43424/).

26. All further numbers reflect the convictions known to us, although, judging from the Supreme Court data, the actual numbers are much higher. But given the volume of available data, it can be assumed that the observed patterns and proportions will hold true for the total number of verdicts.

27. However, on April 8, 2021, the court of appeals completely dismissed the charge against Islyamov under this article.

28. A year earlier, according to the Supreme Court data for the same period, Art. 205.2 was the main article in convictions against 45 people and was applied in combination with other articles in 11 convictions.

29. "Citizens of the USSR" is a community that denies the collapse of the Soviet Union and insists on implementing Soviet laws. In their opinion, the Russian Federation does not exist.

30. Who has been imprisoned for extremist crimes of non-general nature // SOVA Center. Dec. 24, 2013 (http://www.sova-center.ru/racism-xenophobia/publications/2013/12/d28691/).

31. Very likely mostly on Vkontakte.

32. See: N. Yudina. Virtual Anti-Extremism in Russia in 2014–2015 // SOVA Center. Aug. 24, 2016 (https://www.sova-center.ru/files/xeno/web14-15-eng.pdf).

33. Although their descriptions are, regretfully, not always accurate.

34. Including the prisoner who painted graffiti "in a public place in the penal colony."

35. Nikolai Sentsov was also prosecuted in this case; however, his sentence did not include Art. 282.1. He was found guilty under Part 1 of Art. 222 and Part 1 of Art. 222.1 of the Criminal Code (illegal possession of weapons and explosive devices), was sentenced to three years in a penal colony, and was released from the courtroom given time served in the pre-trial detention center.

36. On the justification of the PCU ban, see section Banning Organizations as Extremist.

37. Administrators of public pages that promoted the PCU sentenced in Yekaterinburg // SOVA Center. Sept. 9, 2020 (https://www.sova-center.ru/misuse/news/persecution/2020/09/d42875/).

38. Aleksei Polikhovich, Elena Kriven. The case of New Greatness. Who are these people, and what are they on trial for? // OVD-info. Oct. 27, 2018 (https://ovdinfo.org/articles/2018/10/27/delo-novogo-velichiya-kto-eti-lyudi-i-za-chto-ih-sudyat-gid-ovd-info); Maksim Pashkov. Without purpose or motive: Why the extremist group New Greatness cannot exist // OVD-info. Feb. 20, 2020. (https://ovdinfo.org/opinions/2020/02/20/bez-celi-i-motiva-pochemu-ekstremistskoe-soobshchestvo-novoe-velichie-ne-mozhet).

39. For more information about the activity of *Artpodgotovka*, see: Vera Alperovich. This is a fiasco, gentlemen! The Russian Nationalist Movement in the summer and autumn of 2017 // SOVA Center. Dec. 26, 2017 (http://www.sova-center.ru/racism-xenophobia/publications/2017/12/d38558/).

40. One other person was released from criminal responsibility since he had tipped off the authorities.

41. Thirty-one were convicted under Art. 282.2; for 28 of them it was the main charge. Four were charged under Art. 282.1. 53 charged under Art. 205.5; for 43 of them it was the main charge. Nine people were charged under Art. 205.4; for three of them it was the main charge.

42. See: Ruling of the Plenary Session of the Supreme Court of the Russian Federation "On Judicial Practice in Criminal Cases Regarding Crimes of Extremism" of June 28, 2011, No. 11 // Rossiiskaya Gazeta. July 3, 2011 (https://rg.ru/documents/2011/07/04/vs-dok.html).

43. Prosecution against Polyudova under Art. 280.1 of the Criminal Code was terminated in February 2021 due to the partial decriminalization of this article.

44. See: Belgorod Province: Administrative Sanctions for the Distribution of the Video "Let's Remind the Crooks and Thieves about Their Manifesto-2002" // SOVA Center. 2020 (https://www.sova-center.ru/misuse/news/persecution/2019/10/d41616/).

45. See: Sanctions against Individuals for Online Insults against the State and the Society // SOVA Center. 2020 (https://www.sova-center.ru/misuse/news/persecution/2019/04/d40942/).

46. See: Consolidated statistical data on the activities of federal courts of general jurisdiction and magistrates' courts for the first half of 2020 // Judicial Department at the Supreme Court of the Russian Federation. 2020 (http://www.cdep.ru/index.php?id=79&item=5461); Consolidated statistical data on the activities of federal courts of general jurisdiction and magistrates' courts for 2019 // Judicial Department at the Supreme Court of the Russian Federation. 2020 (http://www.cdep.ru/index.php?id=79&item=5258).

47. As of Feb. 17 2021, the list has 5,133 entries.

48. Including a poem dedicated to CSKA's defeat in a game with Spartak, see: A CSKA fan fined for his poem files a claim with the ECHR // SOVA Center. Nov. 18, 2019 (https://www.sova-center.ru/misuse/news/counteraction/2019/11/d41725/).

Epilogue

In 2021, preceding the parliamentary elections, Russian authorities used the repressive potential inherent in the broad language and various legal instruments of the current anti-extremist legislation and its associated norms against their opponents. The ban on organizations associated with Alexei Navalny and the charges against him and his supporters as an extremist community brought the debate over the enforcement of anti-extremist legislation into the mainstream of Russian politics significantly damaging the political atmosphere in the country.

At the same time, previous trends persisted – tightening control over the Internet, new laws against "foreign agents," and active application of these laws against a wide range of opponents. The "combats pour l'histoire" continued as well: The legislation against the "rehabilitation of Nazism" increased in severity and expanded in scope, and the corresponding article of the Criminal Code was actively implemented, although not on a massive scale. The intensified sanctions for "insulting the feelings of believers" reflected the growing role of moral conservatism in the law enforcement. In general, the enforcement of anti-extremist laws continued to increase its potential as repressive means of propaganda and schooling of citizens.

As for the overall 2021 statistics in the center's area of interest, SOVA noted a greater than twofold increase in the number of criminal verdicts that we viewed as inappropriate both under articles that cover public speech and under articles that pertain to involvement in banned organizations. The number of penalties inappropriately imposed under the anti-extremist articles of the Code of Administrative Offenses grew as well. However, this growth was not uniform across articles.

All law enforcement agencies escalated their fight against associations and groups that they perceived as dangerous, and this campaign led to a much greater number of inappropriate sentences compared to the preceding years. As to prosecutions for public speech, SOVA recorded a sharp increase in the number of criminal cases under articles that were purely ideological in nature, such as the one pertaining to historical narrative or the one on "offending the feelings of believers." Meanwhile, the judicial practices under the criminal articles on incitement to terrorism, extremism and hatred demonstrated a different trend: Despite the overall significant increase in the number of verdicts, SOVA found almost none of them completely inappropriate. Many verdicts punishing speech rose serious doubts over the adequacy of the sanctions or extent of public danger of a given statement.

The outbreak of hostilities in Ukraine in late February 2022 caused noticeable and widespread discontent in Russian society that found expression in public actions on the streets, numerous open letters, personal public statements, dissemination of information, and various forms of visual protest. In this situation, the authorities took various steps, both reactive and proactive. All three branches – the legislative, the executive, and the judiciary – were involved in countering the protest. Nevertheless, the protest activity continued on a daily basis. Subsequently, in the course of the year, thousands of people were charged in criminal and administrative cases, which utilized the old anti-extremist legal norms as well as the newly adopted legislation restricting civil liberties.

The fight against extremism fit quite organically with the general repressive policy of the state. In many ways, the anti-extremist norms formed the core, the basis of legislation on ideological and political control as well as its enforcement. This legislation expanded, and many new restrictions applied to acts that had not been classified as "crimes of an extremist nature" in the Law on Combating Extremist Activity. However, SOVA's analysis has always gone beyond the formal boundaries: The center defines anti-extremist policy as one that criminalizes actions motivated politically or ideologically. SOVA expanded the scope of its monitoring to include the enforcement of new legal norms that punished calling for sanctions against Russia and discrediting the actions of the Russian Army and officials abroad. On the other hand, SOVA only partially included in its review the cases related to "fake news" against the Russian Army and officials, taking into account only the subset for which the relevant charges included the hate motive. It must be noted that in 2022 the courts managed to issue only about a dozen verdicts under new criminal articles, but over 100 such cases were opened. In connection with the events in Ukraine, about three dozen people were prosecuted for vandalism and hooliganism motivated by political or ideological hatred; half of these cases went to trial and ended in guilty verdicts in 2022, others were left for the following year.

In general, SOVA classified 119 criminal sentences against 192 people issued in 2022 under articles on extremism and other closely related norms as inappropriate. Meanwhile, over 250 people became defendants in criminal cases newly opened without due cause.

An unprecedented number of people – about 4,400 – were fined under the administrative article on discrediting the Army and government officials, which was used for the first relevant prosecution of the year. The overall number of administrative sanctions for displaying prohibited symbols and inciting hatred also exceeded 5,000. Besides the article on discreditation, SOVA's monitoring revealed about 300 cases of inappropriate sanctions under other articles of the Code of Administrative Offenses relevant the center's area of interest. Citizens and organizations were punished primarily for anti-government statements in various forms.

Of course, the targeted persecution of opposition activists continued as well. The number of defendants in the case of the community of supporters of Alexei Navalny increased. Members of the opposition faced charges in numerous cases, both criminal and administrative. The youth opposition movement *Vesna* (Spring) was recognized as an extremist organization.

According to the statistics of the Ministry of Internal Affairs, in 2022 almost 500 crimes were classified as calls for terrorism on the Internet (55% more than a year earlier) and almost 500 crimes were prosecuted under the article on calls for extremist activity on the Internet. Thus, the alarming trend towards intensifying law enforcement under these articles, which had emerged in the previous years, continued unabated. SOVA hardly ever included these cases in its "Misuse of Anti-Extremism" section, since in the vast majority of known cases, the statements that caused complaints from law enforcement agencies, in fact, contained calls for violent actions – very often against representatives of the authorities. However, as was the case for Art. 282 CC on incitement to hatred, SOVA believed that the public danger of these statements was not always sufficient to merit criminal liability. Moreover, the punishments imposed by the courts were disproportionately severe. It is worth reminding readers that Art. 282 was partially decriminalized under public pressure. Thus, there had been a precedent for shifting the approach in the fight against online propaganda, but the situation in the country changed dramatically since then. The authorities did not even consider liberalization, and, given the ideological pressure against citizens and organizations and the complete suppression of the independent media, the public could not convey its opinions to the state. In its report for 2022 SOVA reported on the internal information blockade established by the authorities and the further development of the legislation on "foreign agents."

As law enforcement agencies largely concentrated their efforts on suppressing protests against the "special operation," their activity in other, more "traditional" directions somewhat decreased. Contrary to expectations, the ideologically important article on the "rehabilitation of Nazism" did not grow much in terms of the scale of its application, although two dozen sentences issued under it still gave it the leading position in the center's statistics of inappropriate criminal verdicts. The number of prosecutions for insulting the feelings of believers also remained quite the same as the previous year.

At the same time, however, prosecutions for involvement in the PCU criminal subculture, recognized as an extremist organization in 2020 on unclear grounds, continued throughout the year. The school shooter subculture was banned as a terrorist organization known as "Columbine," and teenagers faced charges for involvement in it. Individuals who romanticize criminality or mass murder obviously cannot be viewed as members of organized structures with a particular ideology. Thus, enforcement of anti-extremist and anti-terrorist legislation has increasingly been crossing into the realm of the unreasonable, not only in showing a disproportionate repressive response but also in determining its targets.

Repressive trends continued through the first half of 2023. with more repressive laws being introduced, the scope of sanctions expanding, and the courts proceeding to tighten penalties.

Index

Page numbers in italics apply to entries that appear in figures; page numbers followed by *t* apply to entries that appear in tables.

About the Authors

Maria Kravchenko and **Natalia Yudina** were researchers and report writers at the SOVA Center for Information and Analysis, directed by Alexander Verkhovsky. The SOVA Center is a Moscow-based nonprofit organization founded in 2002. It specialized in monitoring and analysis in the areas of nationalism, racism, hate crimes and hate speech; the relationship between religious organizations, the state and the secular society; and the government's misuse of anti-extremism legislation. The SOVA Center was involved in promoting human rights standards in enforcement of anti-terrorism and anti-extremism legislation.

On December 30, 2016, the Ministry of Justice forcibly included the SOVA Center on the list of "nonprofit organizations performing the functions of a foreign agent." On April 27, 2023, the Moscow City Court met to consider the request filed by Russia's Ministry of Justice to liquidate the SOVA Regional Public Association and ruled to approve the request. The formal reason for the liquidation of the organization was its participation in events outside its region of registration (Moscow). The decision came into force and the SOVA Center staff, including the authors of the book, continued their work as SOVA Research Center.

www.ingramcontent.com/pod-product-compliance
Lightning Source LLC
Chambersburg PA
CBHW050330270326
41926CB00016B/3386